Crime and Justice in the City as Seen through *The Wire*

Crime and Justice in the City as Seen through *The Wire*

Edited by

Peter A. Collins
Seattle University

David C. Brody
Washington State University

Carolina Academic Press
Durham, North Carolina

Library of Congress Cataloging-in-Publication Data

Collins, Peter A. (Peter Alan)
  Crime and justice in the city as seen through The Wire / Peter A. Collins and
David C. Brody.
      pages cm
  Includes bibliographical references and index.
  ISBN 978-1-61163-033-6 (alk. paper)
  1. Wire (Television program) 2. Social problems on television. I. Brody,
David C. II. Title.
  [DNLM: 1. Social Problems--Baltimore--Autobiography.]

  PN1992.77.W53C65 2013
  794.45'72--dc23

                              2012050911

                    CAROLINA ACADEMIC PRESS
                          700 Kent Street
                  Durham, North Carolina 27701
                    Telephone (919) 489-7486
                       Fax (919) 493-5668
                       www.cap-press.com

                          2014 Printing

Printed in the United States of America

This book has not been endorsed or authorized by HBO or the creators of *The Wire*.

Contents

Section 2
Police Culture, Ethics, and Intelligence

Section 4
Criminological Theory and *The Wire*

Foreword

Peter Moskos

In a place like Baltimore, word travels fast when David Simon and Ed Burns are seen around town filming a new police series. After all, they were the same guys who made *The Corner*, so I was excited! I had watched *The Corner* while I was cop policing the same streets of East Baltimore featured in many of the episodes of that series (and later in *The Wire*). I even watched the show on a quiet night while I was supposed to be policing, as my notes confess: "humping out at the [police station] desk with George (well at least *he* was supposed to be there)." On the street, we police knew which corners were used for *The Corner* because they were often spruced up with paint. In American ghettos, even something as simple as fresh paint can stand out.

The Wire followed the desolate themes of *The Corner* but filled and expanded the picture in a true-to-life style with a focus on police and poor, urban America. Rarely in TV history has this ravaged landscape been presented with any realism—but *The Wire* was different. The style, writing quality, and depth of *The Wire* have earned it the deserved appreciation of legions of fans, myself included.

Some of my favorite scenes concern the often mundane world of policing. Take, for instance, the effort McNulty makes at the start of the second season to "dump a body"—push the responsibility for a hard-to-solve murder—onto his old homicide squad. And there is the concern of the Southeast District commander when his legacy (and ego) are threatened by a church's display of the union's stained glass. Faced with such absurdity police often say, "You can't make this shit up." *The Wire* shows you can. And take the casual, laughable, and entirely believable conversations between the police knuckleheads, Hauk and Carver. In the first episode Carver describes their role as police officers: "What [Hauk] means to say is that we are effective deterrent in the war on drugs when we are on the street." Hauk interjects, "Fucking mothafuckers up." In the end, Carver, usually the sharper of these two tacks in the box, concludes, "You can't even call this shit a war.... Wars end."

The Wire is not and does not purport to be one hundred percent realistic, but it gets much more right than wrong, especially from a police perspective. Even a decade after I last heard the real thing, I still perk up anxiously when the show occasionally broadcasts the two-toned Signal-13 sound indicating an officer potentially in danger. "The location ... what's the 'twenty'?" I think before reminding myself that I am a civilian, hundreds of miles away ... and watching a TV show. From my perspective the show is about eighty percent realistic. Though this percentage declined somewhat in the faster-paced final season, this still is the most realistic cop TV show or movie ever made, *fiction or non-fiction*.

I do, admittedly, have a few minor (read: petty) complaints about realism in *The Wire*. For instance I wish more characters spoke with a Baltimore accent. And the police Marine Unit, which the seasick McNulty finds himself on at the start of the second season, is a highly coveted assignment, never a punishment post (for that, we have foot patrol). And in the real world the grapevine of the Baltimore City Police Department could never, not even for a day, keep a secret like the drug free-for-all zone "Hamsterdam." But the writer of this episode admitted as much to me.

When *The Wire* takes a deliberate turn away from reality, it does so to present a greater truth. Through Hamsterdam, *The Wire* presented an alternative vision of illegal drug distribution, one that isolates the harms of drug-dealing violence away from greater society. For a short while, in season three, the rest of the district was free from violent drug dealers! If only this could happen in real life. Of course it could ... but we would need major changes in law enforcement's approach to drug laws. And that, of course, is the very real point.

If there is a single underlying theme of *The Wire*, it is the disastrous effects of the war on drugs on post-industrial urban America. Well-paying manufacturing jobs are gone for good; the show's unflinching gaze highlights not America's winners but the police officers, the working stiffs, the junkies, the street hustlers and the strivers who fail to succeed because the game is rigged. One message of *The Wire*, one that needs to be better understood, is that when drug selling is criminalized, only criminals sell drugs. The show does not wrap up every hour with the guilty repentant and a hero making a stirring speech about protecting the innocent. In contrast with television that typically thrives on American optimism, *The Wire* can be downright depressing. And yet we can't turn away.

The Wire presents irreplaceable firsthand perspectives and does so without condescension or pandering. The worldview of police officers, for instance, is very much shaped by their forced interactions with society's least wanted. When I was working in Baltimore, an officer once told me, "If you're documenting this for your research or whatever, get this down: ... I mean, this raid we did today, you pull up a sheet and cockroaches are running around the bed. Who can sleep like this? Everyone is drugged out, like that zombie movie: 'Brains, I want brains!'" Another time an officer called the Eastern District residents, "drugged-out, lazy motherfuckers." Then he spelled out the full stereotype: "These people don't want to work. They want to sit on their ass, collect welfare, get drunk, and make babies. Let them shoot each other." But after a brief pause he turned to me and said with faux sincerity mirrored by Carver in the first episode, "I think the problems here are caused by social conditions, which can be solved by better education." Finally he concluded: "That's so when you write down all this stuff for your book I don't come out like an asshole." In truth, many officers who know him—even those who agree with his questionable views on social responsibility and public safety—think he *is* an asshole. And, boy, he would make a great character in *The Wire*, because the show breaks through the uniform exterior of any police department to show the diverse characters of the blue family. As I learned in the academy, "We're one big happy family, right? Dysfunctional as hell; but what family isn't?"

Fortunately, in 2013, Baltimore and its police department aren't quite as hopeless as one may think from watching *The Wire*. Charm City has had a recent influx of immigrants, which is very promising. And, even after a massive population drop over several decades, the city has held on to a healthy, albeit struggling middle class, both black and white. These groups are underrepresented in *The Wire*. Also given short shrift is the entire half of the police department assigned to patrol. This is unfortunately typical of TV shows and movies, which tend to focus on police detectives because they give writers greater freedom of plot. The average Baltimore officer has no wiretaps or long-term investigations in progress. A patrol officer drives around for most of eight hours, answers 311 and 911 calls for service, clears drug corners, backs up other officers, and fills out paperwork for anything that comes out "domestic related." Maybe once a week somebody is arrested.

Though firmly set in Baltimore, *The Wire* could be about any American city in post-industrial decline. Even more dramatic (and depressing) stories are found in Camden, New Jersey; East Saint Louis, Illinois; or most any city in Michigan. Large neighborhoods and even entire cities have been swallowed and destroyed by a combination of joblessness and drug prohibition which leads almost inevitably to poverty, segregation, violence, and incarceration. *The Wire* helps show how human despair does not simply happen—it comes from bad personal choices often rooted in decades and centuries of choices the powerful have made and imposed on others. Social mobility is the exception in America, not the rule. And *The Wire* does not pretend otherwise.

Having faith in humanity, I prefer to think that Americans' tolerance of this kind of suffering is rooted more in ignorance than malice. Society may lack the political and moral will to regulate drug distribution, provide employment opportunities, and reduce incarceration levels, but *The Wire* lets us imagine how our world might be different if the poorest among us did not grow up in the shadows of violence, poverty, and prison. *The Wire* presents not only the problems but also an aspirational vision of an unrealized future.

By the time I finished *Cop in the Hood*—my book on the subject of police and the war on drugs in Baltimore—*The Wire* had wrapped up its final season. I half-jokingly proposed to my editor that my soon-to-be-published book should be titled *Like* The Wire: *Season Six, but Real!* (It wasn't, though it might have sold better had it been.) I quit the police department before season one, after I got civil-service protection and gathered enough material for my dissertation and book.

I still have mixed feelings about leaving, even though that was always my plan. Baltimore was good to me. I made life-long friends and return when I can. But like hundreds of thousands of those before me who had the means to leave Baltimore, I did. And once you leave, the problems of Baltimore seem very far away, out of sight and almost out of mind. *The Wire* kept me feeling close to the police, people, and problems of the city I loved and left. Of course I had a good excuse to leave—I needed to earn my PhD in sociology, after all—but aren't excuses something we all have?

The Wire paints a pointillist picture of life in urban America without excuses or apology. Individual characters in *The Wire* coalesce into a striking group portrait which brings to mind something I heard in Baltimore time and time again: "When you get back to Harvard, tell 'em what it's really like!" Of course I tried; I wrote a book. But *The Wire* did it better and streamed this reality into more than four million living rooms simultaneously. Yes, as critics have pointed out, some dirty laundry was aired (stereotypes often have some basis in truth). And yes, the show can be a quick and perhaps too easy slumming tour. But such a tour can be the first step to a greater understanding of the world. Like a good liberal arts education, *The Wire* provides a strong foundation for academic discourse. But unlike academia, *The Wire* is effective in part because it ignores the traditional camps and rivalries of academic disciplines and public-policy efforts.

Consider our current national discourse in which police are dichotomized as either saviors or oppressors; unions are demonized by the right; and the ghetto is such a toxic mix of race, poverty and dysfunction that national politicians dare not even talk about "poor people" except in the context of cutting social services. In the pages of this wonderful compendium you will learn not just about a TV show, but about American society. This book breaks new ground because it provides, through *The Wire*, a common language by which we can once again discuss issues of poverty, race, crime, gender, drugs, justice, and economic inequality in America. *The Wire* presents the humanity and daily struggles of characters who are empathetic and even sympathetic. This book, like *The Wire*, will allow us once again to care.

Acknowledgments

First and foremost, this project would have never been possible had it not been for all of those individuals who worked to bring us such a provocative and entertaining experience in *The Wire*. So, to the show and its creators, actors, and all those behind the scenes, we say thank you. Next, we would like to sincerely thank each of the authors for sharing our vision for this work and for contributing their time, expertise, and unique points of view. We are deeply grateful for your efforts and creative input and any success that comes as a result of this endeavor is due directly to your hard work. We would like to thank a few of our graduate student assistants who helped with various tasks on this project, namely: Heather Burns and Naomi Rosenburg (from the Seattle University Master of Arts in Criminal Justice Program), who drafted most of the end of chapter study questions, and Lauren Block (a PhD candidate from the Department of Criminal Justice and Criminology at Washington State University), who not only contributed a chapter, but also provided a great deal assistance on various editorial tasks. We would also like to additionally thank Wendy Molyneux for her substantive input and editorial assistance in the inception stages of this project. We would like to thank the editors and staff at Carolina Academic Press for sharing our interest in this book. Finally, we would like to thank our families for their support while we completed this project.

Crime and Justice in the City as Seen through *The Wire*

Chapter 1

Introduction:
Using *The Wire* to
Contemplate Urban Crime
and Criminal Justice

David C. Brody and Peter A. Collins

When *The Wire* premiered on June 2, 2002, it was viewed as much more than a typical police procedural. While its plot is centered on crime, drug dealers, and the police, the show's true focus was on the city of Baltimore, Maryland, and the institutions that operated within it. Over its five season run it was praised by critics for its intricate examination of crime, life in the inner city, the criminal justice system, and the functioning of public institutions and the people who work in them. Though *The Wire* was praised by media critics, it was largely ignored by the viewing public. It seems the factors that led to critical acclaim also led to low viewership. Unlike other police and crime dramas, the police in *The Wire* did not solve cases on a weekly basis. The hardships faced by millions of people struggling to survive in the inner city were not softened. Rather than portraying characters as simply good or bad, *The Wire* did not flinch from portraying the good and bad sides of the police, criminals, educators, judges, lawyers, elected officials, or labor unions. Indeed, it presented an unvarnished view of the complex nature of the criminal justice system and the web of institutional linkages that impact individuals and society.

The show's willingness to take the time to address complex issues and institutions in non-simplistic ways has led academics and scholars from a myriad of disciplines to make *The Wire* a component of their scholarship and university teaching. Over the past five years there have been several academic

3

conferences, as well as dozens of college classes and scholarly publications examining various aspects of *The Wire*. These activities have crossed a wide variety of disciplines, including political science, linguistics, sociology, literature, law, African American studies, urban affairs, education, public administration, and of course, criminal justice.

The reason for this, regardless of the field of study, is due to *The Wire*'s focus on a city's institutions and the people who work within them, which leads to deep questions and far-reaching implications. While this book examines the problem of urban crime and an inefficient criminal justice system from the perspective of legal and social science scholars, it presents divergent and unique examinations of these oft-studied issues. Whether it is individual decision-making under institutional pressure, or institutional policy established for non-altruistic reasons, *The Wire* takes the time to present the ineffectiveness of a network of disparate yet cross-cutting institutions in addressing how to keep the public safe. In this opening chapter, we examine these concepts briefly and lay the groundwork for the essays that make up the rest of the text.

Institutional Obstinacy

During the opening scene of the last episode of *The Wire*, Mayor Tommy Carcetti's top aide Norman Wilson provides an eloquent summary of the systemic problems that the Baltimore government, criminal justice system, and citizenry face. Upon learning that the existence of a serial killer was a fabrication made by several detectives in an effort to obtain increased resources, Mayor Carcetti and his aides decide not to make this information public because it would be politically damaging. Summing his view of the situation, and perhaps the entire system, Wilson states, "I wish I was still at the newspaper so I could write on this mess. It's too fucking good." Although this is in reaction to an acute dilemma brought on by system-based pressures and the actions of individuals, it encapsulates a dominant theme of the series: the relentless problem of crime and the justice system's reaction to it. As is clearly recognized, there are indeed persistent and permeating "messes" seen throughout the episodes, the seasons, and the series as a whole. The relentless and cyclical nature of these depictions within *The Wire* provides a rich context in which to introduce students, researchers, practitioners and all types of readers to key problems, concepts, and theories that are of central importance to social scientists and should be both informative and important to the general public.

The stories depicted throughout the life of the show have been uniquely lauded by the general public, practitioners, and academics alike, as they all have raved over how closely the show's content reflects real-life patterns and practice. Moreover, the fact that it is a work of fiction permits *The Wire* to portray a series of events that resemble real world happenings in a clear and coherent manner. This linkage of real-life experiences from the show to reality and vice versa is a big reason why the show has been celebrated by academics as a unique pedagogical tool, as it provides rich examples and a unique and "safe" context that teachers can use to facilitate learning.

For example, while viewing *The Wire*, one might note that the many institutions that make up the formal-legal or law enforcement system lack strong collaborative partnerships. In fact, the partnerships that do surface are often tenuous, taboo, tainted, and in many respects, non-tolerated—these partnerships may be better termed collaborative manipulations! The problem of non-collaborative partnership is played out from the very beginning of the show, as evidenced by McNulty's revelation of the "truth" to Judge Phelan, and then his (McNulty's) subsequent scolding from Colonel Rawls. Viz., as Rawls stands above McNulty, both fists curled under his middle fingers he states: "don't major me you back-stabbing-smartass-piece of shit! What the fuck are you doing over at the courthouse anyway? Why the fuck are you talking to some shit-bag judge?" The colorful words continue as McNulty defends (and instructs) his reasons for sharing the information with the judge and Rawls continues to chastise him for speaking out of turn. One leaves this scene with the sense that collaboration, or any possibility of it within *The Wire's* crime control/justice system, is fragmented and dysfunctional—a theme that persists throughout the entirety of the show.

It is such unwillingness of institutions to collaborate in addressing these types of issues that is at the root of many urban problems. Institutions tend to focus solely on themselves and how they are impacted by specific issues rather than looking outside their universe at the system or city as a whole. Faced with budget cuts and demands to do more with less, institutions conduct internal examinations and look for ways to alter reality to give the appearance of increased effectiveness and productivity. This focus on statistics, which has become increasingly popular in the past decade, fosters, and even encourages myopic decision-making. As explained by David Simon, the show's creator,

> You show me anything that depicts institutional progress in America, school test scores, crime stats, arrest reports, arrest stats, anything that a politician can run on, anything that somebody can get a promotion on. And as soon as you invent that statistical category, 50 people in that institution will be at work trying to figure out a way to make it look as if progress is actually occurring when actually no progress is (Moyers, 2009).

Beyond a general unwillingness to cooperate with other institutions and an overreliance on internally generated measures to evaluate effectiveness, institutions tend to focus on and demand individuals adhere to a number of codes and rules maintained by the institution. This reality is a dominant theme in virtually every episode of *The Wire*, and spans the gamut of institutions portrayed, including the police, the schools, politicians, and even the street criminals.

The concept is presented in the opening scene of the show's first episode. In the scene below, Detective James McNulty is interviewing a teenage boy on the stoop of a row house about the shooting death of another teen named Snot Boogie which arose from a dispute at a back alley dice game:

McNulty: So, who shot Snot?

Kid: I ain't goin' to no court ... Mothafucka didn't have to put no cap in him though.

McNulty: Definitely not.

Kid: He coulda just whooped his ass like we always whoop his ass.

McNulty: I agree with you.

Kid: He killed Snot. Snot been doing the same shit since I don't know how long. You don't kill a man over some bullshit. I'm sayin', every Friday night in an alley behind the Cut Rate, we rollin' bones, you know? I mean all them boys, we roll till late.

McNulty: Alley crap game, right?

Kid: Like every time, Snot, he'd fade a few shooters, play it out till the pot's deep. Snatch and run.

McNulty: What, every time?

Kid: Couldn't help hisself.

McNulty: Let me understand. Every Friday night, you and your boys are shootin' craps, right? And every Friday night, your pal Snot Boogie ... he'd wait till there's cash on the ground and he'd grab it and run away? You let him do that?

Kid: We'd catch him and beat his ass but ain't nobody ever go past that.

McNulty: I've gotta ask you: if every time Snot Boogie would grab the money and run away ... why'd you even let him in the game?

Kid: What?

McNulty: Well, if every time, Snot Boogie stole the money, why'd you let him play?

Kid: Got to. It's America, man.

Throughout the series, incidents of adherence to institutional norms without regard for long-term, external consequences are depicted. For example, rather than effectively engaging and teaching their students, teachers in public schools are required to spend weeks teaching children how to answer the questions that will appear on standardized tests. Failure to do so is punished, regardless if it inhibits actual teaching and learning.

Within the police departments, it is the norm for commanders to manipulate crime statistics to give the appearance of effective law enforcement. Failure to do so has serious repercussions. There are many other instances involving the police that mimic real world codes. For example, under the code there it is expected that officers who observe a person assault another officer will join in on a retributive beating of the offender; that when an act of police misconduct takes place, officers will lie to insulate themselves and their fellow officers from reprimand and punishment; and that when strategy, however foolhardy, is set by command staff, it will be followed despite its ineffectiveness. Each of these examples has a negative impact on the police officer working in the community. They lead to a lack of trust in the police and a general unwillingness to assist law enforcement in crime fighting efforts.

Beyond looking at the inefficiencies of institutions, *The Wire* and this text explore the issues and conflicts faced by individuals working and operating in these organizations. *The Wire* sheds light on the many complex social, community, and individually-based problems that people of all walks of life face on a daily basis. Indeed, the show greatly succeeds at unearthing inconstancies and ironies in how the criminal justice system attempts to control crime and criminal behavior. Each season presents a major theme and each episode eloquently and forcefully presents a piece to the problem-puzzle. Tension is applied on an inter-personal level across episodes and the larger problems that many of the characters face do find some level of resolve, which makes for one hell of an entertaining show. The overall focus, however, does not take into account many of the support-based functions and reactions found in reality. Truthfully, one could characterize the show as an example of reactionary control-based policies. Could this focus—that of utter failure of the system and the many "flawed" actors who must operate in a rigid control-based criminal justice apparatus—be the reason why so many of us students, academics, and practitioners can relate to the show?

This is obviously a normative question that should be left up for each of us to decide. The information presented in the following chapters, however, can and should be used as a "jumping-off" point for readers to begin fashioning their own opinions about the nature of the criminal justice system, public policy, the media, and politics. Likewise, we have organized the rest of the book with these general considerations in mind and we turn now to an overview of the contents to follow.

Organization of the Book

It should be clear that we are both fans of the show. That said, because we ourselves share both a critical and blind admiration for the show's topics and characters, and we have spent quite a bit of time discussing the linkages between the show and academics (and drawing inspiration from them), we wanted to approach the book in a similar laid-back and approachable way. That is, rather than force a structure on the authors, we asked that they write on topics and themes from the show that interested them the most—we wanted our authors to be fully engaged and passionate about the material and we truly believe that it shows in each of the following chapters.

After getting an idea of topical coverage, we divided the book into four separate sections. Each section contains an introduction and overview. Although the chapters were grouped in thematic sections, as you read on, you will see that they are all truly interconnected! The first section focuses on the systemic and institutional impact on crime. In this section, Susan Bandes, Anmol Chaddha, William Julius Wilson, Alafair Burke, and Dawinder Sidhu address the interconnectedness of our justice system, the impacts of urban inequality and poverty, the many institutional failures that plague our cities, and the impacts these systematic patterns have on individuals.

In the second section, the authors cover some of the main policing-related themes depicted in the show, such as noble-cause corruption, ethics, and the rise of intelligence led policing. In this section, Peter Parilla, Wendy Wyatt, Jonathon Cooper, Jonathan Bolen, and Gennaro Vito discuss the portrayal of policing from organizational to individual points of view. As has been noted elsewhere, *The Wire* is "not about policing" but rather about larger issues pertaining to "the city." Policing does, however, take a central role in nearly every episode's storyline. Given this coverage, many fans and critics have focused on the portrayal of the day-to-day institutional operations and individual actions of the police. So it is to these exciting themes that the authors draw your gaze and capture your interest.

The third section focuses on politics and the war on drugs. In this section, Sarah Reckow, Jennifer Balboni, Zachary Hamilton, and Lauren Block turn the reader's attention to issues surrounding politics at the city level and the interplay between politics and policy formation, how similarly-based decision-making, as well as other social forces, influenced the United States' plunge into the War on Drugs, and the repercussions of the drug war policies. Like with the previous section on policing, this group of chapters covers perhaps the most salient theme of the show—illicit drug trade, use, and abuse. More importantly, where the show leaves the viewer questioning "what is to be done" about the drug problem, this section provides some of the most current research on harm reduction strategies and offers some insight into their applicability in supplanting the now debunked policies surrounding the war on drugs.

In the final section, Stephen Rice, Gabriel Cesar, Kevin Wright, Kyle Thomas, Matthew Nobles, Laurie Drapela, Christopher Sullivan, and James McCafferty all provide excellent linkages from the various scenes and themes from *The Wire* to criminological theory and practice. All of the chapters in this volume are useful in linking material from the show to academic concepts; however, the section four chapters all do a particularly excellent job providing critical insight into the theoretical development and the practical application of these ideas. Each chapter tackles a different topical focus area (such as procedural injustice, community-to-individual level factors which impact offender reintegration, social disorganization, the portrayal of women in the show, and juvenile justice) and they all do an excellent job in citing the relevant research as well as contemporary issues surrounding the chosen subject matter.

In preparing this book, we operated under the assumption that the reader has viewed some (or all) episodes of *The Wire*. While we encourage readers to watch the entire series (available in DVD or streaming format), this is not a prerequisite for one to fully grasp the substance of the individual essays. As an alternative to watching multiple episodes of the show before diving in the text, there are several sources available to help individuals get up to speed on the plots, characters, and themes presented over the course of the show's five seasons (listed below under the resources heading).

References

Moyers, B. (2009). Interview transcript, Bill Moyers Journal, PBS, 17 April 2009, obtained from www.pbs.org/moyers/journal/04172009/watch.html.

Resources

Alvarez, R. (2009). *The Wire: Truth be Told*, Home Box Office, Inc.

Busfield, S. and P. Owen. (2009). *The Wire Re-up: The Guardian Guide to the Greatest TV Show Ever Made*, Guardian Books.

HBO: The Wire: Homepage: http://www.hbo.com/the-wire/index.html.

The Wire Wiki: http://thewire.wikia.com/wiki/The_Wire_on_HBO.

Section 1

Criminal Justice and Urban Institutions

As discussed in the previous chapter, a number of social and governmental institutions have direct and indirect impact on crime and quality of life in America's cities. Through inaction or through inappropriate or poorly executed actions, political, social, and economic institutions that exist to serve the public oftentimes exacerbate the very problems they are meant to address. The four essays presented in this section use *The Wire* as a backdrop to examine the reasons behind institutional and systemic ineffectiveness, and the unintended effect they have on crime and quality of life in urban communities.

In Chapter 2, Susan Bandes focuses on *The Wire's* unique portrayal of the criminal justice system, the other institutions undeniably intertwined with the system, and their impact on the lives of individuals. Bandes first discusses one of the most memorable scenes from the first season of *The Wire*, the comparison D'Angelo Barksdale makes between his uncle's drug organization and the game of chess. She uses this comparison to demonstrate the ways in which institutions use similar tactics to maintain their power and the status quo, in which "the king stay the king." Bandes describes how this often comes at the expense of the "pawns" or citizens whose own lives and decisions are ultimately shaped by these institutions: institutions focused on self-preservation, not on individual well-being. Bandes concludes by illustrating the often tragic consequences and the unending cycle for the pawns trapped in the game.

In Chapter 3, Anmol Chaddha and William Julius Wilson highlight one of the most important themes in *The Wire*, the role of social, economic, and political institutions in creating systemic urban inequality that then shapes the lives of individuals. Chaddha and Wilson begin by discussing how high incarceration rates are concentrated across certain populations, including African Americans, the urban poor, and disadvantaged neighborhoods, how these trends exacerbate the problems of inequality that already exist within these populations, and how these long-term negative factors affect individuals and their families, friends, and neighborhoods. They also examine the role of a declining economy and the creation of disadvantaged urban areas, including the ways in which deindustrialization and improvements in transportation contributed to the migration of the upper and middle classes from inner cities to the suburbs and the consequences that joblessness, social isolation, and concentrated disadvantage have had on those left living in urban areas.

Chaddha and Wilson discuss the lack of support from the federal government in helping these disadvantaged urban areas, the consequences of a market-approach to assistance, and the barriers the residents face in building political power within their communities. The authors also examine how the education system has failed to provide opportunities to children living in disadvantaged areas, which additionally serves to reinforce inequality. By providing such a thorough explanation of how systemic urban inequality is created through our social, economic, and political institutions and the consequences of this inequality, Chaddha and Wilson remind us of the importance of considering the context of individuals' lives.

In Chapter 4, Alafair Burke focuses on one of most intriguing ideas *The Wire* raises—that differentiating between the "good guys" and the "bad guys" is not always easy. Perhaps the best representation of the moral gray area many of *The Wire* characters reside in is the character of Omar Little, the "rip and run" artist who robs drug dealers but has a strict moral code of not harming innocent citizens. Burke focuses on the sometimes less than ethical behavior of the actors working within the criminal justice system, specifically law enforcement and prosecutors. While these institutions are typically represented as the "good guys" in many crime dramas, *The Wire* questions their legitimacy. Burke uses examples of situations where law enforcement and prosecutors fail to abide by ethical standards and sometimes even violate the law in order to pursue their own version of "justice." She also discusses the dangerous repercussions of unethical behavior for the criminal justice system, and concludes with an important reminder that the actors within these institutions are meant to administer justice fairly and without bias.

In the final chapter in this section, Dawinder Sidhu uses key themes from *The Wire* to argue that our civil liberties and the checks and balances on executive power laid out by the U.S. Constitution are far too important to our nation to be trampled on, even in times of war. He uses Richard Posner's provocative book, *Not a Suicide Pact: The Constitution in a Time of National Emergency* to illustrate the contrary argument, that in order to protect the nation from harm, national security concerns should trump the Constitution during wartime.

Sidhu begins with a thorough introduction to the drug problems that plague the city of Baltimore, including a discussion of both the reality of Baltimore and the Baltimore shown to us through *The Wire*. He compares the questionable tactics used by law enforcement to target the drug trade in Baltimore to tactics used by the U.S. in the war on terror such as illegal search and seizures, racial profiling, the unlawful detainment of citizens, and torture, arguing that they demonstrate the negative consequences of allowing the unlimited and unchecked executive power that Posner advocates.

Sidhu discusses the great importance of the legislative and judiciary branches of government in providing the proper oversight of the executive branch in order to protect our country from a tyrannical government, disagreeing with Posner's argument that the judiciary lacks the knowledge needed to make decisions concerning security and should refrain from interfering on executive power. Sidhu concludes that by allowing executive power to violate the Constitution in order to preserve national security, we are actually violating the very principles we seek to represent as a nation. Instead, he argues that both liberty and security can and must exist together.

Chapter 2

And All the Pieces Matter: Thoughts on *The Wire* and the Criminal Justice System[*]

Susan A. Bandes[**]

Introduction

"Whatever it was, they don't teach it in law school."[1]

The standard police procedural, even including great dramas like *NYPD Blue* and *Hill Street Blues*, adheres to time-honored narrative conventions. It focuses on good if sometimes imperfect cops trying to find the real bad guys—the perpetrators—and bring them to justice. A crime had ruptured the social fabric, and at the end of the episode, guilt is determined and things are put to right. The standard procedural is concerned mainly with individual fault and individual heroism. It does not raise disquieting questions about the criminal

---

* Reprinted with permission from: Susan A. Bandes, "And All the Pieces Matter: Thoughts on The Wire and the Criminal Justice System," *Ohio State Journal of Criminal Law*, 8: 435–445 (2011).

** I am grateful to Bennett Capers and Joshua Dressler for organizing and publishing this written symposium, to Bennett, Alafair Burke, Jeff Fagan and David Sklansky, who joined me in channeling our shared enthusiasm for *The Wire* into a panel at Law and Society, and of course to David Simon, for participating in our panel and for *The Wire*. And heartfelt thanks to my sons Daniel and Andrew, for watching all five seasons of *The Wire* with me—twice—and for countless wonderful discussions about it.

1. Season 5, Episode 7 (Prosecutor Rhonda Pearlman, responding to Rupert Bond's question "What the fuck just happened?" after Clay Davis is acquitted).

justice system, the legal system, or the social and political arrangements that lead to a permanent underclass. There are eight million stories in the Naked City,[2] and in the police procedural, every one of them stands on its own.

This standard cop show narrative reflects and reaffirms a deeply ingrained, reassuring view of the world. *The Wire* is a different kind of television. It aims not to reassure but to unsettle, or as David Simon once put it, "to pick a fight."[3] On its surface a police procedural, *The Wire* has been aptly described as a portrayal of "the social, political and economic life of an American city with the scope, observational precision and moral vision of great literature."[4] Unlike the standard police procedural, which presents and resolves a discrete problem every week, *The Wire* keeps widening its lens to reveal the context in which crime and policing take place. Although the show begins as a description of an actual wiretap, the series soon turns out to be about a series of interlocking systems, wired for dysfunction.

The Wire is deeply concerned with institutions, how they constrain the shape of individual lives, and how they perpetuate themselves, often at the expense of achieving their legitimate goals. However, although the show's most cherished subject is the institutional roadblocks to good policing, *The Wire* rejects the standard paradigm in this regard as well. It is not one of those cop shows that reflexively portrays constitutional rights as annoying hindrances to law enforcement. Other shows tell us that cops need free rein; that we ought to trust their instincts and keep the government and the Constitution off their backs. This show vividly demonstrates that those instincts are sometimes misguided or self-protective and that the right kinds of limits can play an important role in good police work.

In order to dramatize the criminal justice system *as a system*, the show radically revises the narrative conventions of the genre. Against all odds, it creates a compelling narrative about institutional dynamics and bureaucratic dysfunction. For those of us who study and care about issues of policing and crime, *The Wire* is indispensable for both its remarkable portrait of the criminal justice system and its demonstration that complexity and social context can make for a gripping tale. This short essay is an exploration and an appreciation of *The Wire's* portrait of the criminal justice system, using "The King Stay the King," the chess lesson scene from Season One, as a starting point.

---

2. The tag line from The Naked City, a TV drama that ran from 1958 to 1963.

3. From Simon's introduction to "The Wire: Truth be Told," as quoted in Dan Kois, Everything you were afraid to ask about The Wire, Salon, October 1, 2004.

4. Jacob Weisberg, The Wire on Fire, Slate, September 13, 2006.

"The King Stay the King"

Early in the first season, D'Angelo Barksdale, a young lieutenant in his uncle Avon Barksdale's drug organization, attempts to teach two street level dealers, Preston 'Bodie' Broadus and Wallace, to play chess:[5]

D: Yo, what was that?

Wallace: Hm?

D: Castle can't move like that. Yo, castle move up and down and sideways like.

Bodie: Nah, we ain't playing that.

Wallace: Yeah, look at the board. We playing checkers.

D: Checkers?

Wallace: Yeah, checkers.

D: Yo, why you playing checkers on a chess set?

Bodie: Yo, why you give a shit?

D: Now look, check it, it's simple, it's simple. See this? This the kingpin, a'ight? And he the man. You get the other dude's king, you got the game. But he trying to get your king too, so you gotta protect it. Now, the king, he move one space any direction he damn choose, 'cause he's the king. Like this, this, this, a'ight? But he ain't got no hustle. But the rest of these motherfuckers on the team, they got his back. And they run so deep, he really ain't gotta do shit.

Bodie: Like your uncle.

D: Yeah, like my uncle. You see this? This the queen. She smart, she fast. She move any way she want, as far as she want. And she is the go-get-shit-done piece.

Wallace: Remind me of Stringer.

D: And this over here is the castle. Like the stash. It can move like this, and like this.

Wallace: Dog, stash don't move, man.

D: C'mon, yo, think. How many time we move the stash house this week? Right? And every time we move the stash, we gotta move a little muscle with it, right? To protect it.

Bodie: True, true, you right. All right, what about them little bald-headed bitches right there?

---

5. Season 1 Episode 3.

D: These right here, these are the pawns. They like the soldiers. They move like this, one space forward only. Except when they fight, then it's like this. And they like the front lines, they be out in the field.
Wallace: So how do you get to be the king?
D: It ain't like that. See, the king stay the king, a'ight? Everything stay who he is. Except for the pawns. Now, if the pawn make it all the way down to the other dude's side, he get to be queen. And like I said, the queen ain't no bitch. She got all the moves.
Bodie: A'ight, so if I make it to the other end, I win.
D: If you catch the other dude's king and trap it, then you win.
Bodie: A'ight, but if I make it to the end, I'm top dog.
D: Nah, yo, it ain't like that. Look, the pawns, man, in the game, they get capped quick. They be out the game early.
Bodie: Unless they some smart-ass pawns.

Several years later, Bodie finally understands the chess lesson. Bodie's realization and rejection of his status as one of the "bald headed bitches" leads to his murder:[6]

Bodie: I feel old. I been out there since I was 13. I ain't never fucked up a count, never stole off a package, never did some shit that I wasn't told to do. I been straight up. But what come back? Hmm? You'd think if I get jammed up on some shit they'd be like, "A'ight, yeah. Bodie been there. Bodie hang tough. We got his pay lawyer. We got a bail." They want me to stand with them, right? But where the fuck they at when they supposed to be standing by us? I mean, when shit goes bad and there's hell to pay, where they at? This game is rigged, man. We like the little bitches on a chessboard.
McNulty: Pawns.

For five seasons the show meticulously illustrates D'Angelo Barksdale's insight in one bureaucratic context after another. There is an ironbound internal logic to the institutions portrayed in *The Wire*. This logic—the rigged chessboard in which the king stays the king, everyone had better know his proper moves, and the pawns are infinitely replaceable—drives every institution *The Wire* portrays: the drug culture, families, neighborhoods, labor unions, politics, social welfare agencies, law enforcement agencies, the schools, and

---

6. Season 4 Episode 13. This brief reference to the chess scene marks the first time it is mentioned in three years. *The Wire* expects its viewers to pay close and sustained attention, and rewards them for doing so.

the media. The main goal of these institutions is to perpetuate and protect themselves. The main goal of the institutional players is to preserve or expand their power. Aims like making the streets safe or covering the news or protecting workers or educating children are consistently subordinated to these primary goals.

The Wire shows us something truly frightening about systemic dysfunction—that most of the harm done is neither dramatic nor venal. Sometimes individuals make heroic or repugnant choices. But *The Wire* insists on complicating not only the notion of villainy, but also the notion of heroism. It repeatedly presents individual choice as severely constrained, even dictated, by the logic of the system. Harm is done, day in and day out, by regular people trying to do and keep their jobs.

As I will discuss below, a central achievement of the series is to replace the flat categories of standard police procedurals with a fully realized world populated with morally and emotionally complex characters. This is not to say that the show withholds moral judgment. But in every case, the viewer is shown how moral choice is shaped and constrained by systemic forces. High level functionaries like the Baltimore Police Department's (BPD's) Major Rawls may be the closest thing to villains in this series, but even as "the king stays the king" by sacrificing justice and progress for institutional expediency and survival, we are shown how these choices are virtually foreordained.[7] Those who attempt to live within an organizational structure but refuse to obey these rules, like the BPD's Bunny Colvin or Baltimore Sun journalist Gus Haynes or student turned drug dealer Michael Lee, are nearly always punished: demoted, forced to resign, banished, murdered, depending on their trade.

Characters take heroic stands from time to time, but the show subverts the standard narrative expectation for a heroic protagonist. Instead it offers Jimmy McNulty in what appears to be the standard hero's role (the Bobby Simone role in NYPD Blue), consistently forcing the viewer to examine the complex motives driving McNulty's defiance of the departmental strictures that interfere with his investigations, as well as the practical and moral costs of that defiance.[8]

---

7. In several slyly subversive scenes, quintessential outlaw Jimmy McNulty begins running a shadow police department, doling out departmental funds allocated for investigation of his homeless serial killer case, and finds himself understanding some of the frustrations of supervising people like him and his fellow officers. See e.g. Season 5, Episode 8.

8. Indeed, by the end of Season 5, McNulty has thoroughly unsettled the viewer's assumptions and, for many viewers, betrayed their trust just as he betrayed the trust of his coworkers.

Just as the show locates its individual characters in the broader institutional context of the criminal justice system, it also locates the criminal justice system within a broader network of crisscrossing institutions. The standard cop show not only erases the bureaucratic constraints on the individual cop; it also erases the larger bureaucratic landscape within which law enforcement institutions operate. All the pieces matter, as Detective Lester Freamon remarks.[9] *The Wire* begins by showing us the symbiotic relationship between the cops and the drug trade. It then keeps widening the lens. Unless we look at the wider symbiotic relationship between the police, the schools, the street corner, the various levels of government, the media and other institutions, we can't even scratch the surface of what's wrong here.

But crucially, even as *The Wire* painstakingly reveals the internal wiring of each institution, and the myriad ways in which the institutions are wired together, it also shows the viewer, time and again, how much energy is spent on keeping those wires hidden. Statistics are manipulated ("juked"). Money trails are not followed. High value targets are not pursued. Whistleblowers are severely disciplined and usually banished.[10] Explorations into root causes are tabled in favor of quick fixes or showy press conferences.[11] The police culture and the drug culture align in a happy symbiosis—it is in everyone's interest to keep picking off the pawns, who are then simply replaced. It is in nobody's interest to follow the money to the high value targets—a road that ends at the seats of power in Annapolis, in Baltimore, and in the corporate boardrooms.

It turns out that the king stays the king in the police department by appeasing the government officials who control the purse strings—that is, by not putting the pieces together. This is the abstract concept of dysfunction made concrete: a show about the institutional imperative to turn away knowledge of systemic failure rather than risk disturbing the status quo. *The Wire* is about the effort that is put, not into solving the crimes that just happen to present themselves at the beginning of each show, but into keeping the "red" (open) cases off the board, keeping the bodies buried, and keeping the patterns of violence that tie the bodies together buried too. That thematic point

---

9. Lester spends his spare time building intricate doll house furniture.

10. Indeed the series is essentially set in motion by Jimmy McNulty's nearly accidental revelation to Judge Phelan that high value targets are not being properly pursued, a revelation that violates the departmental code of loyalty. See also Susan Bandes, Loyalty to One's Convictions: The Prosecutor and Tunnel Vision, 49 Howard Law Journal 475 (2006) for a discussion of institutional loyalty and systemic injustice.

11. Or in the case of the Baltimore Sun, explorations into root causes are tabled in favor of colorful "Dickensian" anecdotes (Season 5, Episode 6).

is made quite literally in this show, which in the final seasons depicts the strenuous efforts of top brass to avoid learning about the bodies in the vacant houses or how they got there.[12]

The bureaucratic refusal to put the pieces together is often counterpoised, in this series, against misguided, counterproductive tracking of useless or non-existent patterns. The plot line in which top brass keep the bodies in the vacants out of sight is counterpoised against one in which these same officials pull out all the stops to investigate a faked pattern of serial killings. Although the pattern of killings is entirely illusory, the "discovery" of the pattern and the response to it advance a number of careers in the police department, the newspaper, and electoral politics. The use of COMSTAT (see Chapter 8, this volume) to track patterns of crime and to hold officials accountable for crime rates is repeatedly portrayed as increasing the territoriality, the juking of statistics, and the concern with keeping clearance rates down that create disincentives to actually investigating and fighting crime. In the schools, standardized testing not only measures illusory "progress," but actively impedes the ability to teach anything of value. In each institution, energy is devoted to creating an illusion of measurement, coherence and progress in ways that impede legitimate institutional goals.

We Got Our Thing but It's Just Part of the Big Thing[13]

Although the show's most cherished subject is the institutional roadblocks to good policing, *The Wire* is not one of those cop shows that reflexively portray constitutional rights as annoying hindrances to law enforcement.[14] It is not cynical about the importance of standards of behavior. Other shows tell us that cops need free rein; that we ought to trust their instincts and keep the government and the Constitution off their backs. This show vividly demonstrates that those instincts are sometimes misguided or self-protective and that the right kinds of limits can play an important role in good police work.

Criminal procedure is concerned, at least ostensibly, with how law guides police behavior. However, it makes only a halfhearted attempt to grapple with

---

12. Sgt. Jay Landsman orders the unit to stop looking for bodies: "We do not go looking for bodies, especially moldering John Does. We do not put red up on the board voluntarily ... You will not pull down any more fucking wood." Season 4, Episode 12.

13. The student Zenobia, Season 4 Episode 8.

14. See Susan Bandes and Jack Beermann, Lawyering Up, 1 The Green Bag 5 (1998) (discussing the show NYPD Blue's attitude toward the Miranda warnings).

the criminal justice system as an instrument of social control. As *The Wire* brilliantly depicts, the police presence in certain neighborhoods is a pervasive force shaping the quality of life of those who live there. Criminal procedure has no real framework for addressing questions about policing priorities and police conduct, and tends to relegate these questions to fields like criminology and sociology.[15] It purports to address police conduct and police incentives, yet its main remedy for police illegality is the exclusionary rule, which is ineffectual or beside the point in dealing with a wide swath of police street-level conduct and supervisory decision-making.[16]

The Wire, as it happens, contains a surprising number of scenes depicting the effectiveness of the exclusionary rule. Police and assistant state's attorney Rhonda Pearlman and Judge Phelan spend substantial time discussing the threshold for probable cause, drafting warrant applications, and reviewing arguments for extensions on wiretaps. The warrant process is treated with a fair amount of respect. Cops—notably Thomas "Herc" Hauk—find themselves in serious trouble for doing things like making up informants in warrant affidavits.[17] And in the final season, the BPD's case against drug kingpin Marlo Stanfield's organization is compromised (though his crew is decimated, Stanfield himself walks) because it is tainted by an illegal wiretap.

The exclusionary rule works, but it is doesn't address much of what ails the cop culture or the drug culture. Most of the police work *The Wire* depicts is beyond the reach of the exclusionary rule. The rule doesn't reach the endless *Terry* stops whose point is not to obtain admissible evidence, but to exert control. Nor does it reach the low level misdemeanor arrests whose purpose is to get the suspect to the station for questioning, to create leverage, or to get a weapon off the street. In *The Wire's* Baltimore, cases that do get to court (the most serious felony cases) are often derailed not by suppressed evidence but by witness intimidation and murder. In the great Clay Davis trial scene,[18] the case is derailed by a yawning cultural chasm, inspired oratory, and a deeply ingrained acceptance of corruption.

The Wire captures the irrelevance of standard fourth amendment remedies in another way as well. In standard cop shows, the crime is a given—it appears, unbidden, at the beginning of the episode. *The Wire* shows a world in

---

15. For a general discussion of what criminal procedure can learn from criminology see OSJCL Volume 7 Issue 1 (2009).

16. http://balkin.blogspot.com/2010/09/challenges-of-quality-of-life-policing.html

17. Hauk's confidential informant in Season Four is the fictional Fuzzy Dunlop, named after a tennis ball.

18. Season 5, Episode 7.

which police are inundated with cases and information. The question is not how the police will solve "the case," but how caseload priorities will be determined. Much of the drama takes place in cubicles, where street level police and supervisors spend much of their time arguing about resource allocation, begging functionaries to do their jobs, and engaging in jurisdictional disputes about who gets saddled with open cases. See, for example, the scene in which Jimmy McNulty consults tide reports to prove that the floating dead body really was in the BPD's jurisdiction rather than the Harbor Patrol's.[19] Questions of which cases get prioritized, deep sixed or sidelined are well outside the ambit of constitutional criminal procedure. But *The Wire* illustrates the point: a jurisprudence that attempts to address police incentives mainly through excluding evidence at trial is in danger of being sidelined or marginalized.

Even as it shows the myriad multi-institutional barriers to good policing, *The Wire* also carefully depicts the importance of internal police culture to defining and enforcing policing norms. The point is driven home in the final episodes, when Kima Greggs, the moral compass of the BPD ensemble, turns in McNulty and Freamon for their rogue behavior in the serial killer scheme. Likewise, in one beautiful small exchange, Ellis Carver, who has been promoted to sergeant, informs his former partner Herc, who has been fired for his incompetence and repeated refusal to respect limits, that he is about to discipline another officer in a way that will create problems for Herc.

> **Herc:** He knows he fucked up. He knows this. He's proud, you know? He doesn't wanna beg.
> **Carver:** It's not about that.
> **Herc:** Carv, you cannot do one of your own guys. I mean, I know you got rank now. You're damn-near lieutenant. But still.
> **Carver:** It ain't about the rank. I never told you, Herc. Never said a fuckin' word. But when I gave you that kid to debrief last year. Whatshisface? You were supposed to get him to Bunk Moreland, you remember that?
> **Herc:** Yeah. I fucked up. So what?
> **Carver:** So it mattered.
> **Herc:** So what the fuck does this have to do with Colicchio?
> **Carver:** It all matters. I know we thought it didn't, but ... it does ...[20]

---

19. Season 2, Episode 1.
20. Season 5, Episode 4.

You Feel Me?: Empathy and Moral Complexity on TV

I have long been fascinated by the problem of how media can effectively portray complex entities without devolving into simple stories with heroes, villains and an easy, cathartic resolution (Bandes, 1999).[21] Likewise I've been interested in the question of empathy—both the problems of bridging empathic divides across race and class and other barriers, and the problem of evoking empathy for cops, victims and suspects, all at the same time (Bandes, 1996; Bandes, 2006).[22] I've observed elsewhere that:

Television ... has a particular grammar, and the nature of the information we receive is to a great extent shaped by that grammar. I do not suggest that this grammar is inherent in the technology: there are complex explanations having to do with corporate imperatives, audience psychology, and the political and social landscape. But descriptively, we can say that TV uses an episodic frame that "fragments information into isolated, dramatic particles and resists longer and more complex messages."[23]It emphasizes immediacy, and discrete occurrences. It prefers simple, dramatic messages that resonate with what we already know—heroes, villains and other familiar stock figures, right and wrong, easily identifiable problems with simple solutions. It is better at showing the status quo than the need for change, better at the concrete than the abstract or nuanced (Bandes, 2004: 585–586).[24]

I am now grateful that I included the caveat. *The Wire* is a testament to the fact that the hurdles to nuance and complexity are not inherent in the medium.[25] It is possible to tell a compelling story that defies the standard narrative rules

---

21. Susan A. Bandes, Patterns of injustice: Police brutality in the courts. 47 Buffalo Law Review 1275 (2009).

22. Susan A. Bandes, Empathy, narrative, and victim impact statements. 63 The University of Chicago Law Review 361 (1996); Susan A. Bandes, Repression and denial in criminal lawyering 9 Buffalo Criminal Law Review 339 (2006).

23. Jeffrey Scheuer, The Sound Bite Society: Television and the American Mind at 9 (1999).

24. Susan A. Bandes, Fear factor: The role of media in covering and shaping the death penalty. 1 Ohio State Journal of Criminal Law, 585, 585–586 (2004).

25. There are interesting discussions to be had about the role of subscriber television in this new golden age of television. Subscriber television, for example, gave *The Wire* time to build an audience. It enabled the audience to catch up on previous episodes so it could give the story the attention it required. These were important elements in the ability to present a subtle, complex, long running serial narrative.

of the medium. Indeed, *The Wire* is a pioneer in creating a new kind of serial television, in which multiple intersecting stories involving a huge case of characters play out, not only from one episode to another, but over a span of several seasons.

The feat *The Wire* achieves is to draw us deeply into the lives of individual characters while at the same time drawing back and showing us the roles these characters occupy in a larger system. This systemic focus doesn't work against the viewer's ability to empathize with individual characters. It provides additional context for their perspectives and their decisions. At times it even helps create understanding (if not exactly compassion) for powerful characters like Police Commissioner Erwin Burrell or Mayor Tommy Carcetti, who might elsewhere be portrayed simply as ruthless or clueless bureaucrats, but whom this show portrays as institutionally constrained and readily replaceable.

But *The Wire* distinguishes itself from the usual police procedural most notably by the complex, nuanced world it creates, and by the empathy it evokes for those whom other shows simply portray as crooks, thugs and perpetrators. By the time D'Angelo Barksdale gets killed off in the second season, the audience has become invested in his well-being. It is clear that he has been raised to fill a certain role. It is evident that despite his moral qualms and deep unease about that role, he has no real grasp of what other options might be available to him—and the show leaves entirely ambiguous the question of what those other options might be. Much later, when boxing coach Dennis "Cutty" Wise assures student Dukie Weems that there is a world outside drug dealing, and Dukie asks "How do you get from here to the rest of the world?," Cutty responds "I wish I knew."[26]

D'Angelo Barksdale is a pawn, an infinitely replaceable commodity. This is the message he tries to teach Bodie Broadus. By Season 4 the viewer has been acquainted with Bodie for a long time. He's been a drug dealer and a cold blooded killer—in one searing early scene, he killed his sweet, out-of-his-depth friend Wallace—but by now we understand that isn't all he is. The viewer mourns Bodie's death. By Season 4 we begin to feel in a visceral way what it means to be an expendable pawn in the game, and what it means to watch the game unfold. We can get attached to the characters. But no matter what happens to them, there will be others just like them, with the same set of circumscribed moves in the same game, already mapped out for them.

The characters learn this lesson along with the viewer. When the teacher Roland "Prez" Pryzbylewski wants to adopt his student Dukie, the assistant

---

26. Season 5, Episode 5.

principal explains to him that there will be plenty of other students in the same situation who also need his help.[27] The heartbreaking track the kids are on is a systemic problem, not often solvable by individual acts of kindness. The beneficial effect of individual acts of goodness is not ruled out. Bunny Colvin adopts Namond Brice, and it appears that he has successfully saved Namond from a short life as a hopelessly incompetent drug dealer. But for each role, there are replacements waiting in the wings. Dukie is not saved and will replace Bubbles as a street peddler and heroin addict. Michael Lee will replace Omar Little, living outside the rules of the game, robbing drug dealers. Marlo Stanfield, who replaced Avon Barksdale as the drug kingpin, will himself be replaced, as will Cedric Daniels, who resigned from the BPD rather than be forced to juke the stats. And so on. In short, *The Wire* gives us no easy outs, no quick catharsis. In the words of one commentator, "*The Wire* is in the business of telling America truths about itself that would be unbearable even if it were interested in bearing them."[28] For those of us who study and care about the criminal justice system, it is an indispensable exploration of our subject. But don't watch it just for that reason. Watch it because it's a dazzling literary achievement, a riveting show: the greatest television series ever made.[29]

Study Questions

1. David Simon describes *The Wire* as aiming to "pick a fight". What does he mean by this? How does this differ from the standard police procedural drama?

2. How is the game of chess used metaphorically in *The Wire*?

3. Within the context of *The Wire*, how do systemic dysfunction and systemic forces within criminal justice institutions influence and control individual's choices?

4. What complications are associated with using COMPSTAT? Standardized testing in schools? How do these examples encapsulate the challenges found in each institution within the criminal justice system?

---

27. Season 4, Episode 12.

28. J.M. Tyree, Review of The Wire: The Complete Fourth Season, 61 Film Quarterly 32, 38 (2008).

29. There are actually a large number of sources I could cite for this proposition. However, every one of them is an expression of its author's opinion, just as this assertion is an expression of my own opinion.

5. In what ways are the exclusionary rule and the Fourth Amendment utilized, for better or worse, in *The Wire*? As portrayed in *The Wire*, what seems to be the reality of police work? How is that similar or different from other police procedurals?

6. Bandes identifies several ways in which *The Wire* invokes viewers to reach further emotionally, conceptually, and cognitively. What are her observations about how the show challenges its viewers to do this more than other police procedurals?

Chapter 3

"Way Down in the Hole": Systemic Urban Inequality and *The Wire**

Anmol Chaddha and William Julius Wilson**

Introduction

The Wire is set in a modern American city shaped by economic restructuring and fundamental demographic change that led to widespread job loss and the depopulation of inner-city neighborhoods.[1] While the series can be viewed as an account of the systemic failure of political, economic, and social institutions in Baltimore in particular, the fundamental principles depicted in *The Wire* certainly parallel changing conditions in other cities, especially older industrial cities in the Northeast and Midwest. Indeed, it is for this reason that *The Wire* captures the attention of social scientists concerned with a comprehensive understanding of urban inequality, poverty, and race in American cities.

In providing a sophisticated depiction of systemic urban inequality, *The Wire* investigates how key aspects of inequality are interrelated. It offers an in-

* Reprinted from Anmol Chaddha and William Julius Wilson, 2011. "Way Down in the Hole: Systemic Urban Inequality and The Wire," *Critical Inquiry* 38 (Autumn), 164–188. © 2011 by The University of Chicago. Reprinted with permission from The University of Chicago Press.

** The authors greatly benefited from enlightening discussions with the students in our seminar, "Urban Inequality and The Wire" at Harvard University. This article particularly benefited from the valuable insights of Brandon Asberry, Tony Bator, Christen Brown, Dylan Matthews, and Zoe Weinberg.

1. See David Simon, The Wire: The Complete Series, DVD, 23 discs (2002–8).

depth examination of the decline of urban labor markets, crime and incarceration, the failure of the education system in low-income communities, and the inability of political institutions to serve the interests of the urban poor. A central theme of *The Wire* and a fundamental principle of scholarship on urban inequality is that political, social, and economic factors reinforce each other to produce profound disadvantage for the urban poor. By highlighting these connections, *The Wire* sheds light on the persistence and durability of concentrated disadvantage, which is reproduced across generations.[2]

Through the characters of *The Wire*, viewers can clearly see that various institutions work together to limit opportunities for the urban poor and that the actions, beliefs, and attitudes of individuals are shaped by their context. While scholars of inequality often take these ideas as basic assumptions, Americans remain strongly disposed to the idea that individuals are largely responsible for their own economic situations. In a recent survey of American attitudes, "fully two-thirds of those interviewed (67%) say blacks in this country who can't get ahead 'are mostly responsible for their own condition' while only 18% say discrimination is mainly at fault." Nearly three-quarters of U.S. whites (70 percent), a large majority of Hispanics (69 percent), and even a slight majority of blacks (52 percent) believe that "blacks who can't get ahead are mostly responsible for their own condition."[3] In the face of a dominant belief system emphasizing personal inadequacies as the cause of poverty, *The Wire* effectively undermines such views by showing how the decisions people make are profoundly influenced by their environment or social circumstances.

Unlike conventional cop or crime dramas, *The Wire* develops complex characters on each side of the law who cannot be placed in unambiguous moral categories—neither castigated for criminal pathologies and the absence of mainstream values toward work nor valorized as one-dimensional hapless victims of society's cruelty who should command endless liberal sympathy.

To be sure, *The Wire* is fictional, not a documentary, though it takes inspiration from real-life events. It draws on the experiences of its creator David Simon, a former reporter at the *Baltimore Sun*, and his co-writer, Ed Burns, a former police detective and public school teacher in Baltimore. It is part of a

---

2. See Robert J. Sampson, "Racial Stratification and the Durable Tangle of Neighborhood Inequality," *The Annals of the American Academy of Political and Social Science* 621 (Jan. 2009): 260–80, and Patrick Sharkey, "The Intergenerational Transmission of Context," *American Journal of Sociology* 113 (Jan. 2008): 931–69.

3. Pew Research Center, "A Year after Obama's Election: Blacks Upbeat about Black Progress, Prospects" (Washington, DC, 2010), p. 41, pewresearch.org/pubs/1459/year-after-obama-election-black-public-opinion.

long line of literary works that are often able to capture the complexity of urban life in ways that have eluded many social scientists. One need only consider works by Richard Wright, Italo Calvino, Ben Okri, and Charles Dickens, among many others, as examples.[4] As a work of fiction, *The Wire* does not replace rigorous academic scholarship on the problems of urban inequality and poverty. But, more than making these issues accessible to a broader audience, the show demonstrates the interconnectedness of systemic urban inequality in a way that can be very difficult to illustrate in academic works. Due to the structure of academic research, scholarly works tend to focus on many of these issues in relative isolation.

A number of excellent studies analyze the impacts of deindustrialization, crime and incarceration, and the education system on urban inequality. It is often implicitly understood among scholars that these are deeply intertwined, but an in-depth analysis of any one of these topics requires such focused attention that other important factors necessarily receive less discussion. With the freedom of artistic expression, *The Wire* is able to deftly weave together the range of forces that shape the circumstances of the urban poor while exposing deep inequality as a fundamental feature of broader social and economic arrangements.

The idea that cities function as systems in which residents, neighborhoods, and institutions are integrated into a broader ecological unit is central to the paradigmatic Chicago school of urban sociology, led by Robert Park and his colleagues in the 1920s. Emphasizing *The Wire*'s sociological value, Nicholas Lemann argues that it "was about as complete a realization of Park's dream of capturing the full richness and complexity of the city as anyone has ever accomplished. One of *The Wire*'s virtues was that, without denying any of its characters an iota of humanity, it resolutely kept its attention focused on Baltimore as a total system, in which every neighborhood and every institution exists in some relation to every other and people behave according to the incentives and choices they find set before them, more than according to whether they are good guys or bad guys."[5]

---

4. See Richard Wright, *Native Son* (New York, 1940); Italo Calvino, *Invisible Cities*, trans. William Weaver (New York, 1974); Ben Okri, *Dangerous Love* (London, 1996); and Charles Dickens, *A Tale of Two Cities* (London, 1859).

5. Nicholas Lemann, "Charm City, USA." *New York Review of Books*, 30 Sept. 2010, www.nybooks.com/articles/archives/2010/sep/30/charm-city-usa/?pagination=false

Crime and Incarceration

The first season of *The Wire* follows the activities of the Barksdale drug gang and the police unit that set out to bring down the criminal organization. The show casts a critical eye on the war on drugs, which it convincingly depicts as an ill-conceived undertaking whose primary outcome has been the mass jailing of nonviolent offenders. Street-level police officers patrol the neighborhoods where the Barksdale gang operates, and they repeatedly arrest dealers on the corners. Wee-Bey, Cutty, and the gang leader Avon Barksdale are in and out of prison throughout the series. Despite intensive policing, arrests, and jail sentences for many of the key players, the community does not seem safer. The dealers' regular customers, like Bubbles, continue to struggle with addiction, and the drug trade has hardly been curtailed.

This localized drama takes place against the backdrop of an unprecedented scale of imprisonment in the United States, where more than 2.3 million people are incarcerated.[6] The current penal regime is marked by both its magnitude and its rapid expansion in the past decades. While the incarceration rate remained relatively stable from the 1920s to the mid-1970s, it has more than tripled since 1980.[7] The U.S. far outpaces other countries with advanced economies. The incarceration rate is five times higher than that of England, which has the highest rate in Western Europe.[8] The U.S. outranks all other democracies, with an incarceration rate that significantly exceeds that of Russia and South Africa.[9]

Imprisonment, however, is not spread evenly across society; it varies tremendously by race, class, and spatial location. Just less than 1 percent of the national population is incarcerated. By comparison, one in fifteen African Americans are currently in prison or jail, with even higher rates for black men under the age of thirty-five. Considering the disproportionate severity across social groups, some scholars describe the phenomenon as "racialized mass incarceration."[10] About 10 percent of young African Americans who did not com-

---

6. See Matthew Cooper, William J. Sabol, and Heather C. West, "Prisoners in 2008," 8 Dec. 2009, bjs.ojp.usdoj.gov/content/pub/pdf/p08.pdf.

7. See Bruce Western and Becky Pettit, "Incarceration and Social Inequality," *Daedalus* 139 (Summer 2010): 8–19.

8. See Nicola Lacey, "American Imprisonment in Comparative Perspective," *Daedalus* 139 (Summer 2010): 102–14.

9. See Marc Mauer, "Comparative International Rates of Incarceration: An Examination of Causes and Trends" (2003), www.sentencingproject.org/doc/publications/inc_comparative_intl.pdf.

10. See Lawrence D. Bobo and Victor Thompson, "Racialized Mass Incarceration:

plete high school were in prison or jail in 1980; by 2008, the rate had increased to 37 percent. These men, therefore, are nearly fifty times more likely to be incarcerated than the average American. Indeed, research suggests that going to prison "has become a normal life event for African American men who have dropped out of high school."[11] Among the cohort of African American men now in their early thirties, 68 percent of those who dropped out of high school have spent some time in prison.

In terms of spatial location, it should not be surprising that residents of some neighborhoods are more likely to be incarcerated than others, since crime rates also vary across neighborhoods. Robert Sampson and Charles Loeffler, however, find that even among neighborhoods with comparable levels of crime, the incarceration rate is substantially higher for residents in neighborhoods with higher levels of concentrated disadvantage.[12] Taken together, this research makes clear that the incarceration boom in recent decades has been concentrated among certain social groups.

Beyond the unprecedented magnitude of the prison population, the social implications of mass incarceration extend beyond the individuals currently behind bars. Each inmate is tied to a number of people in the general population, with relationships to spouses, children, other family members, and friends in their communities. Given the disparities in incarceration, social exposure to the phenomenon of large-scale imprisonment is also felt most sharply by some sections of society. In a survey conducted in 2001–2 cited by Lawrence Bobo and Victor Thompson, one in ten whites reported having a close friend or relative who was incarcerated.[13] By comparison, half of African Americans had a friend or relative in prison. Class is also an important factor in who goes to prison and therefore who has social exposure to incarceration. Among high school dropouts with incomes below $25,000, one in five whites and nearly three in five blacks had a close relationship with someone behind bars. At higher-class positions, among college-educated respondents making at least $60,000, less than 5 percent of whites were tied to someone in prison. Among comparable African Americans, nearly one in three had a friend or relative in prison. While the higher end of the class hierarchy has less exposure to the incarcerated population in general, "the impact of racialized mass incarceration

Poverty, Prejudice, and Punishment," in *Doing Race: Twenty-One Essays for the Twenty-First Century*, ed. Hazel Rose Markus and Paula M. L. Moya (New York, 2010), pp. 322–55.

11. Western and Pettit, "Incarceration and Social Inequality," p. 11.

12. See Sampson and Charles Loeffler, "Punishment's Place: The Local Concentration of Mass Incarceration," *Daedalus* 139 (Summer 2010): 20–31.

13. See Bobo and Thompson, "Racialized Mass Incarceration."

reaches across boundaries of class in black America."[14] In fact, the highest status African Americans were substantially more likely to have a close friend or relative in prison than whites at much lower class positions.

In addition to disparities in who is incarcerated and the social exposure to friends and relatives in prison, mass incarceration also has the effect of exacerbating existing social inequality. The standard economic measures mask the devastating impact on poor black communities, in particular. Official statistics reveal that joblessness and unemployment are regularly more than twice as high for blacks as for whites. Since inmates are excluded from employment statistics, however, these troubling figures do not even fully capture the economic conditions of black communities.[15] Spending time in prison significantly hinders the future prospects of ex-offenders, which compounds disadvantages they faced before their incarceration. Using longitudinal data to isolate the impact of serving time in prison, Bruce Western and Becky Pettit find that incarceration is associated with 40 percent lower earnings and higher unemployment, corroborating similar findings by other researchers.[16]

A fundamental feature of the era of mass imprisonment is that incarceration has effectively been decoupled from crime. The dramatic expansion in the prison population is not accompanied by a corresponding increase in crime. Western shows that the incarceration rate has grown consistently since 1970, while official measures of crime increased in the 1970s and declined in 1990s.[17] At the level of individual offenders, one might expect a direct link between crime and punishment, so that an increase in incarceration should be the result of greater crime. At the macro level, however, political shifts since the 1960s have created the climate for a more punitive approach to crime, so much so that incarceration has increased independently of trends in actual crime. Indeed, the chances of an arrest resulting in prison time and the average time served by violent offenders have risen over time despite a decline in the level of violent crime.[18]

Recent research on mass incarceration explicitly draws attention to the role of state policy in generating and exacerbating key dimensions of urban in-

---

14. Ibid., p. 350.

15. See Western, Punishment and Inequality in America (New York, 2006).

16. See Western and Pettit, "Incarceration and Social Inequality," and Harry J. Holzer, "Collateral Costs: Effects of Incarceration on Employment and Earnings among Young Workers," in *Do Prisons Make Us Safer? The Benefits and Costs of the Prison Boom*, ed. Steven Raphael and Michael A. Stoll (New York, 2009), pp. 239–69.

17. See Western, *Punishment and Inequality in America*.

18. See ibid.

equality. Current sociological research generally emphasizes how economic and labor market processes have combined with demographic factors to produce enduring racial inequality and poverty in American cities.

Through direct state action, the boom in incarceration interacts in critical ways with deindustrialization, joblessness, and other threats to family stability and the social organization of poor inner-city neighborhoods, including the significant decline in social provision through traditional social policy.[19]

Several scenes in *The Wire* connect this macro-level analysis of mass incarceration in academic research to key processes that produce these outcomes at the micro level. Perceptions of crime and the lack of safety have been consistent challenges for political leaders throughout the era of urban decline. Elected officials place pressure on their local police departments to produce measureable results in fighting crime and typically track progress with statistics. This approach was made famous by the CompStat system of the New York Police Department and was subsequently adopted by local police around the country.

Faced with the expectation of producing numbers, police departments are encouraged to focus on poor, inner city neighborhoods to provide a greater number of arrests, especially by targeting the open-air drug trade. Much police activity in *The Wire* is intended to "juke the stats," as the officers describe it. With media attention on crime and the pursuit of measurable results, greater public pressure makes more intense policing a political necessity. Since imprisonment directly constrains the economic opportunities of ex-offenders and has deleterious consequences for their families, the social conditions of inner-city communities deteriorate even further. In cities across the country, mass incarceration has an enduring effect on the concentration of disadvantage.

Gangs and Street Culture

In his ethnographic research on the social order of an inner-city community, Elijah Anderson argues that activity and behavior in the neighborhood are characterized by one of two codes.[20] The street code places the highest value on interpersonal respect and makes the regular use of the threat of physical violence a means of self-assertion. While outsiders commonly stereotype all

19. See Loic Wacquant, Punishing the Poor: The Neoliberal Government of Social Insecurity (Durham, N.C., 2009).

20. See Elijah Anderson, Code of the Street: Decency, Violence, and the Moral Life of the Inner City (New York, 2009).

inner-city residents as acting in accordance with this code, Anderson argues that many residents in fact follow the decent code, which affirms middle-class values, personal responsibility, and participation in the mainstream economy. Subsequent ethnographic research has challenged this framework as overly simplistic and inadequate in explaining how the social organization of inner-city neighborhoods corresponds to greater violence.[21]

In the first two seasons of *The Wire*, viewers see the tension between D'Angelo's active participation in the worst aspects of the drug trade and his desire to pursue a different life path. As he develops sympathy for the victims of violent conflicts, he is unable to convince the gang leaders to change their approach. D'Angelo never reconciles these inner tensions, and, as he takes the fall for the gang's activities at the same time that he charts out a decent life for himself, he cannot be placed in either moral category. Wallace, a teenager who takes orders from D'Angelo, similarly undermines this street-decent dichotomy. While he pursues a life in the drug trade and seeks to prove his street orientation to the gang leaders, he simultaneously oversees a household of several young neighborhood children. He feeds them in the mornings, gets them ready for school, and helps with their homework. Wallace is deeply troubled by the gang's killing of a perceived adversary and doubts whether he is suited to continue in the drug trade. Unable to find an exit from that trajectory, Wallace is himself killed when the gang's leaders question his loyalty to their enterprise. The moral dichotomy is perhaps most significantly undermined by Omar, a stick-up artist who regularly robs drug dealers but follows a personal code that prevents him from harming any resident not involved with the drug trade.

D'Angelo and Wallace are not able to freely act on their personal misgivings because they are both situated within the Barksdale gang. The organization of the gang is generally in line with the "business" model of street gangs described by Sudhir Venkatesh and Steven Levitt.[22] It has a well-developed internal hierarchy with high-level executives like Avon Barksdale and Stringer Bell, managers like D'Angelo, and lower-level corner dealers like Bodie and Poot. To a significant degree, the structure of the Barksdale gang parallels that of other organizations in *The Wire*, including the police department and the dockworkers union. Internal hierarchy is central to the operations of these or-

---

21. See David J. Harding, The Living Drama: Community, Conflict, and Culture among Inner-City Boys (Chicago, 2010), and Sudhir Alladi Venkatesh, Off the Books: The Underground Economy of the Urban Poor (Cambridge, Mass., 2006).

22. See Venkatesh and Steven D. Levitt, "'Are We a Family or a Business?' History and Disjuncture in the Urban American Street Gang," *Theory and Society* 29 (Aug. 2000): 427–62.

ganizations, as reflected by the entrenched norm of following the chain of command in the police department. Each organization demands unwavering loyalty from its members, although tensions inevitably arise among those at the low end, who are expected to implement the decisions made by leaders at the top, who are removed from the day-to-day reality on the ground.

Viewing the drug gang as an organization with specific objectives—in this case, maximizing profit from the sale of drugs—helps to explain many of the actions by gang members. Some of their violent acts are rooted in the organization's objectives, such as protecting its segment of the drug market from competitors and punishing those who cooperate with police efforts to obstruct its operations in the drug trade. These motivations are distinct from psychological, emotional, or cultural sources of violence. Some of the murders carried out by the Barksdale gang are not motivated by anger or a vague personal desire for respect on the street. To the extent that an analysis fails to distinguish a gang's institutional objectives from personal and individual-level factors, explanations of social organization and inner-city violence will necessarily be incomplete.

Joblessness and Work

The Wire also examines the declining economic prospects of Baltimore and many of its residents. Cities like Baltimore were economically devastated by deindustrialization in the 1970s and 1980s. Manufacturing jobs had been a source of decent wages, and the strong demand for labor had attracted migration to these cities in earlier decades. However, in the last quarter of the twentieth century federal transportation and highway policies made it easier for industries to relocate to cheaper labor production areas in the suburbs. And the out-migration of industries was accompanied by the out-migration of higher income families to the suburbs, aided by mortgage interest tax exemptions and home mortgages for veterans.

Improved transportation and the suburbanization of employment accelerated the out-migration of central city manufacturing. With manufacturing jobs no longer readily available in central-city and inner-city areas, the Great Migration wave of blacks from the South to northern urban areas abruptly ended around 1970. With the cessation of migration from the South and the out-migration of higher income families, many poor, black, densely populated inner-city neighborhoods were physically transformed by depopulation, as abandoned homes and storefronts became common markers of the visual landscape. By 2000, there were 60,000 abandoned buildings in Philadelphia, 40,000 in Detroit, and 20,000 in Baltimore.[23] The depopulated inner city is the visible backdrop for much of the action in *The Wire*.

In addition, the end of the Great Migration from the South and the out-migration of higher income families resulted in inner-city ghettos with a much larger proportion of poor families and significantly higher levels of joblessness. These developments were in part due to the following: (1) the exodus of higher income families who were more likely to be employed, including black middle-and working-class families whose departure was also aided by antidiscrimination measures in housing; (2) the decline of industrial employment in the inner city; and (3) the decline of local businesses that depend on the resources of higher income groups, many of whom had departed.

In previous years—prior to the cessation of the Great Migration, massive industry relocation from central city neighborhoods, and the civil rights revolution—poor, working-class, and middle-class blacks had generally lived in the same section of the city, as reflected in the classic research on race and the city during this time.[24] This class heterogeneity in black neighborhoods was rooted in the intense residential segregation whereby even black families with greater resources were confined to black neighborhoods by direct discrimination in the real estate markets: redlining practices by banks that denied home loans to black applicants and restrictive covenants that prevented the sale of designated property to black buyers.[25] However, with the gradual exodus of higher income blacks, poor blacks were left behind in neighborhoods hardest hit by the disappearance of jobs.[26]

The unprecedented concentration of poverty produced the profound social isolation of poor blacks in the inner city.[27] They had little meaningful employment nearby, inadequate schools and training opportunities for higher-skill jobs, and spatial barriers to employers that had relocated to the suburbs. As joblessness climbed, formal organizations that had depended on the sup-

---

23. See Radhika K. Fox, Sarah Treuhaft, and Regan Douglass, Shared Prosperity, Stronger Regions: An Agenda for Rebuilding America's Older Core Cities (2006), www.policylink.org/atf/cf/%7B97c6d565-bb43-406d-a6d5-eca3bbf35af0%7D/SHAREDPROSPERITY-CORECITES¬FINAL.PDF.

24. See St. Clair Drake and Horace R. Cayton, *Black Metropolis: A Study of Negro Life in a Northern City* (New York, 1945).

25. See Douglas S. Massey and Nancy A. Denton, *American Apartheid: Segregation and the Making of the Underclass* (Cambridge, Mass., 1993).

26. See William Julius Wilson, *When Work Disappears: The World of the New Urban Poor* (New York, 1996).

27. See Wilson, *The Truly Disadvantaged: The Inner City, the Underclass, and Public Policy* (Chicago, 1987).

port of middle-class residents were weakened, thus undermining social organization in the inner city, including important institutions such as churches, schools, businesses, and civic clubs. As a greater percentage of the residents were jobless, they had fewer social ties to individuals employed in the formal labor market who could provide information on and access to job opportunities. With all of these developments occurring simultaneously, urban sociologists developed the concept of concentration effects to signify that the various processes associated with concentrated poverty work together to produce uniquely severe disadvantage for residents of these neighborhoods.[28]

One of the greatest strengths of *The Wire* is that it captures this analytic perspective. The Barksdale gang dominates the drug trade on Baltimore's West Side, where economic decline and the failure of political institutions have had harmful social consequences that work together to constrain the opportunities of residents. As a result of the disappearance of work, there are few economic opportunities in the mainstream economy for neighborhood residents. Many poor black residents live in public housing projects where they are generally confined to interactions with their neighbors and remain socially isolated from the rest of the city. Other than the police, there are almost never visitors from other neighborhoods.

The loss of jobs was not exclusively a problem for black workers, though. White workers were also hit by the wave of factory closings across the Northeast and Midwest during this period. Deindustrialization and the decline of manufacturing fundamentally altered the economic prospects of the white working class, especially men who had not gone to college. With labor unions in decline, workers were unable to resist the downward pressure on their wages brought about by these structural economic shifts and competition through international trade.[29] These economic factors have had important social implications for white working-class communities, as shown in ethnographic research on the impact of plant closings in white towns.[30]

The Wire examines the declining fortunes of white workers through the storyline of the dockworkers in the second season of the series. The ports had

---

28. See ibid.

29. See Richard B. Freeman, "How Much Has De-Unionization Contributed to the Rise in Male Earnings Inequality?" in *Uneven Tides: Rising Inequality in America*, ed. Sheldon Danziger and Peter Gottschalk (New York, 1993), pp. 133–63, and Bennett Harrison and Barry Bluestone, The Great U-Turn: Corporate Restructuring and the Polarizing of America (New York, 1988).

30. See Kathryn Marie Dudley, *The End of the Line: Lost Jobs, New Lives in Postindustrial America* (Chicago, 1994)

long been a source of stable jobs for the white working class, who loaded and unloaded cargo from the ships that had docked in Baltimore. With the decline in production at the steel mills, a local manifestation of the nationwide deindustrialization, activity at the ports had dropped dramatically. The stevedores depicted in *The Wire* go day to day without knowing whether they will have any work. And much of the work still remaining at the port is quickly being mechanized through technological innovation. Faced with limited economic prospects, they eventually turn to illicit activities to earn money. The union itself colludes with a smuggling ring, which delivers payments in exchange for the union's assistance in moving contraband through the port. Some individual workers also look for opportunities to make money in the local drug trade.

In many ways, the experiences of the dockworkers parallel those of the black poor depicted in *The Wire*, as both groups struggle with the disappearance of work in the formal economy. In the absence of stable employment opportunities, both the white dockworkers and black residents in the show are drawn to illicit activities to provide income. There are also clear similarities in their lack of trust in mainstream institutions and the sense that they have been abandoned in the face of economic hardship. In an economy that places a much greater premium on high levels of education and credentials than on manual skills, both the white working class and inner-city black residents sense that they have been made superfluous by deindustrialization. Bodie, a teenager who works in the drug trade, likens himself to a sacrificial pawn on a chessboard.[31] Lamenting the loss of reliable employment, the leader of the dockworkers union, Frank Sobotka, complains, "we used to make shit in this country."[32] The parallel trajectories of these two groups point to important similarities based on their class position with regard to the impact of economic restructuring.

While recognizing these similarities, we need to pay special attention to the sharp impact of rising joblessness on African American communities. Indeed black workers have borne the brunt of deindustrialization. John Bound and Harry Holzer estimate that the shift away from manufacturing accounts for nearly half of the decline in employment for less-educated young black men in the 1970s.[33] The social implications of high joblessness for many African Americans, including those formerly in manufacturing jobs, are unique because the concentration of disadvantage in black neighborhoods creates fundamentally different contexts than those in urban white neighborhoods.

---

31. See Simon, "The Buys," dir. Peter Medak, 2002, *The Wire*, Season 1, Episode 3.

32. Simon, "Bad Dreams," dir. Ernest Dickerson, 2003, *The Wire*, Season 2, Episode 11.

33. See John Bound and Holzer, "Industrial Shifts, Skills Levels, and the Labor Market for White and Black Males," *The Review of Economics and Statistics* 75 (Aug. 1993): 387–96.

In an analysis of Chicago neighborhoods, Sampson found that even the poorest white neighborhood has an income level higher than that of the median black neighborhood. This stark inequality leads him to conclude that "the bottom-line result is that residents in not one white community experience what is most typical for those residing in segregated black areas with respect to the basics of income:.... Trying to estimate the effect of concentrated disadvantage on whites is thus tantamount to estimating a phantom reality."[34]

An analysis of Baltimore neighborhoods reveals an identical pattern. Figure 1 plots Baltimore neighborhoods by their per capita income. Among black neighborhoods (that is, those in which at least 75 percent of residents are black), the median neighborhood has a per capita income of $12,588 (in 2000). The lowest per capita income of any white neighborhood is $13,550. As in Chicago, there is not a single white neighborhood in Baltimore that faces the economic conditions that characterize the typical black neighborhood (Figure 1).

When considering the neighborhood contexts of poor families, it is clear that the black poor face even greater disadvantage than poor white families in Baltimore. Among all families below the poverty line, the average poor white family lives in a neighborhood that has a poverty rate of 22.7 percent. By comparison, the average poor black family lives in a neighborhood in which 32.5 percent of the families are below the poverty line. More than a quarter of poor black families (27.7 percent) live in neighborhoods in which more than 40 percent of the residents are living below the poverty line; 6.8 percent of poor white families live in neighborhoods with such high levels of poverty. Thus, the neighborhood context differs for even poor white and poor black families. The absence of stable employment opportunities in poor black neighborhoods exacerbates this concentration of disadvantage, thereby presenting uniquely difficult challenges for its residents.

The disparate neighborhood context is not the only factor that takes us beyond the apparent similarities between the black poor and the white dockworkers in *The Wire*. The different social implications of economic hardship for the two groups are also evident. While the status of employment on the docks is certainly in decline, the stevedores maintain an attachment to jobs and are ready to report whenever work does materialize. However unpredictable their actual employment, this attachment to a job and the community

---

34. Sampson, "Racial Stratification and the Durable Tangle of Neighborhood Inequality," p. 265.

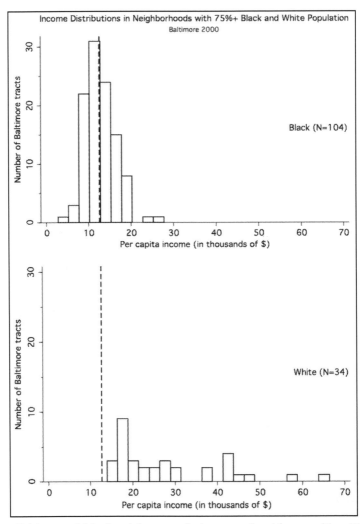

Figure 1. Baltimore neighborhoods by per capita income and racial composition. Note: the dashed line represents the per capita income of the median black neighborhood ($12,588).

of fellow union members are significant buffers against the social isolation that has accompanied economic decline in the inner city.

The union members have meaningful ties in a well-developed social network and are less isolated from mainstream institutions. The leaders of the union maintain access to political leaders in local and state government, although their political influence has diminished with their declining economic prospects. By comparison, political institutions have not been vehicles for pursuing meaningful improvements in the conditions of the black urban poor, even when black officials have been elected to office.[35] In short, whites with diminishing employment prospects still maintain fundamental advantages in social capital and access to political institutions that are not similarly available to their African American counterparts.

Politics and Urban Policy

While economic factors are central to the urban social problems examined in *The Wire*, the political context of urban decline must also be incorporated in an analysis of systemic urban inequality. As jobs were leaving urban centers in the 1980s, the Reagan administration aggressively pursued its political project of New Federalism through which the federal government dramatically reduced fiscal support for city governments and spending on programs that mainly targeted urban residents. In 1977, federal aid accounted for 17.5 percent of local government revenues in cities; by 1990, that share had dropped to a mere 5.0 percent.[36] Without this support, cities were stripped of the capacity to deal with the serious challenges presented by the crack epidemic, public health crises, and widespread homelessness in the 1980s.[37] The economic decline that accompanied deindustrialization weakened revenues for city governments, which inevitably reduced services and programs for those in need. The drastic cuts in federal aid to cities were not restored during the Clinton administration; federal support comprised 5.4 percent of city budgets in 2000.[38]

The federal abandonment of cities at the same time that joblessness became widespread in the inner city exacerbated the problems of urban decline. This political context is essential for understanding the subsequent course of urban policy and the contemporary nature of urban inequality several decades later.

In this same period, federal urban policy underwent a fundamental shift toward an explicit emphasis on the market as the preferred source of social welfare in distressed neighborhoods. Initiated by the Carter administration in

---

35. See Thompson, *Double Trouble: Black Mayors, Black Communities, and the Call for a Deep Democracy* (New York, 2005).

36. See Bruce A. Wallin, *Budgeting for Basics: The Changing Landscape of City Finances* (Washington, DC, 2005).

37. See Demetrios Caraley, "Washington Abandons the Cities," *Political Science Quarterly* 107 (Spring 1992): 1–30.

38. See Wallin, *Budgeting for Basics.*

the late 1970s, the Urban Development Action Grant (UDAG) program promoted public-private coordination of local urban development and required that local authorities work with private developers in attempts to revitalize poor neighborhoods. This market-based approach was extended through the Reagan and Clinton administrations, most notably through enterprise zones that provided tax incentives to attract developers and private firms to invest in profitable opportunities in the inner city.[39]

This marked a significant break from previous federal policy. Whereas the earlier state-sponsored antipoverty programs were essentially counter-cyclical, the new emphasis on economic development meant that urban policy had become fundamentally pro-cyclical. With the focus of urban policy shifting to economic development through a supply-side approach, inner-city neighborhoods would be dependent on the private sector rather than the state and therefore be even more vulnerable to structural economic shifts. As this explicit turn to the private sector and a market-based approach to urban policy took place in the late 1970s, inner-city neighborhoods became particularly vulnerable to the widespread problems of joblessness, which are typically viewed as an economic process.

With the decline of their industrial sectors and federal support, cities turned to urban economic development as a source of revenues to make up for their budget deficits. These strategies increasingly emphasized commercial and housing development to generate revenues from sales and property taxes. Many cities sought to develop major projects to attract revenue from outside investors and tourists.[40] With limited capacity for redistributive policy, local governments sought to attract middle-class residents through high-end residential development that could provide increased property taxes, while giving little attention to the conditions of low-income residents.[41]

Along with the strategy to attract middle-class residents, many cities also sought to deconcentrate poverty in the 1990s—mainly through the demolition of high-rise public housing projects. In cities like Baltimore and Chicago, these buildings were home to thousands of poor residents living in highly concen-

---

39. See Deirdre Oakley and Hui-Shien Tsao, "A New Way of Revitalizing Distressed Urban Communities? Assessing the Impact of the Federal Empowerment Zone Program," *Journal of Urban Affairs* 28 (Dec. 2006): 443–71, and Michael E. Porter, "The Competitive Advantage of the Inner City," *Harvard Business Review* 73 (May–June 1995): 55–71.

40. See *Cities and Visitors: Regulating People, Markets, and City Space*, ed. Lily M. Hoffman, Susan S. Fainstein, and Dennis R. Judd (Malden, Mass., 2003).

41. See Kathe Newman, "Newark, Decline and Avoidance, Renaissance and Desire: From Disinvestment to Reinvestment," *Annals of the American Academy of Social and Political Sciences* 594 (Jul. 2004): 34–48.

trated poverty. The physical structures were often in disrepair, and high rates of crime and violence threatened the safety of public housing residents. The demolition of public housing projects was supported by federal assistance, including the HOPE VI program that replaced the buildings with mixed-income developments. Local officials typically promoted the demolition of housing projects by highlighting the problems of concentrated poverty and the need to improve conditions for poor residents. Indeed, in the opening scene of the third season of *The Wire*, the mayor of Baltimore addresses residents and the media just before the high-rise projects are demolished. With local developers at his side, he emphasizes the detrimental social conditions of poor families as the basis for tearing down the buildings.[42]

Understood in the context of the pressures on local governments to generate sufficient revenue after the federal disinvestment from cities, the demolition of public housing projects was linked to urban economic development strategies. Many of the buildings were located near redeveloped downtown areas, which could attract middle-class residents who, unlike public housing residents, would pay property taxes on market-rate housing. In Chicago, for example, the infamous Cabrini-Green housing projects were located less than one mile from downtown; they were demolished and replaced with mixed-income housing. Considering that many former residents of public housing in cities like Baltimore, Chicago, St. Louis, and Atlanta had not been relocated to other areas several years after their public housing projects were demolished, they were apt to question whether the discourse of deconcentrating poverty had been cynically employed to promote high-end real estate development instead.[43] As the mayor in *The Wire* announces the demolition of the housing projects with great fanfare, three teenagers debate the costs and benefits of losing the towers.[44] Beyond the problems posed by the restructured labor market and broader economic forces, political institutions have also failed to improve the conditions of the urban poor.

The period of urban decline also coincided with the ascent of an urban black political elite, as black mayors were elected in many large cities for the first time. However, this apparent political empowerment has not seemed to produce meaningful improvements in the conditions of the urban black poor.

---

42. See Simon, "Time after Time," dir. Ed Bianchi, 2004, *The Wire*, Season 3, Episode 1.

43. See Jeff Crump, "Deconcentration by Demolition: Public Housing, Poverty, and Urban Policy," *Environment and Planning* D 20, no. 2 (2002): 581–96, and Edward G. Goetz, *Clearing the Way: Deconcentrating the Poor in Urban America* (Washington, DC, 2003).

44. See Simon, "Time after Time."

In a detailed study of urban politics in postwar Atlanta, Clarence Stone describes a long-running alliance between the white business elite and black middle class that has shaped local policymaking and constrained the policy options available to elected officials.[45] This alliance has negotiated a compromise through which the white business elite benefits from pro-growth policy while the black middle class has reaped gains in minority business opportunities. Even when Maynard Jackson was elected in 1973 with the support of progressive, neighborhood-based voters, he was unable to implement redistributive policies that would have benefited poor black residents. Stone emphasizes the distinction between an electoral coalition and a governing coalition; although they may be significant in their electoral power, residents of poor, black neighborhoods cannot contribute much in governing capacity, and elected mayors are consistently dependent on the entrenched regime for governing authority.

In the fictional depiction of Baltimore politics in *The Wire*, the incumbent black mayor, Clarence Royce, makes symbolic appeals to black voters when he is threatened by an electoral challenge from a white candidate. While in office, however, Mayor Royce never prioritized policies that would benefit the black poor. The influence of governing coalitions on local policies points to the significance of political processes and shows that macroeconomic forces do not solely determine urban inequality. In analyzing the waves of black mayors in recent decades, Thompson also emphasizes the divide between the black political elite and the urban poor.[46] While the black political elite depend on low-income black voters to get elected, once in office they actually demobilize the black poor by building coalitions with business interests and the middle class; and consequently they prevent the black poor from effectively demanding policies that improve their conditions.

Even in cities with a substantial share of low-income black residents, elected officials have tended to cater to middle-class residents and business interests that can provide valuable governing capacity and economic resources that are crucial in local politics. Nonetheless, while political institutions have not effectively improved the conditions of the urban poor, the magnitude of the underlying structural problems may in fact be beyond the capacity of local government to address. Deindustrialization has devastated the economic base of many large cities, and federal disinvestment from the cities further weakened the ability of local governments to address urgent problems. The combined impact of these changes—declining economic and social institutions

---

45. See Clarence N. Stone, *Regime Politics: Governing Atlanta, 1946–1988* (Lawrence, Kans., 1989).

46. See Thompson, *Double Trouble*.

and the failure of political institutions—on the residents of poor inner-city neighborhoods is fully captured in *The Wire*'s portrayal of systemic urban inequality.

Education and Youth

In his classic 1965 text on the conditions of the black poor in inner-city ghettos, Kenneth Clark devotes a chapter to "ghetto schools" and the unequal educational achievement of black and white students.[47] More than four decades later, much of his analysis applies to present-day urban schools, which are examined in the fourth season of *The Wire*. Clark points to the de facto segregation of schools as the fundamental factor at the root of educational inequality. He strongly criticizes popular arguments that emphasize cultural deprivation as the cause of lower black achievement. In his view institutional practices of schools and the structure of the education system are much more significant in explaining educational inequality than cultural explanations. As schools develop lower expectations for black students, he argues, these become self-fulfilling prophecies as black students then inevitably underachieve.

The public school depicted in *The Wire* lacks the necessary resources to truly educate students and help them develop skills that prepare them for jobs that would pay decent wages. Even before the students reach high school, their trajectories are seriously constrained by the poor quality of the elementary and middle schools and the limited economic opportunities available to them. The students themselves seem aware of their likely outcomes, and the teachers are often resigned to accept their fate. In a comment that describes the antagonistic dynamics in the school, one teacher in the show reflects, "no one wins. One side just loses more slowly."[48] The students also recognize that even if they were able to learn skills in their schools, they would be thwarted by the absence of well-paying jobs in the surrounding area.

At a systemic level, economic factors and educational institutions work together to shape this dimension of urban inequality. Although some students might overcome these obstacles and attain some upward mobility, the broad pattern of social stratification is reproduced and remains durable. The school essentially prepares the students for the social positions they occupy. For students who are already involved in the drug trade, the school is actually a site of learning the habits of disobeying rules and dealing with authority.

---

47. See Kenneth B. Clark, *Dark Ghetto: Dilemmas of Social Power* (New York, 1965).
48. Simon, "Refugees," dir. Jim McKay, 2006, *The Wire*, Season 4, Episode 4.

Through an in-depth historical analysis of inner-city education, Kathryn Neckerman emphasizes that the problems of inner-city schools are fundamentally linked to policy choices made by the school system throughout the twentieth century.[49] Using the case study of inner-city schools in Chicago, she highlights the inadequate response to de facto segregation in the school system, the implementation of vocational education that relegated black students to a lower tier of skills training, and the failure of schools to provide adequate remedial education for low-achieving students. Her analysis makes clear that the problems of inner-city schools were not necessarily and inevitably determined by the concentration of disadvantage in the surrounding communities; instead, these institutions pursued specific policies that had detrimental impacts on the achievement of black students. While urban decline was an important condition that contributed to failing schools, the practices of educational institutions resulted in even greater inequality.

This focus on institutional practices effectively challenges alternative explanations that overemphasize the role of individual actors, especially those that attribute low achievement to the behavior or attitudes of teachers, families, or students. A common view is that, in the context of racial segregation and social isolation, black students have developed an oppositional culture toward schools and teachers. According to this explanation, the cultural perspective of black students entails a devaluing of education, which is presumed to be a significant factor in their low achievement. A specific version of this explanation holds that black students stigmatize educational success as acting white; rather than accept the social penalty that supposedly comes with educational achievement, black students are hypothesized to favor social acceptance over education.[50] While there may be evidence of oppositional or antagonistic relationships between some students and the schools, these explanations do not adequately explain racial disparities in educational achievement.[51]

An overemphasis on attractive but inadequate cultural explanations mistakenly draws attention away from structural, institutional, and environmental factors that are fundamental to understanding educational inequality. Prudence Carter connects the cultural orientations of students to institutional practices of schools by demonstrating that the schools and teachers actually

---

49. See Kathryn M. Neckerman, *Schools Betrayed: Roots of Failure in Inner-City Education* (Chicago, 2007).

50. See Signithia Fordham and John U. Ogbu, "Black Students' School Success: Coping with the 'Burden of "Acting White,"'" *Urban Review* 18 (Sept. 1986): 176–206.

51. See Roland G. Fryer, "'Acting White': The Social Price Paid by the Best and Brightest Minority Students," *Education Next* 6 (Winter 2006): 53–59.

link cultural patterns of students to their educational outcomes. She distinguishes between "dominant" and "non-dominant" forms of cultural capital and argues that teachers mistakenly interpret the "non-dominant" cultural capital of inner-city students as evidence of lower academic ability.[52] This profoundly shapes the expectations that teachers hold, which then constrains the academic performance of poor, black students. Even if a student does value education and is committed to succeeding in an inner-city school, the structural barriers in the education system as depicted in *The Wire* present tremendous obstacles.

Outside of the schools, the neighborhood context is also an important factor in the cognitive and educational development of students. As an illustration of the impact of the neighborhood environment, researchers analyzed longitudinal data on 750 black students in Chicago and found that "residing in a severely disadvantaged neighborhood cumulatively impedes the development of academically relevant verbal ability in children."[53] An important finding in this research is that the negative effects of concentrated disadvantage on the cognitive development of the students persisted even for those who had moved out of these neighborhoods.

In addition to the economic and demographic components of neighborhood disadvantage, the high levels of violence characteristic of many poor urban neighborhoods may also adversely affect students. In a recent study, Patrick Sharkey finds that performance on cognitive assessments was significantly lower for students who lived in areas in which a homicide had occurred in the week before they were given the test.[54] This study estimates only the effect of a very recent murder near a student's home on his or her cognitive performance. The long-term effects of cumulative exposure to high levels of violence may also have significant implications for the development of children in poor urban neighborhoods.

Beyond these acute effects of violence on student achievement, the prevalence of violent conflicts has important implications for the social organization of these neighborhoods, especially for youth. Based on ethnographic research in inner-city neighborhoods, David Harding shows that the perceived threat

---

52. See Prudence L. Carter, "'Black' Cultural Capital, Status Positioning, and Schooling Conflicts for Low-Income African American Youth," *Social Problems* 50 (Feb. 2003): 136–55.

53. Sampson, Patrick Sharkey, and Stephen W. Raudenbush, "Durable Effects of Concentrated Disadvantage on Verbal Ability among African-American Children," *Proceedings of the National Academy of Sciences*, 23 Jan. 2008, p. 846.

54. See Sharkey, "The Acute Effect of Local Homicide on Children's Cognitive Performance," Proceedings of the National Academy of Sciences, 26 June 2010, pp. 11733–38.

of violence leads poor youth to seek protection by developing more neigh-borhood-based bonds among youth of different ages. Whereas young people in other neighborhoods tend to create relationships with peers of their same age, youth in poor neighborhoods are more likely to develop social ties with people who are a few years older. These bonds facilitate the "cross-cohort so-cialization" that Harding argues is an important mechanism for the transmis-sion of certain worldviews about education and the labor market.[55]

In a notable scene in *The Wire*, two teenage drug dealers marvel at the in-genuity of their boneless Chicken McNuggets and imagine that they must have made their inventor extremely wealthy. An older dealer, D'Angelo, derides their naïveté. "The man who invented them things, just some sad ass down at the basement of McDonald's thinking up some shit to make money for the real players," he tells them. Disillusioned with a formal labor market comprised mainly of low-wage jobs, D'Angelo rejects it as fundamentally unfair since people are not rewarded according to their true worth. In his view, powerful institutions regularly exploit those with less power, and social inequality is the inevitable result. His understanding of how society works shapes his approach to how one should operate in such a world. When a younger dealer objects to the inadequate compensation of the McNuggets inventor, D'Angelo teaches them, "it ain't about right. It's about money." In this way, D'Angelo transmits his view of how the world works to the dealers who are several years younger.[56]

Given the scale of mass imprisonment, poor urban youth are also exposed to family members and older friends who are or have been incarcerated. Christo-pher Wildeman estimates that 25 percent of black children born in 1990 had a parent in prison by the time they reached the age of fourteen; by compari-son, approximately 4 percent of white children had a parent in prison.[57] For black children born to parents who had not completed high school, more than 50 percent had a father in prison. The risk of having a parent or family mem-ber who is incarcerated therefore is especially concentrated among low-income black youth. Having an incarcerated parent has detrimental, long-term im-pacts on these children, who already confront other forms of disadvantage.[58] In *The Wire*, the young character Namond is shown visiting his incarcerated father, Wee-Bey, who had been active in the drug trade. Namond is identified

---

55. Harding, *The Living Drama*, p. 4.

56. Simon, "The Detail," dir. Clark Johnson, 2002, *The Wire*, Season 1, Episode 2.

57. See Christopher Wildeman, "Parental Imprisonment, the Prison Boom, and the Concentration of Childhood Disadvantage," *Demography* 46 (May 2008): 265–80.

58. See Megan Comfort, "Punishment beyond the Legal Offender," *Annual Review of Law and Social Science* 3 (2007): 271–96.

by the school as a particularly troubled student and soon thereafter enters the drug trade himself as a street-level dealer.[59]

The low educational achievement of poor urban youth can be traced to the social dimensions of their neighborhood context, the economic factors underlying urban decline, the institutional practices of the school system, and the reliance on mass imprisonment in the criminal justice system. This set of factors undermines the "achievement ideology" that promotes a belief in the equality of opportunity and assumes that schooling itself can provide a route for upward mobility. In this framework, education is regarded as the solution to social inequality. With an understanding of how unequal education reproduces social inequality, acceptance of the "achievement ideology" is a key mechanism through which existing inequality is legitimated.[60] The entangled connections among these institutions are at the core of systemic, multigenerational urban inequality.

Urban Inequality beyond *The Wire*

By placing crime and the drug trade at the center of its depiction of urban inequality, *The Wire* runs the risk of reinforcing stereotypical depictions of the urban poor. Some writers have maintained that the show promotes biased views of poor African Americans as dependent on welfare, lazy, criminal, and immoral.[61] A degree of caution about the broader implications of how the black poor is represented is certainly well-founded. These negative perceptions have dominated popular discourse on urban inequality, and they, too, often influence decisions about who is deemed worthy of assistance through social policy.[62]

A careful assessment, however, reveals that *The Wire* actually powerfully undermines these dangerous stereotypes. By examining the institutions that shape the characters, it convincingly demonstrates that the outcomes of the

---

59. See Simon, "Soft Eyes," dir. Christine Moore, 2008, *The Wire*, Season 5, Episode 2.

60. See Jay MacLeod, *Ain't No Makin' It: Aspirations and Attainment in a Low-Income Neighborhood* (Boulder, Colo., 1987).

61. See Mark Bowen, "The Angriest Man in Television," *Atlantic Monthly* 301 (Jan.--Feb. 2008): 50–57, and Ishmael Reed, "Should Harvard Teach 'The Wire'? No, It Relies on Cliche s about Blacks and Drugs," *Boston Globe*, 30 Sept. 2010, www.boston.com/bostonglobe/editorial_opinion/oped/articles/2010/09/30/no_it_relies_on_clichs_about_blacks_and_drugs/.

62. See Martin Gilens, *Why Americans Hate Welfare: Race, Media, and the Politics of Antipoverty Policy* (Chicago, 1999), and Michael B. Katz, *The Undeserving Poor* (New York, 1989).

lives of the black poor are not the result of individual predispositions for violence, group traits, or cultural deficits. Through a scrupulous exploration of the inner workings of drug-dealing gangs, the police, politicians, unions, and public schools, *The Wire* shows that individuals' decisions and behavior are often shaped by—and indeed limited by—social, political, and economic forces beyond their control.

To be sure, *The Wire* does not provide a comprehensive portrayal of the various complex dimensions of life in the inner city. As one example, the influx of immigrants in recent decades has reshaped urban America. A thorough understanding of contemporary urban inequality needs to include an examination of how recent immigration continues to transform American cities. The racial landscape of urban inequality is far more complex than an exclusive focus on poor black ghettos. In its depiction of the poorest of the poor, the series does not provide an in-depth portrayal of the challenges faced by those who do hold jobs in the formal economy and who may be above the poverty line but nevertheless struggle in the context of deep urban inequality. As others have noted, many residents of these neighborhoods are actively engaged in political efforts to improve their conditions; rather than adapt to their circumstances, they work to improve the opportunities that should be available to residents.[63]

In fact, metropolitan poverty itself is no longer a fundamentally inner-city phenomenon. In recent years, the share of the nation's poor living in the suburbs has actually surpassed that of the cities. Of the 39.1 million people below the poverty line in 2008, 31.9 percent were in the suburbs, 28.0 percent lived in "primary cities," and the rest were in small metropolitan and rural areas.[64] In portraying the lives of the urban poor, *The Wire* also gives relatively little attention to families and parents, which have long been the subject of considerable research on urban poverty.

There are undoubtedly several substantive topics that are relevant to urban poverty but receive less attention in the series. That said, we must not lose sight of an important recurring theme in the series: given a limited set of available opportunities, there is often no exit from the predetermined life trajectories of residents in poor urban neighborhoods. This is vividly illustrated in the lives of D'Angelo, Wallace, and many other characters. By the end of the series, the problems remain unsolved, and the cycle repeats itself. Disadvantages become more deeply entrenched over time and across generations.

---

63. See John Atlas and Peter Dreier, "Is The Wire Too Cynical?" *Dissent* 55 (Summer 2008): 79–82.

64. See Elizabeth Kneebone and Emily Garr, *The Suburbanization of Poverty: Trends in Metropolitan America, 2000 to 2008* (Washington, DC, 2010).

A fundamental objective of social scientists is to generate explanations of social conditions. Outside of academia, ordinary people also form explanations about their conditions and how the world works, and *The Wire* takes their explanations seriously.

A key lesson from the series is that people's circumstances are shaped by the institutions that govern their lives—despite their best efforts to demonstrate individual autonomy, distinctiveness, and moral and material worth. Accordingly, the conditions of the urban poor cannot be understood as somehow existing outside the political and economic arrangements of the broader society. By depicting the interrelationship of social, political, and economic institutions that work together to constrain the lives of the urban poor, *The Wire* effectively illustrates the fundamental nature of systemic urban inequality.

Study Questions

1. *The Wire* investigates systemic urban inequality within an urban setting. What factors within political, economic, and social institutions are known to lead to this inequality?

2. What have real-world studies been shown to find regarding such inequalities? How does this compare with the Chicago School and Robert Park's ideas of inequality?

3. What are the social implications of mass incarcerations seen within certain social groups and communities? How does this inequality manifest itself within economic the structure of the affected communities? What are the characteristics of the affected social groups and communities?

4. Describe the "codes" characterizing activity and behavior within inner-city neighborhoods. How are these codes embraced or undermined by various characters in *The Wire*?

5. Discuss the history of the Great Migration that occurred in relation to deindustrialization in the 1970's and 1980's. What factors contributed to a larger number of poor families and higher unemployment?

6. How do policy choices and economic limitations contribute to the inequality of inner-city schools and their ability to prepare students for life within, or beyond, their community? What other factors outside of educational inequality effect the development of individual students?

Chapter 4

I Got the Shotgun: Reflections on *The Wire,* Prosecutors, and Omar Little[*]

Introduction

The Wire, although it features police and prosecutors, is not a show that sets out to be about the law or the criminal justice system. Instead, the series creator, David Simon, views *The Wire* as a critique of the excesses of unencumbered capitalism:

> Thematically, it's about the very simple idea that, in this postmodern world of ours, human beings—all of us—are worthless.... Whether you're a corner boy in West Baltimore, or a cop who knows his beat, or an Eastern European brought here for sex, your life is worthless. It's the triumph of capitalism over human value. This country has embraced the idea that this is a viable domestic policy. It is. It's viable for the few. But I don't live in Westwood, L.A., or on the Upper West Side of New York. I live in Baltimore.[1]

* Reprinted with permission from: Alafair S. Burke, "I Got the Shotgun: Reflections on *The Wire,* Prosecutors, and Omar Little," *Ohio State Journal of Criminal Law,* 8: 447–458 (2011).

** I am thankful to Professors Susan Bandes, Bennett Capers, Jeffrey Fagan, and David Sklansky for including me on the panel at the annual conference of the Law & Society Association that influenced this essay, and to Stephen Cheng, Sean Doherty, and Erin Mitchell for their valuable research assistance. I also want to thank David Simon for participating on the panel and for creating hours of thoughtful television viewing.

1. Meghan O'Rourke, *Behind* The Wire: *David Simon on Where the Show Goes Next,* SLATE (Dec. 1, 2006, 2:27 PM), http://www.slate.com/id/2154694/pagenum/all/#p2.

The Wire is also a show about institutions, the people trapped inside of them, and a society made static by their inaction, indifference, and ineptitude. Whether the series was exploring the drug trade, police departments, city hall, unions, or public schools, the individual actors within those systems were depicted as having little control over either the institutions or their individual fates within them. As a result, the constituencies supposedly served by those institutions continually "got the shaft."

To say that *The Wire* is about the tolls of unmitigated capitalism and inflexible bureaucracies is not to say that the show is silent on, or indifferent to, the criminal justice system that encompasses its main characters. Perhaps because I am a former prosecutor who now teaches criminal law and procedure and writes about the discretionary decisions of law enforcement, I have a tendency to focus on the series' messages about the criminal justice system. I became especially intrigued by an episode in the first season in which police and prosecutors rely on the testimony of Omar Little in a murder trial, despite doubts about Omar's first-hand knowledge of the crime. This essay is a reflection on the depiction of law enforcement in *The Wire*, both generally and with respect to the single scene that first made me a *Wire* addict.

Reflections on the Legal System

Perhaps because *The Wire* was not intended to be primarily about the criminal justice system, the directness of *The Wire*'s assault on that system differentiates it from shows that are actually about law enforcement. *Law and Order*, for example, lionizes police and prosecutors, the two separate yet equally important groups that represent the people. More importantly, it largely celebrates the system in which those two actors operate. Sure, Jack McCoy was once brought up on ethical charges for hiding a material witness from the defense, but he was cleared.[2] ADA Serena Southerlyn also stretched ethical bounds by pretending to be a defense lawyer, but she did so to resolve a life-threatening hostage situation.[3] Similarly, when Detective Lennie Brisco stretches the truth on the stand, he does so to gloss over an immaterial fact that threatens the conviction of a dangerous stalker.[4] For the most part though, in the world of

---

2. *See Law & Order: Monster* (NBC television broadcast May 20, 1998); *Law & Order: Cherished* (NBC television broadcast Sept. 23, 1998).

3. *See Law & Order: DR 1-102* (NBC television broadcast Jan. 30, 2002).

4. *See Law & Order: Stalker* (NBC television broadcast Apr. 15, 1998). When Lieutenant Van Buren scolds Briscoe that he was "an inch away from perjury," he responds, "More like a foot, foot and a half." *Id.*

Law and Order, bad guys are arrested, good guys prevail, order is restored, and justice usually prevails—all within the system. Even a more rebellious show like *The Shield* assumes that the criminal justice system is presumptively legitimate, but then explores the havoc that a rare bad apple like Vic Mackey can reap from inside of it.

The Wire, in contrast, does not simply nip at the grey edges of a black and white legal system that differentiates between good and evil. Instead, as it does with seemingly all bureaucracies, the show subtly asks its viewers to question the entire law enforcement enterprise. How can we trust detectives who would contemplate faking their own injuries in order to retire early?[5] How can we trust a judge who would let his own political ambitions affect decisions about whether to approve a wiretap?[6] How can we trust a corrections system that allows D'Angelo to be murdered and then faults his death a suicide?[7]

No other piece of pop culture has ever had as much to say about our nation's drug policy as *The Wire*. When D'Angelo Barksdale resists pressure to flip on his Uncle Avon, but is later murdered in custody for his perceived disloyalty, *The Wire* teaches its viewers something about the Catch-22 suffered by would-be informants and the failure of our corrections system to protect even the best-intentioned prisoners.[8] As soldier upon soldier in the drug dealing operation is either killed or incarcerated, only to be replaced on the same corner and in the same role, *The Wire* directly takes on the assumptions underlying our War on Drugs. Indeed, *The Wire*'s writers have expressed their distrust of prevailing legal norms publicly, embracing jury nullification in non-violent drug cases as a form of "legitimate protest."[9]

5. *The Wire: Old Cases* (HBO television broadcast June 23, 2002). Detectives Mahone and Polk, two "humps" on the squad, celebrate a minor injury Mahone suffers because it will allow him to retire early. Mahone suggests that Polk throw himself down a flight of stairs to enable him to do the same. *Watching The Wire: Episode Four: Old Cases*, REV/VIEWS: DVD & TELEVISION, http://rev-views.blogspot.com/2008/11/watching-wire-episode-four-old-cases.html (last visited Mar. 6, 2011).

6. Judge Daniel Phelan is initially a friend to Detective McNulty and supports the use of wiretaps in a sprawling investigation of Avon Barksdale's operation. When he realizes that his authorization is costing him political goodwill, he pulls back on his support, but ultimately supports the police again by authorizing a tap on Stringer Bell's telephone. *Daniel Phelan*, WIKIA, http://thewire.wikia.com/wiki/Daniel_Phelan (last visited Mar. 6, 2011).

7. *See The Wire: All Prologue* (HBO television broadcast July 6, 2003); *The Wire: Backwash* (HBO television broadcast July 13, 2003).

8. *See The Wire: All Prologue* (HBO television broadcast July 6, 2003).

9. Ed Burns et al., *Saving Cities, and Souls*, TIME, Mar. 17, 2008, at 50. *Cf.* Paul Butler, *Racially Based Jury Nullification: Black Power in the Criminal Justice System*, 105 YALE L.J. 677, 679 (1995) (advocating jury nullification in trials of African-American defendants for non-violent offenses).

One way in which *The Wire* subtly calls into question the legitimacy of sup-posedly legitimate enterprises is by drawing narrative parallels between the drug game on the street and the rules of government and recognized institu-tions and bureaucracies. It is no coincidence that Avon's number two, Stringer Bell, continually applies lessons from his economics classes at the local com-munity college to his neighborhood trade and runs meetings of his soldiers using Robert's Rules of Order. In Season 2, Episode 5, "Undertow," Bell is wor-ried about the operation's market share because of concerns about the repu-tation of its product on the street.[10] In a discussion with his professor, he realizes that a name change is in order after the professor invokes the example of WorldCom adopting the MCI corporate name in an attempt to ditch the stigma of its infamous accounting fraud scandal.[11] In a subsequent scene of the episode, *The Wire*'s writers cut to the image of a government seal for Im-migration and Naturalization being removed from the wall only to be replaced by a new Department of Homeland Security sign.[12]

You Got the Briefcase

It is through the lens of *The Wire*'s overall challenge to recognized bu-reaucracies in general and to the criminal justice system in particular that I viewed one of my favorite scenes from the series, in Season 2, Episode 6, "All Prologue."[13] The scene's star is Omar Little,[14] a self-described "rip and run"

---

10. *See The Wire: Undertow* (HBO television broadcast June 29, 2003).

11. *Id.*

12. *Id.*

13. The title refers to D'Angelo's comments about *The Great Gatsby*, shortly before he was murdered for trying to put his life with Avon behind him: He's saying that the past is always with us. Where we come from, what we go through, how we go through it—all this shit matters.... Like at the end of the book, ya know, boats and tides and all. It's like you can change up, right, you can say you're somebody new, you can give yourself a whole new story. But, what came first is who you really are and what happened before is what really happened. And it don't matter that some fool say he different cuz the things that make you different is what you really do, what you really go through. Like, ya know, all those books in his library. Now he frontin with all them books, but if you pull one down off the shelf, ain't none of the pages have ever been opened. He got all them books, and he hasn't read nearly one of them. Gatsby, he was who he was, and he did what he did. And cuz he wasn't ready to get real with the story, that shit caught up to him. That's what I think, anyway. *The Wire: All Prologue* (HBO television broadcast July 6, 2003).

14. While running for president, then-candidate Barack Obama identified Omar Little as his favorite television character. Perhaps demonstrating the cautiousness that restrains po-

4 · I GOT THE SHOTGUN

artist.[15] When asked to explain the meaning of that term, he says, "I robs drug dealers."[16] As demonstrated by his chosen profession, Omar is guided by his own moral code—"Robin Hood shit," as Bell complains.[17] He boasts to Detective William "Bunk" Moreland that he targets Barksdale's crew because of its practice of murdering civilians: "I ain't never put my gun on nobody that wasn't in the game."[18] Even Bunk has to concede, "A man must have a code."[19] We see Omar's code in action when he robs a shopkeeper of his drug stash but then takes the time to pay cash for a pack of cigarettes, waiting for proper change.[20]

In "All Prologue," Omar agrees to testify for the prosecution against a Barksdale soldier named Bird who has been charged with murdering a state witness. Omar's testimony is vengeance for Bird's involvement in the murder of his boyfriend, Brandon, whose death Barksdale ordered in retaliation for a robbery that Omar and Brandon had committed. Omar's cross-examination by drug lawyer, Maurice Levy, is one of the most memorable courtroom scenes in television:

> **Levy:** You are feeding off the violence and the despair of the drug trade. You're stealing from those who themselves are stealing the lifeblood from our city. You are a parasite who leeches off the culture of drugs...
> **Omar:** Just like you, man.
> **Levy:** Excuse me? What?
> **Omar:** I got the shotgun. You got the briefcase. It's all in the game though, right?'[21]

The most obvious comparison in Omar's cross-examination scene is between Omar and Levy, but whether intentionally or not, *The Wire's* writers also hint at parallels between Omar and members of law enforcement. Like Omar and Levy, law enforcement can also be said to profiteer from the drug war. Individual officers benefit from the quick and easy overtime racked up from felony drug busts. In the first season, the writers depict a lazy detective's comment that cases go from "red to black" (meaning open to closed, as noted

---

litical candidates, Obama felt the need to add the phrase, "[t]hat's not an endorsement." Sam Delaney, *Omar Little is the Gay Stick-Up Man Who Robs Drug Dealers for a Living in The Wire...*, THE GUARDIAN, July 19, 2008, (The Guide), at 5.

15. *The Wire: All Prologue* (HBO television broadcast July 6, 2003).
16. *Id.*
17. *The Wire: Game Day* (HBO television broadcast August 4, 2002).
18. *The Wire: One Arrest* (HBO television broadcast July 14, 2002).
19. *Id.*
20. *See The Wire: Home Rooms* (HBO television broadcast Sept. 24, 2006).
21. *The Wire: All Prologue* (HBO television broadcast July 6, 2003).

by the color of ink used to list a case on the whiteboard) "by way of green" (meaning overtime paid to officers).[22] Police departments also skim money from the drug trade through asset forfeiture, frequently evading local mandates that forbid the use of such assets for non-law enforcement purposes by funneling the cases to federal prosecutors through "adoption" procedures.[23]

But the comparison I find most subtle and intriguing is the parallel between the moral codes of Omar and the cops and prosecutors who would put him on the stand despite doubts about whether he actually saw Bird pull the trigger. By using Omar as a witness, Detective McNulty and Assistant State's Attorney Ilene Nathan, like Omar, create their own moral code. Like Omar, they decide for themselves what is right. They entrust themselves to be the arbiters of truth outside of the formal legal system.

Perhaps it is because I worked as a prosecutor and often write about prosecutorial decision-making that I was so interested in an earlier scene in which McNulty brings Omar to ASA Nathan for a proffer. Nathan asks Omar to leave the room and then asks McNulty whether Omar is telling the truth. Despite her concerns, she agrees to use Omar as a government witness but on one condition—that McNulty purchase Omar proper courtroom attire, "anything with a tie."[24] What ultimately matters to her is that she and McNulty both know Bird is guilty. Once that determination is made—by them, not a jury—the challenge is to prove his guilt, even if it means relying on the obviously self-interested Omar.

Police and Prosecutors as Omar Little

That prosecutors believe they are entitled to determine for themselves what is just is a point that a show like *Law and Order* makes far less subtly than *The Wire*. Consider, for example, this representative exchange between District Attorney Adam Schiff and Assistant District Attorney Ben Stone from an early episode of the former:

---

22. *The Wire: The Detail* (HBO television broadcast June 9, 2002).

23. *See* Eric Blumenson & Eva Nilsen, *Policing for Profit: The Drug War's Hidden Economic Agenda,* 65 U. CHI. L. REV. 35, 40?41 (1998); Karen Dillon, *State's Forfeiture Woes Trace to Federal Officials,* K.C. STAR, May 22, 2000, at A7, *available at* 2000 WL 7733243 (describing how law enforcement can evade local rules for forfeiture by handing off proceedings to federal agencies).

24. *See The Wire: Undertow* (HBO television broadcast June 29, 2003).

Schiff: You want the jury to ignore the evidence.

Stone: No, Chris and Amy [the defendants] want the jury to look at the law. I'll get the jury to look at Chris and Amy.

Schiff: The law's supposed to be a shield, not a sword. They're despicable, yes. But by the letter of the law, they're not guilty.

Stone: The legislature could never have conceived of anything like this. Wrong should not win by technicalities. You know that yourself.

Schiff: Get these bastards off the street.[25]

The beauty of the writing on *The Wire* is that the show does not hit viewers over the head. It makes its points not in a single line of dialogue or even a single scene or episode, but across the course of five seasons. We watch the evolution of Omar Little, Witness for the Government, from beginning to end—his first meeting with the skeptical but unscrutinizing prosecutor, his shopping trip with McNulty to peruse possible suit purchases for his transformation to the witness stand, his direct and cross examination, and, finally, the scene in which he is rewarded for his cooperation. Outside the courtroom, we watch the prosecutor and McNulty celebrate Bird's conviction with Omar.[26] As the prosecutor hands Omar a "Get Out of Jail Free" card for future use, Bird passes them in the hallway and threatens Omar's life.[27] Even though Omar responds by telling Bird to "think on Brandon," neither Nathan nor McNulty inquires into Omar's apparent grudge against Bird.[28] After Nathan is gone, McNulty finally asks Omar whether he really witnessed Bird pull the trigger.[29] Omar's response: "Are you really asking?"[30] McNulty walks away in silence.[31]

With the government's tactics against Bird, we see the harsher side of law enforcement's "we decide who's innocent" tendencies. But in a later episode, we see its softer side as law enforcement uses its discretion to show leniency towards street junkie Bubbles.[32] Tormented by another vagrant's assaults and robberies, Bubbles concocts a "hot shot" of heroin and sodium cyanide that he assumes his enemy will steal and then use.[33] Instead, Bubbles' beloved

---

25. *Law & Order: Misconception* (NBC television broadcast Oct. 29, 1991).

26. *See The Wire: All Prologue* (HBO television broadcast July 6, 2003).

27. *Id.*

28. *See id.*

29. *Id.*

30. *Id.*

31. *See id.*

32. *See The Wire: Final Grades* (HBO television broadcast Dec. 10, 2006).

33. *The Wire: That's Got His Own* (HBO television broadcast Dec. 3, 2006).

protégé Sherrod stumbles upon the tainted drugs and dies from an over-dose.[34] Wracked with guilt (and apparently understanding the doctrine of transferred intent), Bubbles turns himself into police and confesses.[35] How-ever, a sympathetic sergeant decides not to charge him, even though the de-cision will adversely affect the homicide unit's all-important clearance statistics.[36]

The joy of watching Maurice Levy cross-examine Omar is that we know as view-ers that Omar does in fact have a moral code when he explains, "I ain't never put my gun on no citizen."[37] And like Omar, ASA Nathan also distinguishes be-tween a true innocent and someone in the game, deciding for herself what amounts to justice. But where a self-created, Robin-Hood-style vision of justice might be admirable in a rip-and-run artist, it is not so desirable in a prosecutor.

Why Prosecutors Might
See Themselves as Omar Littles

A prosecutor's duty to do justice is well-known.[38] So is the fact that some prosecutors do not live up to that obligation, so it may be tempting to attrib-ute ASA Nathan's decision to call someone like Omar Little to the stand as an example of failing to do justice. However, an alternative explanation for that decision is that prosecutors have a peculiarly prosecutorial understanding of their do-justice mission. Bruce Green, for example, has written that because of a "tradition of machismo," it is important to the prosecutorial culture to do jus-tice in a "muscular," "unsentimental" way.[39] I have used the term "prosecutor-ial passion" to describe a prideful, warrior-like aspect of the culture.[40] Prosecutors

---

34. *Id.*

35. *The Wire: Final Grades* (HBO television broadcast Dec. 10, 2006).

36. *Id.*

37. *The Wire: All Prologue* (HBO television broadcast July 6, 2003).

38. *See* STANDARDS FOR CRIM. JUSTICE §3-1.2 cmt. (1993). *See also* MODEL RULES OF PROF'L CONDUCT R. 3.8 (2004); Berger v. United States, 295 U.S. 78, 88 (1935) (holding that the prosecutor carries dual obligations both to punish the guilty and to pro-tect the innocent).

39. Bruce A. Green, *Why Should Prosecutors "Seek Justice"?*, 26 FORDHAM URB. L.J. 607, 609 (1999).

40. Alafair S. Burke, *Prosecutorial Passion, Cognitive Bias, and Plea Bargaining*, 91 MARQ. L. REV. 183, 187 (2007). *See also* Andrew E. Taslitz, *Eyewitness Identification, Democratic Deliberation, and the Politics of Science*, 4 CARDOZO PUB. L. POL'Y & ETHICS J. 271, 304 (2006) (observing a prosecutorial tendency toward a "warrior mindset").

have a tendency to see their lawyering not just as a form of employment, but as a calling.[41]

Consider, for example, an anecdote that Professor Angela Davis shares from her days in practice as a defense attorney.[42] Her client was accused of rape.[43] He insisted that the sex was consensual and told Professor Davis that the victim-witness was deaf.[44] Professor Davis asked her investigator to contact the woman for a statement, but the victim's mother turned the investigator away.[45] Professor Davis subsequently learned from the victim's mother that the woman was incapable of speech and did not know any accepted form of sign language.[46] Instead, she and her mother had developed their own mode of communication.[47]

Meanwhile, the defendant could not make bail.[48] Professor Davis attempted to persuade the prosecutor to dismiss the case, arguing that the victim's inability to testify about the allegations rendered a conviction at trial impossible.[49] The prosecutor did not appear to dispute Professor Davis's conclusion.[50] Rather than arguing that he might somehow produce an admissible prima facie case at trial, the prosecutor simply stated that he was under no obligation to make his case yet and had nine months under local law within which to indict the defendant.[51] Predictably, at the end of the permissible nine-month period, the defendant had still not been indicted and was therefore released.[52] The prosecutor admitted to Professor Davis, "I know your client is guilty. At least he did nine months in jail."[53]

Professor Davis describes her reaction as "stunned": "When this prosecutor was unable to prove my client's guilt legally, he took it upon himself to act as judge and jury—single-handedly finding him guilty and 'sentencing' him to

---

41. *See* Mary Patrice Brown & Stevan E. Bunnell, *Negotiating Justice: Prosecutorial Perspectives on Federal Plea Bargaining in the District of Columbia*, 43 AM. CRIM. L. REV. 1063, 1080 (2006) (reporting that colleagues at the U.S. Attorney's Office "view being a prosecutor as more of a calling than a job" and as "part of their personal identity").

42. Angela J. Davis, *Arbitrary Justice: The Power Of The American Prosecutor* 27‒30 (2007).

43. *Id.* at 27.

44. *Id.* at 28.

45. *Id.*

46. *Id.* at 29.

47. *Id.*

48. *Id.* at 27.

49. *Id.* at 29‒30.

50. *Id.* at 30.

51. *Id.*

52. *Id.*

53. *Id.*

nine months in jail."[54] I am not stunned at all. Nor would I be stunned if a real-world prosecutor, like the fictional one in *The Wire*, decided to call an Omar Little to the stand.

Although prosecutors have an obligation to seek justice, that responsibility is nebulously defined. Moreover, there is a tendency to interpret a prosecutor's special role in the adversarial system by emphasizing prosecutorial responsibility to protect the innocent. For example, in perhaps its most famous discussion of prosecutorial ethics, the Supreme Court described the prosecutor as "in a peculiar and very definite sense the servant of the law, the twofold aim of which is that guilt shall not escape or innocence suffer."[55] Similarly, many prosecutors believe that their unique obligation to do justice morally obligates them to serve as what I have called "supreme jurors," refraining from prosecuting a defendant until they first form a personal belief in the defendant's guilt.[56] Although a supreme juror requirement is not explicitly mandated by law, many legal ethicists believe that the obligation flows from the prosecutor's unique role in the adversarial system.[57]

Similarly, the innocence movement's high-profile exonerations based on exculpatory DNA evidence[58] have invited us to view the aim of justice as preventing wrongful convictions, where "wrongful" means "inaccurate." In this innocence-focused model of prosecutorial virtue, prosecutors do justice so long as they refrain from prosecuting the innocent. Rather than shun this special ethical obligation, prosecutors find honor in it, often boasting about their power to charge or not to charge, based on their personal determination of what is right—meaning who is innocent and who is guilty.

---

54. *Id.*

55. Berger v. United States, 295 U.S. 78, 88 (1935).

56. Alafair S. Burke, *Prosecutorial Agnosticism*, 8 OHIO ST. J. CRIM. L. 79, 79 (2010).

57. *See, e.g.*, MONROE H. FREEDMAN & ABBE SMITH, UNDERSTANDING LAWYER'S ETHICS § 11.04, at 300 (2d ed. 2002) ("[C]onscientious prosecutors do not put the destructive engine of the criminal process into motion unless they are satisfied beyond a reasonable doubt that the accused is guilty."); Bennett L. Gershman, *A Moral Standard for the Prosecutor's Exercise of the Charging Discretion*, 20 FORDHAM URB. L.J. 513, 524 (1993) ("[A] responsible prosecutor should be morally certain that the defendant is guilty and that criminal punishment is appropriate."); Bruce A. Green, *Prosecutorial Ethics as Usual*, 2003 U. ILL. L. REV. 1573, 1588 (2003) (noting that a prosecutor's role as "minister of justice" ... is generally thought to imply a "gate-keeping function"); Kenneth J. Melilli, *Prosecutorial Discretion in an Adversary System*, 1992 BYU L. REV. 669, 700 (1992) ("Prosecutors do not serve the interests of society by pursuing cases where the prosecutors themselves have reasonable doubts as to the factual guilt of the defendants.") (footnote omitted).

58. *See* The Innocence Project, Know the Cases, http://www.innocenceproject.org/know/Browse-Profiles.php (last visited Mar. 6, 2011) (listing 258 exonerations since 1989).

The harmless error test also signals to prosecutors that outcomes matter more than processes. When prosecutors use inadmissible evidence and make impermissible arguments before the jury, the convictions they obtain are reversed on appeal only if an appellate court concludes that a fair process would have created a reasonable probability of a different outcome. The *Brady* standard explicitly links prosecutorial ethics to outcomes, requiring prosecutors to disclose exculpatory evidence "only if there is a reasonable probability that, had the evidence been disclosed to the defense, the result of the proceeding would have been different."[59] This obsession with innocence creates a model of prosecutorial justice that can justify questionable processes used to punish those who are determined (by police and prosecutors) to be non-innocents. My guess is that the prosecutor in Professor Davis's case would defend his decision not to dismiss the charges against her client earlier by saying that he was in fact doing justice because he believed the defendant was guilty. The rules of evidence that prevented him from proving his case in court were subverting true justice—meaning punishment of the guilty and protection of only the innocent—and he followed the jurisdiction's timing rules in a manner that served the interests of justice.

Similarly, an innocence-focused model of "justice" permits prosecutors to defend the common practice of overcharging, in which the prosecutor includes charges that are not likely to be proven at trial, either to gain leverage in plea negotiations or to give the jury a compromise verdict. If the prosecutor believes the defendant to be guilty, overcharging is a strategy to ensure that the charges of which the defendant is eventually convicted will reflect his true level of culpability, even if the defendant receives plea-bargaining consideration or jury mitigation. An overemphasis upon protection of the innocent might also explain prosecutors' tendency to remain blissfully ignorant of questionable police tactics, so long as those tactics are unleashed only against people who deserve punishment because they are guilty and not innocent. Or they may, as with Omar Little, accept the testimony of a cooperating witness despite doubts about its veracity, as long as they believe that the target of the testimony did in fact commit the crime.

---

59. United States v. Bagley, 473 U.S. 667, 682 (1985).

Conclusion

Scholars who study prosecutorial ethics have emphasized that the model prosecutor should adopt the mindset of an "inquisitive neutral"[60] and "should approach the preparation of a case with a healthy skepticism."[61] However, the amorphous and ill-defined concept of prosecutorial justice too frequently emphasizes outcomes over process. Prosecutors are told to protect the innocent without sufficient clarification that the mechanisms through which they should do so are the legal processes in place, not their own personal judgments about who is or is not "in the game." Prosecutors should instead be trained to strive for neutrality, refraining from forming personal beliefs about a defendant's guilt and working to protect the fairness of the process through which all defendants—even the guilty—are judged and sentenced. Prosecutors should not, in short, behave like Omar Little.

Study Questions

1. Describe the ways in which *The Wire* deals with the criminal justice system and how it differs from other "cop" shows, such as Law and Order or The Shield. Is one show more or less accurate or truthful than another?

2. How does *The Wire's* Stringer Bell apply his economic lessons to call into question the legitimacy of supposedly legitimate enterprises?

3. Burke indicates that *The Wire* perhaps unintentionally indicates that there are parallels between those involved in the drug trade and members of law enforcement and prosecutors. What are those parallels? Do you think this is a fair assessment?

4. Describe the ways in which *The Wire* demonstrates the discretionary flexibility of law enforcement and prosecutors.

5. It has been said that prosecutors should have an "inquisitive neutral" mindset and should remain skeptical. How does the example of Professor Angela Davis illustrate the importance of this opinion?

---

60. H. Richard Uviller, *The Neutral Prosecutor: The Obligation of Dispassion in a Passionate Pursuit*, 68 FORDHAM L. REV. 1695, 1704 (2000) (asserting that prosecutors should review their cases with "the mindset of the true skeptic, the inquisitive neutral").

61. Bennett L. Gershman, *The Prosecutor's Duty to Truth*, 14 GEO. J. LEGAL ETHICS 309, 342 (2001) (footnote omitted).

Chapter 5

Wartime America and *The Wire*: A Response to Posner's Post-9/11 Constitutional Framework*

Dawinder S. Sidhu

Introduction

In the groundbreaking legal text *The Common Law*, Justice Oliver Wendell Holmes observed that "[t]he life of the law has not been logic: it has been experience."[1] Years later, fellow pragmatist Richard A. Posner similarly noted that there is undoubtedly "a considerable residue of cases ... against which logic and science will be unavailing and practical reason will break its often none-too-sturdy lance."[2] "Practical reason," according to Posner, consists of "anecdote, introspection, imagination, common sense, empathy, imputation of motives, speaker's authority, metaphor, analogy, precedent, custom, memory, 'experience,' intuition, and induction," among other things.[3] It lies, Posner adds, somewhere "[b]etween the extremes of logical persuasion and emotive persuasion ..."[4]

---

* Reprinted from Dawinder S. Sidhu, "Wartime America and *The Wire*: A Response to Posner's Post-9/11 Constitutional Framework," *George Mason University Civil Rights Law Journal*, 20: 37–82 (2009). Reprinted with permission of George Mason University Civil Rights Law Journal.

1. Oliver Wendell Holmes, Jr., *The Common Law* 1 (1881).
2. Richard A. Posner, *The Problems Of Jurisprudence* 78 (1990).
3. *Id.* at 73.
4. Richard A. Posner, *Law And Literature* 272 (rev. & enlarged ed. 1998).

Posner, a well-regarded law professor and circuit court judge, is also a pro-lific scholar who has offered to the academy profound ideas on some of the law's most vexing problems.[5] In his book, *Not a Suicide Pact: The Constitution in a Time of National Emergency*, Posner presents a "pragmatic response"[6] to the pressing, unsettled question of how national security and constitutional rights should intersect in this perilous, post-9/11 age.[7] He specifically argues that in a balance between national security and competing constitutional interests such as individual liberty, the former invariably takes precedence during times of war.[8] Viewed from this lens, Posner indicates that civil libertarians must toler-ate security measures—including torture[9]—implemented to protect the home-land from catastrophic terrorist events, even if those measures infringe upon constitutional rights or depart from established legal rules.[10] Posner also con-tends that the boundaries of executive power are expansive and that the role of the judiciary as a check on the executive is limited in times of war. Surveillance and profiling of Muslims, he argues, are constitutional, as are coercive interro-gation techniques. Posner's pragmatic response logically culminates with the as-sertion that the Constitution is flexible to the extent that the executive may permissibly invoke a "law of necessity" to authorize extra-constitutional acts.[11]

---

5. *See, e.g.*, Jeffrey Rosen, *Overcoming Posner*, 105 YALE L.J. 581, 610 (1995) (calling Posner "the most prolific and creative judge now sitting on the federal bench.").

6. RICHARD A. POSNER, NOT A SUICIDE PACT: THE CONSTITUTION IN A TIME OF NA-TIONAL EMERGENCY 147 (2006) [hereinafter POSNER, NOT A SUICIDE PACT]. The pragmatic, individualized character of the book is plain. For example, Posner acknowledges that "con-stitutional theory is inherently subjective," and that constitutional decision-making is in-formed by "life experience and other personal factors." *Id.* at 26; *see also id.* at 19 (positing that judges "make constitutional law rather than just apply[ing] preexisting rules.").

7. *See id.* at 125 ("this is not a book about how best to respond to the terrorist threat. It is a book about the limitations that constitutional law places on the government's re-sponses to the threat.").

8. *See id.* at 6 ("[r]ooting out" our enemy "might be fatally inhibited if we felt con-strained to strict adherence to civil liberties ...").

9. *See id.* at 86 (arguing that there may be situations in which a president has "the moral and political duty ... to authorize torture."); *see also id.* at 81 ("[There is] abundant evidence that torture *is* often an effective method of eliciting true information...."); *id.* at 83 ("Almost everyone ... accepts the necessity of resorting to [torture] in extreme situa-tions."); *id.* at 81 ("[O]nly a die-hard civil libertarian will deny the propriety of using a high degree of coercion to illicit" information from a suspect).

10. *See id.* at 41 ("[C]ivil libertarians ... are reluctant to acknowledge that national emergencies in general, or the threat of modern terrorism in particular, justify *any* cur-tailment of civil liberties that were accepted on the eve of the emergency. They deny that civil liberties should wax and wane with changes in the danger level.").

11. *See generally, id.* at 111–25, 158.

This chapter challenges *Not a Suicide Pact* by using a single component of practical experience that has factored into legal reasoning: television.[12] In particular, it will invoke various themes from *The Wire*[13] to demonstrate the problematic nature of the aforementioned arguments set forth in Posner's book.[14]

The application of *The Wire* to *Not a Suicide Pact* suggests that the promises of Posner's constitutional framework, however intuitively appealing, are unlikely to be a satisfactory direction of our constitutional development in the post-9/11 world. In particular, this chapter argues that liberty and security are not locked in a zero-sum game in which the former must be sacrificed for the latter: Both interests can and must be preserved at all times. The chapter further contends that the judiciary must robustly perform its role as a check on the executive in order to safeguard individual rights against possible overreaching, that surveillance and profiling of Muslims absent any evidence of wrongdoing are discriminatory and inconsistent with lessons from America's wartime past, and that the use of torture not only is counterproductive from a security standpoint but also conflicts with the nation's assumed legal obligations. Finally, the chapter asserts that the executive has no legal or moral authority to "preserve" the Constitution by breaking its solemn strictures.

As noted above, the post-9/11 liberty-security dynamic is largely undefined in the United States. The use of "enhanced interrogation techniques" and the suitability of civilian courts to try suspected terrorists, for example, remain contentious and unresolved questions.[15] To be sure, Posner's particular attempt

---

12. *See, e.g.*, Muscarello v. United States, 524 U.S. 125, 144 n.6 (1998) (Ginsburg, J., dissenting) (quoting an episode of the television series "M*A*S*H"); *id.* at 148 n.11 (referring to the children's television program "Sesame Street").

13. *See generally* Home Box Office, *The Wire: About the Show*, http://www.hbo.com/thewire/about/.

14. It is worth noting that *The Wire* has previously been invoked in judicial decisions, *see, e.g.*, United States v. Fiasche, 520 F.3d 694, 695 n.1 (7th Cir. 2008); Twentieth Century Fox Film Corp. v. Cablevision Sys. Corp., 478 F. Supp. 2d 607, 615 (S.D.N.Y. 2007), and in academic legal argument, *see e.g.*, D. Marvin Jones, *The Original Meaning of* Brown: *Seattle, Segregation and the Rewriting of History*, 63 U. MIAMI L. REV. 629, 651 (2009); Ronald J. Krotoszynski, Jr., *The Perils and the Promise of Comparative Constitutional Law: The New Globalism and the Role of the United States in Shaping Human Rights*, 61 ARK. L. REV. 603, 611 (2009); Colin Miller, *Even Better than the Real Thing: How Courts have been Anything but Liberal in Finding Genuine Questions Raised as to the Authenticity of Originals Under Rule 1003*, 68 MD. L. REV. 160, 213 (2008).

15. As to torture, *compare* George's Bottom Line, http://blogs.abcnews.com/george/2009/01/obama-on-cheney.html (Jan. 11, 2009, 9:12 EST) (containing a statement from President Barack Obama that, "Vice President Cheney I think continues to defend what he calls extraordinary measures or procedures and from my view waterboarding is torture. I

in *Not a Suicide Pact* to frame how these and other relevant issues may be examined and perhaps settled serves as a useful contribution to the legal field. This chapter aims to offer additional thoughts on the recommended course of constitutional law advanced by Posner, thoughts that may give pause to those initially in agreement with Posner's formulation in *Not a Suicide Pact*. In that sense, this chapter, though critical of Posner's proffers, hopes to modestly advance the state of our understanding of national security and individual rights such that the nation may be closer to reaching a consensus on the permissibility and propriety of important post-9/11 policies and programs.

Given Posner's stature in American law, when he speaks, people listen. Unsurprisingly, then, prominent judges, scholars, and others in the legal community responded in short order to *Not a Suicide Pact*.[16] This chapter differs from those responses in at least two critical respects. First, Posner penned his book in 2006 with the Bush administration's post-9/11 constitutional model as the canvas for his conversation on civil liberties and wartime governance. While others reacted to *Not a Suicide Pact* during the administration,[17] those efforts may be considered premature particularly as details of the security techniques

---

have said that under my administration we will not torture...."), *with Cheney Defends Enhanced Interrogation Techniques* (National Public Radio broadcast May 13, 2009), *available at* http://www.npr.org/templates/story/story.php?storyId=104079567&ft=1&f=1001 (quoting former-Vice President Dick Cheney regarding the Obama administration's ban on the Bush administration's interrogation program as saying, "I think that we are stripping ourselves of some of the capabilities that we used in order to block, if you will, or disrupt activities by al-Qaida that would have led to additional attacks"). As to the detainees, *compare* Remarks of Matthew G. Olsen, Executive Director of the Guantanamo Review Detainee Taskforce, Panel Discussion, "Are Military Commissions the Right Answer?" Georgetown University Law Center, Sept. 10, 2009 (noting, as the official responsible for assessing whether over two-hundred remaining Guantanamo detainees are to be tried or released, that Article III courts, courts martial, *and* military commissions are viable options for where Guantanamo detainees may be tried), *with* Remarks of Major Jon Scott Jackson, Defense Counsel, Office of Military Commissions, at the same panel discussion (arguing in his personal capacity that military commissions are a "failure" and as such are not an appropriate forum to administer justice with respect to these detainees).

16. Reviews of NOT A SUICIDE PACT include Stephen Reinhardt, *Weakening the Bill of Rights: A Victory for Terrorism*, 106 MICH. L. REV. 963 (2008); Thomas P. Crocker, *Torture, with Apologies*, 86 TEX. L. REV. 569 (2008); MAJOR MATTHEW R. HOVER, *Not a Suicide Pact: The Constitution in a Time of National Emergency*, 197 MIL. L. REV. 164 (2008); David Cole, *How to Skip the Constitution*, 53 N.Y. REV. BOOKS, Nov. 16, 2006, at 20.

17. There does not appear to be any articles dedicated to exploring NOT A SUICIDE PACT in the aftermath of the Bush administration's policies that necessarily formed the landscape for Posner's discussion.

employed by the administration and the legal cover prepared by administration attorneys have come to light only after the end of Bush's second term in 2009.[18] With the Bush administration's security efforts and accompanying legal approach fully behind us, it is now appropriate to consider the merits of Posner's proposed paradigm. Second, aside from timing, the content of this chapter is undoubtedly unique in that it extracts information from a source that has garnered praise for its commentary on the law and crime, but that has not yet been comprehensively applied as an instrument to illuminate open areas within the law.

Before discussing how *The Wire* should lead one to reconsider *Not a Suicide Pact*, it would be helpful to briefly introduce the reader to this critically acclaimed show, especially for those unfamiliar with the series, and to examine why *The Wire* is a valuable resource or reservoir of ideas for examining the course of constitutional law urged by Posner.

The Wire

"It's a thin line 'tween heaven and here."[19]

—Bubbles

"Perhaps no city in the United States is more closely identified with drug addiction than Baltimore, Maryland[,]" observed Ellen M. Weber, law professor at the University of Maryland and head of the university's Drug Policy Clinic.[20] Although Baltimore has had a long history of widespread drug problems,[21] reviewing statistics on the city's drug trade in 2002–2003 — around

---

18. For example, official Bush administration memoranda that have been declassified and released during the Barack Obama administration are providing new and insightful information on the Bush government's security response and related legal views.

19. Season 1, Episode 4.

20. Ellen M. Weber, *Bridging the Barriers: Public Health Strategies for Expanding Drug Treatment in Communities*, 57 RUTGERS L. REV. 631, 702 (2005).

21. *See, e.g.*, William D. Mccoll, *Baltimore City's Drug Treatment Court: Theory and Practice in an Emerging Field*, 55 MD. L. REV. 467, 478 (1996) (commenting on a 1990 report, which produced startling facts, including that "fifty percent of felony prosecutions in Baltimore City were direct drug offenses, while eighty-five to ninety-five percent of all felony prosecutions were drug-driven offenses," and that "[f]ifty-five percent of all murders were drug related.") (citing THE BAR ASS'N OF BALTIMORE CITY, THE DRUG CRISIS AND UNDERFUNDING OF THE JUSTICE SYS. IN BALTIMORE CITY 3 (1990)).

when *The Wire* first premiered in mid-2002[22]—provides a useful window into the underlying subject matter of the series.

A 2003 Grand Jury Charge Committee Report commissioned by the Circuit Court for Baltimore City contained several staggering figures on the degree to which the drug trade factored into the city's existence.[23] According to a city court factual determination, there were "approximately sixty thousand substance abusers in the city, primarily addicted to heroin and cocaine";[24] this "equates to about nine percent of city residents needing drug treatment."[25] With respect to heroin alone, an Urban Institute Justice Policy Center study ascertained that "Baltimore has the highest concentration of heroin use in the country"[26] and that "about forty percent of arrested males and nearly half of arrested females test positive for heroin."[27]

The report addressed not only pure drug use in the city but also its impact on Baltimore's criminal justice system. The Maryland State's Attorney's office found that an estimated "5,867 individuals were charged with felony narcotics violations in the City of Baltimore in 2002,"[28] which "represents 51.2% of the total number of defendants charged for all felony crimes."[29] Moreover, "at least seventy percent of *all* cases heard in the Circuit Court for Baltimore City were directly or indirectly related to drug abuse."[30] A Justice Policy Institute study calculated that "[t]he arrest rate in Baltimore for drug crimes was nearly *triple* the rate for other large U.S. cities, with heroin and cocaine arrests *ten times* the national average."[31]

When it comes to drug-related crime, what is most disturbing is the number of "bodies"—that is, the number of homicides: "[A]pproximately 90% of

---

22. The series' first episode was: *The Wire: The Target* (HBO television broadcast June 2, 2002).

23. GRAND JURY FOR THE CIRCUIT COURT FOR BALTIMORE CITY, GRAND JURY CHARGE COMMITTEE REPORT (Jan. 2003), *available at* http://www.courts.state.md.us/baltgrandjuryreport_03.pdf.

24. *Id.* at 5 (citing NANCY G. LA VIGNE ET AL., URBAN INS. JUSTICE POLICY CTR., A PORTRAIT OF PRISON REENTRY IN MARYLAND, 51–52 (2003), *available at* http://www.urban.org/UploadedPDF/410655_MDPortraitReentry.pdf).

25. *Id.* (citing LA VIGNE ET AL., *supra* note 24, at 52).

26. *Id.* (citing LA VIGNE ET AL., *supra* note 24, at 52).

27. *Id.* at 6 (citing LA VIGNE ET AL., *supra* note 24, at 52).

28. *Id.* at 3.

29. *Id.* at 5.

30. *Id.* (citing GRAND JURY FOR THE CIRCUIT COURT FOR BALTIMORE CITY, GRAND JURY CHARGE COMMITTEE REPORT, (Sept. 2002)) (emphasis added).

31. *Id.* at 6 (citing JUDITH GREENE & TIMOTHY ROCHE, JUSTICE POLICY INS., CUTTING CORRECTLY IN MARYLAND 13 (Feb. 2003), *available at* http://www.prisonpolicy.org/scans/jpi/cc_md.pdf) (emphasis added).

homicides in Baltimore are drug related."[32] The Baltimore-based Johns Hopkins University published an article noting that, for a decade, the city was home to at least 300 homicides per year and that, in 2002, Baltimore was "the second most violent big city in America" and the murder rate stood "at *seven times* the national average."[33]

These numbers provide a snapshot of the city that David Simon, a thirteen-year veteran of the *Baltimore Sun*,[34] and Edward Burns, a former Baltimore police detective and Baltimore city public school teacher,[35] intended to portray when they created *The Wire*.[36] The drugs, crime, and resultant law enforcement response are not a loose backdrop for *The Wire* but form the basis for the actual plots and characters in the series. As Simon noted after the series' fifth and final season aired, "All the things that have been depicted in *The Wire* over the past five years—the crime, the corruption—actually happened in Baltimore.... The storylines were stolen from real life."[37]

The Wire begins by focusing on police efforts to crack down on a major Baltimore drug ring through the use of surveillance technology and street-level interactions.[38] As the series unfolds, Simon and Burns delve deeper into the investigation of the Baltimore drug trade while adding into the mix its impact on the city's blue collar working class and on the political leadership called upon to reduce crime.[39] *The Wire* then takes us into the city's public schools and introduces us to four Baltimore middle-school students contending with the appeal of the "corners," the street locations at which drugs are sold, on one hand, and the limited benefits of a broken school system and imperfect family settings on the other.[40] Finally, the series brings us into the media, com-

---

32. *Id.* (citing City of Baltimore, Baltimore City Police Dep't, Homicide Unit, Grand Jury Tour, (Jan. 24, 2003)).

33. *Baltimore Finally Has a Reason to Believe*, The Johns Hopkins News-Letter, (The John Hopkins Univ., Baltimore, Md.,), Dec. 6, 2002, at ¶6, *available at* http://media.www.jhunewsletter.com/media/storage/paper932/news/2002/12/06/Features/Baltimore.Finally.Has.A.Reason.To.Believe-2247801.shtml (emphasis added).

34. *See* Home Box Office, *The Wire: About the Show*, http://www.hbo.com/thewire/about/.

35. *See id.*

36. *See id.*

37. *The Wire: Arguably the Greatest Television Programme Ever Made*, Daily Telegraph, Apr. 2, 2009, at ¶6, *available at* http://www.telegraph.co.uk/news/uknews/5095500/The-Wire-arguably-the-greatest-television-programme-ever-made.html.

38. *See* Home Box Office, *supra* note 34.

39. *See id.*

40. *See id.*

menting on the sad state of newspaper journalism and depicting the *Baltimore Sun* as more interested in winning Pulitzer prizes than in reporting the nuanced truth on the ground.[41]

Although *The Wire* explores tragedies of individual characters and circumstances throughout its five-season run, perhaps the ultimate tragedy is that the significant drug trade, related crime, ineffective criminal justice approaches, poor schools, and corrupt political practices in a major American city had gone so unnoticed by those outside Baltimore's city limits. Simon explained in 2008 that "[e]verything that you know about *The Wire* up to this point never appeared in the newspaper.... Watching a TV drama to get the truth, that's the real joke...."[42] In that sense, *The Wire* functions as a documentary on the city of Baltimore. It informs the blissfully oblivious about the hell that is Baltimore, Maryland.

What converts *The Wire* into an attractive and useful repository of raw information is that it highlights the complexities and realities of law enforcement efforts to curb the serious and seemingly endless criminal, legal, and societal problem of the drug trade. In doing so, *The Wire* knowingly and necessarily draws parallels between the "war on drugs" and the "war on terror," as others have recognized.[43] Accordingly, the series' depiction of Baltimore's wide-ranging struggle with this pandemic is a helpful tool by which we may analyze a proposed response to a broader criminal, legal, and social predicament—terrorism.[44]

---

41. *See id.* at 4.

42. Show Tracker: The Wire, http://latimesblogs.latimes.com/showtracker/the_wire/ (Mar. 4, 2008, 9:07 PST).

43. *See, e.g.,* Aziz Z. Huq & Christopher Muller, *The War on Crime as Precursor to the War on Terror*, 36 INT'L J.L. CRIME & JUST. 215, 215 (2008) (alluding to *The Wire* in introducing its discussion on the war on crime and the "war on terror"); Robert David Sullivan, *Slow Hand*, THE BOSTON PHOENIX, Aug. 15–22, 2002, at ¶ 7 ("Series creator [David] Simon, who developed the story line with Edward Burns, isn't the first to express skepticism toward the War on Drugs, but *The Wire* has a fresh resonance because of its implicit parallels to the new War on Terrorism."), *available at* http://www.bostonphoenix.com/boston/ arts/tv/documents/02394694.htm; *see also* Daniel R. Williams, *Who Got Game?* Boumediene v. Bush *and the Judicial Gamesmanship of Enemy-Combatant Detention*, 43 NEW ENG. L. REV. 1, 2 (2008) (discussing "the game" as it pertains to the drug trade and as it is portrayed in *The Wire*, and noting that "[j]udging from the folly of the War on Drugs, we have good reason to worry about what we are unleashing in this new game, this so-called 'War on Terror.'").

44. It should be noted that a number of substantive points emerge from *The Wire* and that while this article references a defined set of themes from the show, it does not purport to present an exhaustive account of the possible ways in which the series may be applied to NOT A SUICIDE PACT, or to the anti-terrorism debate more generally. Moreover, I readily acknowledge that even those themes which I selected are open to interpretation and may have different meanings for others. I have attempted, however, out of an unwavering respect for

Common Ground

"This is what makes a good night on my watch.
Absence of a negative."[45]
— Major Howard "Bunny" Colvin

On September 11, 2001, nineteen Muslim men hijacked commercial airplanes and used them to attack the World Trade Center and the Pentagon; in all, the attacks killed close to three thousand civilians.[46] The Supreme Court noted, "Americans will never forget the devastation wrought by these acts."[47] The attacks upon the United States triggered a military conflict[48] and placed the nation under a specter of future acts of terrorism.[49]

---

the creators and through meticulous research, to be as faithful as possible to the purpose of the series as I understand it to be. In working with the editors of this publication, who share my significant interest in and appreciation for the series, I am confident that my understanding of the series is well within reason. To the extent others disagree, it is my hope that this article may serve as a useful starting point for further conversations on *The Wire* and contemporary issues within the American legal system, including the post-9/11 relationship between national security and individual rights.

45. Season 3, Episode 2.

46. *See* Hamdi v. Rumsfeld, 542 U.S. 507, 511 (2004) ("On September 11, 2001, the al Qaeda terrorist network used hijacked commercial airliners to attack prominent targets in the United States. Approximately 3,000 people were killed in those attacks.").

47. Hamdan v. Rumsfeld, 548 U.S. 557, 568 (2006).

48. On September 18, 2001, Congress authorized the President to "use all necessary and appropriate force against those nations, organizations, or persons he determines planned, authorized, committed, or aided the terrorist attacks" or "harbored such organizations or persons, in order to prevent any future acts of international terrorism against the United States by such nations, organizations or persons." Authorization for Use of Military Force, Pub. L. 107-40, § 2, 115 Stat. 224, 224 (2001). Although it did not formally declare war, Authorization for Use of Military Force (AUMF) arguably "activated the President's traditional war powers in the conflict against al Qaeda...." David J. Barron & Marty Lederman, *The Commander in Chief at the Lowest Ebb—Framing the Problem, Doctrine, and Original Understanding*, 121 HARV. L. REV. 689, 731 (2008) (citing *Hamdan*, 548 U.S. at 594 (citing *Hamdi*, 542 U.S. at 507 (plurality opinion))). AUMF also "helps satisf[y] modern de jure and de facto requirements for a state of war." J. Andrew Kent, *A Textual and Historical Case Against a Global Constitution*, 95 GEO. L.J. 463, 536 (2007) (citing Authorization for Use of Military Force, § 2). Indeed, President George W. Bush invoked his authority under the AUMF to, among other things, deploy "Armed Forces into Afghanistan to wage a military campaign against al Qaeda and the Taliban regime that had supported it." Rasul v. Bush, 542 U.S. 466, 470 (2004). President Bush also invoked his authority under the AUMF to designate individuals, including Jose Padilla, as "enemy combatants" and thereby hold them in a military—not civilian—detention system. Rumsfeld v. Padilla, 542 U.S. 426, 431 (2004).

49. *See* Cass R. Sunstein, *On the Divergent American Reactions to Terrorism and Climate*

There is little doubt that those in charge of the security of the nation were pressed with an awesome responsibility: to keep America safe by thwarting a relatively obscure, scattered, global network of fundamentalists from attacking again. In his memoir, Jack Goldsmith (2007: 67–69, 75), a former Assistant Attorney General under President George W. Bush, wrote that the administration was "under pressure to stop a second attack by an enemy it couldn't see and didn't fully understand," that the president held the "ultimate obligation" to ensure another attack did not take place, and that the government was "largely in the dark about where or how the next terrorist attack [would] occur."[50] David Addington, legal counsel to then-Vice President Dick Cheney, warned Goldsmith that if a second attack occurred, "the blood of the hundred thousand people who die[d]" would be on his hands (2007: 71).[51] To Goldsmith, then, the success of his efforts and those of his colleagues would be evidenced by "the absence" of a second attack.[52]

Posner uses the unimaginably dire national situation in which Goldsmith and others were operating as the starting point for his analysis, reminding the reader of the urgent and gripping nature of their task.[53] He writes, for example, that "terrorist leaders may even now be regrouping, and preparing an attack that will produce destruction on a scale to dwarf 9/11"[54] and "wielding nuclear bombs, dirty bombs, biological weapons capable of killing millions of people, or other weapons of mass destruction...."[55] Posner stresses that the threat of terrorism faced by the United States is very real and from Goldsmith (2007: 175) we understand that those public servants who assumed the mantle of American security attempted, in good faith and under trying

---

Change, 107 COLUM. L. REV. 503, 516 (2007) ("In the period shortly after the 9/11 attacks, 88% of Americans believed that it was either very likely or somewhat likely that there would be 'another terrorist attack ... within the next few months'—*with about half of Americans worrying about the possibility that a family member might 'become a victim of a terrorist attack,' and over 40% worrying that 'terrorist attacks might take place where [they] live or work.'"* (*quoting* PROGRAM ON INT'L POLICY ATTITUDES, AMS. AND THE WORLD, TERRORISM ¶¶ 1–2, http://www.americans-world.org/digest/global_issues/terrorism/terrorism_perception.cfm) (alteration in original)).

50. Jack Goldsmith, *The Terror Presidency* 67–69, 75 (2007).

51. Season 3, Episode 3. Similarly, in *The Wire*, an acting police commissioner rather ominously reminds his district commanders that their satisfactory performance is expected regardless of how difficult their tasks on the streets may seem by stating, "the Gods will not save you."

52. GOLDSMITH *supra* note 50, at 188.

53. POSNER, NOT A SUICIDE PACT, *supra* note 6, at 148.

54. *Id.*

55. *Id.* at 47.

circumstances, to prevent subsequent terrorist catastrophes from taking place on the homeland.[56]

There can be little doubt that security branches of the government are faced with an outstanding duty for which the only measure of success may be "nothing"—that is, the non-existence of an event. Such was the case with the Baltimore law enforcement community's response to the war on drugs in *The Wire*.[57] In one particularly telling scene, when the city police's creative and frustrated efforts to cripple the drug trade were coming to a head, a police officer attempting to effectuate a drug bust is shot by his criminal targets.[58] The officer's commander, Howard "Bunny" Colvin, learns of the shooting in the middle of the night, and shortly thereafter reflects, "Tonight is a good night. Why? Because my shot cop didn't die. And it hit me ... This is what makes a good night on my watch: absence of a negative."[59] Whether in the "war on terror" or the "war on drugs," the powers that be may be oddly reassured by non-existence of anything "bad" occurring during their tenure.

What must be disputed is not the starting point of Posner's analysis, but his logical progression.[60] For starters, Posner makes two improvident leaps from the accepted propositions that the terrorist dangers to America are clear and that the security arm of the American government is performing a daunting task. First, he argues that identifying whether security responses to 9/11 are constitutional requires a straight balancing of civil liberties and security.[61] Second, he effectively contends that ensuring security is more important than safeguarding civil liberties.[62] Put differently, according to Posner, the post-9/

---

56. Noting, with respect to Addington, that "[d]espite our many fights, and despite what I view as his many errors of judgment, large and small, I believe he acted in good faith to protect the country."

57. Season 3, Episode 2.

58. *Id.*

59. *Id.*

60. *See, e.g.*, Richard A. Clarke, *The Trauma of 9/11 is No Excuse*, WASH. POST, May 31, 2009, *available at* http://www.washingtonpost.com/wp-dyn/content/article/2009/05/29/AR2009052901560.html (rejecting the notion that the trauma of 9/11 and the high-level responsibilities that arose from the attacks justify the government's response to the terrorist threat).

61. Posner argues that the terrorist attacks of 9/11 have created an opportunity in which the balance between liberty and security must be modified. "The challenge," he writes, "is to [strike at] the balance between liberty and safety." POSNER, NOT A SUICIDE PACT, *supra* note 6, at 31. Posner also noted that "[a] national emergency, such as war, creates disequilibrium in the existing system of constitutional rights." *Id.* at 147.

62. That liberty must recede in the post-9/11 climate is an effective afterthought in the Posner analysis. Posner's inquiry therefore boils down to the extent to which liberty must

11 world requires a balancing of civil liberties and security responses which must come out in favor of enhancing security at the cost of limiting liberty.

The Zero Sum Game

"No one wins. One side just loses more slowly."[63]
—Roland "Prez" Pryzbylewski

Posner suspects that Supreme Court Justices generally "base their decisions on a balancing of anticipated consequences, pro and con...."[64] In *Not a Suicide Pact*, he explores one particular type of judicial balancing: the extent to which "civil liberties based on the Constitution should be permitted to vary [based on] the threat level."[65] Posner suggests that "readjustment[s]" between liberty and security occur "from time to time as the weights of the respective interests change."[66] The terrorist attacks of 9/11, according to Posner, demand a recalibration of the "constitutional balance between liberty and safety."[67] In short, in the context of post-9/11 America, Posner believes that "the proper way to think about constitutional rights in a time such as this is in terms of the metaphor of a balance."[68] An important consequence of this balancing paradigm is that it necessarily presumes that tipping the balance to enhance one side must harm the other. Posner admits this, stating "The scope of governmental power to take actions to protect national security is the reciprocal of the individual's rights to liberty and privacy."[69]

On a related note, throughout *Not a Suicide Pact*, Posner describes the debate about the relationship between liberty and security as a purely bifurcated tussle between two players: civil libertarians and national security hawks.[70] He appears to do this, at least in part, to simplify the discussion and to label and criticize, with greater ease, any who express concerns for liberty in times

---

wane. *See id.* 50–51 ("[T]he relevant question is not whether curtailing civil liberties imposes costs, to which the answer is obvious; it is whether the costs exceed the benefits.").

63. Season 4, Episode 4.

64. Posner, Not a Suicide Pact, *supra* note 6, at 28.

65. *Id.* at 7.

66. *Id.* at 148; *see also id.* at 152 ("Constitutional law is a looser garment, continually rewoven by Supreme Court justices mindful (one hopes) of the need to balance security and liberty concerns as the weights of these concerns shift.").

67. *Id.* at 148.

68. *Id.*

69. *Id.* at 8.

70. *See id.* at 67.

of war. Posner defines civil libertarians as those who believe that: (1) "[T]he Constitution is about protecting individual rights rather than about promoting community interests";[71] (2) "[P]ast curtailments of civil liberties were gratuitous responses to hysterically exaggerated fears";[72] (3) The Bush administration abused civil liberties without any evidence;[73] (4) "[G]overnment always errs on the side of exaggerated threats to national security;"[74] (5) The current threat is exaggerated, and post-9/11 security measures require no changes in order to adequately cope with the current threat;[75] and (6) Any curtailment of civil liberties during an emergency will continue once the emergency has passed,[76] and, thus, any curtailment of civil liberties will lead to a "slippery slope."[77]

The zero-sum game frame of reference, however sensible on its face when two parties are in apparent opposition, does not comport with the complex realities of actual law enforcement. *The Wire* illustrates the folly of using a win-loss scorecard in the wartime context. Baltimore City public middle school teacher and former City police officer Roland "Prez" Pryzbylewski, comments on the plight of urban Baltimore's war on drugs.[78] He states that tradeoffs between seemingly competing interests do not yield a positive result for one side but rather degrade both to different degrees, thereby permitting the impression that one side is a legitimate beneficiary of any exchanges between the two.[79] For example, the Baltimore City police invested significant resources and time into infiltrating drug camps, only to capture mid-level operatives and low-end dealers who shield those higher in the food chain from prosecution by "taking" charges and not "snitching" or divulging information about others in the enterprise; these bottom-drawer dealers will simply be replaced by other "soldiers."[80] Although removing some dealers from the streets may suggest that the police have hurt the drug trade, in truth they have only temporarily interrupted the normal operations of the drug ring and, in the process,

71. *Id.* at 41–42.

72. *Id.* at 42.

73. *See id.* at 47.

74. *Id.*

75. *Id.*

76. *Id.* at 47 ("[Civil libertarians] are also being inconsistent, for they consider the post-9/11 security measures particularly ominous because the struggle against terrorism may never end.").

77. *Id.* at 44.

78. Season 4, Episode 4.

79. *Id.*

80. Season 1, Episode 4.

diverted its attention from more productive techniques.[81] In short, there is no outright winner.

Just as the loss by one side in *The Wire* does not translate into an actual gain to the other, liberty and security in the post-9/11 America are not necessarily mired in a zero-sum game. Our liberties, for instance, would certainly wane if al-Qaeda used weapons of mass destruction to kill innocent civilians on American soil, but security programs and practices may just as surely threaten to erode individual liberties.[82] Accordingly, Posner's "either-or" proposition wrongly implies that the people must choose between safety and individual rights; by doing so, it condones Posner's preferred option, that security may be maintained at the expense of civil liberties.

As the National Commission on Terrorist Attacks Upon the United States (9/11 Commission) noted, "The choice between security and liberty is a *false* choice...."[83] On one hand, as the 9/11 Commission observed, "[N]othing is more likely to endanger America's liberties than the success of a terrorist attack at home."[84] On the other, "[I]f our liberties are curtailed, we lose the values that we are struggling to defend."[85]

The latter concern has resounded in the post-9/11 Supreme Court. In 2004, the Court made clear that "[i]t is during our most challenging and uncertain moments that ... we must preserve our commitment at home to the principles for which we fight abroad."[86] It also is shared by those in the security community. For example, Royce C. Lamberth, the presiding judge of the United States Foreign Intelligence Surveillance Court (FISA Court) at the time of 9/11 and current chief judge of the U.S. District Court for the District of Columbia, advised that, "We have to understand you can fight the war [on ter-

---

81. Season 1, Episode 7. (Demonstrating that, when a street-level dealer is arrested with a large quantity of drugs, the Barksdale gang stops doing business over pay-phones; otherwise, it continues dealing drugs as normal).

82. For example, the use of torture, the indefinite detention of individuals without formal charge, warrantless domestic surveillance of Americans, and blanket profiling of Muslims and those perceived to be Muslim may be part of a security response, but may diminish individual liberties. More specifically, these security practices suggest that several American values and constitutional protections may be compromised, including an insistence on humane treatment for all, habeas rights, providing due process in the deprivation of liberty, Fourth Amendment's prohibitions on warrantless searches, and equality under the law.

83. Nat'l Comm'n on Terrorist Attacks upon the U.S., The 9/11 Commission Report 395 (2004), *available at* http://www.9-11commission.gov/report/ (emphasis added).

84. *Id.*

85. *Id.*

86. *Hamdi* 542 U.S. at 532 (citing Kennedy v. Mendoza-Martinez, 372 U.S. 144, 164–165 (1963)).

rorism] and lose everything if you have no civil liberties left when you get through fighting the war."[87] He further pointed out that the FISA Court has "worked to protect civil liberties while protecting the country itself. The judges asked themselves: Are we going to lose our liberties if we approve this kind of surveillance?"[88] Indeed, Tom Ridge, the first head of the Department of Homeland Security—the agency formed after 9/11 to assemble relevant information from federal, state, and local governmental bodies to detect and dismantle terrorist operations—noted in his farewell remarks to the Pennsylvania General Assembly, "We must reject the false choice of liberty versus security. We can and must have both. We will be safe. And we will not let the terrorists change our essential way of life."[89] Edwin Meese, former attorney general of the United States during the Cold War, likewise remarked after 9/11, "Government's obligation is a dual one: to protect civil safety and security against violence and to preserve civil liberty. *This is not a zero-sum game....*"[90] The nation's ability to serve the "dual" interests of national security and individual rights refutes Posner's insistence that a balancing test must be employed.[91]

The concept that a secure nation may be maintained and individual rights simultaneously preserved dates back before 9/11. In 1962, Chief Justice Earl Warren declared that "as always, the people, no less than their courts, must

---

87. Michael J. Sniffen, *Ex-Surveillance Judge Criticizes Warrantless Taps*, Wash. Post, June 24, 2007, at A07, *available at* http://www.washingtonpost.com/wp-dyn/content/article/2007/06/23/AR2007062301125.html.

88. Mary Jo Patterson, A View from Inside the FISA Court, The Star-Ledger, Aug. 21, 2005, *available at* http://www.nj.com/news/ledger/index.ssf?/news/ledger/stories/patriotact/insidefisa.html.

89. *Federally Speaking* (W. Pa. Chapter of the Fed. Bar Ass'n & Allegheny County Bar Ass'n, Pittsburgh, Pa.) at 1, *available at* http://www.pawd.uscourts.gov/Documents/Misc/fsp09.pdf.

90. Edwin Meese, *Patriot Act's Bum Rap*, Wash. Times, July 8, 2004, at A17, *available at* http://www.washingtontimes.com/news/2004/jul/07/20040707-090159-8291r/print/ (emphasis added).

91. Both the security of the people and the principles to which the American people subscribe can be upheld in concert. Allow me to use the security practices noted in footnote 82 as the operative examples. As to torture, interrogation techniques that do not rise to the level of torture may be used to extract information from detainees; as to indefinite detention of detainees, such detainees should proceed through some civilian or quasi-legal system that safeguards classified information while still providing them with basic legal rights to ensure a fair and just trial; as to surveillance, information gathering in America may take place pursuant to tailored warrants provided by a specialized national security court or the existing FISA court; and lastly as to profiling, intelligence measures should rely on evidentiary behavior, not race or religion, as the touchstone for a finding that an individual should be subject to different treatment or additional scrutiny.

remain vigilant to preserve the principles of our Bill of Rights, lest in our desire to be secure we lose our ability to be free."[92] In fact, it extends to the time of the Framers, men fresh from their experiences with the oppressive King George III who were intent on creating a lasting experiment in political order that derived its powers from the consent of the governed. Benjamin Franklin, an elder statesman among them, famously wrote in a letter to a state official, "Those who would give up essential Liberty, to purchase a little temporary Safety, deserve neither Liberty nor Safety."[93]

Furthermore, Posner's dichotomy of civil libertarians and national security hawks serves as an inaccurate representation of the manner in which the debate regarding liberty and security actually takes place. One cannot reasonably claim that the 9/11 Commission, which was composed of former lawmakers, judges, and others of different political stripes, a former presiding judge of the FISA court and Reagan-appointee to the federal bench, an attorney general appointed by and who worked directly under President Reagan, a former chief justice, and a principal American Revolutionary of the very system of governance in which we now live, were either civil libertarians or national security hawks. Rather, just like Posner, they were quite simply Americans interested in the welfare of the nation.[94]

Positioning the debate as one between civil libertarians and aggressive defenders of national security programs is problematic not only in its characterizations, but also in its practical consequences with respect to formulating relevant policy. To assign certain recommendations to a civil libertarian or national security camp will legitimize the two-camp system to which all policymakers are assigned and soil those very substantive ideas with preconceived, fixed

---

92. Earl Warren, *The Bill of Rights and the Military*, 60 A.F. L. REV. 5, 27 (2007) (article was delivered as the third James Madison Lecture at the New York University Law Center on February 1, 1962).

93. *Respectfully Quoted: A Dictionary of Quotations Requested from the Congressional Research Service* 73 (Suzy Platt ed., 1989) (quoting Benjamin Franklin, Pennsylvania Assembly: Reply to the Governor (Nov. 11, 1975), in 6 The Papers of Benjamin Franklin, at 242 (Leonard W. Labaree ed., 1963), available at http://www.bartleby.com/73/1056.html.

94. It is ironic that Posner would resort to the use of such broad labels in the first instance. In previous works, Posner decried the invocation of value-laden sentiments precisely because they serve merely as restatements of one's views and therefore do not enrich or advance the legal debate at hand. *See generally* Dawinder S. Sidhu, *The Immorality and Inefficiency of an Efficient Breach*, 8 TRANSACTIONS: TENN. J. BUS. L. 61, 81–82 (2006) (summarizing Richard A. Posner, *The Problematics of Moral and Legal Theory*, 111 HARV. L. REV. 1637 (1998), and POSNER, THE PROBLEMS OF JURISPRUDENCE, *supra* note 2, in so far as Posner addresses the unhelpfulness of making value judgments in legal argument).

notions regarding what the recommendations entail. The ultimate result will be a reflexive support or disdain for the ideas, and policymaking will be robbed of an open, impartial, and thorough discussion process.

Daniel B. Prieto, Director of the Independent Task Force on Civil Liberties and National Security at the Council on Foreign Relations, noted, "[I]ssues of national security and civil liberties are akin to theological issues. That is, opinions are so strongly held that they are nonnegotiable."[95] As a result, "Divides over national security and civil liberties have become so deep that they stand in the way of America's ability to forge a critical national foreign policy consensus on how to deal with the strategic challenge of transnational terrorism and defeat al-Qaeda."[96] Prieto adds, "[A]lthough security considerations and civil liberties protections are often in tension, the two need not exist in zero-sum, something that is too readily implied when policymakers discuss the need to balance security and civil liberties."[97]

Robert Chesney, who served on the Detainee Policy Task Force, described the real-life problems of a polarized debate with respect to the government's detention policy. He writes, "the national dialogue has been dominated by a pair of dueling narratives that together reduce the space available for nuanced, practical solutions that may require compromise from both camps."[98] Put differently, "the public receives the message that detention policy ... involves a binary choice between black-and-white alternatives, with apocalyptic stakes. The net effect is to shrink the political space within which reasonable, sustainable policies might be crafted with bipartisan support."[99] As a result, the possibility of achieving a resolution over the detention policy diminishes: "The path to sound and sustainable detention policy almost certainly will require compromises and a willingness to incur political risk at both ends of Pennsylvania Avenue; however, today's culture of distrust and polarization makes this far more difficult than it needs or ought to be."[100]

---

95. Daniel B. Prieto, Council On Foreign Relations, War About Terror: Civil Liberties And National Security After 9/11 2 (2009), *available at* http://www.cfr.org/content/publications/attachments/Civil_Liberties_WorkingPaper.pdf.

96. *Id.* at 6.

97. *Id.*

98. Robert Chesney, A Detention Debate in Black and White, Wash. Post, Sept. 12, 2009, available at: http://www.washingtonpost.com/wp-dyn/content/article/2009/09/09/AR2009090902214.html.

99. *Id.*

100. *Id.*

If Posner continues to insist that post-9/11 homeland policies are decided by pushes and pulls between civil libertarians and national security hawks as they trade off liberty for security and vice versa, one side may appear to realize a short-term gain, as *The Wire's* Prez observed with respect to the war on drugs. But with an absence of a cohesive perspective that embodies both liberty and safety considerations and that is the product of meaningful, flexible debate, genuine, lasting advancement will remain elusive. In that sense, the American people will ultimately suffer both in the present and in the eyes of posterity.

Rigging the Game

"Juking the stats."[101]

—Roland "Prez" Pryzbylewski

In *Not a Suicide Pact*, Posner not only presents an unhelpful balancing scheme between liberty and security, a contest that is attended only by civil libertarians and hawkish security folks, but then also stacks the deck against the preservation of liberty such that security will invariably be dominant and liberty must consequently give way.[102] In particular, Posner posits that in times of war, security measures acquire greater value due to the heightened interest in protecting the homeland. He writes, "In times of danger, the weight of concerns for public safety increases relative to that of liberty concerns, and civil liberties are narrowed."[103] He continues, "[A] decline in security causes the balance to shift against liberty,"[104] and "the more endangered we feel, the more weight we place on the interest in safety...."[105]

Moreover, according to Posner, elevating security concerns above liberty interests may be necessary to ward off future terrorist activity. He speculates that "[a] minor curtailment of present civil liberties, to the extent that it reduces the probability of a terrorist attack, reduces the likelihood of a major future cur-

---

101. Season 4, Episode 9.

102. Posner discusses the fate of several individual liberties, including freedom from torture, surveillance, airport profiling, and chilled religious speech, which will be examined, *infra*.

103. POSNER, NOT A SUICIDE PACT, *supra* note 6, at 9.

104. *Id.* at 46–47.

105. *Id.* at 148.

tailment of those liberties."[106] Otherwise, "rooting out" the enemy "might be fatally inhibited if we felt constrained to strict observance of civil liberties...."[107] From the government's point of view, Posner notes in basic terms, "[I]t is better to be safe than sorry...."[108]

Prez and others in *The Wire* often expressed their disappointment with the concept of "juking the stats."[109] This refers to a situation in which the powers that be—police commanders, high-level public school officials, or politicians—would manipulate perspectives or information to ultimately achieve a predetermined, preferred outcome.[110] It refers to the rigging of the system; it is result-oriented decision-making by those at the top of the power structure to the detriment of those stakeholders with little or no bargaining ability.[111] For example, in an effort to appease the city's political leadership and the pub-

---

106. *Id.* at 46.

107. *Id.* at 6.

108. *Id.* at 45.

109. Season 1, Episode 6; *see also* Season 4, Episode 10 (involving an example of "jukin' the stats" where students were "taught" the standardized test, rather than the underlying skills, in order that the test scores may indicate high teaching quality and student achievement).

110. *The Wire* co-creator David Simon expressed his views on the concept of "jukin' the stats":

> You show me anything that depicts institutional progress in America, school test scores, crime stats, arrest reports, arrest stats, anything that a politician can run on, anything that somebody can get a promotion on. And as soon as you invent that statistical category, 50 people in that institution will be at work trying to figure out a way to make it look as if progress is actually occurring when actually no progress is.... In the same way that a police commissioner or a deputy commissioner can get promoted, and a major can become a colonel, and an assistant school superintendent can become a school superintendent, if they make it look like the kids are learning, and that they're solving crime. And that was a front row seat for me as a reporter. Getting to figure out how the crime stats actually didn't represent anything, once they got done with them.

See generally Bill Moyers Journal, Interview with David Simon (PBS television broadcast Apr. 17, 2009) [hereinafter PBS-Simon Interview], *available at* http://www.pbs.org/moyers/journal/04172009/transcript1.html.

111. As reflected by Simon's comments, PBS-Simon Interview, *supra* note 110, the illegitimate furtherance of a goal by the powerful and the simultaneous disservice to the powerless spans various contexts of *The Wire*, from the schoolhouse, to the police station, to city hall. It is also consistent with the operations of the drug trade. *See* Season 4, Episode 13 (including a soliloquy by Preston "Bodie" Broadus, a lower-level drug dealer, in which he comments on his steadfast loyalty to senior drug bosses and their reluctance to reciprocate: "This game is rigged, man.").

lic to which the politicians were accountable, the high-level police officials implemented a strategy to increase the absolute number of arrests; in essence, they manufactured the impression that they were making a dent in city crime.[112] Although the number of arrests did increase, the arrests were of minor users and offenders; as such, police resources were drawn away from infiltrating the primary sources of the city's drug and related crime problems.[113] Even when the police furnished statistics that supported the suggestion that they were successful in addressing crime, in actuality the drug camp was unfazed and the public remained vulnerable to widespread drug trafficking and associated criminal activities.[114] The campaign, though successful on its face, was in truth ineffective and counterproductive.

Just as information could be "juked" to support a self-fulfilling outcome in *The Wire*, legal commentators recognize that the constitutional equation suggested by Posner is not objectively calibrated, but instead will yield only one pre-determined answer: Civil liberties must defer to security programs or policies. David Cole of the Georgetown University Law Center observed that "constitutional interpretation for Posner is little more than an all-things-considered balancing act—and when the potential costs of a catastrophic terrorist attack are placed on the scale, the concerns of constitutional rights and civil liberties are almost inevitably outweighed."[115] Two other academics criticize Posner's law and economics approach to security issues because his "method works largely through a cost-benefit analysis where equality and antisubordination never quite measure up to the concerns against which they are being measured."[116] Another commentator similarly writes that Posner's "method ... tilts in the favor of security more often than not."[117]

In proposing that post-9/11 constitutional questions implicating the security of the nation be reduced to a balancing of purportedly competing interests, Posner offers a mechanism that is not only faulty in design, as both security and liberty can be simultaneously managed, but also troublesome in its ap-

---

112. Season 3, Episode 1.

113. Season 3, Episode 5.

114. Season 3, Episode 8.

115. David Cole, *The Poverty of Posner's Pragmatism: Balancing Away Liberty after 9/11*, 59 STAN. L. REV. 1735, 1737 (2007) (book review).

116. Mario L. Barnes & F. Greg Bowman, *Entering Unprecedented Terrain: Charting a Method to Reduce Madness in Post-9/11 Power and Rights Conflicts*, 62 U. MIAMI L. REV. 365, 387 (2008).

117. Jarrod Stuard, Book Review, 39 N.Y.U. J. INT'L L. & POL. 475, 504 (2006) (reviewing POSNER, NOT A SUICIDE PACT, *supra* note 6).

plication, as security invariably subjugates other constitutional interests, specifically individual rights. Accordingly, Posner's recommendation is consistent with the "rigging" exhibited and discredited in *The Wire*—giving the impression of an objective approach to produce a pre-determined outcome, but in essence depriving the people of a legitimate debate on the proper relationship between national security and individual rights.

Executive Authority

"The king stay the king."[118]

—D'Angelo Barksdale

Thus far, Posner has argued that constitutional questions implicating national security are to be decided through a balancing of liberty and security, whereby security invariably is the prevailing American interest. What role does Posner envision for the courts—the institution charged with preventing the executive from encroaching on the Constitution—in his balancing scheme? In short, for Posner, it is one of judicial abdication.

Himself an appellate judge, Posner claims the courts are incompetent to perform their function as arbiters of the law in national security cases and, thus, effectively asks judges to trust those advancing the security programs or policies under review. In particular, he writes that judges "[know] little about the needs of national security" and thus will be "unlikely" to substitute their judgment for "that of the executive branch."[119] For example, in the context of indefinite detention, Posner candidly states that "the greater the *perceived* terrorist menace, the greater will be, and should be, the judges' inclination to resolve doubts in favor of detention and its continuation unless and until the danger diminishes significantly."[120] Moreover, Posner claims that it is Congress that should serve as the more effective check on executive authority.[121]

In the third episode of *The Wire*, the writers created a scene that co-creator David Simon called the "preamble" of the series.[122] In it, D'Angelo Barksdale,

---

118. *The Wire: The Buys* (HBO television broadcast June 16, 2002).

119. Posner, Not a Suicide Pact, *supra* note 6, at 9.

120. *Id.* at 66 (emphasis added).

121. *See id.* at 150 ("Congress knows more about national security and so may perform a more effective checking function on the president than the courts are able to do.").

122. PBS-Simon Interview, *supra* note 110.

a mid-level operative in a major Baltimore drug ring led by his cousin, teaches two "hoppers" (younger, low-level dealers) how to play the game of chess, using characters in "the game" (the code within the drug universe) as reference points the youngsters would understand.[123] Barksdale explains that the pawns are like the "soldiers," the loyal low-level dealers on "the front lines."[124] The pawns, Barksdale continues, can become queens if they proceed to the other end of the chessboard; however, pawns don't live long and are get killed off by way of jail or death—in Barksdale's words, the pawns "get capped quick," they are "out of the game early."[125] Accordingly, without any rivals, "the king stay the king."[126] Simon states that the scene is a comment on the stratified system in which "nobody moves" and "there is no improvement in anyone's station."[127] As those on the bottom possess insufficient power to correct those at the top, and given the absence of any moderating agents of comparative power, the king remains in full control.

The existence of an all powerful monarch is fundamentally what the American constitutional tradition seeks to avoid. It is one of checks and balances— the existence of co-equal branches of government empowered to prevent impermissible overreaching by the other two. As James Madison, quoting Montesquieu, declared in *Federalist* No. 47, "There can be no liberty where the legislative and executive powers are united in the same person, or body of magistrates...."[128] The Supreme Court has echoed this concept, stating, "The Constitution sought to divide the delegated powers of the new federal government

---

123. *The Wire: The Buys* (HBO television broadcast June 16, 2002).

124. *Id.*

125. *Id.*

126. *Id.*

127. PBS-Simon Interview, *supra* note 110.

128. The Federalist No. 47 (James Madison); *see also* The Federalist No. 51 (James Madison) ("[T]he great security against a gradual concentration of the several powers in the same department, consists in giving to those who administer each department the necessary constitutional means and personal motives to resist encroachments of the others.... This policy of supplying, by opposite and rival interests, the defect of better motives, might be traced through the whole system of human affairs, private as well as public. We see it particularly displayed in all the subordinate distributions of power, where the constant aim is to divide and arrange the several offices in such a manner as that each may be a check on the other...."). This was a viewpoint seemingly followed in practice by the Framers. *See e.g.,* David McCullough, 1776 80 (Simon & Schuster 2005) (discussing George Washington's decision to confer with Congress regarding the extent of his powers, as Washington "was not fond of 'stretching' his powers;" opining of Washington that "such sensitivity to and respect for the political ramifications of his command were exactly what made him such an effective political general.").

into three defined categories, legislative, executive, and judicial"[129] and that "[e]ven a cursory examination of the Constitution reveals ... that checks and balances were the foundation of a structure of government that would protect liberty."[130] Justice Robert H. Jackson—a man whose words on the interplay of liberty and security from the mid-twentieth century have come to be viewed as highly instructive in today's post-9/11 America[131]—understood that the purpose of separating federal power into three co-equal parts was to "diffus[e] power the better to secure liberty."[132] Put differently by the full Court decades later, "[T]he greatest security against tyranny ... lies ... in a carefully crafted system of checked and balanced power within each Branch."[133]

Constitutional scholar Akhil Reed Amar has perhaps described the constitutional design most clearly: "The structure of separation of powers ... protects constitutional values by providing three separate, overlapping, and mutually reinforcing remedies—legislative, executive, and judicial—against unconstitutional federal conduct."[134] This structure calls for the active participation of each branch; otherwise, a branch asleep at the switch may permit the others to infringe upon the liberty of the people and thus degrade the entire republic. As Alexander Bickel wrote, "Our government consists of discrete institutions, but the effectiveness of the whole depends on their involvement with one another, on their intimacy, even if it often is the sweaty intimacy of creatures locked in combat."[135] This is particularly true in the context of wartime decisions. As the 9/11 Commission noted in this respect, a "shift of power and authority to the government calls for an *enhanced* system of checks and balances to protect the precious liberties that are vital to our way of life."[136] Justice Holmes's colleague on the Supreme Court, Justice Louis D. Brandeis, simi-

---

129. INS v. Chadha, 462 U.S. 919, 951 (1983).

130. Bowsher v. Synar, 478 U.S. 714, 722 (1986).

131. *See, e.g.,* Eric L. Muller, *12/7 and 9/11: War, Liberties, and the Lessons of History,* 104 W. VA. L. REV. 571, 592 (2002) ("Justice Jackson's instruction from sixty years ago must guide our steps today.").

132. Youngstown Sheet & Tube Co. v. Sawyer, 343 U.S. 579, 635 (1952) (Jackson, J., concurring).

133. Mistretta v. United States, 488 U.S. 361, 381 (1989).

134. Akhil Reed Amar, *Of Sovereignty and Federalism,* 96 YALE L.J. 1425, 1504 (1987).

135. ALEXANDER M. BICKEL, THE LEAST DANGEROUS BRANCH: THE SUPREME COURT AT THE BAR OF POLITICS 261 (Yale Univ. Press 2d ed. 1986) (1962).

136. NAT'L COMM'N ON TERRORIST ATTACKS UPON THE U.S., THE 9/11 COMMISSION REPORT 191 (2004) (emphasis added); *but see* POSNER, NOT A SUICIDE PACT, *supra* note 6, at 149 ("[T]he cornerstone of judicial interpretation of the Constitution in emergency situations ... is judicial modesty.").

larly said, "Experience should teach us to be *most on our guard* to protect liberty when the government's purposes are beneficent."[137] More recently, Justice Sandra Day O'Connor memorably quipped in 2004 that "a state of war is not a blank check for the President."[138]

With respect to Posner's proposition that Congress be an energetic check on the executive in wartime situations, the constitutional concept of the separation of powers among three co-equal branches does not contemplate that Congress alone or primarily be entrusted to protect the people from improper federal conduct. Indeed, in *Federalist* No. 78, Alexander Hamilton holds that "the courts were designed to be an intermediate body between the people and the legislature, in order, among other things, to keep the latter within the limits assigned to their authority."[139] Thus, it is only through the robust performance of the respective functions of *each* arm of the federal government that the nation as a whole may properly move forward in times of peace as well as uncertainty.[140]

Posner's view of the judiciary's function in national security cases hardly reflects the notion that the courts are an essential part of the checks and balances constitutional design. By suggesting that judges should respond not to the law and the proven facts of the particular case but rather to *perceptions* of threats, Posner would have the judiciary limit its role due to threats that may be speculative and inherently subjective. Moreover, these perceptions of threats will be projected by the very party purportedly seeking to counter the threats. The judge's decision may as well be determined by the government's color-coded threat chart.[141]

Rather than rely on others, the courts should perform their traditional, independent[142] duty to ascertain the constitutionality of the government's programs or policies, even if they are in the realm of national security. The courts are routinely presented with complicated cases, such as ERISA matters, chal-

---

137. Olmstead v. United States, 277 U.S. 438, 479 (1928) (Brandeis, J., dissenting) (emphasis added).

138. *Hamdi*, 542 U.S. at 536.

139. THE FEDERALIST No. 78 (Alexander Hamilton); *see also id.* ("The interpretation of the laws is the proper and peculiar province of the courts.").

140. *See* BICKEL, *supra* note 135, at 261.

141. *See* DEP'T OF HOMELAND SEC., HOMELAND SECURITY PRESIDENTIAL DIRECTIVE 3 (March 11, 2002), *available at* http://www.dhs.gov/xabout/laws/gc_1214508631313.shtm (creating the Homeland Security Advisory System).

142. *See* Marbury v. Madison, 5 U.S. 137 (1803) (asserting the independence of the judicial branch by reviewing and ultimately nullifying the congressionally-enacted Judiciary Act of 1789).

lenges to environmental regulations, and intellectual property disputes. In those instances, it is incumbent upon the parties to provide the courts with accessible, reliable information that will enable them to reach an appropriate decision. The importance or intricacy of the national security programs or policies at issue should not discharge the courts from determining the constitutionality of the government's actions, but rather should compel the parties to take greater care in presenting their legal arguments and the factual predicates for their contentions to the courts.

That the courts should play a vital role in constitutional questions of a national security nature is more than a theoretical hope or abstract goal. It is a function that the courts have traditionally performed without any evidence that doing so has truly harmed the security pursuits of the other coordinate branches. As former constitutional law professor and Obama administration official Cass Sunstein observed in 2005, "American practice suggests that judges are most unlikely to err by protecting civil liberties; in our history, it is hard to find even a single case in which judicial protection of freedom seriously damaged national security."[143]

For Posner, the courts are ill-suited to decide national security issues and should therefore rely on Congress to serve the legitimate checking function. The federal judiciary, however, is the very branch entrusted by the people and designed by the Framers to safeguard liberty against legislative overreaching, even in difficult national circumstances. Without a meaningful role for the courts in national security matters, the executive, like a "king" over security decisions and the fate of individual rights, will remain the king.[144] President Harry Truman's impermissible seizure of steel plants during the Korean War reflects the dangers of an unfettered wartime executive to private rights.[145] With a power-

---

143. Cass R. Sunstein, *National Security, Liberty, and the D.C. Circuit*, 73 Geo. Wash. L. Rev. 693, 702 (2005).

144. The "King" is, in effect, the executive branch as a whole. More specifically, if the policy arm of the executive (e.g., the president, Cabinet, senior executive agency officials) is relatively free to design its security policies at will, those implementing the policies (e.g., homeland security and immigration agents at borders, transportation authority officials in airports, spies in mosques) similarly may carry out their security functions without fear of legal resistance or accountability. *See The Wire: Misgivings* (HBO television broadcast Nov. 19, 2006) ("The patrolling officer on his beat is the one true dictatorship in America.").

145. *See* Youngstown Sheet, 343 U.S. 579 (striking down the President's executive order to seize privately owned steel mills, in the course of the American conflict in Korea, holding the President did not act pursuant to an act of Congress or constitutional grant of authority). *Youngstown* illustrates the judicial limitation placed on the President's powers during the Korean War. *Youngstown*, thus, serves as a contrast to Posner's arguments that

ful executive unrestrained by the federal judiciary or legislature, the "pawns" in modern American society will be without recourse and may have their rights abridged.[146] This is a result that, as will be examined in the next section, Posner is willing to accept.

Profiling

"They're dead where it doesn't count."[147]

—Mike Fletcher

Posner finds little trouble equating the terrorist threat with Muslims. By doing so, he finds that Muslims in America are appropriate targets of national security measures. He writes, "Terrorism and religion are highly entwined in Muslim extremism today; the juncture cannot be ignored by our security services."[148] Furthermore, because it is Muslims who pose the terrorist threat to the United States, it is prudent for those security services to track the Muslim-American community for suspicious behavior: "[W]hen one reflects that there are several million Muslims in the United States and that a tiny number of terrorists may be able to cause catastrophic harm to a nation, the government should not have to stand by helplessly" while extremism spreads.[149] Posner therefore argues that the government may, without running afoul of constitutional mandates, surreptitiously intercept and sift through a Muslim-American's electronic communications and personal information, subject Muslim-Americans to additional security procedures in the airport setting, and shadow Muslim priests in American mosques to listen for provocative religious lectures.

With respect to electronic communications, Posner claims that "surreptitious eavesdropping need impose no costs at all on people who don't know they're being eavesdropped on, or who know but don't care because they have nothing they particularly care to hide from the eavesdropper."[150] He also contends

---

the judicial branch is ill-equipped to judge, or should refrain from interfering with, the executive's decisions concerning national safety.

146. *See* discussion *infra* pp. 48–49 on the inadequacy of a political check on the executive by the right to vote.

147. *The Wire: Not for Attribution* (HBO television broadcast Jan. 20, 2008).

148. POSNER, NOT A SUICIDE PACT, *supra* note 6, at 116.

149. *Id.* at 124.

150. *Id.* at 90.

that any constitutional complications with surreptitious eavesdropping of electronic communications can be eased with a two-pronged system in which a
computer program first filters the communications, and a human then reviews
only those aspects of the communications identified by the computer.[151]

As to the effect on those subjected to the surveillance, Posner argues, "An
electronic search no more invades privacy than does a dog trained to sniff out
illegal drugs, though the dog's 'alerting' to the presence of drugs in a container
provides probable cause for a (human) investigator to search the container."[152]
Posner suggests that even if an individual's privacy is invaded, the individual
is not truly "harmed ... in any practical sense."[153] It "might," according to Posner, "cause ... at least transitory emotional distress, and that is a harm even if
it has no rational basis."[154]

Finally, Posner argues that the government's intelligence entities may "want
to maintain a close watch on radical imams in the U.S. Muslim community of
several million people ... *even if there is no basis* for thinking that *any* of these
imams has yet crossed the line that separates advocacy [which may not be constitutionally suppressed] from incitement" of violence, which may be constitutionally suppressed.[155] Posner acknowledges that roaming the mosques for
such incitement may chill the speech of Muslim worshippers, who may be less
inclined to express themselves or to join the congregation in the first place.[156]
Posner contends, however, that the cost to speech may be worth it depending
"on the importance of the investigative activities to national security."[157]

It is doubtless that those who count least today, the "pawns" in American post-
9/11 security chessboard, are the innocent Americans who are Muslim or are
perceived to be Muslim.[158] *The Wire* powerfully speaks to the absence of consideration for the "pawns" in Baltimore, including those without the political

---

151. *See id.* at 99–100.
152. *Id.* at 130.
153. *Id.* at 131.
154. *Id.*
155. *Id.* at 111–12 (emphases added).
156. *Id.* at 112.
157. *Id.* at 112–13.
158. *See* Leti Volpp, *The Citizen and the Terrorist*, 49 UCLA L. Rev. 1575, 1576 (2002)
("Th[e] article suggests that September 11 facilitated the consolidation of a new identity
category that groups together persons who appear 'Middle Eastern, Arab, or Muslim,'
whereby members of this group are identified as terrorists and disidentified as citizens.");
see also Muneer I. Ahmad, *A Rage Shared by Law: Post-September 11 Racial Violence as
Crimes of Passion*, 92 CAL. L. Rev. 1259 (2004) (discussing the extent of the public and private racial violence against Muslims, Arabs, South Asians, and Sikhs after 9/11).

clout or the social status to be taken seriously by others. In the series' final season, a *Baltimore Sun* reporter was disappointed to learn that her article on a triple murder, which had been slotted as a front-page story, was instead buried deep inside the paper and edited down considerably.[159] A fellow reporter explained the article's placement by stating that the victims were "dead where it doesn't count."[160] In other words, they were pawns in the blighted parts of Baltimore whose lives had been marginalized in the existing social structure. In condoning the minimized constitutional protections to be afforded to Muslim-Americans, Posner targets a people who have been placed on the fringe of our collective conscience when it comes to a full recognition of individual rights in the post-9/11 world. Posner's proposition that infringements upon the constitutional rights of Muslim-Americans do not count, however, cannot be squared with the basic legal system within which we live.

Even if Muslim-Americans are not cognizant of the fact that they are being eavesdropped on, they may still have a sense that they are being profiled on the basis of their religion. In a recent article, I released the results of a study that shows that 70.7% of Muslim-American respondents believe, 45.0% strongly, that their online activities are being monitored by the government.[161] The same study reveals that 8.4% of Muslims have altered their online behavior as a result of the belief that their electronic behavior is being monitored by the government.[162] Even if Muslim-Americans are not aware of any monitoring, they are nevertheless chilled in their speech. Extrapolating these numbers to the "several million" Muslims in the United States figure Posner references yields a large number of Muslims who believe that they are under surveillance and who have chosen to limit their online activities as a consequence.[163] Furthermore, people with "nothing to hide" do not become indifferent towards the government's eavesdropping on them. This is why the Fourth Amendment to

---

159. *The Wire: Not for Attribution* (HBO television broadcast Jan. 20, 2008).

160. *Id.*

161. Dawinder S. Sidhu, *The Chilling Effect of Government Surveillance Programs on the Use of the Internet by Muslim-Americans*, 7 U. Md. L.J. Race, Religion, Gender & Class 375, 390–91 (2007).

162. *Id.* at 391.

163. U.S. Dep't of State, Muslims in America—A Statistical Portrait (2008), *available at* http://www.america.gov/st/peopleplace-english/2008/December/20081222090246jmnamdeirf0.4547083.html ("The size of the Muslim-American population has proved difficult to measure because the U.S. Census does not track religious affiliation. Estimates vary widely from 2 million to 7 million. What is clear, however, is that the Muslim-American population has been growing rapidly as a result of immigration, a high birth rate, and conversions.").

the Constitution[164] generally requires the *government* to possess an appropriate basis to search an individual and does not first require that the *individual* establish that he has nothing to hide.[165]

Posner's creative suggestion regarding a bifurcated computer/human review of communications does not resolve the possibility that harmless speech may be flagged by the electronic part of the surveillance mechanism and thereafter transmitted to a human reviewer. Although the computer, as a filter of communication, is an inanimate entity and preserves some semblance of privacy, it is still fallible. In particular, it is susceptible to over-inclusiveness of allegedly suspicious communications. Thus, a human may ultimately read electronic information of a legitimate or personal nature. In this respect, Posner's two-pronged system may, at best, reduce the number of false positives, but it does not eliminate the constitutional difficulties with respect to surreptitious eavesdropping.

Posner's comparison of electronic surveillance to a dog sniffing for drugs, although perhaps reasonable on the surface, does not upon deeper inspection alleviate any genuine constitutional concerns. The surreptitious eavesdropping contemplated by post-9/11 security measures is not random; it is targeted at members of one community or those perceived to be members of that com-

---

164. The Fourth Amendment provides:

> The right of the people to be secure in their persons, houses, papers, and effects, against unreasonable searches and seizures, shall not be violated, and no Warrants shall issue, but upon probable cause, supported by Oath or affirmation, and particularly describing the place to be searched, and the persons or things to be seized.

U.S. CONST. amend. IV.

165. *See, e.g.*, *Thirty-Second Annual Review of Criminal Procedure: Overview of the Fourth Amendment*, 91 GEO. L.J. 5, 5 (2003) ("The Fourth Amendment of the United States Constitution governs all searches and seizures conducted by government agents. The Amendment contains two separate clauses: A prohibition against unreasonable searches and seizures, and a requirement that probable cause support each warrant issued."); Orin S. Kerr, *Lifting the "Fog" of Internet Surveillance: How a Suppression Remedy Would Change Computer Crime Law*, 54 HASTINGS L.J. 805, 811 (2003) ("[T]he Fourth Amendment ... generally requires a search warrant or special factual circumstances for the government to go into private spaces that are protected by a reasonable expectation of privacy."). *See generally* Samuel D. Warren and Louis D. Brandeis, *The Right to Privacy*, 4 HARV. L. REV. 193, 195 (1890) (expressing the view that there exists a "right to be let alone"). To the extent that the concept of consent in Fourth Amendment jurisprudence captures an individual's affirmative willingness to allow the government to search him, consent is inapplicable to Posner's argument, which is premised on surreptitious eavesdropping—one cannot consent to what one does not know. *See, e.g.*, Katz v. United States, 389 U.S. 347, 358 (1967) ("[O]f course, the very nature of electronic surveillance precludes its use pursuant to the suspect's consent.").

munity. To use a more apt metaphor, a police car that stops some people, but not all, for speeding is fine so long as the officer is genuinely attempting to survey all cars or, say, every tenth car for speeding. The situation becomes problematic when the officer stops some people because the officer is looking only at cars driven by certain people, based on characteristics such as ethnicity or skin color.[166] The selective application by government security or investigative efforts on one class of individuals—even if initially conducted by a non-human—is unjust because it is based on actual or perceived race, religion, or national origin.[167]

Contrary to Posner's assertion that any harm suffered by stricter airport security measures is at most "transitory emotional distress," such harm extends beyond the targeted individual to all members of that community who may realize that they are now subject to different rules and to the prospect of being treated less than equally on account of their actual or perceived race, religion, or national origin. Not only is this harm more extensive in scope, it is also more expansive in depth; a Muslim profiled in an airport walks away with more than hurt emotions. The qualitative and quantitative aspects of his experiences with a public accommodation supposedly open on equal terms to all Americans are significantly affected, a situation reminiscent of the African-American plight with public accommodations in the 1960s.[168] As a result, Muslims may use other modes of transportation to avoid harassment or may not travel at all.

With regard to Posner's acceptance of surveilling Muslim clerics, the importance of such investigative activities can be determined only after the fact, after the government has scoured mosques and chilled the speech of adherents to Islam. In other words, it is acceptable in Posner's formulation to chill the speech of Muslims at mosques, even without any evidence that the speech contains incitement or a resemblance of incitement on the spectrum of religious rhetoric. Such curtailment would be justified if it is later found that there was objectionable speech being uttered. Although such justification would extend to those mosques at which radical teachings took place, it would not apply to those mosques innocent of such teachings, making those mosques victims of

---

166. *See* Stephen Nathanson, An Eye for an Eye: The Immorality of Punishing by Death 64 (Rowman & Littlefield Publishers 2d ed. 2001) (1992) (postulating that such enforcement punishes people based on appearance and constitutes an abuse of power).

167. *See id.*

168. *See* Sidhu, *supra* note 161, at 379 (drawing parallels between the civil rights findings in the landmark case of Heart of Atlanta Motel, Inc. v. United States, 379 U.S. 241 (1964), and the post-9/11 climate facing Muslims and others).

an unnecessary, presumptive invasion. The approach offered by Posner erroneously presupposes that a Muslim mosque is a potential breeding ground for incitement of violence against the United States.[169]

Posner acknowledges that generally "more speech" is preferable to the chilling of speech but writes, "[I]t is unclear what counterarguments are available to opponents" of instructional, appealing rhetoric from imams.[170] What is the antidote to such speech, Posner asks.[171] Posner underestimates the attractiveness of the fundamental principles of liberty and religious freedom that form the intellectual foundation of the American republic. The concept, that man is free to live in America and develop a relationship with God in accordance with the dictates of his conscience and without government interference or coercion, is one that should be offered in response to those who "hate" the United States.[172] American values and ideals can resonate with the hearts and minds of all men and can commensurately diminish the misguided intention to cripple the greatest experiment in liberty and religious freedom ever known.[173]

The arguments put forth by Posner with respect to profiling Muslims in the United States do not pass constitutional muster. They are not only legally infirm, but may also be counterproductive as a practical matter. First, and perhaps most evident, these arguments if implemented would alienate the very community from which cooperation is necessary for the threat of terrorism to be properly averted.[174] Posner recognizes this possibility but nonetheless contends that the benefits of his suggestions outweigh the costs and, thus, must

---

169. A more constitutionally accepted alternative would be one requiring investigative powers to possess some degree of evidence that particular imams should be monitored.

170. POSNER, NOT A SUICIDE PACT, *supra* note 6, at 122.

171. *See id.*

172. *See* Abington Sch. Dist. v. Schempp, 374 U.S. 203, 226 (1963) ("The place of religion in our society is an exalted one, achieved through a long tradition of reliance on the ... inviolable citadel of the individual heart and mind. We have come to recognize through bitter experience that it is not within the power of the government to invade that citadel...."); Schneider v. Smith, 390 U.S. 17, 25 (1968) (noting that the First Amendment "creates a preserve where the views of the individual are made inviolate."); *see also* JON MEACHAM, AMERICAN GOSPEL: GOD, THE FOUNDING FATHERS, AND THE MAKING OF A NATION 6 (Random House 2006) (positing generally that the American "public religion" is one in which the Founders believed there was a Creator God, but that the individual was free to decide whether there was a God, gods, or no God at all).

173. It is this appeal to conscience that regrettably is not part of the battle against fundamentalists. *See* POSNER, NOT A SUICIDE PACT, *supra* note 6, at 5 ("[W]e have no strategy for defeating them, only for fighting them.")

174. *See* Kevin R. Johnson, *Protecting National Security Through More Liberal Admission of Immigrants*, 2007 U. CHI. LEGAL F. 157, 187–88 (2007) ("The many measures the U.S. gov-

be brought within the Constitution.[175] Second, such profiling would induce terrorists to recruit and employ individuals who defy the operative 'Muslim male' profile.[176]

There are doctrinal as well as pragmatic reasons to dispute Posner's proposals, which are predicated on the notion that Muslim-Americans are a rightfully marginalized community whose constitutional rights are less meaningful in the post-9/11 context.[177] In ensuring that the rights of Muslim-Americans "count" in the modern constitutional design, we will not only safeguard our legal principles but will also aid our anti-terrorism efforts moving forward.

Discrimination

"Deserve got nuthin' to do with it."[178]
—Felicia "Snoop" Pearson

Posner suggests that due to the terrorist threat, the government can permissibly surveil the communications and information of Muslims in the United States, profile Muslims in airports, and stake out mosques for inflammatory teachings.[179] These suggestions are based solely on shared religious identity, not on any evidence of terrorism.[180] For instance, Posner writes that inevitably "some of the personal information gathered by intelligence agencies pertains to people who have no links to terrorism"[181] and that "radical imams" should be monitored "even if there is no basis for thinking" that they have incited vi-

---

ernment directed at Arabs and Muslims after September 11 estranged these communities, thereby damaging the nation's efforts to collect necessary intelligence.").

175. *See* POSNER, NOT A SUICIDE PACT, *supra* note 6, at 50, 117–19. The temptation for and danger of the authorities viewing the people they are to serve as the enemy has been explored in *The Wire*. *See The Wire: Reformation* (HBO television broadcast Nov. 28, 2004) ("[W]hen you're at war, you need a fucking enemy. And pretty soon, damn near everybody on every corner is your fucking enemy. And soon the neighborhood that you're supposed to be policing, that's just occupied territory.").

176. *See* POSNER, NOT A SUICIDE PACT, *supra* note 6, at 117–18.

177. *See id.* at 50.

178. *The Wire: Late Editions* (HBO television broadcast Mar. 2, 2008).

179. *See* POSNER, NOT A SUICIDE PACT, *supra* note 6, at 117–20 (suggesting that profiling of "Islamic terrorism" is less problematic as compared to "ordinary crimes").

180. *See id.* at 111–12, 130.

181. *Id.* at 130.

olence against the United States.[182] To justify his position, Posner states that profiling of Muslims is "mild" in comparison to other civil rights violations, such as the internment of the Japanese and the segregation of African-American students.[183] To diminish the actual or perceived burden on Muslims, Posner volunteers that non-Muslims should be subject to heightened surveillance as well so Muslims do not feel singled out.[184]

Posner's suggestions call into question what may constitute an acceptable basis for negative treatment and specifically whether religion may be the sole factor in a judgment that surveillance and profiling of Muslims is permissible legally or sensible practically. In the penultimate episode of *The Wire*, Michael Lee, a teenage product of the Baltimore streets, asks a superior in his drug crew's hierarchy, Felicia "Snoop" Pearson, why he's been singled out by the drug ring's leader to be executed even though he didn't violate any internal code of conduct warranting any punishment, much less death.[185] Snoop curtly responds, "[D]eserve got nuthin' to do with it."[186] In other words, actual guilt is an irrelevant consideration. It is enough that the powers that be, the "king" in this case, suspected that Michael was guilty.[187]

Especially in times of crisis, mere suspicion has served as the basis for adverse actions and decisions irrespective of evidence. Such suspicion generally is premised on a single characteristic—race, ethnicity, or national origin—that individuals share with America's enemies. When the judiciary fails to meaningfully check the other two branches, race, religion, or national origin may be legitimized as a proxy for suspicion, and the adverse actions or decisions consequently attain the imprimatur of the Constitution.

This was perhaps most evident during World War II. In response to the attack on Pearl Harbor, over 100,000 individuals of Japanese descent on the West Coast of the United States were taken from their homes and were placed into internment camps pursuant to an executive order signed by President Franklin

---

182. *Id.* at 111–12.

183. *Id.* at 119.

184. *See id.* at 118.

185. *See The Wire: Late Editions* (HBO television broadcast Mar. 2, 2008). Michael's alleged transgression was providing the police with information that led to the arrest of the principals of a drug organization. *Id.* In truth, Michael was not a "snitch" or police informant. *Id.*

186. *Id.*

187. *See id.* Bodie, another character on *The Wire*, encountered a similar issue, as he was suspected of wrongdoing (in his case sharing confidential information with the police, even though he did no such thing) and was executed as a result. *The Wire: Final Grades* (HBO television broadcast Dec. 10, 2006).

D. Roosevelt.[188] In the infamous 1944 case *Korematsu v. United States*, the Supreme Court upheld the constitutionality of the executive order that had given rise to the internment, deferring significantly to the government's arguments regarding the military necessity of the relocation.[189] The Court noted that the petitioner, who was born in California to Japanese parents, was subject to the order and interned not because of any racial animus towards the Japanese, but rather:

> [B]ecause we are at war with the Japanese Empire, because the properly constituted military authorities feared an invasion of our West Coast and felt constrained to take proper security measures, because they decided that the military urgency of the situation demanded that all citizens of Japanese ancestry be segregated from the West Coast temporarily ...[190]

In another case upholding the conviction of an American citizen of Japanese ancestry for violating the exclusion order and curfew requirements imposed after the attack on Pearl Harbor, the Court observed, "We cannot close our eyes to the fact, demonstrated by experience, that in time of war residents having ethnic affiliations with an invading enemy may be a greater source of danger than those of a different ancestry."[191]

---

188. *See* Korematsu v. United States, 323 U.S. 214, 216–18 (1944); *see also* Exec. Order No. 9066, 7 Fed. Reg. 1407 (Feb. 19, 1942).

189. *See Korematsu*, 323 U.S. at 218 ("Nothing short of apprehension by the proper military authorities of the gravest imminent danger to the public safety can constitutionally justify [the exclusion].... The military authorities, charged with the primary responsibility of defending our shores, concluded that curfew provided inadequate protection and ordered exclusion. They did so ... in accordance with Congressional authority to the military to say who should, and who should not, remain in the threatened areas.").

190. *Id.* at 223.

191. Hirabayashi v. United States, 320 U.S. 81, 101 (1943). Recently, the Supreme Court issued a decision in a case brought by a Muslim detained after 9/11 who alleged discrimination by high-level government officials. *See* Ashcroft v. Iqbal, 129 S. Ct. 1937 (2009). In the course of its discussion on whether the detainee's complaint satisfied the pleading standard of Federal Rule of Civil Procedure 8(a)(2), the majority noted:

> The September 11 attacks were perpetrated by 19 Arab Muslim hijackers who counted themselves members in good standing of al Qaeda, an Islamic fundamentalist group. Al Qaeda was headed by another Arab Muslim—Osama bin Laden—and composed in large part of his Arab Muslim disciples. It should come as no surprise that a legitimate policy directing law enforcement to arrest and detain individuals because of their suspected link to the attacks would produce a disparate, incidental impact on Arab Muslims, even though the purpose of the policy was to target neither Arabs nor Muslims.

Id. at 1951. Given that the ruling centered around the sufficiency of the complaint (i.e., did

Justice Jackson dissented from the Court's ruling in *Korematsu*, forewarning that the majority had validated a principle of racial discrimination that:

> [L]ies about like a loaded weapon ready for the hand of any authority that can bring forward a plausible claim of an urgent need. Every repetition imbeds that principle more deeply in our law and thinking and expands it to new purposes. All who observe the work of courts are familiar with what Judge [Benjamin] Cardozo described as "the tendency of a principle to expand itself to the limit of its logic." ... [I]f [the courts] review and approve, that passing incident becomes the doctrine of the Constitution. There it has a generative power of its own, and all that it creates will be in its own image.[192]

Posner's suggestions that Muslims can be singled out for surveillance and additional security measures, which absent any evidence of wrongdoing or suspected wrongdoing amount to blanket racial discrimination, are difficult to reconcile with Justice Jackson's guidance from another wartime moment in America's history.

Posner's proposition that the profiling of Muslims is somehow less severe than the discriminatory measures faced by Japanese- and African-Americans is unconvincing.[193] That the form of the discrimination may seem less invidious does not deflect from the fact that profiling is discriminatory in substance. Profiling in the post-9/11 may not seem as "bad" as other practices, but this comparison does not change the nature of profiling from discriminatory to non-discriminatory.

Regarding the idea that security measures applied to Muslims should be applied to non-Muslims to furnish the appearance of equal treatment,[194] the result would be just that—nothing more than an appearance. Tricking Muslims into believing they are subject to non-discriminatory security policies does not change the intent of the policies in the first instance, namely to target Muslims. Posner's proposal may not only fail to alter the discriminatory content of the security efforts, it may also make things worse: The pernicious effects would be to conceal discrimination from its victims, to effectively prohibit any resultant complaints, and, therefore, to immunize the government from having to answer for its discriminatory tactics.

---

the complaint comply with Federal Rule 8(a)(2)) and did not pass on the merits of the claims of discrimination (i.e., were the detainee's constitutional rights violated), it is unclear what the import of this excerpt is, if any. This question will require resolution elsewhere.

192. *Korematsu*, 323 U.S. at 246 (Jackson, J., dissenting) (footnote omitted).

193. *See* POSNER, NOT A SUICIDE PACT, *supra* note 6, at 119.

194. *Id.* at 118.

The terrorist attack upon the United States necessitated a response both internal and external to America's borders. The clear threat to national security required the government to determine how best to prevent a subsequent attack from occurring. As modern as the attack was, the security elements of the government do not operate on a blank slate. It has its own history from which to glean the proper limits of America's security measures. A lesson from the World War II era applies today despite the social, economic, and technological advancements in the interim: Suspicion of guilt premised on race, religion, or national origin alone is impermissible and runs against the very Constitution and pluralistic republic we seek to defend. Posner suggests that Muslim rights may be sacrificed on the margins even in the absence of any evidentiary support for suspecting Muslims of wrongdoing.[195] This is a fate they do not deserve and that our system of laws should not permit.

Torture

"You play in dirt, you get dirty."[196]
—James "Jimmy" McNulty

Posner's post-9/11 constitutional construct, in which liberty may be sacrificed if marginal gains to national security may result, allows for the mistreatment of people as well as the use of a highly controversial practice: torture. Posner supports the notion that torture may be used in "extreme situations" or in an "extreme emergency" where information can be elicited.[197] He contends that the "propriety" of using a "high degree of coercion" cannot be reasonably denied and that the reply of those who do entertain such a denial is that 'torture never works.'[198] Posner further states that while some may have moral objections to torture, they "should not be allowed to occlude consideration of instrumental considerations."[199]

The propriety of using aggressive tactics with suspects is another theme present in *The Wire*. For example, Baltimore city officer Eddie Walker employed questionable deterrent methods in dealing with younger troublemak-

---

195. *Id.* at 130.

196. *The Wire: A New Day* (HBO television broadcast Nov. 26, 2006).

197. POSNER, NOT A SUICIDE PACT, *supra* note 6, at 83.

198. *Id.* at 81.

199. *Id.* at 83; *see also id.* at 85 (suggesting that whether torture "shocks the conscience" is a subjective, relative judgment).

ers in the community: Breaking the fingers of a youth who routinely stole cars and pocketing the money of another who was fleeing police.[200] A number of the youth sought revenge and were successful in pouring yellow paint on Officer Walker, publicly embarrassing him.[201] His colleague, James "Jimmy" McNulty, later commented on the situation, "You play in dirt, you get dirty."[202] The motive to retaliate was understandable given the manner in which Officer Walker engaged those subject to his authority. *The Wire* thus touches on the practical realities of the abuse of power and the natural inclination to contemptuously respond to it.[203]

With respect to torture, it is quite clearly impermissible on legal, principled, and practical grounds. Professor Jordan J. Paust notes:

> "[C]ustomary and treaty-based human rights law requires, *without exception*, that no persons shall be subjected to torture or to cruel, inhumane, or degrading treatment. The same absolute prohibition exists in customary and treaty-based laws of war." For example, common Article 3 of the Geneva Conventions requires that all persons detained "shall in all circumstances be treated humanely," and that "[t]o this end ... at any time and in any place ... cruel treatment and torture" are proscribed in addition to "outrages upon personal dignity, in particular, humiliating and degrading treatment." Article 5 of the Geneva Civilian Convention reiterates that "[i]n each case" persons detained as security threats shall "be treated with humanity," a requirement that is also reflected in Article 27. Additionally, Article 31 requires that "[n]o physical or moral coercion shall be exercised against protected persons, in particular to obtain information from them," and Article 33 prohibits "all measures of intimidation."[204]

---

200. *The Wire: Misgivings* (HBO television broadcast Nov. 19, 2006).

201. *The Wire: A New Day* (HBO television broadcast Nov. 26, 2006).

202. *Id.*

203. Ironically, Officer McNulty later conceived a plan to make it seem as if there was a serial killer on the loose in Baltimore so as to ensure that greater resources would be dedicated to the police department, resources that could be used in the apprehension of a drug "king." *The Wire: Not for Attribution* (HBO television broadcast Jan. 20, 2008). Officer McNulty's efforts, although well-intended, were clearly illegal. He not only lost his job, but the "king" was not prosecuted due to the inadmissibility of the evidence produced by the plan. *The Wire: -30-* (HBO television broadcast Mar. 9, 2008).

204. Jordan J. Paust, *Judicial Power to Determine the Status and Rights of Persons Detained Without Trial*, 44 Harv. Int'l L.J. 503, 530–31 (2003) (alteration in original) (internal footnotes omitted) (emphasis added).

The United States is a signatory of the Geneva Conventions.[205] As such, these prohibitions are not simple pronouncements of international human rights norms that lie in ether beyond the borders of the United States. Rather, they are commitments the nation has obligated itself to comply with and brought well within the realm of the American legal landscape.[206]

Furthermore, the problem is not that 'torture never works.' Instead, it is that information extracted from the use of torture can be obtained by other means that do not rise to the level of torture and that therefore allow the American intelligence services to stay within the bounds of applicable American legal obligations and comply with the prevailing views of the international human rights community. As President Obama noted after reviewing materials on waterboarding, "[W]e could have gotten this information in other ways,"[207] ways that perhaps would not run afoul of those obligations. President Obama added, "[W]e can still get information" using other techniques, even though "[i]n some cases, it may be harder" to do so.[208]

Posner likely does not accept President Obama's view that the use of torture "corrodes the character of [our] country" and stands in opposition to "our ideals."[209] If only arguments related to the success or failure of torture—again, a simple cost-benefit analysis—are admissible, then it would be necessary to bring to the balance the distinct possibility that the use of torture by the United States serves as a recruitment tool for terrorist elements.[210] If the nation em-

---

205. *See* International Humanitarian Law, International Committee of the Red Cross (ICRC), States Party to the Geneva Conventions (2005), *available at* http://www.icrc.org/ihl.nsf/WebSign?ReadForm&id=375&ps=P.

206. *See* United States v. Khadr, CMCR 07-001, at 4 n.4 (Ct. Mil. Comm'n Rev. Sept. 24, 2007), *available at* http://www.scotusblog.com/movabletype/archives/CMCR%20ruling%209-24-07.pdf.

("The United States is a signatory nation to all four Geneva Conventions. The Geneva Conventions are generally viewed as self-executing treaties (i.e., ones which become effective without the necessity of implementing congressional action), form a part of American law, and are binding in federal courts under the Supremacy Clause." (citing U.S. Const. art VI, §2) ("This Constitution, and the laws of the United States which shall be made in pursuance thereof; and all treaties made, or which shall be made, under the authority of the United States, shall be the supreme law of the land....")).

207. President Barack Obama, 100th-Day Press Briefing (Apr. 29, 2009) (transcript available on Westlaw at 2009 WL 1145265).

208. *Id.*

209. *Id.*

210. *See e.g.*, Louis Fisher, *Extraordinary Rendition: The Price of Secrecy*, 57 Am. U. L. Rev. 1405, 1446 (2008) (discussing El-Masri v. United States, 479 F.3d 296 (4th Cir. 2007), and arguing that "[a]busive, illegal, and unconstitutional actions by the Executive Branch do

ploys techniques that are known to be considered by the enemy as contemptible or "dirty," we essentially shroud ourselves in the very dirt that exists as a marker for hatred and violence. This is true irrespective of our own subjective value judgments of the usefulness of that investigative practice. That taint will be difficult to undo, the hate commensurately difficult to neutralize.[211]

The adoption of an official policy permitting the executive to authorize torture in some situations—even in "extreme" ones—may prove counterproductive and ultimately more harmful to the American security cause than information elicited from torture. Given that the information may be obtainable by less drastic means, means that may not lead to terrorist recruitment or the retaliation that *The Wire* portends, it seems imprudent based on a purely pragmatic analysis to bring torture under the standard of the Constitution.

Extra-Constitutionalism

"The tree that doesn't bend breaks."[212]

—Marla Daniels

Francis Biddle, Roosevelt's attorney general during World War II, once opined, "[T]he Constitution has never greatly bothered any wartime President."[213] Biddle expressed the practical reality that presidents will do whatever it takes to defend the United States even if those actions technically transgress lines drawn by the Constitution.[214] For his part, Posner endorses the view that, in times of war, the executive is empowered to act outside the law if doing so would help ensure the preservation of the nation.[215] Indeed, the title of the book, *Not a Suicide Pact*, is derived in part from the Supreme Court's statement in *Kennedy v. Mendoza-Martinez*: "[W]hile the Constitution protects against in-

---

not maintain national security. They undermine it. To allow the Executive Branch to engage in extraordinary rendition and torture serves to recruit terrorists and spread hate against the United States.").

211. *See, e.g.*, *The Wire: All Prologue* (HBO television broadcast July 6, 2003) (regarding reputational harm, one character remarks, "[T]he past is always with us. Where we come from, what we go through, how we go through it, all this shit matters.... [Y]ou can change up..., you can say you're somebody new, and you can give yourself a whole new story. But, what came first is who you really are and what happened before is what really happened, and it don't matter that some fool say he different....").

212. *The Wire: -30-* (HBO television broadcast Mar. 9, 2008).

213. Francis Biddle, *In Brief Authority* 219 (1962).

214. *See id.*

215. *See* POSNER, NOT A SUICIDE PACT, *supra* note 6, at 158, 170.

vasions of individual rights, it is not a suicide pact."[216] In the opening paragraph of the book, Posner writes that civil liberties are flexible and must give way to public safety interests because "a Constitution that will not bend will break."[217] Elsewhere, Posner echoes Biddle's observation and writes that those responsible for the nation's security will not, on their own, give much weight to individual rights in reaching security decisions;[218] the executive will use torture to gain information even if there is no cognizable right to do so.[219]

In reference to President Abraham Lincoln's decision to suspend habeas corpus rights during the Civil War, Posner notes that "to violate one constitutional provision (the suspension provision) in order to save the Constitution as a whole" is "not a legal argument" because there is "no such grant of authority" to violate the Constitution.[220] Instead, it is a pragmatic response to the dire conditions precipitating the extra-constitutional action.[221] There is a "law of necessity" that "supersedes the law of the Constitution."[222] Put differently, the "law of necessity" is not a "law" but the "trumping of law by necessity."[223] As Lincoln himself asked rhetorically, "[A]re all the laws, *but one*, to go unexecuted, and the government itself to go to pieces, lest that one be violated?"[224]

With regard to such extra-constitutional acts, Posner thinks it unwise to codify situations or moments when the government may sidestep the Constitution because those rules may be ill-defined and may be tested to their outer limits.[225] Instead, Posner finds it preferable to let stand an implicit, default rule that the executive can suspend the laws when necessary.[226] He reasons that prescribed rules generally are meant to be broken and that a president will pay a higher political price if he abuses the default rule.[227]

Posner dedicates the "main task" of his book "to suggest[ing] the direction that the law should take, by assessing the relevant consequences and hoping that the Supreme Court will be convinced by the assessment and shape the law ac-

---

216. Kennedy, 372 U.S. at 160.
217. POSNER, NOT A SUICIDE PACT, *supra* note 6, at 1.
218. *See id.* at 61.
219. *See id.* at 38.
220. *Id.* at 40.
221. *See id.*
222. *Id.* at 70 (quoting Martin Sheffer).
223. POSNER, NOT A SUICIDE PACT, *supra* note 6, at 158.
224. *See* DORIS KEARNS GOODWIN, TEAM OF RIVALS: THE POLITICAL GENIUS OF ABRAHAM LINCOLN 355 (2005).
225. *See* POSNER, NOT A SUICIDE PACT, *supra* note 6, at 86–87, 154.
226. *See id.* at 154.
227. *See id.*

cordingly."[228] In *Not a Suicide Pact*, however, Posner argues that the executive can engage in extra-constitutional acts because it has a "moral duty to violate positive law...."[229] To that end, Posner claims that presidents who disobey the law are engaging in "civil disobedience" much in the same way that "Gandhi and Martin Luther King, Jr." did in their situations.[230]

In the final episode of the series, Marla Daniels, an aspiring local politician and ex-wife of Cedric Daniels, a deputy commissioner in city police department, asks Cedric to consider resigning due to a potential scandal in order to save her career.[231] She reminds Cedric of the need to be flexible in the face of unfavorable and emerging circumstances: "The tree that doesn't bend breaks," she advises.[232]

Chief Justice William H. Rehnquist once noted, "The laws will ... not be silent in time of war, but they will speak with a somewhat different voice."[233] The courts called upon to resolve constitutional questions during these difficult times will likely cede the point that the executive possesses great power and greater power when it acts with congressional approval.[234] Accordingly, Posner's opening salvo—that "a Constitution that will not bend will break"[235]—is relatively innocuous, but his additional step of declaring that the law may be permissively disregarded in favor of the "law of necessity"[236] must be disputed.

Although Posner suggests that there exists a law of necessity that may be invoked even if it violates the Constitution,[237] the fact remains that, since its

---

228. *Id.* at 29.

229. *Id.* at 85.

230. *Id.*

231. *The Wire*: *-30-* (HBO television broadcast Mar. 9, 2008).

232. *Id.*

233. William H. Rehnquist, All the Laws but One: Civil Liberties in Wartime 225 (1998).

234. *See* Youngstown Sheet, 343 U.S. at 635–37 (Jackson, J., concurring) ("When the President acts pursuant to an express or implied authorization of Congress, his authority is at its maximum, for it includes all that he possesses in his own right plus all that Congress can delegate.... When the President acts in absence of either a congressional grant or denial of authority, he can only rely upon his own independent powers, but there is a zone of twilight in which he and Congress may have concurrent authority, or in which its distribution is uncertain.... When the President takes measures incompatible with the expressed or implied will of Congress, his power is at its lowest ebb, for then he can rely only upon his own constitutional powers minus any constitutional powers of Congress over the matter.").

235. Posner, Not a Suicide Pact, *supra* note 6, at 1.

236. *See id.* at 158.

237. *Id.*

founding, the United States has been a nation of laws. Chief Justice John Marshall, writing for the nascent Supreme Court in *Marbury v. Madison*, proclaimed, "The government of the United States has been emphatically termed a government of laws, and not of men."[238] Marshall, in that same case, declared famously, "It is emphatically the province and duty of the judicial department to say what the law is."[239]

The Supreme Court has spoken to the question of whether the Constitution is a straightjacket on government action in the security realm. In *Aptheker v. Secretary of State*, the Court, quoting *Mendoza-Martinez*, said that "'while the Constitution protects against invasions of individual rights, it is not a suicide pact.'"[240] But the Court added in the very next sentence that "[a]t the same time the Constitution requires that the powers of government 'must be so exercised as not, in attaining a permissible end, unduly to infringe' a constitutionally protected freedom."[241] In other words, legitimate governmental ends, such as securing the nation, cannot be pursued by means that infringe an individual right.[242]

Moreover, even if a "law of necessity" were to be considered an inherent source of authority that existed outside American positive law, in practice this "law" should not be advanced because of the expediency within which it can be invoked and the dangers that may result from its improvident use. Indeed, in reflecting on the *Korematsu* decision, Justice Jackson stated that the executive order "was an unconstitutional one which the Court should not bring within the Constitution by any doctrine of necessity, a doctrine too useful as a precedent."[243]

Posner's preference for an implicit rule that the President may suspend laws when necessary is also untenable. Although it may be the case that rules are meant to be broken, this proposition cannot be held with respect to the Constitution. The Constitution was not intended to be read as having holes in it or to

---

238. Marbury v. Madison, 5 U.S. 137, 163 (1803).

239. *Id.* at 177.

240. Aptheker v. Sec'y of State, 378 U.S. 500, 509 (1964) (quoting Kennedy, 372 U.S. at 160).

241. *Id.* (quoting Cantwell v. Connecticut, 310 U.S. 296, 304 (1940)). Although *Mendoza-Martinez* gave rise to the "suicide pact" language, it was similar to *Aptheker* in that it concerned an act of Congress.

242. The Court in *Aptheker* addressed the relationship between congressional power and the right to travel. 378 U.S. at 507. One can imagine that the Court's pronouncement would be more compelling with other individual rights that may be at stake in the context of 9/11, including the right of equal protection under the law.

243. Robert H. Jackson, Associate Justice, United States Supreme Court, *Wartime Security and Liberty Under Law*, Address at the Buffalo Law School (May 9, 1951) *in* 1 Buff. L. Rev. 103, 116 (1951).

be disregarded on a whim.[244] To the contrary, it is the binding and highest law of the land.[245]

It is the belief in the rule of law that distinguishes the American republic from other forms of government and that serves as a vital tool in post-9/11 campaign against extremist elements. As deputy solicitor general Neal Katyal observed, "[I]f we're going to win the war on terror, we are going to win it through our soft power, we're going to win it through saying to the world that we actually have a better model than you because in your countries you settle these things through force and fiat, and here we settle them through law, we settle them through law."[246] An executive bypassing the law would be to deny the country this instrument of international diplomacy and of attraction to American principles and interests.

With regard to Posner's contention that the executive will be subject to political costs for extra-constitutional acts, even if an executive suffers voter retribution for abusing his power, there are additional costs that go beyond a political death. These externalities include the precedent set for successive executives to take risky steps outside of the bounds of the Constitution and the loss of public confidence in the executive office (not just in the administration of a single executive). More fundamentally, winning a subsequent election or staying in relatively good public graces does not serve as ad hoc approval of any extra-constitutional conduct. As the Supreme Court noted in *Aptheker*, a legitimate end does not sanction impermissible means,[247] and the public cannot, through political speech, bring executive action within the law. Independent courts insulated from popular will, not popular will by itself, are

---

244. *See, e.g., Saikrishna Prakash, The Constitution as Suicide Pact*, 79 NOTRE DAME L. REV. 1299, 1300 (2004) (commenting on the fact that the Constitution does not have a general escape clause granting the President "authority to sacrifice constitutional provisions in order to preserve and defend the Constitution and nation as a whole").

245. *See e.g.,* THE FEDERALIST No. 78 (Alexander Hamilton) ("Until the people have, by some solemn and authoritative act, annulled or changed the established form, [the federal Constitution] is binding upon themselves collectively, as well as individually; and no presumption, or even knowledge, of their sentiments, can warrant their representatives in a departure from it, prior to such an act."). To the extent that the question is one of a default rule or established rules, the people should favor a situation in which there are expressly enumerated constitutional provisions that the executive can ignore in times of war, as opposed to one in which all provisions are up for grabs and can be potentially transgressed. To limit the universe of areas in which the executive can frolic would be to circumscribe the possible abuses of extra-constitutional executive action.

246. Neal Katyal, Comments at the American Enterprise Institute (May 24, 2006).

247. *Aptheker*, 378 U.S. at 509 (quoting Cantwell v. Connecticut, 310 U.S. 296, 304 (1940)).

charged with the duty to define what is legal. The law is not an entity sub-servient to the executive; to the contrary, the executive is sworn to "preserve, protect and defend the Constitution of the United States," not the nation.[248] In other words, the president is duty-bound to preserve the Constitution, ir-respective of any political consequences.

Turning to Posner's moral imperative argument, there are critical differ-ences between presidents, such as Lincoln, and individuals like Gandhi and Dr. King.[249] The former have authority not only to execute laws but also to change them through the political process and through their exercise of con-stitutional power. The latter are those challenging discriminatory laws and the oppressive effects of the use of power by institutions and officials with power and authority. The former have many legal tools at their disposal, while the latter are forced to rely on civil disobedience precisely because they lack polit-ical clout. The former are elected by way of the majoritarian democratic process, while the latter represent marginalized members of society without the rights enjoyed by others. Ultimately, the former are kings, and the latter are pawns.[250]

In sum, the Constitution may bend in times of crisis, although there are lim-its on the degree to which it is flexible. Perhaps most important are the inher-ent limits set forth by the law itself. Practical considerations also cut against Posner's proposition that the extra-constitutionality is permissible in the wartime era. Specifically, as Justice Jackson pointed out, stepping outside the Constitu-tion establishes a dangerous precedent subject to executive abuse.[251] In addition, an element of "soft power" in the current war is denied if we fail to remain faith-ful to the Constitution. Finally, the moral underpinnings for civil disobedience do not support an alleged executive duty to act outside of the law, but rather entitle the relatively powerless to object to oppressive laws through non-compliance.

Conclusion

Justice Felix Frankfurter observed, "The words of the Constitution ... are so unrestricted by their intrinsic meaning or by their history or by tradition or by prior decisions that they leave the individual Justice free, if indeed they do not

---

248. U.S. CONST, art. II, §1.

249. *See* POSNER, NOT A SUICIDE PACT, *supra* note 6, at 85.

250. Posner's moral argument seems odd, not only because of the stated legal purpose of the book, but also because in other works Posner has likened morality to purely subjec-tive, value-judgments that lack intrinsic value in ascertaining objective truths. *See* Sidhu, *supra* note 94, at 81–82.

251. See Korematsu, 323 U.S. at 246 (Jackson, J., dissenting).

compel him, to gather meaning not from reading the Constitution but from reading life."[252] This article has attempted to invoke one aspect of my life—knowledge of *The Wire*—to challenge Judge Richard A. Posner's book, *Not a Suicide Pact*.

Posner characterizes his book as an attempt "to suggest the direction that the law should take...."[253] Posner's book, therefore, is one about the law—particularly, about how the courts should decide questions of constitutional law that implicate national security and individual rights in the post-9/11 world. To more fully appreciate Posner's arguments, this article has offered additional thoughts from a legal and practical perspective on some of the major contentions in Posner's wartime constitutional framework.

The most disquieting aspect of Posner's overall analysis is the extent to which he views executive authority in times of war. Posner allows for the executive to not only stretch the law but also ignore it when any allegedly troublesome circumstances or subjective moral views tempt the executive to do so. In Posner's scheme, there are no meaningful checks on the executive, even with the knowledge that the executive is significantly inclined to serve national security without regard for protected rights. In a nation of laws and not men, and in a nation where the Constitution is the supreme law of the land, Posner's framework allows the law to be reduced to a nullity if the practical benefits outweigh the "costs" of exhibiting faithfulness to the law. This is not an exercise in law so much as a recipe for executive abuse, judicial abdication, and constitutional meaninglessness.

"The tree that doesn't bend breaks,"[254] Marla Daniels noted to Cedric. We must not forget his response: "Bend too far, and you're already broken."[255] This is an outcome that Posner blesses yet one this article hopes this constitutional republic will avoid.

Study Questions

1. According to research conducted by several universities, the Circuit Court for Baltimore City, and The Maryland State's Attorney's office, how does the drug trade affect all facets of the criminal justice system and the health care system?

---

252. The Supreme Court, vol. 3, no. 1, Parliamentary Affairs (1949).
253. POSNER, NOT A SUICIDE PACT, *supra* note 6, at 29.
254. *The Wire*: *-30-* (HBO television broadcast Mar. 9, 2008).
255. *Id.*

2. Discuss Posner's views on balancing civil liberties and security responses to localized or national crises. Do you feel that this is a fair trade? Under which circumstances? How does this apply in the zero-sum frame of reference?

3. Posner argues that in the balancing of liberty and security, security should be the America's greater concern. How does Posner suggest American courts approach this dilemma? In a system of checks and balances, what is the importance of separating the legislative, executive, and judicial branches?

4. It is suggested that because Muslim extremists perpetrated that attack on the World Trade Center on 9/11, that all Muslims living in this country should be monitored in various ways. And that these monitoring systems are no more intrusive than a trained dog sniffing luggage at an airport. How do or don't these suggested monitoring systems encroach on all Americans' constitutional rights? How does Posner's "two-pronged" system fit into the debate about liberty versus security?

5. How do the Japanese internment camps of World War II mirror the concerns of Posner today?

6. Discuss Posner's views on torture being used in "extreme situations" or an "extreme emergency". How do these views conflict with or align with the Geneva Convention?

Section 2

Police Culture, Ethics, and Intelligence

A central component of *The Wire* draws attention to the many efforts of local police, individually and at the departmental level, to combat drug sales and violent crime. Through the show's sixty episodes, many aspects of policing are portrayed, far too many to completely cover in this text. The chapters presented in this section, however, cover three areas of policing that we believe are of great significance from an applied perspective, and are a fundamental part of *The Wire*. The general topics covered in this section, such as police ethics and discretion, police subculture, and intelligence based policing, are representative of interrelated concepts police officers and departments face on a daily basis.

Consider the following scenario. Based on an analysis of crime statistics, and for political reasons, a police department's command staff determines that it is critical to strictly enforce all laws, regardless of how petty, in certain areas of the city. In other words, there will be zero tolerance for illegal behavior. As this edict is conveyed to a unit's officers at roll call, there is wide spread moaning and snickering at the perceived futility and ineffectiveness of a zero tolerance policy.

Once on patrol the officer sees people violating open bottle laws, littering, jay walking, and loitering. While she is under orders to cite and/or arrest each violator, based on her training and experience she knows this is a waste of resources and will likely alienate members of the community, making her job more difficult in the future. Moreover, she realizes that if she goes ahead and does what she is supposed to do her fellow officers will be quite upset with her. Beyond making them look bad, she will be polluting the community for all police officers. Based on the subculture maintained by the department's rank and file, she is to produce fake paperwork and lie about her shift and why she didn't make dozens of arrests. She knows that if she doesn't abide by cultural expectations she will be ostracized and alienated.

In this example, in deciding what to do, our officer must weigh her ethical values (honesty) and the command staff's expectations based on statistical evidence, against the cultural expectations of her fellow officers and members of the community which she serves. It is such balancing acts, which police officers encounter on a routine basis, that are presented throughout *The Wire* and are addressed in this section.

In Chapter 6 Peter Parilla and Wendy Wyatt examine police culture. The authors define police culture, and discuss its actual prevalence as revealed in policing research. Weaving the academic literature on police culture with a number of examples from *The Wire*, the chapter goes on to explore the components of police culture and subcultures and the effects such subcultures have on police officers, departments, and the communities they serve.

In Chapter 7 Jonathon Cooper and Jonathan Bolen examine the concept of noble cause corruption, unethical acts committed in the pursuit of worthwhile goals. In examining the recurrent instances of such acts in *The Wire*, Cooper and Bolen consider whether noble cause corruption rises up from individual officers or is part of an organization's culture that officers are expected to follow. The authors also examine whether repeated yet isolated acts of noble corruption can become habit-forming to the extent that police officers lose the ability (or desire) to consider the morality, let alone legality, of their unethical actions.

In Chapter 8, Gennaro Vito takes on one of the most interesting questions surrounding the inception and past and current integration of Compstat-style police and public agency management policies. Compstat involves incorporating computers into the collection and analysis of crime statistics and information. The information obtained and analyses conducted are then used to identify troubled locations and patterns of criminal activity, to prioritize crime prevention actions, and hold individuals accountable for not meeting expectations. Vito considers the impact of Compstat on crime, and considers whether the decline in crime rates in the late 20th and early 21st centuries was due to use of Compstat or because of other, non-police related factors.

Professor Vito also discusses the history behind the widespread adoption of Compstat (or similar named programs) as a set of strategic management policies for police and public agencies, and how it revolutionized police management. The chapter also highlights potential problems associated with the Compstat process, by examining how Compstat was portrayed in *The Wire*.

Chapter 6

Representations of 'Po-lice' Culture in *The Wire*

Peter F. Parilla and Wendy N. Wyatt

Introduction

"... when a policeman dons his uniform, he enters a distinct subculture governed by norms and values designed to manage the strains created by his unique role in the community." (Van Maanen, 1974: 85)

As viewers of *The Wire*, we are treated to more than a glimpse of the subculture Van Maanen describes. Through 60 episodes over five seasons, we are offered a kind of all-access pass to a club known as the Baltimore Police Department. Other TV shows and movies have purported to offer the same kind of view into police departments and their cultures, but few have managed to do so with such authenticity and verisimilitude. In *The Wire's* Baltimore, the crimes aren't always solved, the bad guys aren't always caught, and the police aren't always the heroes. But in *The Wire's* Baltimore, you can find "real po-lice," those whose lives are fundamentally shaped by the decision they made to become a cop.

Every profession is marked to some extent by a subculture or collection of subcultures. Professional socialization is a well-recognized phenomenon. But can police be characterized by one uniform, unvarying culture? Most scholars say it's more complicated than that. Researchers comparing police work across departments find that important differences exist (e.g. Wilson, 1968; Paoline, 2001, 2003). This discovery—that norms, values, and approaches to policing vary among organizations—challenges the notion of a universal culture in favor of a view that police in different departments subscribe to distinctive organizational subcultures that mediate the effect of overarching occupational factors. In other words, we can't assume that the culture of the Chicago Police Department is identical to that of Baltimore's. Other researchers have stressed that even within a single department, multiple subcultures may exist. In her study of the New York Police Department, for example, Reuss-Ianni (1983) found evidence of two separate cultures within the organization—one shared by officers on the street; the other by those in administration. Reuss-Ianni also found that these separate cultures were a source of tension and conflict. Still other researchers have identified different styles of policing among rank and file officers, making the case that even officers of the same rank think about and approach the job very differently (see Mastrofski and Willis, 2010; Paoline, 2001; Worden, 1995).

Even with these divergent research findings, however, the belief that police share a strong occupational culture or subculture has persevered in academic studies of the police. For more than fifty years, social science researchers have posited that the challenges of police work have led to the creation of a unique set of norms and values that help officers cope with the strains of the job. Police culture, like any culture, is long-standing; it is passed relatively unchanged from one generation to the next. As recruits join the ranks, they learn the culture from the veterans who socialize them, and the recruits then interpret their own experiences in light of this shared worldview. New officers learn the importance of loyalty and solidarity among officers and a sense of distrust and wariness for those who don't carry a badge. They develop an understanding that they can count on each other and only on each other in times of trouble. They learn that "real" police work involves fighting crime. Maintaining order and providing service are of secondary importance. Finally, they discover that higher-ups in administration are more likely to hinder their work than facilitate it. Just as line officers must protect each other from criminals, those officers must do the same from those in command.

The elements of police culture described by social scientists are also commonly featured in television shows, movies, and novels about the police. *The Wire* is no exception. The fictional account of the Baltimore Police Department offers a portrayal of police work that is consistent with the view often found in the more scholarly literature on the topic. In this chapter, we use the characters in *The Wire* as a way to make the notion of police culture come alive. By analyzing how the series depicts the police, we can better understand what many scholars consider the content and effects of police culture. We begin by reviewing what sociologists and criminologists have learned about police culture. We then move to a description of the police in *The Wire* as a way of demonstrating how police culture influences their outlook and behavior.

Police Culture

By culture, we mean shared beliefs, norms, and values that help provide meaning for a group and are transmitted over time (also see Crank, 2004; Paoline, 2001). Many occupational groups develop cultures around the work they do. Police are believed to have an especially strong culture, which distinctly influences those who do the job. The traditional view of police culture claims that being a cop is different than being in any other line of work. The demands of the job create a highly stressful work environment, which leads to the development of a culture that helps police cope with this stress. Although researchers are not in complete agreement about the occupational characteristics responsible for the emergence of the culture, several aspects commonly appear. Here we draw upon Paoline's review of the literature, which identifies four key elements of police work that make it so stressful and are the source of the culture (2001, 2003).

The first is danger. Images of policing from the media convey the impression that police work is incredibly dangerous. But those who study the police challenge this conventional view (Kappeler, Blumberg, and Potter, 1993). On-the-job injuries or deaths are relatively rare events in policing, and are often, in fact, much lower than in other occupations not normally perceived as dangerous (e.g. working in agriculture or mining) (Reuss-Ianni, 1983). However, if we looked purely at statistical data, we would miss the point. For police, it is the *potential* that a situation may become life threatening that is important. The nature of the job means that police must be constantly alert for the possibility of danger, even if it never materializes. Police are aware that even the most routine of encounters can quickly escalate into life or death struggles. Thus, they must be ever vigilant in their interactions with others.

The second element of police work that is commonly thought to lead to a strong occupational culture relates to the authority that officers possess (Paoline, 2001, 2003). When police arrive on the scene, it is their responsibility to "take charge" of events. Whether it's arresting a felon, resolving a domestic dispute, or telling a group of unruly teenagers on a corner to disperse, the police expect that persons will comply with their commands so that law and order can prevail. Unsurprisingly, they sometimes meet hostility and resistance to their orders. In such situations, police differ from other members of society in that they have the legal right to use coercive force to achieve compliance. Police can legally stop and frisk people judged to be suspicious, arrest persons when probable cause exists, and even shoot persons who pose a threat of deadly harm. Often, decisions about how much force is necessary and legal need to be made very quickly and in highly tense, uncertain conditions. Police realize that the wrong decision can produce catastrophic consequences. Exercising too little authority can lead to the officer or bystanders being injured or killed and a criminal escaping. Using too much can result in charges of brutality or false arrest. In either instance, the conduct can bring about official recriminations against an officer for incompetence and failure to perform adequately on the job. And in rare cases, unwarranted use of force can lead to criminal charges against the officer.

The stress of policing is not restricted to work on the street. The third and fourth stress-inducing factors—those relating to supervisor scrutiny and role ambiguity—are organizational (Paoline, 2003). Police department administrations expect that police officers will excel in the multiple roles they perform—i.e. law enforcement, order maintenance, and service. These roles, however, can be in tension. Succeeding in some may jeopardize the achievement of others, and this can lead to stressful conditions for multiple reasons. First, police officers feel that superiors removed from the street may second-guess their actions unfairly. Officers are expected to enforce the law, yet those who act aggressively in doing so may be criticized if they don't strictly adhere to legal procedures and departmental policies. Line officers often are left with feelings of uncertainty about how their performance will be evaluated. Second, departments expect that officers, especially patrol officers, will perform multiple functions, juggling the need to enforce the law with demands that they maintain order (e.g. deal with a dispute between neighbors) and engage in service (e.g. medical emergencies). The effect is that police can find themselves in a no-win situation because of the difficulty of performing all roles successfully.

Each of the above factors, alone and in combination, escalates levels of stress for officers. As a way to cope, a unique culture, which influences conduct both on and off the job, has developed. It is a culture defined by the values of loyalty and solidarity among officers, the normative expectation that police will have each others' backs in times of trouble, the belief that all police work is not equal—some duties are more worthy than others—and the realization of the need to maintain distance between the administration and the line officers. In the next sections, we examine five core themes of this culture in more detail by showing how they are manifested in *The Wire*.

"We are the only crime fighters. Crime fighting is what the public wants from us."

(Sparrow, Moore, and Kennedy, 1990: 51)

The most common view of police is that their job is to fight crime and protect us as citizens from those who would do us harm (Barlow and Barlow, 2006). This is the perception promoted by television shows and movies, which routinely show police matching wits with criminal masterminds, being involved in high speed chases, engaging in shootouts, and eventually bringing the offender to justice (Kappeler, Blumberg, and Potter, 1993). This view is also regularly found in newspapers and TV news accounts, which similarly emphasize the role of police in investigating and solving serious crime. Yet this portrayal of the police as law enforcers and crime fighters is greatly at odds with empirical studies of police work. A significant body of research has found that relatively little of what police actually do is related to crime. In fact, less than 20 percent of an officer's time is devoted to enforcing the law (Kappeler et al., 1993).

Although far more sophisticated in its treatment of the police than the typical cop show, *The Wire* does tend to reinforce the myth that police spend most of their time fighting serious crime. The show's title reinforces this idea—it is only through using a wiretap that serious crimes can be solved and bad guys can be caught—and the plotlines of each season revolve around serious crime. Yes, we as viewers occasionally see police patrolling the streets, engaging in community policing, and completing routine administrative duties, but the show's emphasis is on the homicide and major crimes units. And through these units, we are introduced to some of Baltimore's finest: crime fighters such as Officer Jimmy McNulty and Detectives Kima Greggs, Bunk Moreland, and Lester Freamon. Throughout the series, in fact, we get to witness these crime fighters taking on gangsters, traffickers, murderers, and, of course, drug lords. In *The Wire*, it's clear that the police who matter are the ones out on the streets fighting the criminals.

The view of police as crime fighters is not only key to how police are viewed by outsiders; it's also central to how they view themselves. Within the police culture, it is the crime fighting/law enforcement role that is paramount. Other activities such as maintaining order and providing service to the public are derogatorily referred to as "babysitting" and "social work" and are viewed as being less important and less prestigious for officers (Cochran and Bromley, 2003). "Real" police work is oriented toward investigating serious crime and apprehending dangerous felons, and anything else is a bum deal. In *The Wire*, McNulty makes this abundantly clear when at the end of Season 1 he gets demoted out of Major Crimes and sent to the Baltimore Police Harbor unit. Although his partner calls it the "sweetest detail in the whole damn department," Mc-Nulty knows it's not work for a "real police." As we watch McNulty going through the motions, we see only a shadow of the cop he was when he was taking on the Barksdale drug cartel.

The primacy of the crime-fighting role in police culture is partly due to the fact that police themselves are not immune from the media-produced images of police work as crime fighting. Individuals are not drawn to police work because they want to write tickets and settle neighborhood disputes. They want to protect the public by catching "bad guys." In addition, police realize that the reward structure within departments emphasizes the ability to clear crimes by arrests. As described earlier, police feel stress because of the role ambiguity associated with their work. One way to relieve this is to emphasize the part of the job that is most likely to elicit praise from superiors and least likely to provoke criticism; that is fighting crime (Paoline, 2003).

For police in *The Wire*, clearing crimes is an administrative edict, a professional goal, and, for some, even a personal obsession. The Baltimore of *The Wire* is a city plagued with crime, and nothing is emphasized more than "bringing in the arrests." In Baltimore's homicide department, the importance of clearing crimes is visually symbolized by a white board, which lists the city's unsolved murders. The board appears repeatedly throughout the series, and it serves as a striking indication of how things are going in the homicide unit. The goal of the detectives in Homicide is crossing names off that list; it's, quite simply, the sign of a job done right. Sergeant Jay Landsman, the man in charge of the unit, may not appear entirely on top of things, but he knows the white board, and he knows when things on it are moving and when they're standing still.

In Major Crimes, the goal is also arrests, but here the *kind* of arrests becomes important. The police department's top brass is looking for productivity in terms of numbers; the more arrests, the cleaner the streets. Statistics tell it all; arresting 10 "corner boys" for dealing drugs on Baltimore's streets means something, even if 10 more will replace them the next day. For detectives in the major crimes unit, arrests are important, but McNulty, Greggs, Freamon, and others are far less interested in the corner boys, who occupy the lowest level of Baltimore's drug trade. For them, it's about the men at the top, the people running the organizations. Bringing down Avon Barksdale, Stringer Bell, or Marlo Stanfield means more than doing the job or meeting an administrative decree; it means the cops have what it takes to catch the actual bad guys. In many ways, the pursuit becomes personal and, for at least one cop, McNulty, a fixation. As *The Wire* moves through five seasons, it becomes increasingly evident that Mc-

Nulty's quest to bring down Baltimore's drug trade is intimately tied with his own identity and sense of self-worth. The irony is that even putting away the drug kingpins solves nothing because others quickly step in to replace them.

"It is impossible to win the war on crime without bending the rules."

(Sparrow et al., 1990: 51)

Police are expected to rely on their experience, investigative skills, and even hunches to identify suspects, collect evidence against them, and bring them to justice; especially when crime rates rise, politicians and the press communicate the public's outrage over the failure to protect society, and they exert considerable pressure on police administrators to "do something" about crime. The administration, in turn, demands that those further down the chain of command produce results. *The Wire* gives viewers a unique glimpse into the way these expectations to "do something" are conveyed. It begins with the politicians: Mayor Clarence Royce, in this case, who is trying to hold onto public support and his office. From there, it feeds down through Police Commissioner Ervin Burrell and Deputy Commissioner William Rawls to the commanders in charge of "The Western" and Baltimore's other districts. In *The Wire's* tense Compstat scenes, we hear Rawls tell his men that "felony cases must drop by five percent for the year, and murders must be kept under 275 ... There is no excuse I want to hear. I don't care how you do it. Just fucking do it." And if his commanders can't? Rawls promises they'll be replaced by someone who can. So with that threat looming, commanders take their order to "do something" to their rank and file officers on the streets.

Yet, those who are most responsible for actually dealing with criminals on the street—i.e. patrol cops and investigators—often find themselves in a "no-win" situation. They agree that catching criminals ought to be a priority, yet they fear that aggressive law enforcement will be criticized by the very people who are pressuring them to lower crime. Law enforcement efforts are constrained by a variety of due process safeguards, departmental policies, and ethical codes that govern police work. Police may know that incriminating evidence can be found in a residence, but they can't perform a search without the probable cause needed to obtain a warrant. They may pursue an offender in a high-speed car chase only to be ordered to call it off because departmental policy restricts such pursuits. They are expected to act professionally in their dealings with a suspect even when the person has caused unspeakable harm to others and acts toward them with utter disrespect. It's not surprising, then, that a cultural belief has emerged, which claims that the courts, police administrators, and the public at large act in a way that "handcuffs the police," preventing them from doing their work in an aggressive and effective manner (Cochran and Bromley, 2003). This belief is consistent with another: No one but the police themselves understands the real nature of police work (Sparrow et al., 1990).

In *The Wire*, handcuffs to good police work often come in the form of policies and procedures that must be followed to get a wiretap up and to keep it up. McNulty and his fellow officers are convinced it will take a wire to bring the Baltimore drug trade to its knees, but the wire is never quick in coming. First, a wire has to be endorsed by the powers that be in the police department. Then it requires the approval of a judge based on the sworn testimony of an officer that the facts submitted are true. As we watch *The Wire*, we see the time ticking by and the case that "could have been" at risk of slipping away. The drug gangs always seem one step ahead of the cops. By the time the wire is up, the gangs have often changed their tactics.

As a way to relieve the stress associated with the conflicting signals that police receive, the cultural remedy takes the form of rationalizations supporting the idea that the ends justify the means. To catch criminals, it is acceptable to bend and even break the rules and still receive the support of co-workers. Deception, perjury, and abuse are tolerated, even expected, under the right conditions because they ultimately lead to justice, defined as the guilty being punished for their transgressions. In an ideal world, this would mean that the accused is convicted in a court of law. However, it can also mean "street justice"—e.g. a cop confiscates a dealer's drugs but doesn't arrest him because the search was illegal. In their zeal to catch criminals, police may trick suspects to obtain a confession, stretch the truth to convince a judge that probable cause exists for a warrant, or tack on charges to legitimate an arrest (see Crank, 2004; Van Maanen, 1978/2010; see also the next chapter, as Cooper and Bolen describe the corruption of noble cause).

For cops in *The Wire*, bending the rules is the norm, and everyone does it. Sometimes the incidents are small: Bunk shows pictures of his own children to a suspect in an effort to convince that suspect that a murdered witness was a "family man," and Sergeant Ellis Carver refuses to chase the corner kids who are dealing drugs because "until the handcuffs fit, there's still talking to be done." At other times, bending the rules amounts to major schemes: Sergeant Howard "Bunny" Colvin legalizes drugs in "Hamsterdam" to bring order to the rest of his district, and McNulty manufactures a serial killer in order to get resources for his drug investigation, then using those resources to put an illegal tap on Marlo Stanfield's phone. In Baltimore, bending the rules seems to be the only way to get anything accomplished, and we as viewers become sympathetic to the cops' actions as we begin to understand this. When Colvin informs Carver that he and his cops need to get the drug dealers on board with the "free zones," we sympathize when the cops throw the dealers' shoes into the sewers, tow their cars, and round them up in a van only to drive them far out of town and leave them in a forest. We understand when Greggs buries drug money subpoenas in a pile of mundane paperwork that needs Lieutenant Asher's signature. And we're with Freamon when he uses extortion against Senator Clay Davis, telling him he'll ignore evidence on Davis' illegal loan if Davis helps with future information. Even police aggression can begin to look justifiable after we've spent some time with the cops in *The Wire*. We empathize with Officer Thomas "Herc" Hauk's frustration in trying to get back the camera stolen by Marlo's gang, and when he fires a nail gun into the asphalt next to Snoop's leg, we almost understand. And even though Donut didn't deserve broken fingers, we wonder whether the "street justice" Officer Walker gave Donut when he stole an SUV and rammed it into several parked cars would be more effective than the kind of justice a court could give.

Police learn that it's appropriate, even expected, to use force against those who challenge their authority or act in disrespectful ways, even if such force violates departmental policy or criminal law (Hunt, 1985/2009). To justify its use, police will resort to filing false charges such as resisting arrest, disorderly conduct, or assaulting an officer. When police act in a proactive manner—i.e., on their own volition rather than responding to a complaint—such tactics become even more common. Enforcing laws regarding victimless crimes like drug possession or prostitution pose special challenges for the police because there are rarely voluntary witnesses and no complainants. In these situations, police may push the limits even further as they seek to build a case against a criminal (Crank, 2004).

This pushing of limits is seen in McNulty's series-long quest to bring down the West Side drug trade. While some of his fellow cops have resolved themselves to the "war that never ends," McNulty is obstinate. Barksdale, Bell and Stanfield are the targets. They do not get to win; he gets to win. But to do this, McNulty—sometimes with accomplices, sometimes on his own—must improvise. That's what it will take to make the case. McNulty is less about bending the rules than he is about failing to acknowledge their very existence. He views working within the chain of command as a mere suggestion, and he gets testy when his colleagues don't adopt the same attitude. And if he's challenged about his renegade attitude, he's quick with a response: "Fuck the chain of command." For McNulty, it's far better to ask for forgiveness than permission. To build his case against Baltimore's drug lords, McNulty ignores the chain of command to acquire a court order for a wiretap, to investigate the "suicide" of drug dealer D'Angelo Barksdale, and to pursue Stringer Bell, Avon Barksdale, and Marlo Stanfield through a "back door" approach. And, of course, Mc-Nulty's coup de grace is his invention of a serial killer, designed to get more resources pumped into the homicide unit, which can then be used in his covert drug investigation.

McNulty takes the "bending the rules" philosophy to the extreme. He is clearly one of *The Wire's*, protagonists, but he is motivated by more than the idea of justice. He wants to prove he's smarter than the drug dealers he's chasing. Former cop Pam Newton (2011) said:

> McNulty was no hero, but he was a lot like a lot of cops I knew. They see The Job as a cross between a game and a business, and they play to win. They believe they are the smartest person in the room, and they'll bend and break a lot of rules to guarantee they come out on top.

While bending the rules is a cultural norm, it is important to note that the police culture does not provide police with carte blanche to act any way they please when enforcing the law. What the culture provides are shared understandings that in some contexts, police can violate ethics, policy, and even the law with the assumption that their co-workers will support them and, in the case of an internal investigation, protect them.

"... 'to maintain one's edge' is a key concept vis-à-vis the how to of police work. And, as all policemen know, to let down ... is to invite disrespect, chaos and crime."

(Van Maanen, 1978/2010: 95)

The potential for danger and the need to exercise coercive control has led to a number of cultural prescriptions regarding how police should act in their encounters with non-police. These function to lessen job-related stress by giving police a greater sense of security and control in their dealings with others. The belief that police should be suspicious is one such cultural mandate (Paoline, 2003; Skolnick, 1994). Good cops are constantly aware of their surroundings, distinguishing what is normal from what is not. A supermarket door left ajar after hours, a nervous person pacing outside a liquor store before it closes, a car filled with minority kids cruising in an all-white neighborhood at 2:00 a.m. can all trigger police action to learn more. Police develop a "sixth sense" for identifying untoward behavior and then dealing with it. Similarly, unlike most of us who may be willing to give the benefit of the doubt to others, police do the opposite, taking little for granted and bestowing trust reluctantly. After all, police are well aware that people who interact with them often have powerful incentives to lie or distort the truth. Cynicism and skepticism are valued traits that enable them to cut through evasions of the truth.

McNulty, Freamon, Moreland, Greggs, Carver, Herc—they're all skeptics and cynics. D'Angelo's "suicide" in prison couldn't be *just* a suicide. Stringer Bell's copy shop must be doing more than making copies. A corner kid with a pocket full of cash couldn't really have received the money from his foster mom to do school shopping. And when bodies stop dropping in the West Side, it's impossible that the gang warfare has simply ceased. In *The Wire*, this attitude is what makes for good police work. There's always more to the story; cynicism and skepticism help uncover what that real story is.

Police also operate under the belief that anticipating problems and preparing for them can lessen the risk of danger and challenges to authority (Herbert, 1998; Paoline, 2003). As police enter a situation, they need to quickly size it up, determine whether the participants are likely to be a threat, and then act in a manner to dissuade them from doing so. In Van Maanen's (1978/2010) terms, they seek to create and maintain an "edge" over others—i.e. to have an interactional advantage over the conduct of others as a way to increase the odds of compliance. Thus, police will come on stronger when approaching a group of gang members on an inner-city corner than preppy high school students in a middle class suburb. As the interaction continues, police can adapt their approach depending on whether participants behave in a respectful, cooperative manner or a belligerent, abusive one. Maintaining an edge is crucial for police. When others challenge an officer's authority and control, that officer must successfully deal with this affront (Van Maanen, 1978/2010). Failure to do so means others have gained control of the situation. When this occurs, police may suffer not just physical harm, but also a loss of face as competent law enforcers. Cops who can't control a situation lose the respect and confidence of fellow officers.

The cops who police Baltimore's West Side constantly work to maintain their edge over the hoppers, soldiers, and leaders of the city's drug trade, and their authority is constantly challenged. It's part of the game. As we watch, we begin to understand how having that edge is critical; if you lose it, the results can be disastrous. When Greggs goes undercover to make a drug buy, we know the risks, and we hope she's in prime form. When she gets shot, we see how quickly a situation can deteriorate. The same thing happens when Officer Dozerman is shot in a drug bust gone bad, and one of the criminals makes off with his gun. And when Carver, Herc, and Officer Roland "Prez" Pryzbylewski make a late-night visit to the Towers, command central for Barksdale's drug ring, and begin hassling anyone who happens to cross their paths, the situation quickly spins out of control. Prez hits a 14-year-old boy in the face with the butt end of his pistol, and just as Carver says to him "What the fuck is the matter with you?" the retaliation begins. In the end, Herc is injured, a Crown Vic is destroyed, several pieces of police property are lost, a brutality charge is filed, and the respect the officers have for Prez has been lost. For Prez, the effort to maintain an edge has gone too far.

It's not only the raids, the busts, and the chases that require an edge. It's essential for cops' day-to-day life in the Western. One way Baltimore's cops gain and maintain their edge is by always keeping their foes guessing. One day, everyone on the corner gets rounded up and sent downtown; another day, it's just a discussion. Sometimes a kid in a stolen car gets chased; sometimes he's left to his own devices. Cops may deliver aggression, or they may deliver mercy. The point is, the cops decide how and when they'll exert their authority. Through that, they also maintain some degree of control.

It's important to understand that disputes over authority between police and non-police are not just a question of police being tougher or more macho than the opponent. Much more is at stake. "In a very real sense, the patrolman-to-citizen exchanges are moral contests in which the authority of the state is either confirmed, denied, or left in doubt" (Van Maanen, 1978/2010: 96). Here we see another important cultural perspective at work. In the worldview of the police, their job is to defend the moral/legal order against those who refuse to abide by it. It's a pitched battle between right and wrong, good and evil. In his ethnographic study of the Los Angeles police, Herbert found that police officers regularly " ... nest discussions and justifications of their behavior within a discourse of morality that portrays them as proud and noble warriors protecting the peace from the chaotic and turbulent anarchy of evil" (Herbert, 1996: 805). There are multiple implications when the police view of the world is based on such stark contrasts. They are more likely to demonize others, viewing them solely in terms of the wrongs that they do. The pejorative labels that police commonly use to describe those who break the law or challenge their authority offer insight into such perceptions: "bad guys," "knuckleheads," "idiots," "assholes," "mopes," and "scumbags," (Herbert, 1988, 1996; Van Maanen, 1978/2010). Identifying others using such negative categories helps sharpen moral boundaries that distinguish good and evil (Herbert, 1988). Doing so also increases the likelihood that offenders will be treated as less than fully human, opening the door to disrespectful treatment and abuse (Kelman and Hamilton, 1970/2009). When offenders are viewed as enemies in the wars on crime and drugs, it supports the use of street justice or other forms of misconduct as a way to mete out punishment when legal means are unavailable. Finally, when the police define themselves as the "good guys" in contrast to the "bad guys" they need to control, it supports the perception of a "we-they" mentality, leading to police closing ranks and increasing solidarity.

For viewers of *The Wire*, the distinction between good and evil isn't always clear, but Baltimore's cops are convinced they're on the side of good and will eventually triumph. This is demonstrated through one of Carver's most memorable speeches—what some have called a soliloquy—delivered from the top of a car and designed to set everyone within shouting distance straight on what the moral order should be:

> Hey, listen to me you little fuckin piece of shit. I'm going to tell you one thing and one thing only about the Western boys you are playing with. We do not lose, and we do not forget. And we do not give up. Ever. So I'm only going to say this one time. If you march yourself out here right now and put the bracelets on, we will not kick the living shit out of you. But if you make us go into them reeds for you, or if you make us come back out here tomorrow night, catch you on the corner, I swear to fuckin Christ, we will beat you longer and harder than you beat your own dick. Because you do not get to win shitbird, we do.

"Loyalty to colleagues counts above everything else."

(Sparrow, 1990: 51)

Perhaps the best-known characteristic of police culture relates to the intense sense of loyalty and solidarity that police share. In a study of police, the vast majority of cops agreed that "the most important obligation that a patrolman has is to back up and support his fellow officers" (Brown, 1981: 83). Most importantly, it means that in times of trouble, police will "have each others' backs." This cultural expectation for loyalty and solidarity is not the same as friendship or the absence of conflict. It's true that many police develop close friendships with others in law enforcement—McNulty and Bunk, and Carver and Herc are examples of cops on *The Wire* whose loyalty extends beyond their professional lives—but the cultural mandate extends even to police who personally can't stand each other. McNulty has few real fans in the police department because, as Freamon points out, "You put fire in everything you touch, McNulty. Then you walk away while it burns." Yet McNulty has the loyalty of his fellow cops. This loyalty is played out in small ways when, for example, his partner Santangelo refuses to snitch on him because "It's not my job to fuck another cop." But it also plays out in dramatic fashion when Freamon, Bunk, and Detective Leander Snyder cover for McNulty who, in the name of finally bringing down the Baltimore drug trade, fabricates a serial killer and begins running an illegal wiretap.

Once again, this cultural expectation is a direct offshoot of the stressful occupational conditions related to potential danger and the exercise of authority (Paoline, 2003). The fears and anxieties associated with the job can be partly offset by the confidence that backup is available if needed. In addition, other dimensions of the culture serve to reinforce the sense of solidarity police feel. The goal of protecting society from criminals and the belief that police are the guardians of public morality promote a common identity and purpose. "We are po-lice," the cops from Baltimore declare again and again. That one word, pronounced in two distinct syllables, carries with it a world of meaning.

The fact that police often feel under siege also draws them closer together. Not only must they battle those who violate the law or disrupt public order, they also come under attack from politicians, the media, and the public at large whose criticisms are perceived to be unfair because their critics are incapable of understanding the nature of police work (see Sparrow et al, 1990). Finally, the belief that aggressive law enforcement requires "bending the rules" leads to situations where cops expect other cops to cover for them when they come under scrutiny from police administrators, internal affairs, civilian review boards, and even the courts. Crank (2004) refers to this as the "dark side to solidarity," since it acts to pressure police to remain silent in the face of corruption and misconduct by co-workers.

We are introduced to solidarity's dark side in the scene at the Towers when Prez loses control and seriously injures the 14-year-old boy. At the end of the melee, Cedric Daniels, the three cops' lieutenant, arrives at the scene to get to the bottom of what happened. Daniels demands to know who "cold-cocked the kid," and neither Herc nor Carver gives up Prez. When Prez does confess, he says he did it because the kid pissed him off. "No," Daniels says:

> He did not piss you off. He made you fear for your safety and that of your fellow officers. I'm guessing now, but maybe he was soon to pick up a bottle and menace officers Herc and Carver, both of whom had already sustained injury from flying projectiles. Rather than use deadly force in such a situation, maybe you elected to approach the youth, ordering him to drop the bottle. Maybe when he raised the bottle in a threatening manner, you used a Kel-Lite, not the handle of your service weapon, to incapacitate the suspect.

Daniels then tells Prez to "go practice" the story that will protect the three from an Internal Affairs shakedown. Despite Daniels' anger and utter frustration, he has his cops' backs.

Yet another way that police are expected to protect each other relates to the emotional and psychological toll that the job produces. In the course of their work, police encounter a wide variety of experiences and emotions ranging from boredom—days upon days of monitoring a silent wire—to adrenaline-producing excitement—busting in on a Barksdale stash house. They experience bizarre situations that are hilarious—learning from a drug dealer that the dead kid lying on the street was always allowed into the craps game even though he repeatedly tried to steal the pot because "This is America, man." But they also face tragic situations that are traumatic—Greggs gets shot as her fellow cops listen in through the wire she's wearing. When police get off work, they often feel the need to decompress, to talk about what they saw and felt. Partly because of the vicissitudes of shift work where police are on totally different schedules than most people and partly because police believe that non-police (including spouses) are incapable of empathizing with them or understanding their experiences, cops will often gravitate toward other police for socializing. Over the course of a career, this means that police may become increasingly isolated from persons outside the profession (see Paoline, 2003; Skolnick, 1966). In fact, in *The Wire*, we see few personal relationships, and most we do see are dysfunctional. Greggs' partner Cheryl wants her to leave the police force and go to law school. In a late-night drinking session with McNulty, one of many we witness throughout the series, Greggs gives voice to her dilemma:

> How come … they know you're police when they hook up with you. And they know you're police when they move in. And they know you're police when they decide to start a family with you. And all that shit is just fine. Until one day it ain't. One day, it's "you should have a regular job. You need to be home at 5 o'clock."

McNulty isn't exactly one to give advice. His wife Elena has already left him when the series begins. And while Bunk stays married throughout the series, he is bailed out more than once by a sympathetic partner when he strays. When social isolation occurs, it may intensify the effects of police culture as police lose the perspective that can be given by those outside the profession.

Police solidarity is often manifested through ritual. These rituals are not only the product of solidarity, they also serve a "solidarity-building" function. Crank (2004) singles out ritualized activities related to the death of an officer as a particularly compelling example of the role of rituals in enhancing solidarity.

Nowhere is this truer than in funeral ceremonies for those killed in the line of duty. Thousands of officers from throughout the country can come together to honor an officer slain while doing the job. Such highly publicized ceremonies are a public manifestation of the honor due to police and serve to re-establish their authority and power in the eyes of the public (Lord, Crank, and Evans, 2004).

As viewers of *The Wire*, we get more than one invitation to take part in a special ritual that precedes a cop's funeral: the wake at Kavanaugh's bar. Baltimore cops who have died or been killed always spend some time with their police family before being taken by funeral home attendants to the more public ceremonies. Cops in attendance eulogize their dead colleague (who is laid out on a pool table); sing tributes, and drink, often to excess. When McNulty and Freamon, leave the police department at the end of *The Wire*, this special ritual is held for them as well. McNulty's death is only symbolic, but he still gets the eulogy, the singing, and the drinking. Landsman sends him off with these words, eloquently delivered with a shot of whiskey in hand, Irish music playing in the background, and more-than-occasional heckles from the cops who crowd the bar:

> He was the black sheep, permanent pariah. He asked no quarter of the bosses, and none was given. He learned no lessons. He acknowledged no mistakes. He was as stubborn a Mick as ever stumbled out of the Northeast parish just to take up a patrolman's shield. He brooked no authority. He did what he wanted to do, and he said what he wanted to say, and in the end ... he gave me the clearances. He's natural police. And I don't say that about many people, even when they're here on a felt, I don't give that one up unless it happens to be true. Natural po-lice ... But Christ, What an asshole.

"Don't trust bosses to look out for your interests."

(Reuss-Ianni, 1983: 16)

Police departments are structured as quasi-military organizations, which place much emphasis on bureaucratic hierarchy and following the chain of command. One theme in police culture is that those occupying lower ranks in a department should not count on those at the top to protect them. Reuss-Ianni (1983) claims that this lack of trust stems from cultural conflict within an organization. For example, she found evidence for the existence of two separate cultures within the New York Police Department: a "street cop culture" and a "management cop culture." In the Baltimore Police Department of *The Wire*, the same differentiation exists. Street cop culture encompasses the various themes addressed so far in this chapter—from the view that bending the rules is essential to get anything done to the belief that, above all, cops must have each others' backs. While *The Wire* clearly introduces us to the street cop culture, it also gives us a glimpse into the culture of management. During the course of the series, we get to know some of the men at the top of the Baltimore Police organization chart: Commissioner Ervin Burrell and Deputy Commissioners William Rawls and Stanislaus Valchek. We learn what their mandates are and from whom they come. And we see the difference in worldviews between them and the rank and file cops under their command. For Burrell, Rawls and Valchek, the job is more about politics than it is about crime fighting.

Management cop culture emphasizes the use of "scientific" approaches to managing organizations. Rather than valuing knowledge gleaned from working the streets, this culture stresses modern managerial techniques in public administration. Norms of cost effectiveness, accountability and productivity govern the work of police leaders whose job is to use empirical data in making decisions (Reuss-Ianni, 1983). For Baltimore's top cops, it's all about managing the numbers: crime statistics, budgets, clearance rates, and—not to be ignored—polls. To do this, Burrell and Rawls give edicts to their commanders such as "felony rates, district by district, will decline by five percent before the end of the year" and "we will hold this year's murders to 275 or less." When administrators create departmental policies and practices, they expect underlings to adhere to them. In the Compstat session where district commanders are told to manage the felony and murder rates, Rawls says, if it doesn't happen, "Let no man come back alive." (see also Chapter 8, as Vito details Compstat.)

When those at the bottom have problems or complaints, administrators expect them to follow the chain of command in resolving them. Officers on the street may view administrative pronouncements as being "out of touch" with reality and counterproductive in achieving the goal of law enforcement. The result is that these differing cultural orientations can lead to tension and conflict within a department. In *The Wire*, detectives and officers constantly cause headaches for administrators by going around the chain of command or by ignoring it altogether. No real police want administrative orders to get in the way of good crime fighting. For them, taking orders can mean a wasted shift.

More than a handful of cops in *The Wire* have an exceptionally sophisticated understanding of how the politics of police administration works and many of the show's subplots are driven by conflicts that arise between Baltimore's police administrators and the detectives and officers who work in its homicide and major crimes units. In Season 4, Freamon's decision to stall the investigation of the Barksdale drug money until right before the primary election (because the timing will ensure the investigation won't be impeded) angers the higher ups and eventually results in a whole string of consequences for Freamon's commander (he gets replaced) for Freamon's career (he gets transferred out of Major Crimes back into Homicide), and for the investigation (the case gets closed).

It's important to note that the existence of dual cultures doesn't mean that individual police must be wholly committed to one or the other. In the real world, police are sophisticated enough to appreciate elements of both (Reuss-Ianni, 1983). Yet, as officers move up the ladder, they are likely to be placed in situations where they experience divided loyalties. We watch this happen with Carver, who begins the series as a detective and ends as a lieutenant. As Carver moves up, we see him mature as a cop, but we also see him struggle with how to treat the cops who were once his peers and are now under his command. This sense of divided loyalties is made explicit when Carver, a sergeant at the time, reprimands one of his officers, Anthony Colicchio, for an outburst on the street against a motorist. Colicchio shows no remorse, and Carver decides to write him up, knowing that doing so will make him a "rat." As cops transition into a managerial role, they may feel like they are betraying their roots, a sense that may be exacerbated by having former co-workers accuse them of no longer understanding what "real" policing is all about. In sum, the difference in worldviews of those working at headquarters and those on the street can lead each side to view the other with mistrust and frustration.

Conclusion

The Wire offers one of the richest and most complex views of American policing that the media have ever produced. While it's similar to many cop shows in its focus on the role of homicide detectives solving murders, *The Wire* simultaneously departs from the "cop show formula" by including many other facets of police work. Its exploration of the challenges of drug enforcement— especially the use of electronic surveillance— is unparalleled. Additionally, over the show's five seasons, we as viewers witness police being involved in a wide variety of activities that the media seldom cover. Where else could we view a neighborhood meeting in a community policing program, a depiction of "broken windows" policing, and police supervisors participating in a Compstat meeting? As we have argued, the series provides vivid examples of a number of mainstream themes commonly identified in the criminal justice literature on police culture, including more recent scholarship on the existence of multiple subcultures.

Because culture has been our focus, one caveat is worth noting: The claim that cultural norms and values both exist and exert powerful pressures on police to conform doesn't necessarily mean that all police will respond in the same way. The elements of culture must always be interpreted by individuals, and these interpretations are mediated by a wide variety of factors, including prior socialization and demographic characteristics of race, class, level of education, and gender. The existence of culture does not preclude human agency where individual officers can respond differently to cultural forces. At the same time, those who choose to ignore or disagree with cultural mandates will often pay a price for doing so, as fellow officers will judge their conduct in light of cultural norms and values. In sum, one can argue that culture plays an important role in shaping the attitudes and behavior of police and still agree that culture doesn't totally determine how police will think and act.

The Wire demonstrates this important nuance by giving us interesting examples of police acting in ways that differ from the cultural themes described in this chapter. For example, the show offers at least a few instances where the cultural imperative to assert authority is resisted. When Carver and Herc attempt to bring Marlo Stanfield to Colvin's meeting with drug dealers, Marlo responds, "It ain't gonna happen." Carver, looking around at Marlo's soldiers closing in on the two cops, backs down, telling Herc, "I think he gets a pass this time." On that day in Baltimore, it's the gangsters who appear to win. In another counter-example from the show, the criminals in *The Wire* turn out not always to be the "demons" they're supposed to be, and the norm that says good cops/evil criminals is challenged. When McNulty visits Stringer Bell's harborside condo after the drug dealer's murder, the cop is mystified by what he finds; tasteful furnishings, a collection of antique swords, and a bookshelf that includes Adam Smith's *The Wealth of Nations*. "Who the fuck was I chasing?" McNulty asks as he looks around at the trappings of a life he thought he knew but clearly didn't. And, finally, in an instance of police in *The Wire* challenging the norm of loyalty, Detective Greggs violates a cultural taboo and "snitches" on McNulty when he manufactures evidence for a serial murderer. She is acutely aware that such a betrayal—of a long-term colleague no less—has consequences. In fact, before she blows the whistle, she goes to Carver, who had previously turned in an officer for aggression. "When you spoke up on Colicchio," Greggs asks, "How did that feel?" Carver's reply? "Like shit." But he was okay with it, and Greggs decides she's okay with it too.

The Wire certainly entertains, but it's not *just* entertainment. Writing in *The Atlantic* magazine, Mark Bowden (2008: 51) said David Simon and his collaborators have "conjured the city onscreen with a verisimilitude that's astounding." This is surely one of the reasons the series has been dubbed by many as the best American television show ever made. As ex-cop Pam Newton (2011) said, "It takes a complex and nuanced piece of storytelling to firstly provoke, and then sustain thoughtful, prolonged consideration of its themes, its characters, its flaws and failings, its ambitions and their execution. *The Wire* repays such close attention. Even its imperfections are interesting." Although some plotlines may strain credibility, the show still serves as one of the most authentic and realistic portrayals of urban policing ever produced. It opens a window for viewers into a profession that everyone encounters at one time or another, but few truly do understand. *The Wire* "got some very important things about cops right" (Newton, 2011). Those who view it can learn much about police work and the role of police culture.

References

Barlow, D. E., & Barlow, M. H. (2006). The myth that the role of the police is to fight crime. In R. M. Bohm, & J. T. Walker (Eds.), *Demystifying crime and criminal justice* (pp. 73–80). Los Angeles, CA: Roxbury Publishing Company.

Bowden, M. (January/February 2008). The angriest man in television. *The Atlantic*, 50–57.

Brown, M. (1981). *Working the street: Police discretion and the dilemmas of reform*. New York: Russell Sage Foundation.

Cochran, J. K., & Bromley, M. L. (2003). The myth(?) of the police sub-culture. *Policing: An International Journal of Police Strategies & Management, 26*(1), 88–117. doi:10.1108/13639510310460314.

Crank, J. P. (2004). *Understanding police culture* (Second ed.). United States: Anderson Publishing Co.

Herbert, S. (1988). Police subculture reconsidered. *Criminology, 36*(2), 343–369.

Herbert, S. (1996). Morality in law enforcement: Chasing "bad guys" with the Los Angeles police department. *Law and Society Review, 30*(4), 799–818.

Hunt, J. (2009). Police accounts of normal force. In G. Massey (Ed.), *Readings for sociology* (Sixth ed., pp. 366–381). New York: W.W. Norton & Company. (Reprinted from the *Journal of Contemporary Ethnography, 13*(4), 315–41 1985.)

Kappeler, V. E., Blumberg, M., & Potter, G. W. (1993). *The mythology of crime and criminal justice*. Prospect Heights, Il: Waveland Press, Inc.

Kelman, H. C., & Hamilton, V. L. (2009). The My Lai massacre: A crime of obedience? In G. Massey (Ed.), *Readings in sociology* (Sixth ed., pp. 34–52). New York: W.W. Norton & Company. (Reprinted from *Crimes of Obedience: Toward a Social Psychology of Authority and Responsibility* by H.C. Kelman and V.L. Hamilton 1–21 Yale University Press, 1989.)

Lord, S., Crank, J. P., & Evans, R. (2004). Good-bye in a sea of blue. In J. P. Crank (Ed.), *Understanding police culture* (Second ed., pp. 353–363). United States: Anderson Publishing. Mastrofski, S. D., & Willis, J. J. (2010). Police organization continuity and change: Into the twenty-first century. In M. Tonry (Ed.), *Volume 39 of Crime and Justice: A review of research* (pp. 55–144). Chicago, IL: University of Chicago Press.

Newton, Pam. (April 27, 2011). The Wire Roundtable: Not Anti-Cop. *The Hooded Utilitarian*. http://hoodedutilitarian.com/2011/04/the-wire-roundtable-not-anti-cop/.

Paoline III, E. A. (2001). *Rethinking police culture*. New York: LFB Scholarly Publishing.

Paoline III, E. A. (2003). Taking stock: Toward a richer understanding of police culture. *Journal of Criminal Justice, 31*(3), 199–214. doi: 10.1016/S0047-2352(03)00002-3.

Reuss-Ianni, E. (1983). *Two cultures of policing: Street cops and management cops*. New Brunswick, N.J.: Transaction Books.

Skolnick, J. H. (1966). *Justice without trial: Law enforcement in democratic society*. New York: Wiley.

Sparrow, M. K., Moore, M. H., & Kennedy, D. M. (1990). *Beyond 911*. United States: Basic Books.

Van Maanen, J. (1974). Working the street: A developmental view of police behavior. In H. Jacob (Ed.), *The potential for reform of criminal justice* (pp. 83–130). Beverly Hills, CA: Sage Publications.

Van Maanen, J. (2010). The asshole. In R. G. Dunham, & G. Alpert (Eds.), *Critical issues in policing (sixth edition)* (pp. 90–108). Long Grove, IL: Waveland Press. (Reprinted from P. K. Manning and J. Van Maanen, (eds.) *A View From the Street* 221–238 1978.)

Wilson, J. Q. (1968). *Varieties of police behavior: The management of law and order in eight communities*. Cambridge, MA: Harvard University Press.

Worden, R.E. (1995). Police officers' belief systems: a framework for analysis. *American* Journal of Police, 14(1), 49–81.

Study Questions

1. According to the authors, what does *The Wire* say about police culture?

2. How to the author's compare and contrast the cops who are police administrators and patrol officers?

3. What do the author's mean by the statement: "Good cops are constantly aware of their surroundings, distinguishing what is normal from what is not?" What does this mean in the bigger picture of policing?

4. How do the subcultures of law enforcement, described by Van Maanan, affect the way in which cops interact with citizens?

5. According to the authors, how does *The Wire* explore the complexity of the solidarity that is found between cops?

Chapter 7

Without Regard to the Usual Rules

Jonathon A. Cooper and Jonathan Bolen

Introduction

Police corruption is always a hot topic for the media and citizens, and is typically an uncomfortable topic for those who enforce the law. Yet the types of corruption most citizens think about — brutality and economic corruption — have been on a historic decline since *Serpico* and *Princes of the City* were in theaters. Crank and Caldero (2000) were the first to systematically suggest that there was a moralistic form of police corruption, that they termed *noble cause corruption*. Noble cause corruption involves improper or unethical acts that are committed in the pursuit of good ends and worthwhile goals.

"Noble cause corruption" permeates *The Wire*, becoming such a regular aspect of the show that it is easy to miss: it seems natural, normal, accepted, and hardly worth mentioning. In a way, this suggests to us the inherent danger of noble cause corruption. As with all behavior, however, there are grades of noble cause corruption where some are more "serious" and others less so. The final season of *The Wire* gives us two examples of this pattern. The first incident, seemingly benign and most likely constitutional, occurs in the opening scene of the first episode. Homicide Detective Bunk Moreland has a suspect "hooked up" to a copy machine, while another detective, playing the part of a professor, *interprets* the sham lie detector's "output". In reality, the "professor" is feeding the machine one of two papers: one that indicates the suspect is lying, and one that indicates he is telling the truth. It is all a con, with the Xerox machine acting as the confidence man. In response to the lie detector indicating that he is lying about not being involved in the killing under investigation, the suspect makes a full confession.

Legally, there is nothing wrong with this ruse. Police lying to suspects, in most situations, is not unconstitutional. That being said, the detectives are purposefully deceiving the suspect in an effort to solve a case. As lying is morally wrong, this scenario begs the question, is there a moral dilemma here? In the wake of the Rodney King incident, Skolnick and Fyfe (1993: 62) rhetorically asked, "Should the good end of convicting criminals also justify deception during interrogation? One's answer is likely to depend on the balance of one's attachment to due process or crime-control values. The injunction 'Thou shalt not lie' doesn't seem to apply to trickery in interrogation.... As in the investigation of narcotics dealing, the good end is said to justify the bad means ..."

The second scenario is the main story arc for the fifth season: Detective Jimmy McNulty, in collusion with Detectives Lester Freamon and Leander Sydnor, falsifies the existence and activities of a serial killer in order to force City Hall to fund a specialized unit. They do so by sensationalizing crime scenes where dope fiends have died of an over-dose. This money is diverted to fund an unauthorized wire-tap which is being used to trace down a "real" criminal, Marlo Stanfield. McNulty goes so far as to call a *Sun* reporter—*as* the killer—who, himself, is making things up about the serial killer. This scenario goes way beyond, "it is unethical to lie to a suspect," and into the realm of breaking due process, lying on affidavits, contravening the Fourth Amendment, and creating a moral panic—all in the name of "police work." As Freamon put it: "Who gives a damn if we fake a couple of murders that we're never gonna solve, huh? ... But if it's gonna get the bosses to throw down enough coin to do police work ..." (Season 5, Episode 5). Is there a moral dilemma here?

Although the answer *may* seem more straightforward in the second scenario than in the first, both are rife with nuances. The concept of noble cause corruption can be used to help us understand not only the behavior of police in similar situations, but also to help us see that, in many cases, officers do not perceive a moral dilemma at all, when one is, in fact, readily apparent. For the police, often there is only a *mandate* and *procedural restrictions* to fulfilling that mandate.

As demonstrated by Freamon's statement concerning ways of getting the brass to fund police work, it is also clear that there is more than individual officer agency at work here in the etiology of noble cause corruption. Yet, it is to the individual officer that we typically attribute the source of noble cause corruption: noble cause corruption "happens when police officers care too much" (Crank & Caldero, 2000: 2). Given the voluminous literature on the policing subculture (Manning & Van Mannen, 1978), the us-versus-them mentality of police officers (Skolnick, 1966), discussions of "the number's game" (Skolnick & Fyfe, 1993), the dual police cultures of street cops and the brass (Reuss-Ianni,

1982), and the generally accepted sociological approach to understanding police behavior (Kappeler, Sluder, & Alpert, 1998), it is more likely that the causes of noble cause corruption are to be found in both the individual officer and the organization. Most statements concerning noble cause corruption have focused on the assets of the individual officer over the socializing and political environment of the organization. This chapter asserts that both must be considered. Because the individual has been the topic of previous work, we will instead focus mostly on making the case for the influence of the working environment.

What Is "Noble Cause" and How Is It "Corrupted"?

Television shows are inherently focused on profit from entertainment. Social science, on the other hand, is ultimately concerned with understanding social phenomena. The inconsistency between these two goals should be readily apparent, and therefore begs the question, why draw conclusions concerning social phenomena from a television series? Although criminologists and justicians have used TV and other media as units of observation in their research, they have typically done so in the spirit of answering research questions concerning the relationship between media and crime and the public (Potter & Kappeler, 2006). On the other hand, news media, both print and televised, have also been used to analyze crime and criminal justice trends (White & Ready, 2009). But to employ television as a means for understanding the phenomena which it depicts in the name of entertainment is another matter all together.

Yet, this practice is not without precedence. Klockars (1980) usefully discussed a very specific police behavior by comparing it to the behavior portrayed in the popular movie *Dirty Harry*. Indeed, the article itself is called "The Dirty Harry Problem." This example is pertinent for two reasons; first, because of its success. "The Dirty Harry Problem" has been regularly discussed among policing scholars in both scholarly books and academic journals for over thirty years. This suggests that there is value in considering pressing social phenomena in light of the TV shows and movies which attempt to portray them. It is also important because the topic of this chapter, noble cause corruption, has its nascence in Klockars's seminal piece.

In his article, Klockars (1980: 34) posited a moral dilemma for police officers: a situation that can have no axiomatically correct answer. He stated, "When and to what extent does the morally good end warrant or justify an ethically, politically, or legally dangerous means to its achievement?" In other words, when can a police officer break from due process in the pursuit of the protection of the innocent from the evil? The "noble cause" is therefore a morally good end, and its "corruption" occurs whenever police employ "dirty means" towards its achievement.

To this end, Klockars (1980) suggested that *for a police officer to step over the procedural line*, that officer must answer three questions to his own satisfaction. First, are dirty means the *only* available means? Second, will the dirty means be *effective*? And third, is the "source" reliable? Whereas the first two questions deal with the utility of the dirty means, the third question speaks to the degree to which an officer can trust the information used to answer the first two questions. For example, in *The Wire* McNulty uses known gunman and thug, Omar, to testify against Byrd at his murder trial. McNulty knows who Omar is and appears knowledgeable of Omar's lies, however, he also is aware of the relative untouchability of Avon Barksdale's crew. McNulty appreciates that Omar knows the streets, "knows" that Byrd is guilty and is himself a means to a just end. Each question must further be evaluated according to the following criterion: "... the good to be achieved is so unquestionably good and so passionately felt that even a small possibility of its achievement demands that it be tried" (Klockars, 1080: 36).

Klockars's research was preceded by other important works, such as those published by Hopkins (1931), who explored the idea that police are faced with moral dilemmas during the course of their work week. Arguably the more influential work in this domain, however, was that of Muir (1977). Muir (1977: 3–4) presented the police function using words that would make even Sartre squirm: "A policeman becomes a good policeman to the extent that he develops two virtues. Intellectually, he has to grasp the nature of human suffering. Morally, he has to resolve the contradiction of achieving just ends with coercive means." Taking a Weberian approach, Muir (1977: 51) described these terms as perspective and passion and argued that "[t]he secret to avoiding corruption by coercive power ... was to combine passion with perspective." Although it is unclear if *anyone* perfectly matches this description in *The Wire*, Major "Bunny" Colvin perhaps comes the closest. Bunny struggles throughout the series to intellectually grapple with the immense human misery in his district. Drugs have taken hold on his streets and he is commanded by the administration to confront the steadily climbing felony rate with no additional resource or departmental support. Bunny is a good bureaucrat, but he is in constant strife from his efforts to rectify the abstruse and dissonant logic of his department to create "good numbers" and to make a meaningful impact on the city.

Bunny's love for his community, especially the youth within it, inspires him to be drastic in his decisions to create equilibrium between his bureaucratic demands and his devotion to the citizens under his care. This is most poignantly evidenced by his creation of "Hamsterdam" in season three. Bunny allows drug addicts and their dealers free reign over certain "free zones", which he believes will reduce violent felonies and free up his officers to focus on real police work. For Bunny, drugs are the root of his district's ills, and addressing this issue is not only the most effective way to police, but is the right thing to do. In the end, however, Bunny's superiors disagree, and he is stripped of rank just before retirement.

This line of scholarship was followed up with the work done by Crank and Caldero (2000). Rather than starting from a sociological perspective, as had Muir and Klockars, Crank and Caldero essentially maintained that the seeds of noble cause corruption are to be found, ultimately, within the officer (for this, they relied heavily on the work of Rokeach, 1973). From their perspective, good police officers *want* to protect the innocent. This is the noble cause: something so unquestionably good as to subordinate other concerns. It is this righteous desire that may lead officers to disregard morally good means if they will get in the way of this goal. To a large degree, McNulty is the epitome of this perspective: nothing matters but catching the bad guy. Relationships, due process, personal hygiene, or the needs of other departmental units or public agencies can be cast to the way-side or actively manipulated while "on the hunt." McNulty, however, also demonstrates for us how behavior associated with noble cause corruption comes not only from the individual, but from the organization itself: In Episode 7 of Season 1, McNulty is lamenting his frustration and his sorrow for the command's interference with his righteous path to the prosecutor, and at one time lover, Ronnie: "They're gonna do me, Ronnie. I love this fucking job, and they're gonna do me."

All this notwithstanding, our empirical knowledge of noble cause corruption largely remains unanswered. Much of the discussion surrounding noble cause corruption has been philosophical (Kleinig, 2002; DeLattre, 2006), policy-oriented (Harrison, 1999; Punch, 2000; Sunahara, 2004), or anecdotal (Miller, 1999). To date, the only direct empirical assessments have come from Crank, Flaherty, and Giacomazzi (2007) and Porter and Warrender (2009), with the former trying to disentangle the empirical definition of noble cause corruption and the varying ways in which it manifests, and the latter seeking to uncover the frequency of noble cause corruption relative to other forms of corruption. While limited in sample and methodology, both studies are consonant in suggesting that the concept of noble cause corruption *does indeed* represent a real phenomenon and that it is better understood *situationally* rather than chronically.

The reasons for this lack of research are at least two fold; first, because its existence has largely remained atheoretical. And second, because the focus has been on one dimension of the policing ecology, namely, the individual. The first snag has been discussed elsewhere (Cooper, 2011). For the purposes of this chapter, we want to spend the remainder of our time focusing on the second issue by using *The Wire* to demonstrate just how important the role of the organization is to the ontology and etiology of noble cause corruption, both independent of and in interaction with the individual officer.

Doing Police Work

The Police Mandate

Crank and Caldero (2000) placed the onus of noble cause corruption on the individual police officer, rather than the organization. They argued that the seeds of noble cause corruption were antecedent to an officer's employ. Essentially, they suggested that a certain "type" of person endeavors to be an officer. Such a person is genuinely interested in the well-being of those who cannot protect themselves against crime. Research tends to support this typification (White et al., 2010). When confronted with structural impediments to this noble and compelling end, an officer may simply choose to circumvent procedure or ethical guidelines that might otherwise apply.

While Crank and Caldero (2000) do give place for the socializing influence of police organization and working environment, they do so as a *post hoc* process designed more to reinforce and maintain rather than to create noble cause corruption. This is a bold statement, centered mostly on the work of Rokeach (1973). It also absolves a law enforcement agency of any responsibility. Indeed, it absolves the entire political apparatus under-girding the police agency, and the body politic supporting the political apparatus. But agencies and society cannot get off this easily: there is ample evidence to suggest that it is not *only* the individual who carries with them the seed of noble cause corruption, but the organization itself, in conjunction with its mandate, that facilitate the expression of noble cause corruption.

A mandate can be understood as an organization's right to define the parameters and technology of its occupation (Manning, 1978). For the police, however, their mandate stems from another source. In a broad sense, the police represent the literal manifestation of the state's obligations born from the social contract: individuals relinquish a limited suite of rights, and in return the state promises to protect any and all remaining rights from threats both without and within territorial borders. The police mandate, therefore, is shaped by the democratic process: the government dictates the mandate's terms in light of the needs and desires of the body politic. As Manning (1978) has also pointed out, the police themselves have whole heartily embraced this mandate as their own. Because of their adoption of the policing mandate, Manning's initial definition sticks, albeit in a qualified sort of way.

The policing mandate is to protect the innocent from villains, and to catch the bad guy—that is, to protect and to serve. Further, it is to do so "efficient[ly], apolitical[ly], and professional[ly and through the] enforcement of the law" (Manning, 1978: 8). This mandate, again according to Manning (1978), is an impossible one. It suggests to the police that they can and should have a meaningful impact on the crime rate. As Herbert (2001: 449) points out " ... on their own, police can do little to reduce crime." Further, and as will be discussed in more detail below, although efforts are made to quantify the police mandate, it ultimately remains non-operational (Klockars, 1986), precluding any meaningful comparison of the state of crime *then* versus the state of crime *now* (DiIulio, 1995). The problem with the mandate is that it asks the police to bite off more than they can reasonably chew—yet they do!

Clearly, as Crank and Caldero (2000) pointed out, most police officers begin their careers already with the mandate in their mind: they *want* to help people, they *want* to protect the innocent, and they certainly *want* to catch the villain (White at al., 2010). But this assertion warrants two clarifications. As pointed out above, the police mandate has its impetus in the larger social fabric of the United States. We expect our police officers to look (wear uniforms) and behave (engage in random patrol) a certain way: to suggest otherwise is anathema. What this means is that the source of new recruits' congruence with the noble cause, the police mandate, is just as much societal as it is individualistic. Indeed, it is most likely paralyzingly impossible to disentangle the two. Given this, our first clarification is that we should not throw the baby out with the bathwater: whatever the order of operations, the social environment of the individual police officer clearly matters.

The second qualification is the manner in which it *does* matter. As is clear from the preceding paragraph, socialization into the acceptance of the policing mandate occurs before a recruit even enters the academy. The values that are adopted through this socialization process are at once reinforced and supplemented throughout the academy experience, and later through time on the job with the field training officer (FTO)—to say nothing of the potential impact of other opportunities to spend time with more seasoned officers, such as before and after roll-call, during impromptu car-to-car meetings at gas stations, or meals shared at special "cop friendly" restaurants and diners (for a review of this socialization schema, see Stojkovic, Kalinich, & Klofas, 2003). The working environment of the police officer functions, therefore, as a socializing instrument into acceptance of the noble mandate of police work.

"The Fucking Numbers Game"

As has been alluded to, the police mandate is nebulous, broad, and difficult to operationalize (DiIulio, 1995). It becomes challenging to ascertain the degree to which it is being carried out. This is compounded by the bureaucratic obsession, adopted by the police, with *numbers*. As part of the police professionalization movement in the early 20th century, Vollmer, through the International Association of Chiefs of Police, introduced the uniform crime reports, or UCR, which later would be adopted by the FBI (Skolnick & Fyfe, 1993). At that time, Hoover was doing everything in his power to transform the FBI into *the* standard for police work—both at a federal and a local level. To this end, he utilized the UCR to highlight the professional standard by which the FBI behaved. As agencies across the nation began to emulate the FBI in form and function, local police departments considered their numerical output more closely, as well. This was a great departure from the Peelian model of the early 19th century, which emphasized the absence of crime as a benchmark of police success, rather than police activity itself (Uchida, 2005). This focus would have serious ramifications for police behavior and organization that reverberate today (for an overview, see Skolnick & Fyfe, 1993). For our present purposes, however, we will only focus on what it means for noble cause corruption.

The focus on numbers created a pattern for behavior based on at least three criteria: the numbers game, activity, and how police are themselves rewarded. As one patrol officer stated sardonically to mayor-elect Carcetti during roll-call, "The fucking numbers game." This term ultimately refers to two things: first, that police are judged by numerical output. And second, that in order to achieve an acceptable level of numerical output, police sometimes must "juke the stats"—either through active manipulation of numbers, or through active manipulation of the process. To wit: during the second season of *The Wire*, no agency wants to take the case of the thirteen prostitutes found dead in a shipping container on the docks because to do so would be to decrease their homicide clearance rate. The numbers attempt to quantify the noble mandate, but in the process force police to lose sight of that mandate: the numbers, a means, become ends unto themselves (Merton, 1957). But it is not just any numbers that matter: it is specific numbers. Writing of the Philadelphia police in the 1960s and 70s, Rubinstein (1976: 43–44) notes that:

> The worth of a man to his platoon does not depend on his success in preventing crimes, arresting suspected felons, or even giving service without complaint or injury.... "Activity" is the internal product of police work. It is the statistical measure which the sergeant uses to judge the productivity of his men.... Arrest activity is computed from what the patrolman 'puts on the books' and not by the disposition of his cases in court. Since activity is a measure of his work, his sergeant has no interest in what eventually happens to the cases.

Again, we see that by quantifying the noble cause, we sacrifice its achievement in place of measuring the activity designed to achieve it—even if this activity can "miss the mark."

Finally, officers are often rewarded for engaging in noble cause corruption—typically inadvertently. Police are rewarded for arrests and shootings (Kappeler, Sluder, & Alpert, 1998; Skolnick & Fyfe, 1993). Seldom are they rewarded for crime prevention or dutifully following procedural guidelines. Although procedure is often scrutinized in both arrests and shootings, this focus on morally good ends is *more* pronounced than consideration of legal means. As Fyfe (1997) indicated over two decades ago, many times, the decision to shoot, although legally defensible, was nevertheless avoidable. In an environment that rewards "good" shootings, only the former consideration matters. Major Colvin's "Hamsterdam" in Season 3 demonstrates that thoughtful, prevention focused police work can work—but at a cost too dear to any police agency.

It is worth noting that even such problem oriented police behavior can result in noble cause corruption. "Legalizing" drugs contrary to current statute is the obvious example, as is Sergeant Carver's actions in moving a murder suspect away from the neutral area. Although the analogy obviously falls apart, the principle remains the same: the brass would have been more tolerant of behavior that fell in line with what they believed to be "good police work" even if it was morally questionable. Once outside the bounds of "good police work" or "activity" it became suspect, dangerous, and insoluble.

"The Needs of the System"

The problem for police is that due process and general ethical guidelines often interfere with achieving numbers. Although the emphasis on due process waxes and wanes, it is useful to point out at least two points in policing history where due process received substantial attention, particularly as it relates to numbers. The first came in the wake of the passage of the Pendleton Act in the late 1800s. This act's effects were far-reaching; for police, they resulted in large tomes of standards, benchmarks, and guidelines that, in conjunction with the bureaucratization efforts of reformers such as Vollmer, Wilson, and Hoover, insisted that police agencies be held accountable for their output—an output that, given the Taylorism of the time, could only result in the quantification of the noble mandate (Skolnick & Fyfe, 1993).

The second example came in the mid-1950s and 1960s during the Warren court. Seeing a need to curtail civil rights abuses at the hands of police officers and departments, several decisions came down from the United States Supreme Court that forced agencies to comply with due process, including the Exclusionary Rule and the Miranda rights (Roberg, Novak, & Cordner, 2008). This was later accompanied by new scholarship that called into question not just *what* police were doing, but *if it worked* (Uchida, 2005). Scholars were all too ready to jump on the Supreme Court band wagon in insisting that policing behavior needed to change and conform to standards of due process—in a way, the "way we do things around here" simply did not add up—literally!

And so the police are placed in an insoluble situation: fulfill my mandate and protect the innocent but defy ethical and judicial guidelines, or fail in my mission. For many police, this situation is not so insoluble. But that debate is not the point; that it even *can* be debated *is* the point. Were it not for an institutionally prescribed mandate butting heads with institutionally prescribed behavior, noble cause corruption would not exist. But because police officers are inhered with a noble mandate to protect the innocent—a mandate that is unquestionable and compelling—and because these same officers perceive due process or other ethical guidelines as "handcuffing" them, such a corruption has a place to exist.

> **Freamon:** "I've reached a point, Detective Sydnor, where I no longer have the time or patience left to address myself to the needs of the system within which we work. I'm tired."
> **Sydnor:** "You gonna quit?"
> **Freamon:** "Not yet. Not just yet."
> **Sydnor:** "So what are you talking about?"
> **Freamon:** "[When they took us off Marlo,] I regarded that decision as illegitimate ... And so, I'm responding in kind. I'm going to press a case ... without regard to the usual rules."

As Klockars suggests (1980: 412), "... the department that trains its policeman well and supplies them with the resources—knowledge and material— to do their work will find that the policemen will not resort to dirty means ..." Of course, he takes it one step further, "... 'unnecessarily,' meaning only those occasions when an acceptable means will work as well as a dirty one" (but see Klockars, 1986). Although the rightness or wrongness of noble cause corruption will not be discussed in this particular chapter, we will take some time to discuss some of its consequences beyond the achievement of an actual morally good end.

"If It Makes the Fucking Case, I'm in All the Way"

This chapter is ultimately concerned with the *what* and *why* of noble cause corruption. It seems appropriate however, to include a discussion of the consequences of a behavior that may at first glance seem noble and, as Klockars (1980) put it, desirable. *The Wire* is replete with examples of what can result as a consequence of an officer "caring too much" and subsequently disregarding due process and ethical (even if legal) practices. Crank and Caldero cast the Dirty Harry Problem (Klockars, 1980) and the psychic balancing act between perspective and passion (Muir, 1977) as an issue *of* corruption. This is a distinct change in tone from Klockars' (1980: 37) statement that "I know I would want [Dirty Harry] to do what he did, and what is more, I would want anyone who policed for me to be prepared to do so as well. Put differently, I want to have as police officers men and women of moral courage and sensitivity." By calling it *corruption*, Crank and Caldero were moralizing the issue, just as Klockars had, but in the *opposite* direction. Although not exhaustive, we can focus our attention on the following potential repercussions: dirty means becoming ends unto themselves, an uncomfortable segue into economic corruption, and the solidifying of a subculture which includes silence.

First, As Skolnick and Fyfe (1993) point out, when an officer begins employing dirty means to achieve a just end, it can happen that those dirty means *become* the ends. This happens, for example, when an officer "knows" that the justice system will ultimately let the officer down, resulting in the release of the villain—again. If such a pattern repeats itself often enough, an officer may decide to take on the role of judge and "executioner." Executioner is, of course, too strong of a word: most officers will not result to that extreme unless absolutely necessary. Yet, we have ample anecdotal evidence that this scenario—both generally and in terms of the taking of human life—does occur. The infamous Buddy Boys of the New York Police Department excused stealing money from drug dealers by arguing that the courts would not punish the dealers. Therefore, their actions as corrupt officers were a form of punishment (Kappeler, Sluder, & Alpert, 1998).

Second, some have suggested that noble cause corruption may have a desensitizing effect on officers such that corruption more generally may become acceptable (Crank & Caldero, 2000). Indeed, Ivkovic (2005) suggested that the line between economic and noble cause corruption may be thinner than we assume. We do have some hint that both are situational (although, as the preceding two paragraphs suggest, sometimes systematic) (Crank, et al. 2007; Ivkovic, 2005), which may indicate that an officer's willingness to engage in one or the other is simply the manifestation of an underlying willingness to forgo due process and ethics as the situation allows/demands. Porter and Warrender's (2009) study seems to back this notion up, at least speculatively.

We see the potential connection between noble cause and economic corruption demonstrated in *The Wire* when Detectives Hauk and Carver, who have previously shown their willingness to engage in noble cause corruption (eg. "Fuzzy Dunlap"), each grab a brick of cash after raiding a drug house. Granted, part of their motivation was revenge against Lt. Daniels for having accused them of taking cash in a previous raid when they had not in fact taken the cash. But whatever the motivation for the economic corruption, the juxtaposition of noble cause and economic corruption in this example reinforces the idea that the line between the two may be thin, and that one may lead to, or at least "allow" the other.

Finally, there is the possibility that noble cause corruption may reinforce the police subculture: a subculture noted for its code of silence (Manning & Van Maanen, 1978). Because of the code of silence, many police officers may be unwilling to turn a brother in to supervisors for misconduct—especially misconduct that results in the noble end, which largely binds law enforcement officers together. This reinforcement of the code of silence may only create more opportunities for economic corruption, as well as other forms of misconduct, such as brutality, because it: a) facilitates an environment that lacks accountability; and, b) puts officers in situations where they may be scared to report the inappropriate activities of another officer because the latter has kept his mouth shut for him. We see this in the fifth season where Bunk, although disapproving vehemently of McNulty's activities with the dead bodies, nevertheless does not report it. It is not until a detective opens up to Daniels that it finally comes out—and even then, knowledge of his activity is kept secret from the public and press (who are also incidentally involved in the noble cause corruption, but for less than noble reasons, at this point). McNulty, Freamon, and later Daniels who will not play ball with City Hall after he is named commissioner are all "managed" internally.

In light of these consequences, then, there is serious reason to consider the causes of noble cause corruption. As we indicated earlier in the chapter, by focusing solely on the individual, we miss a big part of the picture, and let police agencies off with no responsibility. More importantly, we let ourselves off because the police mandate does not come out of a vacuum. It is born from the American collective conscious. We have an image of how police should behave, what they should be doing, and to whom they should be doing it. Klockars hit the nail of the American *zeitgeist* on the head when he asserted his desire for police of moral courage who can make the "right" choice when presented with the Dirty Harry problem. Although this chapter has taken Crank and Caldero's assertion that noble cause corruption stems from individual attributes to task, we aver with their conception of noble cause corruption *cum* corruption. Its remedy lies as much with the working environment police must interface with every day as it does with their own ego.

References

Cooper, J.A. (2011). Noble cause corruption as a consequence of role conflict in the police organization. Policing and Society. Forthcoming.

Crank, J.P. and Caldero, M.A. (2000). Police ethics: noble cause corruption. Cincinnati, OH: Anderson Publishing Co.

Crank, J.P., Flaherty, D., and Giacomazzi, A. (2007). The noble cause: an empirical assessment. Journal of Criminal Justice, 35, 103–116.

DeLattre, E.J. (2006). Character and cops: Ethics in policing. 5th ed. Washington, DC: The AEI Press.

DiIulio, J.J. (1993). Measuring performance when there is no bottom line. Performance Measures for the Criminal Justice System, Washington, D.C., 143–156.

Dunham and G.P. Alpert, eds. Critical issues in policing: Contemporary readings. 5th ed. Long Grove, IL: Waveland Press, 20–40.

Fyfe, J. (1997). The split second syndrome and other determinants of police violence. In R. Dunham & G. Alpert (Eds.), Critical issues in policing (3rd ed., pp. 531–546). Prospect Heights, IL: Waveland.

Harrison, B. (1999). Noble cause corruption and the police ethic. FBI Law Enforcement Bulletin, 68, 1–7.

Herbert, S. (1998). Police subculture revisited. Criminology, 36, 343–370.

Hopkins, E. (1931). Our lawless police. New York: Wiley.

Ivković, S.K. (2005). Fallen blue knights: Controlling police corruption. New York: Oxford University Press.

Kappeler, V.E., Sluder, R.D., and Alpert, G.P. (1998). Forces of deviance: understanding the dark side of policing. 2nd ed. Long Grove, IL: Waveland Press.

Kleinig, J. (2002). Rethinking noble cause corruption. International Journal of Police Science and Management, 4, 287–314.

Klockars, C.B. (1980). The Dirty Harry Problem. The Annals of the Academy of Political and Social Sciences, 452, 33–47.

Klockars, C.B. (1986). Street justice: some micro-moral reservations; comment on Sykes. Justice Quarterly, 3, 513–516.

Manning, P.K. (1978). The police: mandate, strategies, and appearances. In: P.K. Manning and J. van Maanen, eds. Policing: a view from the street. Santa Monica, CA: Goodyear Publishing Company, 7–31.

Manning, P.K. and van Maanen, J. (1978). Policing: A view from the street. Santa Monica, CA: Goodyear Publishing Company, Inc.

Merton, R.K. (1957). Social theory and social structure. Glencoe, IL: Free Press.

Miller, S. (1999). Noble cause corruption in policing. African Security Review, 8. Available from: http://www.iss.co.za/Pubs/ASR/8No3/NobleCauseCorruption.html [Accessed 23 November 2009].

Muir, W.K., Jr. (1977). Police: Streetcorner politicians. Chicago: The University of Chicago Press.

Porter, L.E. and Warrender, C. (2009). A multivariate model of police deviance: examining the nature of corruption, crime and misconduct. Police & Society, 19, 79–99.

Porter, L.E. and Warrender, C. (2009). A multivariate model of police deviance: examining the nature of corruption, crime and misconduct. Police & Society, 19, 79–99.

Potter, G.W. & Kappeler, V.E. (2006). Constructing crime: Perspectives on making news and social problems. 2nd ed. Long Grove, IL: Waveland Press, Inc.

Punch, M. (2000). Police corruption and its prevention. European Journal of Criminal Policy and Research, 8, 301–324.

Roberg, R. R., Novak, K. J., & Cordner, G. W. (2005). Police & society (3rd ed.). Los Angeles, Calif: Roxbury.

Rokeach, M. (1973). The nature of human values. New York: The Free Press.

Rubinstein, J. (1973). City police. New York: Farrar, Straus and Giroux.

Russel-Brown, K. (2009). The color of crime (2nd Ed.). New York City: New York University Press.

Sherman, L.W. (1974). Police corruption: A sociological perspective. Garden City, NY: Anchor Press.

Skolnick, J.H. and Fyfe, J.J. (1993). Above the law: Police and the use of excessive force. New York: The Free Press.

Skolnick, Jerome H. (1966). Justice without trial. John Wiley & Sons Inc.

Stojkovic, S., Kalinich, D., and Klofas, J. (2003). Criminal justice organizations: Administration and management. 3rd ed. Belmont, CA: Wadsworth.

Sunahara, D.F. (2004). A model of unethical and unprofessional behaviour. The Canadian Review of Policing Research, 1. Available from: http://aup.athabascau.ca/crpr/index.php/crpr/article/view/17/16 [Accessed 23 November 2009].

Uchida, C.D., 2005. The development of the American police: an historical overview. In: R.G.

Walker, S. (2005). The new world of police accountability. Thousand Oaks, CA: Sage.

White, M.D. & Ready, J. (2009). Examining fatal and nonfatal incidents involving the TASER: Identifying predictors of suspect death reported in the media. Criminology & Public Policy, 8, 865–891.

White, M.D., et al. (2010). Motivations for becoming a police officer: re-assessing officer attitudes and job satisfaction after six years on the street. Journal of Criminal Justice, 38, 520–530.

Study Questions

1. Crank and Caldero were the first to suggest the concept of "noble cause corruption". Discuss the pros and cons of following this moralistic form of police corruption. Is there ever an appropriate time for a police officer to lie?

2. Cooper and Bolen discuss the creation of "Hamsterdam" in order for Major "Bunny" Colvin to regain control of the city. Is this systematic overlooking of ongoing crimes in order to reduce other crimes a process that falls into "noble cause corruption"? Would it be acceptable to ask officers to knowingly ignore the mandate and procedure if the outcome were safer streets for citizens?

3. Is it possible to disentangle the individual officer's internal mandate to protect and serve from the government's literal police mandate to protect and serve when addressing noble cause corruption? If an officer is socialized into the acceptance of the government's policing mandate, do we even need to disentangle the motivation (personal or institutional) for noble cause corruption for a better understanding? Why or why not?

4. How does "the numbers game" promote or detract from noble cause corruption at the officer level? At the institutional level? What does relying solely on numbers do to the shape the rewards obtained by officers?

5. Discuss how the emphasis on due process affected policing and policing agencies during the 1800s and the 1900s. How do these changes contradict what is expected of the police with how they are expected to achieve their goals?

6. Discuss the ways in which noble cause corruption can reach a tipping point in individual officers. How could this reinforced by the police subculture?

Chapter 8

The Compstat Process as Presented in *The Wire*

Gennaro F. Vito*

Introduction

Compstat[1] is a goal-oriented, strategic management process that aims to control crime by holding police officials accountable for organizational performance. It has been recognized as a revolutionary police management paradigm (Henry, 2002; McDonald, 2002; Walsh, 2001). As developed and implemented by the New York City Police Department, Compstat is the most singular police reform program in recent years. In 1996, Compstat was awarded the prestigious *Innovations in American Government Award* from the Ford Foundation and the John F. Kennedy School of Government. The Compstat paradigm has been replicated in numerous police departments throughout the United States, Europe and the Pacific Rim. Among these agencies is the Baltimore Police Department.

---

* I would like to thank Dr. William F. Walsh, Professor Emeritus and former Director of the Southern Police Institute at the University of Louisville for his careful review and thoughtful comments on this chapter.

1. What's in a Name? There is some controversy over what the term "Compstat" actually represents and even how it should be spelled. While the spelling "Compstat" is the most common usage (see Silverman, 1999; Walsh, 2001; Bratton & Knobler, 1998; Timoney, 2010), McDonald (2002) and Kerik (2001) spell it "CompStat." Eterno and Silverman (2006, p. 220) posit that Compstat within the NYPD was a shorthand referral to "compare stats"—a computer file where crime data were originally stored and not "computer statistics." In Baltimore, Mayor O'Malley used the term "CitiStat" to refer to his governmental-wide system of accountability. Yet, in *The Wire*, neither term is used in favor of "Comstat"—the spelling also used by Maple (1999). I use Compstat to refer to the process throughout this chapter.

The Compstat paradigm evolved from New York City Police Department weekly Crime Control Strategy meetings in January 1994 (Henry, 2002; Silverman, 1999). Its aim was to increase the flow of crime information between the agency's executives and the commanders of operational units. NYPD Commissioner William Bratton and his command staff designed these Compstat meetings as a way to make his 76 precinct commanders and their officers accountable for the crime rate within their areas of responsibility (Silverman, 1999). From 1993 through May 5, 2011, index crimes in New York City have declined by about 77 percent under Compstat (New York City Police Department, 2011).

Akin to the high levels of crime faced in New York during the 1990s, Baltimore as presented on *The Wire* and in the real world, faced similar crime problems a decade later. Just as took place in New York, in *The Wire*, reductions in crime were a priority to the Baltimore Police Department and city administration. The use of Compstat, and particularly the Compstat meetings became a significant element of the show during its third season. This chapter reviews the Compstat process as it was implemented in New York City and Baltimore as well as academic research about it. Scenes from Compstat meetings from *The Wire* are examined as examples of how this process operates—its strengths and weaknesses.

The Compstat Process

The underlying concept of Compstat is that police officers and police agencies can have a substantial positive impact on crime and quality of life problems facing the communities they serve if managed strategically. Compstat presents police executives and managers with a new way of looking at police organizations and police activities. It is radically different from the accepted concepts and practices that have guided police administration through most of its existence and it points to new methods and strategies, similar to those used by business managers, that police agencies can use to fulfill their mission (Henry, 2002). Compstat emphasizes the vital link between information, operational decision-making and crime control objectives (McDonald, 2002). As a management tool, however, its impact extends way beyond crime fighting and can be applied to any organizational setting. Its strength is that it is a management process that can adapt to constantly changing conditions.

Compstat, in operation, consists of a four-step process. The first step involves the obtainment and analysis of accurate and time intelligence. Items such as types of crime, reason or motive for the crime, as well as the time and location the commission of the crime took place are entered into the Compstat computer system and analyzed for common themes and criminological factors.

The second step involves rapid deployment of resources to address the criminality or conditions associated with the crimes under review. By providing weekly crime statistics, the Compstat process allows administrators to assess this intelligence so Commanders can then deploy their resources as rapidly as possible.

The third step in the process involves the effective identification and use of appropriate tactics. Tactics such as saturation patrols, differential responses, directed patrol, or hot spot policing may be appropriate in a variety of circumstances. Compstat provides information that can assist in deciding what strategies to use in a given situation.

The final step in the Compstat process consists of relentless follow-up and assessment. The first three steps are only effective if commanders constantly follow up on what is being done, and assess their results. If results are not what they should be, something needs to change.

With such an analytical process, using the data generated, Compstat provides police administrators with the information necessary to foster accountability throughout a police department. As noted by William Bratton:

> There are four levels of Compstat. We created a system in which the police commissioner, with his executive core, first empowers and then interrogates the precinct commander, forcing him or her to come up with a plan to attack crime. But it should not stop there. At the next level down, it should be the precinct commander, taking the same role as the commissioner, empowering and interrogating the platoon commander. Then, at the third level, the platoon commander should be asking his sergeants, 'What are we doing to deploy on this tour to address these conditions?' And finally, you have the sergeant at roll call doing the same thing. All the way down until everyone in the department is empowered and motivated, active and assessed and successful. It works in all organizations, whether it's 38,000 New York cops or Mayberry, R.F.D. (Bratton, 1999: 239).

Regardless of the size of the agency, the heart of the Compstat process is the "Compstat Meeting." Compstat meetings, which are held weekly, are attended by high level police administrators who discuss crime statistics and potential tactics and strategies with division and precinct managers across the agency. In addition to analyzing crime information, Sugarman (2010: 173) notes that the Compstat meeting provides four functions. First, it is the "master classroom for on-the-job training and coaching" with supervision provided by top level administrators who officers may never see on such a regular basis. Second, it is a place for "peer learning among middle managers" who can learn from the experience and thus spread the benefits of successful crime fighting methods. Third, senior managers get the opportunity to obtain a "regular overview of all operations and problems needing special attention" rather than a piece meal approach. Finally, it gives "top brass a bully pulpit and a megaphone to send edicts across agency and a stage to recognize and honor outstanding performers at any rank." That being said, as discussed below and depicted in *The Wire*, the successful implementation and use of Compstat in police agencies can have varied levels of success.

Potential Implementation and Operational Problems in Compstat Systems

While there are a number of potential errors frequently found in the operation of Compstat (see Behn, 2008), two frequently occurring missteps are depicted in *The Wire*. These errors are first, there is no clear purpose behind using Compstat, and second, there is an inability to find balance between the "brutal and the bland" (Behn, 2008: 6) in conducting Compstat meetings.

The effective use of Compstat is limited by implementing and operating it with no clear purpose. Specific questions, such as, "what results are we trying to produce," "what would better performance look like," and "how might we know if we made some improvements" all need to be considered.

In *The Wire* episodes featuring Compstat, the only clear purpose mentioned is to lower the crime rate—particularly the homicide rate in Baltimore. In the Compstat meetings, Acting Commissioner Ervin Burrell and Deputy Commissioner of Operations William Rawls continually pressure their district commanders to lower crime rate statistics in their areas in order to support Mayor Clarence V. Royce's re-election campaign. Overall, after much discussion, it was determined that the number of murders citywide must fall below 275 for the year. Moreover, no excuses for not meeting this target would be tolerated.

In the following scene, Burrell and Rawls hold a Compstat meeting with their district commanders to pass along the mayor's mandate:

> **Burrell:** Gentlemen, the word from on high is that felony rates district by district will decline by five percent by the end of the year.
> **Rawls:** We are dealing in certainties. You will reduce UCR felonies by five percent or more or, and I have always wanted to say this, Let no man come back alive!

Burrell: In addition, we will hold this year's murders to 275 or less.
Foerster: Christ!
Rawls: Feeling a little fazed, Colonel Foerster? A little dyspeptic?
Foerster: Dis-who? No, sir. I'm good to go.
Rawls: Here's a fun fact for you people. If Baltimore had New York's population, we'd be clocking 4000 murders a year at this rate. There is no excuse that I will accept. I don't care how you do it. Just fucking do it.
Colvin: Deputy, as familiar as we all are with the urban crime environment, I think we all understand that there are certain processes by which you can reduce the number of overall felonies. You can reclassify an agg assault or you can unfound a robbery but how do you make a body disappear?
Burrell: There isn't one of you in this room who isn't here by appointment. If you want to continue wearing those oak clusters, you will shut up and step up. Any of you who can't bring in the numbers we need will be replaced by someone who can. (Season 3, Episode 2)

Note that absolutely no attempt at strategy and program development are made. No direction is provided as to how to achieve the goals of reducing the felony rate and limiting homicides to 275 for the rest of the year. The statistical goals are just stated and ordered. Compstat meetings should be strategy sessions where data is analyzed to determine the nature of the problem to develop operational methods to deal with it effectively. It should be a collaborative process.

Additionally, to be effective, Compstat needs to be part of a process where the purpose is to identify and remedy the cause for the crimes. In short, it must be part of a problem-solving process (Godown, 2009). Rather than simply stating homicides must decrease, the appropriate approach would be to use Compstat to identify patterns associated with murders and related crimes.

In *The Wire*, the homicides presented take place as a result of the violent nature of the drug market in Baltimore. They personify Goldstein's (1985: 497) definition of "systemic violence" engendered by the illegal drug trade. These homicides are the result of competition between drug dealers for sales territory, violence used to enforce normative rules of operation, disputes between dealers and consumers, elimination of informers, punishment for selling adulterated or phony drugs, punishment for failure to pay debts, disputes over drug paraphernalia and robberies of drug dealers followed by retaliation (see Varano *et al.*, 2004). It has been clearly demonstrated that illegal drug markets tend to concentrate homicides and other violent incidents both spatially and temporally in those areas of a city where drugs are sold by gangs (Cohen *et al.*, 1998).

Research has also been shown that police operations to reduce homicides related to the systemic violence of the drug trade can be effective. Unlike stranger-to-stranger homicides, research reveals that specific police strategies and problem solving operations have impacted drug related homicides in Phoenix (McEwen, 2009) and Richmond, CA (White *et al.*, 2003). These problem solving operations were well planned and executed efforts that involved not only the police but community representatives and social agency operatives. In *The Wire*, the decrease in homicides was simply declared by Mayor Royce in an attempt to strengthen his re-election bid and echoed by Police Commissioner Burrell and Deputy Commissioner Rawls without any attempt at problem solving type planning. There are clear numerical goals but no direction is provided on how to achieve them.

A second area in which police departments err in the use of Compstat has to do with the nature of the weekly meetings. Ideally, Compstat meetings are used as a collaborative information sharing and problem solving enterprise. Frequently, however, this is not the case, with the meetings drifting toward one of two extremes. On one extreme you have what has been referred to as the bland (Behn, 2008). At this end of the spectrum, meetings resemble a "show and tell", consisting primarily of a series of PowerPoint slides, presenting glowing pictures and statistics of the unit's latest accomplishments. Little feedback is given and little is accomplished.

At the other extreme are meetings that are brutal. Compstat meetings are designed to hold commanders responsible for what occurs under their command. A primary means of promoting accountability is through instilling the fear that those commanders who do not meet expectations will be publicly humiliated (Eterno and Silverman, 2006). This fear, based on how others have been embarrassed at prior meetings, drives commanders to address the concerns of the administration and decrease the level of collaboration and problem solving activity.

The following moments from two Compstat meetings from *The Wire*, are consistent with the way meetings have been reported by police researchers (Willis, Mastrofski, and Weisburd, 2003: 23). In it, Deputy Commissioner of Operations William Rawls, a knowledgeable operative who is ruthless in his pursuit of complete accountability and awareness from his subordinates, and Acting Commissioner Burrell, question a district commander about murders committed in his district.

Rawls: Major, how many people under your command?
Taylor: 278, Sir.
Rawls: 278. And how many felony arrests did they make last month? (Taylor looks at his notes). Don't bother! You made 16. 16 in a month!

Same time period. How many hand guns you pick up? All shifts, all sectors? (Taylor flips through notes.) Once again, don't bother. The answer is none. None. You had four bodies last night in how many hours? (Taylor again checks notes.) Shut the fucking book! How many hours?
Taylor: Seven.
Rawls: Try five. (Picture of black youth shot in the head.) Tell me about this kid.
Taylor: I believe his name is James. James Toney.
Rawls: James Toney. When's the last time he was arrested? With who? Where's he sling? (Another picture of a black youth homicide.) How about this guy? Or him? Or him? (More homicide photos.) You know what? You got four bodies, all within two blocks of each other and you can't even start to connect the fucking dots. You got eight hours to get a grip on this mess or you're done. You hear me? Done! (Rawls makes a neck slitting motion.) (Season 3, Episode 2)

In a follow up Compstat meeting, Deputy Commissioner Rawls continues his assault upon Major Taylor.

Rawls: You're still not connecting the dots, Marvin. Have a look (picture on screen).
Taylor: Hoffman and Holbrook, sir.
Rawls: Very Good. But you had a body dropped there last week and this is what the fuck it looked like yesterday. (Photos show corners crowded with black youth.)
Taylor: Sir, I deployed my resources per your instructions. We've beefed up foot patrols we have our plainclothes squads on 12 hour shifts.
Rawls: And the corners stay full?
Taylor: They move, sir. Every day. They're gonna sell their drugs somewhere.
Rawls: Major Taylor, I look at your numbers, I see the intel reports, the photos. It all tells me that you lack a fucking clue.
Burrell: If you'll permit me. Is your deputy major present?
Taylor: Yes, Sir. (Deputy Creswich stands.)
Burrell: (to Deputy) You now command the Eastern District. Major Taylor, you are relieved. (Points to promoted Deputy.) Take the podium! Anyone else having trouble with the writing on the wall? Dismissed! (Season 3, Episode 3)

The Wire Compstat meetings present continual examples of management by intimidation. Rawls and Burrell make no attempts to coach their district commanders and provide valuable instruction based upon their experience and expertise. In particular, Rawls spends his time on intricate traps of belittle-ment that do nothing to enhance organizational performance. Under Rawls' direction, these Compstat meetings bear the hallmarks of a "status degradation ceremony" where "the public identity of the actor (in this case, the district commander) is transformed into something looked on as lower in the local scheme of social types" (Garfinkel, 1956: 20). There is no coaching or mentoring and no attempt to make accountability functional by bringing people along, build-ing talent and skill. Intimidation by top level managers will only breed contempt among the rest of the staff. The ultimate purpose of these Compstat meetings was to promote the political goals of the mayor and little else.

The Wire Compstat meetings do bear the bitter, albeit unintended fruit planted by intimidation. For example, in the following scene, which takes place in the men's room before the meeting where Taylor is dismissed, he complains to the Western District Commander, Bunny Colvin after he vom-its into a commode:

> **Taylor:** I can't take this shit, Bunny.
> **Colvin:** It'll pass. They're just riding you now. Next week, it will be some-body new. They can't take back your E.O.D., Marvin. The worst they can do is bust you back to lieutenant.
> **Taylor:** I don't even want to think about the worst these motherfuck-ers can do. You don't either. (Season 3, Episode 3)

Fear, not innovating thinking, is produced when Compstat meetings are a the-ater of humiliation. The District Commanders deal with the pressure in rather predictable ways.

It is not the setting of crime rate targets that is the problem in the meeting depicted in the show. The issue is how these targets are used to motivate in-dividuals and hold them accountable for performing operations as directed. Sample (2000: 27) reminds us that "under certain conditions the very process of measurement can affect the outcome of a measurement in unpredictable ways"—the very act of asking the question can dramatically skew the answer. Similarly, Tenbrunsel (2011: 61) describes how setting specific performance targets can affect how employees conduct the process of measurement. Such goals can lead them to neglect other areas, take undesirable "ends justify the means" risks, be dishonest in their reporting, or engage in unethical behavior that they would not otherwise do (such as the behavior mentioned by Cooper and Bolen in the previous chapter).

Eterno and Silverman (2006) believe that NYPD's Compstat process fell prey to some of these evils. Based upon their research and observation of

Compstat in action, they identified several flaws. The most notable problem is that Compstat's focus on crime reduction can lead police to ignore their "most fundamental goal"—protecting legal principles and democratic rights (Eterno and Silverman, 2006: 221). In addition, this focus promoted the perception that Compstat was a numbers game that used fear to drive the process. Berated by high level NYPD command officers, commanders feared presenting their crime information at Compstat meetings and "would do almost anything to escape the embarrassment of crime statistics going up" (Eterno and Silverman, 2006: 223). Furthermore, the commanders then tended to use fear to drive their charges to make arrests and generate statistics to promote crime reduction. Thus, the rank and file typically viewed Compstat as a numbers game where they were required to make more arrests and issue more summonses. They were not motivated by the process to fight crime, unless they were members of specialized crime units designed to address a particular problem, like drugs. In such an atmosphere, reducing crime at any cost can be an outcome.

In a survey and interview study of over 500 NYPD officers (at the rank of captain or above), Eterno and Silverman (2010) examined whether the Compstat process exuded pressure upon officers to record crime statistics in favorable ways—specifically, pressure to downgrade index crimes. The research group included officers who served both before and after Compstat was initiated. The retirees from the Compstat era reported that they felt significant pressure to decrease index crime (Eterno and Silverman, 2010: 434). They also noted that the demand for integrity in crime statistics was significantly less in the Compstat era and that promotions were more likely to be related to demonstrated decreases in the crime rate (Eterno and Silverman, 2010: 442). Thus, pressure and fear can lead subordinates to cheat on statistics, rather than develop inventive ways to reach performance targets. Such cheating on crime statistics was not only a common occurrence by the police in *The Wire*, it was expected, if not demanded by Rawls and Burrell.

Conclusion

Despite its negative portrayal in *The Wire*, performance-based management strategies have great potential and have achieved gains in effectiveness. For example, the use of a Compstat system in the White Plains, NY Police Department between 2002 and 2005 led to a 69 percent increase in arrests that resulted in a 32 percent decrease in crimes against the person and a 33 percent decrease in property crime. In addition, vehicle and traffic summonses rose by 81 percent and a 6.4 percent reduction in motor vehicle accidents (despite an increase in traffic flow) (O'Connell and Straub, 2007: 19). In the NYPD, Compstat remains in place despite a change in Mayors (from Giuliani to Bloomberg) and the three commissioners who have followed Bratton. In addition, it is a process that was manufactured and defined by police administrators with little guidance from academic intelligentsia and absolutely no governmental grant dollar support.

The use of technology is not enough. The technology must be used in a strategic fashion, both responding to current and future problems in innovative ways that build upon collaboration and support between units of the organization to achieve commonly held goals. Here, providing the best quality and most effective possible service to and for the public must be the hallmark, not maintaining political authority and personal power. This is the lesson of how the Compstat process is presented in *The Wire*.

However, the effectiveness of Compstat has been difficult to scientifically ascertain. The Committee to Review Research on Police Policy and Practices (National Research Council of the National Academies, 2004: 185) reached the following conclusion about Compstat:

> Compstat is a recent reform that many police leaders feel will revolutionize the management of police organizations. Very little objective empirical research has been done on Compstat or similar police management strategies. What is available suggests that it has changed the work practices of middle managers responsible for districts or precincts. However, the research also suggests a number of forces at work that limit the effects of Compstat and may even work at cross purposes. Much more research on the implementation of Compstat is needed before conclusions can be drawn.

The Committee drew particular attention to the key role of police middle managers in this process. They are "the mechanism by which the police organization is made responsive to the leadership of top management," they "take responsibility" for closely monitoring crime in their area and "devise and implement" programs to address these problems (National Research Council of the National Academies, 2004: 186; see also Vito, Walsh, and Kunselman, 2005; Walsh and Vito, 2004).

The impact of these approaches must be carefully evaluated. One basic premise is that the results of any operation need to be tied to the implementation of the services provided. In simple terms, crime suppression or prevention efforts are typically targeted at a particular type of crime. In the case of *The Wire*, drug dealing could be the target of a police problem solving operation (See Rengert, Ratcliffe, and Chakravorty, 2005). What was done to target drug dealing (arrests, seizures of both drugs and weapons) could be impact measures. Those measures must be the primary focus and must be considered first. Then, the evaluation can consider secondary measures, like impact upon the homicide rate. Compstat meetings can help coach and supervise the operations of such an effort—bringing the resources and expertise of the department to bear on a particular problem while monitoring its implementation and progress.

Dabney's (2010) observations of a department operating a Compstat model documents the same flaws presented in *The Wire*. Officers did not see the purpose of the Compstat system. They viewed it as a "number's game"—just generating numbers of arrests to make their immediate superiors look good at Compstat meetings, not as indicators of organizational performance under a strategic crime fighting model. From their point of view, there was little collaboration, communication or coordination between districts and their operations (Dabney, 2010: 39). Although the department was engaged in strategic planning and problem solving under a Compstat system, the purpose of accountability was not properly communicated to the line officers. To Dabney (2010: 42), this lack of communication is due to the fact that sergeants (the first line supervisors) were typically excluded from participation in Compstat meetings and were thus uninformed about the "strategic direction of the larger organization." Basically, successful application of Compstat requires that traditional supervisory roles within the police organization must change. The "strategy implementation process" should include all levels of the police organization. After all, the line officers are the people who do the actual work and they must be aware of the purpose of the Compstat process (More, Vito, and Walsh, 2012: 416–417).

Several lessons can be drawn from *The Wire's* version of Compstat. First, the operational flaws portrayed are not simply and solely endemic to Compstat. The focus on crime rate performance targets can become the sole focus of the process and the ultimate goal of effectively dealing with crime and its attendant problems is overlooked and obscured. Indeed, these imperfections would hamper any attempt to establish the foundation of an effective learning organization. Compstat is not a "silver bullet," and organizational panacea. As with any attempt at organizational reform, Compstat can only be as effective as its proper implementation and careful operation permits it to be. Second, more than anything else, Compstat relies upon the ability of the organization to function as a partnership between all members of a police department and the community that it serves in a spirit of collaboration and problem solving. The police can do something about crime problems but they can accomplish more when they work with others and plan their joint operations accordingly.

References

Behn, R. D. (2005). The Core Drivers of CitiStat: It's Not Just About the Meetings and the Maps. *International Public Management Journal*, 295–319.

Behn, R. D. (2008). *The Seven Big Errors of PerformanceStat*. Boston: Harvard University John F. Kennedy School of Government.

Bratton, W., & Knobler, P. (1998). *Turnaround: How America's Top Cop Reversed the Crime Epidemic*. New York: Random House.

Cohen, J., Cork, D., Engberg, J., & Tita, G. (1998). The Role of Drug Markets and Gangs in Local Homicide Rates. *Homicide Studies*, 241–262.

Dabney, D. (2010). Observations Regarding Key Organizational Realities in a Compstat Model of Policing. *Justice Quarterly*, 28–51.

Department, N. Y. (2011, May 15). *Compstat*. Retrieved June 5, 2011, from NYC.gov: http://www.nyc.gov/html/nypd/downloads/pdf/crime_statistics/cscity.pdf.

Eck, J., & Maguire, E. (2000). Have Changes in Policing Reduced Violent Crime? An Assessment of the Evidence. In A. Blumstein, & J. Wallman, *The Crime Drop in America* (pp. 207–265). New York: Cambridge University Press.

Eterno, J. A., & Silverman, E. B. (2006). The New York City Police Department's Compstat: Dream or Nightmare? *International Journal of Police Science & Management*, 218–231.

Eterno, J. A., & Silverman, E. B. (2010). The NYPD's Compstat: Compare Statistics or Compose Statistics? *International Journal of Police Science & Management*, 426–449.

Garfinkel, H. (1956). Conditions of Successful Degradation Ceremonies. *American Journal of Sociology*, 420–424.

Gilbert, J. N. (1983). A Study of the Increased Homicide Rate in San Diego California and Its Relationship to Police Effectiveness. *American Journal of Police*, 149–166.

Godown, J. (2009). "The Compstat Process: Four Principles for Managing Crime Reduction," *The Police Chief*, 76 (8): 36–42.

Goldstein, P. J. (1985). The Drugs/Violence Nexus: A Tripartite Conceptual Framework. *Journal of Drug Issues*, 493–506.

Henderson, L. J. (2003). *The Baltimore CitiStat Program: Performance and Accountability*. Baltimore: University of Baltimore.

Henry, W. E. (2002). *The Compstat Paradigm: Management Accountability in Policing*. New York: Looseleaf.

Hoover, L. T. (1998). Rationale for Police Program Evaluation. In L. T. Hoover, *Police Program Evaluation* (pp. 1–14). Washington, DC: Police Executive Research Forum.

Jacques, S., & Wright, R. (2008). The Relevance of Peace to Studies of Drug Market Violence. *Criminology*, 221–253.

Joanes, A. (1999–2000). Does the New York City Police Department Deserve Credit for the Decline in New York City's Homicide Rates? A Cross-City Comparison of Policing Strategies and Homicide Rates. *Columbia Journal of Law and Social Problems*, 265–311.

Kerik, B. B. (2001). *The Lost Son: A Life in Pursuit of Justice*. New York: Harper Collins.

Maple, J. (1999). *The Crime Fighter: Putting the Bad Guys Out of Business*. New York: Doubleday.

McDonald, P. P. (2002). *Managing Police Operations: Implementing the New York Crime Control Model—CompStat*. Stamford, CT: Thomson.

McEwen, T. (2009). *Evaluation of the Phoenix Homicide Clearance Project*. Alexandria, VA: Institute for Law and Justice.

More, H. W., Vito, G. F., & Walsh, W. F. (2012). *Organizational Behavior and Management in Law Enforcement*. Upper Saddle River, NJ: Pearson Education.

National Research Council of the National Academies. (2004). *Fairness and Effectiveness in Policing: The Evidence*. Washington, D.C.: The National Academies Press.

O'Connell, P. E., & Straub, F. (2007). *Performance-Based Management for Police Organizations*. Long Grove, IL: Waveland Press.

Ousey, G. C., & Lee, M. R. (2004). Investigating the Connections Between Race, Illicit Drug Markets, and Lethal Violence, 1984–1997. *Journal of Research in Crime and Delinquency*, 352–383.

Rengert, G. F., Ratcliffe, J. H., & Chakravorty, S. (2005). *Policing Illegal Drug Markets: Geographic Approaches to Crime Reduction*. Monsey, NY: Criminal Justice Press.

Safir, H. (1997, December). Goal-oriented Community Policing: The NYPD Approach. *The Police Chief*, pp. 31–58.

Sample, S. B. (2002). *The Contrarian's Guide to Leadership*. San Francisco: Jossey-Bass.

Sherman, L. W. (1997). Policing for Crime Prevention. In *Preventing Crime: What Works, What Doesn't, What's Promising—A Report to the Attorney General of the United States* (pp. 8–58). Washington: U.S. Department of Justice, Office of Justice Programs.

Silverman, E. B. (1999). *NYPD Battles Crime: Innovative Strategies in Policing.* Boston: Northeastern University Press.

Sugarman, B. (2010). Organizational Learning and Reform at the New York City Police Department. *The Journal of Applied Behavioral Science,* 157–185.

Tenbrunsel, A. E. (2011, April). Ethical Breakdowns. *Harvard Business Review,* pp. 58–67.

Timoney, J. F. (2010). *Beat Cop to Top Cop: A Tale of Three Cities.* Philadelphia: University of Pennsylvania Press.

Varano, S. P., McCluskey, J. D., Patchin, J. W., & Bynum, T. S. (2004). Exploring the Drugs-Homicide Connection. *Journal of Contemporary Criminal Justice,* 369–392.

Vito, G. F., Walsh, W. F., & Kunselman, J. (2005). Compstat: The Manager's Perspective. *International Journal of Police Science and Management,* 187–196.

Walsh, W. F. (2001). Compstat: An Analysis of an Emerging Police Managerial Paradigm. *Policing: An International Journal of Police Strategies & Management,* 347–362.

Walsh, W. F., & Vito, G. F. (2004). The Meaning of Compstat: Analysis and Response. *Journal of Contemporary Criminal Justice,* 51–69.

White, M. D., Fyfe, J. J., Campbell, S. P., & Goldkamp, J. S. (2003). The Police Role in Preventing Homicide: Considering the Impact of Problem-Oriented Policing on the Prevalence of Murder. *Journal of Research on Crime and Delinquency,* 194–225.

Willis, J. J., Mastrofski, S. D., & Weisburd, D. (2003). *Compstat in practice: an in-depth analysis of three cities.* Washington, DC: Police Foundation.

Study Questions

1. Is there a dark-side to Compstat? If yes, what are its dimensions? How may organizational goals shift from pre- to post-Compstat adoption and implementation? Does the inclusion of a results-based management scheme set the stage for unethical behavior? Why?

2. Should Compstat sessions be used to discipline officers and managers, or should the sessions be more geared towards identifying problems and focusing of the development of methods to deal with problems? Why?

3. Vito states that "the use of technology is not enough." What does he mean by this? How can technology—in particular crime statistics—be used for good and bad?

4. With the adoption of any policy, or group of policies, comes the need to evaluate impact, as Vito clearly notes. The question is … How do we go about evaluating something like Compstat?

5. How does a goal orientation, for example, a strong focus on crime rate performance targets, hamper the efforts of an organization to learn and become reformed? Has seeking answers to these questions changed your perceptions about Compstat and other similar programs? Why or Why not?

Section 3

City Politics and the War on Drugs

In this section, the authors tackle some of the most blaring drug-policy and local-political related issues presented in *The Wire*. The real-life patterns surrounding local politics, drug sales, use, and abuse and treatment in our inner-cities (and suburbs and rural areas) are reflected in nearly every episode of the entire five seasons of the show. These patterns of use and harm to individuals and to their communities did not just occur in the alternate reality of the show; they developed over time and were a result of policies directed towards drug control (policies which also targeted minority communities and the people who lived and still live there).

In Chapter 9, Sarah Reckow provides a glimpse into the world of local politics as depicted in *The Wire*. In taking an additional look at the role of politics in policy formation, we can begin to understand why many policies, such as those tied to the War on Drugs, may be perpetuated. She focuses her analysis on mayoral power, an integral aspect of urban law enforcement and a canopy hanging over the police department and educational system throughout the show's five seasons. As an issue both directly and indirectly referred to throughout the series, Reckow provides evidence of the role of race in city leadership, the bureaucratic reality that in many cases besets reform efforts of mayors (such as Carcetti), and she provides examples of how "political entrepreneurs" can combine formal and informal networks of power to have an increased effect on their objectives. Additionally, Reckow provides some of the background of the widespread adoption of measurement and accountability techniques, such as those discussed in the previous chapter.

In Chapter 10, Jennifer Balboni tackles the topical centerpiece of *The Wire*: the War on Drugs. Throughout the modern era of drug prohibition and the criminalization of drugs and drug addiction, there have been unintended consequences. Many policymakers have held uninformed, and continue to hold unrealistic, expectations of how drug control policies operate. This adherence to empirically unsupported policies has paved a highway to a systematic failure to realistically approach those most vulnerable to drug use and abuse and has led to increased incarceration of urban minorities, overfilled jails and prisons, and increased homelessness and recidivism in ex-offenders, to name just a few consequences.

In Chapter 11, Zachary Hamilton and Lauren Block focus on one of the most memorable and oft-cited occurrences presented in *The Wire*: Hamsterdam. The establishment of Hamsterdam sheds light on the extreme pressures faced by citizens and the criminal justice system in addressing the War on Drugs. In response to environmental/systematic pressures (i.e. revolving door of justice) and the top-down results and data-driven pressures (i.e. Compstat) felt within his own agency, Major Bunny Colvin risks his own career by employing novel methods in dealing with street-level drug dealing and use. As the authors note, Colvin's solution to the repeating patterns of drug sales and abuse, enforcement, incapacitation, and (re-)release was to redirect the behavior, contain it, monitor it, and begin supplying aid and oversight to both dealers and users; a general strategy referred to as *Harm Reduction*.

Hamilton and Block first briefly outline the current issues surrounding Drug Policy in the U.S., and outline a generalized definition and description of an alternative harm reduction strategy. The authors then provide a review of harm reduction as a prevention strategy, what harms are generally considered as targets for such policies (such as drug use, health, and crime), and issues with application and implementation of such programs. Throughout the chapter, they include empirical evidence centered on the impacts or effectiveness that such policies have had on those populations and communities that have risked breaking the failed business-as-usual mold that continues to drive drug-related policy in the U.S. and abroad. The authors conclude by highlighting the major impediments to the adoption and implementation of harm reduction strategies.

Chapter 9

"Respect the Depths": Campaign Rhetoric Meets Bureaucratic Reality

Sarah Reckhow

Introduction

As the fictional Mayor of Baltimore in *The Wire*, Tommy Carcetti is a highly ambitious politician determined to reform the police department in Baltimore and advance his own political career. Carcetti's first appearance in the series occurs at the beginning of Season 3; as chairman of the City Council Subcommittee for Public Safety, Carcetti grills Police Commissioner Burrell and Deputy Commissioner Rawls over rising crime rates. Yet Carcetti's twin ambitions— reforming the police department and seeking higher office—come into conflict once he is elected mayor, and he is faced with tough choices and limited resources.

Shortly after his primary election victory, Carcetti meets briefly with political consultants from Washington, D.C. hoping to groom him for a run as Governor of Maryland. This meeting demonstrates Carcetti's high-flying ambitions as mayor, but also foreshadows the challenges he will face. Everyone agrees that Carcetti should aim for a "ten percent drop in crime" and a major development project with his name on it. One of the consultants comments that "education always polls good." Yet Carcetti's advisor, Norman Wilson, argues that Carcetti should stay away from Baltimore's troubled school system, adding "you gotta respect the depths." Carcetti follows this advice, paying little attention to education while focusing heavily on reforming the police department. Although Wilson was speaking about the school system, Carcetti soon finds that respecting the depths is a much broader lesson, whether those depths are the city's deep social problems or the deeply ingrained and entrenched practices of the bureaucracy he is trying to reform.

This scene highlights several important features of mayoral power and urban bureaucracies. First, mayors do have flexibility when selecting priorities and setting their agenda, such as the choice to focus on public safety and reforming the police department, rather than reforming public education. In particular, mayors in cities with a strong-mayor form of government (such as Baltimore) have considerable power to set the agenda for their time in office. Nonetheless, mayors face substantial constraints when trying to enact their policy priorities, and there are many factors which make urban bureaucracies, including police departments, resistant to change. The experiences of real big city mayors show that there are circumstances when mayors can become "policy entrepreneurs" and implement significant reforms. Yet these circumstances are limited, and mayors are often frustrated by the constraints on their powers and the challenges of reforming large complex institutions like police departments and school systems. Increasingly, mayors are relying on a common set of strategies to monitor and evaluate bureaucratic performance, rather than reforming the internal processes or structure of bureaucracies.

In this chapter, I begin by discussing the powers of big city mayors, and the distinction between formal and informal powers. Next, I highlight the role of the race of the mayor, and discuss how race can shape access to informal power. Then I explain specific factors that make urban bureaucracies, including police departments, resistant to change, such as their importance for city employment, their internal bureaucratic culture, the inherent sources of tension between politicians and bureaucrats, and financial constraints. Acknowledging these limitations, I introduce the concept of political entrepreneurship and show examples of circumstances when mayors do matter. Lastly, I discuss the growing focus on measurement and accountability of bureaucracies among big city mayors, and the role of former Baltimore Mayor Martin O'Malley — often cited as an "inspiration" for Carcetti's character — in leading this trend.

Strong Mayors

Baltimore has a strong-mayor form of government, meaning that the mayor of Baltimore has the power to develop the city's budget and appoint heads of city departments. New York City, Chicago, and Philadelphia are also strong mayor cities. In cities with a weak mayor, or council-manager form of government, the mayor has limited executive authority; the city council has greater control over the city administration, and some administrative agencies may operate independently from city government. A city manager oversees city departments and is responsible for developing the annual budget. Council-manager forms of government are most common in smaller cities, though some larger cities in the South and West, such as Charlotte, NC and San Jose, CA have council-manager systems. Strong-mayor forms of government are more prevalent in large cities like Baltimore, particularly in the Northeast and Midwest, and these mayors have greater formal power to pursue their priorities for the city.

The importance of the strong-mayor form of government is particularly evident when a new mayor is elected. The election of a new mayor in a strong-mayor city leads to greater policy change than re-electing the existing mayor; in contrast, the election of a new mayor does not produce significant policy change in weak-mayor cities (Wolman, Strate, and Melchior, 1996). Drawing on specific examples, there is evidence of changes ushered in by newly elected mayors in strong-mayor cities, seeking to implement their campaign promises and make their mark on city policy. Strong mayors have the power to select city department heads—for new mayors this authority allows them to distinguish their administration and leadership from that of their predecessor. Newly elected mayors, such as Rahm Emanuel in Chicago, Cory Booker in Newark, Adrian Fenty in Washington, D.C., and Michael Nutter in Philadelphia each named new police commissioners at the beginning of their term in office. Mayors often try to set the tone for their approach to crime and public safety with the selection of a new chief of police, such as Mayor Giuliani's selection of William Bratton to implement zero tolerance policing.

As a newly elected mayor who focused on crime and public safety during the campaign, one would expect *The Wire's* fictional mayor—Tommy Carcetti—to begin his term in office by appointing a new head of the police department. Yet unlike several real big city mayors, Carcetti is not able to begin his term as mayor by appointing a new police commissioner. Although he has the formal power to do so, informal constraints tie Carcetti's hands. First, there is the issue of race—as a white mayor in a majority black city, Carcetti's advisors insist that it would be unwise to fire a sitting black police commissioner. Second, there is the issue of Carcetti's rival on the city council, Nerese Campbell, who is unwilling to support a salary increase that would enable Carcetti to initiate a national search for a new commissioner. Thus, Carcetti tries to work within these constraints, promoting Cedric Daniels to groom him as a future police commissioner.

Although Carcetti's story diverges from the experiences of mayors like Giuliani, Booker, Fenty, and Emanuel, Carcetti's struggle over replacing Burrell points to an important distinction between formal and informal powers. Formal powers primarily derive from an individual's position within a hierarchy; informal powers primarily derive from horizontal relationships and are related to factors such as group identity or group membership (Etzioni, 1975). Focusing on formal powers alone, strong mayors can appear quite powerful, with their authority to propose the city's budget, appoint department heads, and oversee day-to-day management of the city. Yet even a strong mayor can be rather weak with respect to informal powers. Carcetti's identity as a white mayor in a majority-black city weakens his informal power, particularly when race is highly salient for a particular issue. Meanwhile, strong ties within Baltimore's black community are a key source of informal power; for example, the city's black church leaders, frequently referred to simply as "the ministers," are an important political constituency which receives frequent attention from the Carcetti administration. How does the race of the mayor affect the ways he or she governs the city? Or does the race of the mayor really matter?

The Role of Race

For Carcetti, a defining feature of his political career in Baltimore seems to be race—he is a white mayor in a majority-black city. From this perspective, it would seem that race plays an overwhelming role in mayoral leadership. Yet research on this topic suggests that the race of the mayor does not matter as much as one might expect. Campaign contests between candidates of different races are often heated and frequently lead to racially polarized voting in the urban electorate (Kaufman, 2004). Nonetheless, governing outcomes do not appear to differ dramatically when a city elects a black mayor rather than a white mayor.

A recent study examined revenue, spending, and employment patterns in cities that elected a black mayor instead of a non-black mayor by a narrow margin (Hopkins and McCabe, 2010). The authors looked for evidence of policy change based on tax rates, city employees, and spending patterns in several policy areas, such as health, housing, and parks, but found no significant differences. The single policy area where the election of a black mayor makes a significant difference is policing. For example, black mayors increase the percent of black police officers, but the authors did not find a significant change in the share of black city employees in other departments. Other scholars have noted that civilian review boards for police departments are frequently promoted and established by black elected officials (Browning, Marshall, and Tabb, 1984). This link is also represented in *The Wire*; in Season 4, a group of African American ministers ask Carcetti to consider establishing a civilian review board for the police after a minister is accosted by Sergeant "Herc" Hauk. One of the ministers reminds Carcetti, "We've asked for a civilian review board for decades now." After the ministers leave the meeting, Carcetti protests to his advisor, Norman Wilson: "If they couldn't get civilian review out of a Royce administration, how can they think they're gonna get it from me?" Carcetti's comments implicitly refer to the role of race in the establishment of civilian review boards for police; Carcetti mentions Clarence Royce, the black mayor who preceded him in office, suggesting that Royce would have been more likely than Carcetti to establish a review board.

Yet the hiring of more black police officers and establishment of civilian review boards are a fairly limited set of policy consequences. Beyond these policies related to public safety and the police department, scholars have shown few links between the race of the mayor and policy outcomes. The lack of findings in this area may be a problem of inadequate data for evaluating the relationship between the race of the mayor and policy outcomes. Most of the outcomes that political scientists have measured are relatively blunt—such as the number of black employees in various city departments or the percent of the city budget devoted to different departments. A more thorough study could examine how resources are distributed within the city by population or geography; for example, investigating how city resources are distributed between predominantly black neighborhoods and predominantly white neighborhoods. Future research may provide more complete answers to questions about how the race of the mayor impacts governing outcomes.

Even so, there are some reasons to expect that electing a black mayor instead of a white mayor may not produce significant policy change. One explanation for the relatively limited policy consequences of electing black mayors is the "hollow prize" problem (Kraus and Swanstrom, 2001). The hollow prize problem focuses attention on the timing and circumstances of the first black mayoral victories. Many cities elected their first black mayor during the 1970s, 80s, and 90s. City budgets became increasingly constrained during these decades, and many cities were ill-equipped to serve an increasingly poor and racially segregated urban population. For central cities, this was a period of economic decline, growing poverty, and diminishing federal aid. On average, cities governed by minority mayors have substantially higher rates of poverty than cities governed by white mayors. Thus, the election of a black mayor in a struggling high-poverty city could be viewed as a hollow prize—the opportunity to govern in a context of severely limited resources. In this context, the race of the mayor could be far less consequential than the constraints that make significant policy change extremely difficult or unlikely.

Although quantitative research has produced limited findings relating the race of the mayor to policy consequences, qualitative case studies of city politics have illuminated links between race, informal alliances, and governing outcomes. Specifically, the concept of an urban regime focuses on the relationships between officials in city government and non-governmental actors who can supply resources and support for policy outcomes. This concept was developed by Clarence Stone through his work in Atlanta. Stone (1989) shows that Atlanta's urban regime involved an alliance between a black mayor, black civil rights leaders, and the white business community. The resulting bi-racial coalition produced some advances in civil rights as well as considerable investment in downtown redevelopment, leveraging public and private resources. Nonetheless, the redevelopment projects led to neighborhood destruction and social disruption, and little was done to address the city's high poverty rate. In *The Wire*, Mayor Royce's term in office shares some characteristics with Atlanta's urban regime. Royce is closely aligned with wealthy developers, and his policies are focused on building up the city's tax base with downtown development projects. He also pursues housing redevelopment, through the removal of Baltimore's high rise public housing projects, and the promise of new mixed income developments. Yet we see little evidence during the Royce administration of efforts to address poverty and or improve conditions in Baltimore's neighborhoods.

Although the race of the mayor appears to have limited policy consequences based on quantitative research, close examination through case studies suggests that race can have important consequences, depending on the particular circumstances that a mayor faces. Based on the hollow prize problem, minority mayors often face substantial challenges in the cities they govern. On the other hand, through coalition building—particularly through coalitions involving the business community—mayors may gain informal power and opportunities to leverage private resources for public projects. These alliances can be particularly attractive in a city with a dwindling tax base. Yet coalitions involve compromise, and the most vulnerable urban residents are often ignored.

Bureaucratic Reality

Informal power can also shape the mayor's ability to reform city bureaucracies. Although the mayor officially has the power to appoint a new department head and guide the policy direction of city departments, these bureaucracies are often guided by their own internal cultures as well as the relationship between the bureaucracy and the community that it serves. If mayors try to disrupt these existing patterns of behavior in order to achieve reform, they are likely to encounter resistance.

Carcetti learns early that his plans to reform Baltimore's police department will be difficult to enact. After Carcetti realizes that he cannot replace Commissioner Burrell, he tries to promote different approaches to policing by going around Burrell. Carcetti works to reorient the department's strategy toward major crimes and community policing, but he soon discovers that a budget crisis in the school system will interfere with his plans. Even before Carcetti learns of the budget deficit, there are signals that his new priorities for policing strategies may not produce significant change. When Deputy Commissioner Rawls shares the mayor's ideas with his commanders, the reaction is cynical; one commander comments, "Our people were raised on stats" (Season 4, Episode 11).

Bureaucracies and large organizations are often characterized by an internal culture, or regularized approaches to tasks and relationships (Wilson, 1989). This internal culture can have positive effects on the bureaucracy—reinforcing a common mission and identity for the agency. Yet bureaucratic culture can also have negative effects, and it can slow down or halt efforts to reform bureaucracies. A specific negative consequence of a strong bureaucratic culture is resistance to new tasks (Wilson, 1989: 107). Bureaucrats who see themselves and their agency a certain way are likely to be reluctant to accept new strategies that suggest a different image of their role. For example, some of the police officers working the Western District in *The Wire* refer to the "Western District way" when they make drug busts and use verbal and physical threats with street level drug dealers. For these officers, the solidarity they enjoy while doing things the "Western District way" reinforces their conception of the police department's culture. For Carcetti and others who hope to reform policing strategies in Baltimore—such as Bunny Colvin—this bureaucratic culture produces considerable inertia.

Another source of resistance to change, particularly in large urban bureaucracies, is their importance as a source of stable well-paying jobs for city residents. Furthermore, access to city jobs in agencies like police departments and school systems became an important way for many African-American families to reach the middle class after the 1960s. This source of upward mobility expanded during a time when other opportunities for social mobility, such as manufacturing employment, were becoming increasingly scarce in U.S. cities (Orr, 1999). According to Marion Orr, the school system was "the linchpin of Baltimore's black employment base" by the 1990s (Orr, 1999: 68). African-American politicians and advocacy groups recognized this important link between jobs that support the black middle class and city bureaucracies. Thus, reform strategies that might pose a threat to these jobs, such as private contracting, restructuring, and hiring non-city residents, often encounter strong opposition.

Moreover, there are sources of tension between politicians and bureaucrats. Politicians and bureaucrats are generally expected to perform different types of tasks, but their roles frequently overlap and intersect, which can create conflict. Scholars often refer to the politics-administration dichotomy. Rather than describing the real world, this dichotomy represents an idealized division of labor between politicians and administrators: politicians are responsible for making policy and administrators are responsible for carrying out these policies. This ideal division of labor was primarily intended to shield administrators from the messy entanglements of politics, allowing them to carry out their tasks with efficient neutrality. In reality, these responsibilities are rarely divided neatly and politics frequently creeps into bureaucratic tasks. For example, administrators often find that policies are vague, forcing administrators to make critical policy decisions in order to implement policy. Sometimes bureaucrats become particularly adept at politics, because their role involves placating multiple constituencies—Commissioner Burrell's actions in Season 4 offer a good illustration of this point. While Carcetti is hoping to sideline Burrell as he prepares Major Daniels for leadership of the department, Burrell suddenly reveals his value to Carcetti for political purposes. Major Daniels had chosen a light punishment for Sergeant "Herc" Hauk in response to the complaints raised by the ministers. Burrell explains the problems with this approach to Carcetti, adding, "I know what a mayor needs." Burrell suggests that Daniels did not fully understand the politics of the situation, and that Burrell can provide a solution that will satisfy the ministers (Season 4, Episode 11). Thus, the mayor finds his position weakened when faced with a politically skillful bureaucrat.

Lastly, mayoral power and efforts to reform bureaucracy are often limited by the reality of city budgets. Unlike the federal government, cities must balance their budgets annually. If the city is receiving fewer revenues from taxes or state and federal grants, then the city must cut spending or raise taxes. If a particular department in city government requires more funds, then other departments must bear the cuts, unless the city is able to raise more revenue. City budgets have become increasingly strained since the financial crisis and the late 2000s recession. Tax revenues declined, and more recently, states and the federal government have started cutting programs that provide funding to local governments. In order to balance budgets in many cities, police officers and school teachers are being furloughed or laid off and hiring freezes have been implemented. Carcetti faces these kinds of tough choices when he learns about the school budget deficit (Season 4, Episode 12).Although the Governor offers Carcetti funding assistance for the schools—in exchange for more state oversight—Carcetti refuses. This plotline is drawn directly from real events in Baltimore. In 2004, the Baltimore City Public Schools faced a $58 million deficit;

Mayor Martin O'Malley refused state assistance and bailed out the schools using the city's "rainy day fund." Like Carcetti, O'Malley regarded the sitting Republican governor, Robert Ehrlich, as a political rival. Yet the consequences of refusing state assistance for the schools end in pain for the police department. By the opening episode of Season 5, we learn that the police department will face additional funding cuts. Meanwhile, Carcetti continues to demand reductions in crime—still hoping to achieve the goals he set when he plotted his course to run for governor.

Thus, even with the formal powers of a strong-mayor, big city mayors face many constraints when they try to change the policies and practices of urban bureaucracies. The internal culture of city agencies, the role of bureaucracies as a source of stable middle-class jobs in the city, the tensions and overlap between bureaucrats and politicians, and the reality of city budgets can limit the mayor's ability to enact reforms. Nonetheless, some mayors do become widely known for major policy initiatives and bureaucratic reforms—how do these mayors overcome constraints to accomplish reform?

Political Entrepreneurs

Robert Dahl (1961) introduced the concept of a "political entrepreneur" in his classic study of city politics, *Who Governs?* Political entrepreneurs are skillful leaders who gather political resources to gain influence; using their heightened influence, these leaders can have substantial effects on policies and institutions. In other words, political entrepreneurs are able to effectively combine formal and informal powers and use these powers to achieve their objectives. Although Carcetti aspires to political entrepreneurship, we never see him achieve an effective combination of political resources or formal and informal powers. Rather than shaping events, Carcetti is forced to deal with crises—the school budget deficit, the bodies found in vacant houses, the fake serial killer—as they arise. Although Carcetti builds some important political alliances during his campaign—for example, gaining the support of Delegate Watkins—he is not able to translate these alliances into sufficient political capital to achieve his objectives. Despite an occasional ribbon cutting and headline-grabbing press conference, Carcetti appears rather weak as mayor.

Unlike Carcetti, a successful political entrepreneur has the skill to gather and use political resources to define the agenda and achieve change. For some mayors, this occurs through single-minded focus on a particular issue. In New York City, Mayor Giuliani cut spending in other areas and privatized some services, while focusing most of his energy on the police department (Flanagan, 2004). Resources within the department were targeted toward policing minor public nuisance crimes, in order to implement zero tolerance policing. Giuliani gained acclaim for the apparent success of the zero tolerance policing strategy, but the substantial reductions in New York City's crime rate during the 1990s likely has many causes, including improving economic conditions (Corman and Mocan, 2005). Despite his success, Giuliani gradually saw his authority erode on public safety issues during his second term. Aggressive policing led to complaints and protests, and high profile cases involving use of lethal force and police brutality drew considerable criticism to the zero tolerance policing. Rather than acknowledging these concerns, Giuliani "refused to take seriously the interest groups and minority leaders that complained about his policing strategies" (Flanagan, 2004: 189). These conflicts eroded Giuliani's ability to advance additional reforms during his second term, and his mayoralty was ultimately defined by his response to the World Trade Center terrorist attacks.

Mayors can also use events to amass the political capital necessary to make difficult changes. In Los Angeles, the mayor is weak, lacking many powers of a strong mayor system; the city council is powerful and city agencies have considerable independence from city government. Mayor Tom Bradley, the first and only African-American mayor of Los Angeles, served from 1973 to 1993. Bradley was a former police officer who hoped to bring the Los Angeles Police Department (LAPD) under greater control of the city government. Yet Bradley could not directly appoint the police commissioner, and commissioners could hold the job for life. For Bradley, a series of devastating events toward the end of his twenty years as mayor provided the political opportunity for far-reaching reform of the police department. The beating of Rodney King by Los Angeles police officers in 1991 was the first crisis. Bradley called for the resignation of the police commissioner and appointed the Christopher Commission to review LAPD practices. The commission's recommendations supported many of the reforms that Bradley favored, such as procedures for civilian complaints against the police and greater oversight of the LAPD by elected officials; the report drew a broader set of supporters toward Bradley's position on police reform (Sonenshein, 1993). Following the acquittal of the officers involved in the beating of Rodney King, the Los Angeles riots led to 50 deaths and $450 million in property damage. Although the riots were deeply destructive for the city and for Bradley's political standing, they offered one last opportunity to reform the LAPD. Under pressure from Bradley, the police commissioner finally resigned, and the city passed a referendum to implement many of the Christopher Commission's recommendations. Bradley's battle with the police department extended through his entire 20 years in office, but "[a]fter years of tension between the mayor and the quasi-independent police department,

Bradley was able to change the bureaucracy on favorable terms" (Flanagan, 2004: 103).

Political entrepreneurship requires considerable skill to amass the required resources and recognize opportunities. Although both strong mayors and weak mayors can act as political entrepreneurs, this type of leadership is most commonly associated with strong mayor systems. In *The Wire*, we largely observe the failure of political entrepreneurship during Carcetti's career as mayor. Yet Carcetti's situation also speaks to a broader set of challenges for big-city mayors. Modern mayors often have fewer resources to support transformational changes to urban policy and city bureaucracies. Thus improving efficiency and doing "more with less" have become dominant preoccupations of mayors and city administrators. Some mayors have focused on data collection and monitoring to hold bureaucracies accountable. This "results-based" approach assumes that bureaucracies will change their practices in order to meet higher standards and deliver services more efficiently.

Measurement and Accountability

The Wire is relentlessly critical of the ways that "stats" are used to monitor performance in both the police department and the school system in Baltimore. Scenes from *The Wire* show police commanders and principals exhorting police officers and teachers that "crime will fall by 10 percent" or "test scores will rise by 10 percent." Yet the officers and teachers know that they are not being asked to make real changes that will significantly improve public safety or education in Baltimore, nor do they receive additional support or resources to reach higher expectations. At a faculty meeting in Roland Pryzbylewski's school, the teachers are informed that they must begin test prep focused on language arts sample questions for the state exams. Prez notes the similarity to the manipulation of crime statistics at the police department, calling the practice "juking the stats" (Season 4, Episode 9).

Although *The Wire* presents an important critique of the use of data for performance evaluation in big city bureaucracies, the show tells only one side of the story. Among public administrators and big city mayors, Baltimore has become a national model for the use of statistics to monitor the delivery of city services and improve bureaucratic efficiency. Shortly after his election as Mayor of Baltimore in 1999, Martin O'Malley introduced CitiStat. The initiative was directly modeled on the Compstat program used by the New York City Police Department (Sanger, 2008). Rather than focusing solely on the police department, CitiStat was a broad performance monitoring strategy for all city agencies. Indicators such as trash collection, snow removal, and pothole abatement are all measured by CitiStat. Considerable cost savings and performance improvements have been attributed to CitiStat since its inception. The program reportedly saved the city $13.2 million in its first year of implementation, including $6 million in overtime pay (Perez and Rushing, 2007). City employee absenteeism dropped significantly. In 2004, CitiStat received an Innovations in American Government award from Harvard's Kennedy School of Government.

Many features of CitiStat will be familiar to viewers of *The Wire*, as they resemble the police department's Compstat (as noted by Vito in the previous chapter) meetings depicted in the series. CitiStat involves specific performance targets, much like the crime reduction targets announced by Rawls and Burrell in Compstat meetings in *The Wire*. For example, O'Malley established a 48-hour target for filling potholes reported by citizens (Behn, 2007). The frequent meetings are also a common feature—CitiStat meetings in Baltimore occur every other week. Another similarity is the room arrangement for CitiStat meetings—much like the Compstat meetings in *The Wire*, the spotlight is on the podium. According to Robert Behn:

> The most obvious feature of Baltimore's Citistat room is the podium. Behind this podium ... stands the director of the agency whose performance is being discussed. Occasionally, the first deputy mayor or the agency director will call other agency managers to the podium. This podium is not essential. A CitiStat session could be conducted with everyone sitting around a large conference table or in a variety of other settings. Nevertheless, the podium does possess symbolic significance. The individual at the podium is the only one in the room who is standing. Everyone else in the room is focused (both visually and mentally) on this person. (Or persons; sometimes two or maybe three people are standing behind the podium.) Thus, the podium dramatizes who is responsible—who is responsible both for answering the specific question now being discussed and for the general overall operation of the broader issue of performance being examined (Behn, 2007: 25).

While agency heads speak from the podium, they face a table where the Mayor, Deputy Mayor, and Director of Citistat are typically seated. Again, this is echoed in scenes from *The Wire*, where Rawls and Burrell are seated with stern faces, while their district commanders squirm at the podium.

One distinguishing feature of CitiStat—as opposed to Compstat—is the central role of mayoral leadership. CitiStat is a broad management strategy for all of city government. By bringing together all major city department heads regularly to review performance data, CitiStat has the potential to centralize mayoral authority and remind the directors of bureaucratic agencies of their accountability to the mayor. A second distinguishing feature is that CitiStat involves systematic data collection from citizens, in addition to data gathered by the city. Through Baltimore's 311 system, citizens can report problems and request city services over the phone or online. These data are gathered, analyzed, and incorporated into CitiStat.

CitiStat has become a model for other big city mayors, and it has spread to several local and state governments. Dozens of mayors have toured the CitiStat office in Baltimore, and several cities have copied the model, including Washington, D.C., Atlanta, Chattanooga, Providence, San Francisco, and Syracuse (Behn, 2006). More recently, Newark Mayor Cory Booker has announced his intention to implement CitiStat in his city. After he was elected Governor of Maryland, O'Malley brought the model to the state level, establishing StateStat. Governor Gregoire implemented a similar system in the State of Washington (Behn, 2007). A few factors have likely contributed to the popularity of CitiStat. First, the system reflects a strong trend among public administration scholars and practitioners toward emphasizing government efficiency and performance. This trend can be traced to the 1990s and the "reinventing government" movement, popularized by a 1992 book by David Osborne and Ted Gaebler as well as by Al Gore's efforts as Vice President to streamline the federal government. Second, CitiStat is compatible with the basic fiscal realities of city government—it is relatively cheap. The start-up cost for CitiStat in Baltimore was just $20,000; operating costs are more substantial—around $500,000—but these funds largely cover salary and benefits of CitiStat staff. Compared to other reform strategies, CitiStat appears remarkably cost effective, and offers the potential to save the city money by improving departmental efficiency.

Thus, although *The Wire* has made a fictionalized Baltimore into a model of "juking the stats," the real city of Baltimore has gained positive national attention for showing how mayors can use data to monitor city agencies. Unfortunately, the reality of data and performance monitoring in Baltimore makes the warning signs depicted in *The Wire* seem prescient. In the spring of 2010, Baltimore police officials decided to suspend use of Compstat while the system was reevaluated. A news article on the suspension reported that Compstat "meetings have been criticized by some officers who say they often devolve into brow beatings" (Fenton, 2010). Meanwhile, in 2011, Maryland state education officials revealed evidence of "widespread cheating" on state assessment tests at two Baltimore elementary schools (Green, 2011). Unfortunately, the cheating scandal in Baltimore's schools appears to be part of a broader pattern, as extensive cheating on standardized tests has also been uncovered in Atlanta and Washington, D.C. public schools.

These incidents are reminders of an important maxim in social science, known as "Campbell's Law," developed by psychologist Donald Campbell. According to Campbell's law, "The more any quantitative social indicator is used for social decision-making, the more subject it will be to corruption pressures and the more apt it will be to distort and corrupt the social processes it is intended to monitor." Thus, although the desire of mayors and other officials to monitor performance may be based on good motives—the promotion of efficiency and improvement of performance—the very act of measuring and linking measurements to evaluation and decision-making creates strong incentives for cheating and distortion. For many new systems for performance monitoring, including No Child Left Behind, Compstat, and CitiStat, Campbell's law creates a serious dilemma. Officials may have to accept the inevitable prospect of cheating, which will compromise the integrity of the monitoring system. Or they may have to invest substantial resources in security and monitoring of cheating, which could be both financially costly and costly for public employee morale.

Conclusion

Mayor Carcetti's character and the political events depicted in *The Wire* effectively show many of the challenges and constraints of governing a large U.S. city. Although Carcetti ultimately succeeds at following his political ambitions to the governor's mansion, his term as Mayor of Baltimore produces disappointing results, given the promises for reform and crime reduction he touted during the campaign. Despite his access to the formal powers of a strong mayor, Carcetti is limited by many factors, some beyond his control, including race, bureaucratic inertia, and fiscal challenges.

The depiction of politics in *The Wire* emphasizes the limits on human agency, and the weakness of individual leaders in the face of dysfunctional and ossified institutions. Similar themes are echoed in many of the subjects tackled in the show, including policing, education, unions, and the media. For viewers of the show, particularly those who are inclined towards urban research or direct engagement with urban policy, *The Wire* is a powerful reminder of the factors that make change so difficult. On the other hand, the show tends to overlook factors that can enable transformative leadership. Mayors who gather political resources, build urban regimes, join together formal and informal powers, and strategically use events to further their agenda, can and do achieve significant policy change in the cities where they govern.

Nonetheless, *The Wire* also provides powerful reminders of the unintended consequences of well-intentioned policy reforms. Martin O'Malley's legacy as Mayor of Baltimore is largely defined by CitiStat. This performance evaluation system has spread to other cities and has been credited with substantial cost savings for city government. However, *The Wire* reminds us of the potential for negative consequences from this type of monitoring system, and the likelihood of cheating and manipulation. Programs like CitiStat are not unique in this regard; policy reforms often lead to unintended consequences, sometimes with far-reaching negative effects that leaders could not anticipate. From the War on Drugs to school reform, this narrative permeates *The Wire*, offering a sobering and important lesson for future political entrepreneurs.

References

Behn, Robert D. 2006. "The Varieties of CitiStat." Public Administration Review. 66(3): 332–340.

Behn, Robert D. 2007. "What All Mayors Would Like to Know About Baltimore's CitiStat Performance Strategy." Managing for Performance and Results Series. IBM Center for Business and Government.

Browning, Rufus P., Dale R. Marshall, and David H. Tabb. 1984. *Protest is not enough: The struggle of Blacks and Hispanics for equality in urban politics.* University of California Press: Berkeley.

Corman, Hope and Naci Mocan. 2005. "Carrots, Sticks, and Broken Windows." *Journal of Law and Economics.* 48(1): 235–266.

Dahl, Robert A. 2005. *Who Governs? Democracy and Power in an American City.* 2nd Ed. Yale University Press: New Haven.

Etzioni, Amitai. 1975. *A Comparative Analysis of Complex Organizations: On Power, Involvement, and Their Correlates.* Simon and Schuster.

Fenton, Justin. 2010. "Baltimore Police Idle Compstat Meetings." *The Baltimore Sun.* April 9. http://articles.baltimoresun.com/2010-04-09/news/bal-md.ci.comstat08apr09_1_comstat-police-department-s-operations-anthony-g uglielmi.

Flanagan, Richard M. 2004. *Mayors and the Challenge of Urban Leadership.* University Press of America: New York.

Green, Erica. 2011. "Cheating, Tampering Found in City Schools." *The Baltimore Sun.* June 23.

Hopkins, Daniel J. and Katherine T. McCabe. 2010. "After It's Too Late: Estimating the Policy Impacts of Black Mayors Using Regression Discontinuity Design." Working Paper. Georgetown University.

Kaufman, Karen. 2004. *The Urban Voter: Group Conflict and Mayoral Voting Behavior in American Cities.* The University of Michigan Press: Ann Arbor.

Kraus, Neil and Todd Swanstrom. 2001. "Minority Mayors and the Hollow-Prize Problem." *PS: Political Science and Politics.* 34(1): 99–105.

Orr, Marion. 1999. *Black Social Capital: The Politics of School Reform in Baltimore: 1986–1998.* University Press of Kansas: Lawrence.

Perez, Teresita and Reece Rushing. 2007. "The CitiStat Model: How Data-Driven Government Can Increase Efficiency and Effectiveness." Center for American Progress.

Sanger, Mary Bryna. 2008. "From Measurement to Management: Breaking Through the Barriers to State and Local Performance." *Public Administration Review.* 68(s1): S70–S85.

Sonenshein, Raphael J. 1993. *Politics in Black and White: Race and Power in Los Angeles.* Princeton University Press: Princeton.

Stone, Clarence N. 1989. *Regime Politics: Governing Atlanta, 1946–1988.* University Press of Kansas: Lawrence.

Wilson, James Q. 1989. *Bureaucracy: What Government Agencies Do and Why They Do It.* Basic Books: New York.

Wolman, Harold, John Strate, and Alan Melchior. 1996. "Does Changing Mayors Matter?" *The Journal of Politics.* 58(1): 201–223.

Study Questions

1. What are the benefits and costs of re-electing an existing mayor in a strong-mayor city? How about when electing a new mayor? How does this differ from a council-manager city?

2. Does the race of a mayor influence policy making? Is the influence stronger just after election? Why or why not?

3. How does the "hollow prize" problem explain policy making in cities electing a black mayor? What impact, if any, does building interracial coalitions have on the "hollow prize" problem?

4. Internal culture often guides city bureaucracies and leads to difficulty in effecting change within them. What are the specific challenges or benefits of an internal culture when trying to effect change?

5. Discuss the concept of a "political entrepreneur". What is needed for a political entrepreneur to be successful? How might certain events affect opportunities for success?

6. Define "Campbell's Law". How does this relate to the use of Compstat or Citistat and the use of these tools in measuring success of a mayor or other city bureaucracy?

Chapter 10

The War on Drugs through *The Wire's* Looking Glass

Jennifer M. Balboni

Introduction

HBO's *The Wire* presents a picture of Baltimore inner city neighborhoods at a particular point in history: the crime and violence, the strained relationships between the police and the community, the kinship, the frustration and (sometimes) hopelessness in the first decade of the new millennium. But this story was, in fact, built in large part upon political decisions made in prior decades. What you see in the characters is a direct consequence of real policies tied to the War on Drugs that began in the seventies, and ramped up in the eighties and nineties. The drug war in many ways changed the culture of America's inner cities, and *The Wire* provides an accurate depiction of that culture. Although these policies may have begun with good intentions (to rid the world of drugs), they have had disastrous unintended consequences, as can be seen in the desperation of so many of the show's characters. Through the on-screen actions of Bubbles, Bodie, Randy, Stringer Bell, and Dukie (among many others), viewers invariably learn to understand life at ground zero in the drug war.

In the following chapter, I first give a brief history of the War on Drugs in the United States and its financial implications; I then discuss the unintended consequences of perpetuating cycles of poverty and crime, as well as explore the role of race in the drug war. Finally, I discuss alternatives to the War on Drugs, including the Hamsterdam model from Season 3, as well as several other models.

Historical Background on the War on Drugs

Although there have been various policies designed to deal with drugs in America dating even before the Harrison Act of 1914 (Walker, 2011), the official start of the War on Drugs began in the 1970s under the Nixon administration when then President Nixon was informed that many Vietnam soldiers were arriving back from foreign duty stoned from marijuana or strung-out on heroin (Wallace-Wells, 2007). Alarmed by what he saw, Nixon convened a panel to study the problem and make policy recommendations to handle it, but the suggestions put forth by the panel—including decriminalization of marijuana and buying up the world's supply of heroin—didn't fit with his "law and order" platform. Like many of the politicians in *The Wire* (consider here Carcetti's mayoral bid in Seasons 3 and 4), Nixon wanted to appear tough on crime, and so he framed it as a criminal justice issue, which demanded a law enforcement response. The Rockefeller Drug Laws of New York, which created mandatory sentences for various types of drug dealers in the 70s, were quickly copied around the country over the next two decades.

President Reagan first used the term "War on Drugs" in 1982, before the crack epidemic (Alexander, 2010). Just a few years later, crack arrived in American cities and brought with it an alarming spike in violence, specifically among young urban minorities like those seen in *The Wire*. In response, the War on Drugs accelerated and became increasingly punitive. During this time, there was an important shift in public sentiment, where the drug user became seen as more of a criminal fiend than a sad victim. The U.S. Congress reacted by passing the Anti-Drug Abuse Acts of 1986 and 1988, marking a watershed in the War on Drugs. With public sentiment at fever pitch over the evils of drug abuse, Congress produced this expansive legislation in just a few weeks' time (Bikel, 1999). The 1988 Act established the Office of National Drug Control Policy (ONDCP), which both expanded the role of the federal government in drug crimes and created a centralized agency which was supposed to spearhead and coordinate the War on Drugs nationally. The Acts, amended in 1990, brought about a variety of responses to drug crimes, including lengthening sentences for convicted drug dealers; establishing and strengthening school zone laws that enhanced penalties for drug crimes committed within a specified reach of schools; curtailing or excluding drug offenders from federal housing assistance; and increasing reporting to Congress about progress on the War on Drugs (Robinson and Scherlen, 2007). At this point, the drug war had officially shifted into high gear.

Throughout the nineties, the drug war continued to expand governmental control with previously unheard of reach. In 1998, the Higher Education Act was amended to exclude convicted drug offenders from receiving financial aid. While the War on Drugs can been viewed as one piece of the broader 'get tough' movement, it should be noted that no similar exclusions have been established for alcohol or even violent offenders, making the penalties for drug use and trafficking particularly punitive (Robinson and Scherlen, 2007).

As the war ramped up, the government also launched a series of media campaigns to attempt to dissuade youth from becoming involved in drugs. Unfortunately, the result of many of these campaigns has been, at best, nearly negligible, and at worst, counterproductive. The first of these was Nancy Reagan's "just say no" campaign. For anyone who's ever spent any time living or working in the inner city—or even anyone who's watched one episode of *The Wire*—such a campaign seems silly, and more to the point, it misses the reality in which many children grow up in America's urban environments, instead reducing complex motivations for drug use to a simplistic slogan. Consider the choices that Avon Barksdale's nephew, D'Angelo, faces in going into the family "business" of drug trafficking (Season 1), or the dilemma Namond (Season 4) finds himself in when his father is sent to prison and his mother insists he "be a man" and sell his own "package" to take care of the family. Similarly, Dukie's descent (also Season 4) into the drug world has much more to do with appalling neglect by his own family to meet even the most basic of his needs (such as providing food and shelter) than any compelling desire on his part. The campaign to "just say no" made for a catchy political sound bite, but the advice was largely irrelevant to anyone living inside communities affected by drugs and the drug war.

Other prevention campaigns followed, including the now famous "this is your brain on drugs" egg-in-the-frying-pan public service announcements. According to a study done by Hornik and his colleagues (2008), kids in his study who were exposed to similar media campaigns during the early 1990s demonstrated either no difference or a slightly higher probability of trying marijuana. Other efforts, including the Drug Abuse Resistance and Education program (DARE) became wildly popular—and were funded with hundreds of millions of dollars—through the 1980s and 1990s, also with dismal empirical results about deterring drug use by youth (Greenwood, 2006).

In addition to dramatically changing domestic policy in the 1980s and 1990s, foreign policy also shifted in accord with U.S.-lead drug war goals during this time. Two main strategies in the drug war during this time were crop destruction and interdiction, using the logic that if you decrease production or intercept supply, the problem will diminish. The scenes in *The Wire* where police and politicians standing proudly around "dope on the table," congratulating one another over a particularly prodigious drug bust, demonstrate the popularity of these tactics. Unfortunately, most analysts agree that these efforts have often amounted to a global game of Whack-a-Mole; just when one country decreases production, some other unstable, corrupt, or impoverished government allows production to climb somewhere else. Supply-side efforts, although intuitively appealing to many, have not reduced the flow of drugs onto American streets. For instance, "Plan Columbia," which was a focal point for the U.S. foreign policy related to the drug war, was heralded as a success in not only in reducing the Columbian production and exportation of cocaine, but also in strengthening the Columbian government (Walker, 2011). However, it did not necessarily translate into significantly less cocaine being available on the open market. Although the interdiction efforts were able to cut supply by more than half in Columbia, Peru and Bolivia filled in much of the vacuum by increasing their production.

Heroin provides a second example of this displacement effect. While the U.S. government was successful in reducing the flow of heroin from South and Central America, Afghanistan then became the leading producer and exporter of heroin. In fact, despite significant governmental attempts to cut supplies, global heroin production has increased fairly steadily from 1987 through to 2009, ballooning from 2,200 metric tons to nearly 7,800 metric tons (UNODC, 2010). The recent Report on the Global Commission on Drug Policy (2011; led by former Prime Ministers, Presidents and dignitaries from an array of hard-hit countries in the drug war) called supply reduction strategies "futile". Perhaps one reason this is so is because there is no shortage of poverty across the globe; and there will always be farmers who need to provide for their families, and people willing to take the risk in trafficking if it means climbing out of abject poverty, even just for a short time. The desperation of the women trafficked in Season 2 demonstrates the steady stream of people willing to engage in drug or human trafficking to escape destitution. This storyline also illuminates how criminal enterprises in global trafficking (of people or drugs) exploit this social structure and thrive in the unstable areas around the globe, leaving multiple law enforcement agencies left to figure out who has jurisdiction, and how to respond.

On the streets in America, a similar game of Whack-a-Mole plays out daily. Policy analyst Sam Walker calls this "the replacement effect" (2011: 314). When one street level drug dealer is arrested, another quickly steps in, rendering the efforts to clean the streets often ineffective. This can be seen over and over again in *The Wire*. When D'Angelo is taken out of circulation (and those of you who've watched the first two seasons understand my not-so-veiled reference here), there are a succession of "corner boys" waiting to take his place. In an interview with Bill Moyers, *Wire* creator David Simon points out that in his observations while working for years in Baltimore, *not one* corner was ever successfully made clean for any extended amount of time from traditional law enforcement tactics. While law enforcement's intentions may be good, looking at the impact over the long term demonstrates that the enforcement-centered approaches to this social problem have been largely unsuccessful in deterring drug use or drug trafficking.

Ironically, if the goals of the drug war were to reduce use of drugs and reduce the potency of drugs available on the street in the United States, then the report released by the White House Drug Policy shows an exact opposite pattern. The 2010 report chronicles how the average purity of cocaine has steadily increased between 1981 and 2007, moving from about 40% purity to 64% purity (for purchases of 2 grams or less). Heroin followed a similar pattern. In just the decade between 1998 and 2008, despite billions spent on the drug war, global opiate consumption was up by 34.5%, cocaine consumption by 27% and cannabis by 8.5% (WHDP, 2011). Furthermore, the relative costs of cocaine, heroin, and methamphetamines have declined significantly over the last three decades. Finally—and perhaps most importantly—death rates from drug-induced causes tripled between 1980 and 2007. In summary, then, the harder drugs on America's streets seem to be cheaper, stronger, and to be causing more deaths than before the drug war started.

Cost and the Drug War: Who Gets a Bigger Slice of Pie?

Question: "Who got mo' money than they know what to do with?"
Answer: "The *gub*-ment"

Home Boy Seminar, *In Living Color*

When *In Living Color* was taped in the 1990s, the government actually *was* spending money on the drug war as if they didn't know what to do with it all, and that spending has continued well into 2011. Estimates of the cost of the war, to date, vary from between 500 billion (Wallace-Wells, 2007) to one trillion dollars (NewsOne, 2011), depending on who's counting, and what they include in the equation. Of those costs, the funds spent in law enforcement and corrections outpace any research-related funding by 100 to 1 (Robinson and Scherlen, 2007). By almost any calculation, drug war costs (including enforcement and incarceration) run into the tens of billions each year.

While the War on Drugs has crept into the goals of numerous government agencies, its effect on our correctional system has been nothing short of profound. In 1970, the Uniform Crime Reports indicated that there were just fewer than 400,000 drug abuse arrests among adults in this country. By 2004, this figure had soared to over 1.6 million. Not surprisingly, there is a similar astronomical increase in the incarceration rates. In 1980, there were less than 25,000 people in state correctional populations for drug related crimes. By 2005, this number multiplied tenfold to 250,000 and although skyrocketing incarceration rates were part of a larger get tough movement, the War on Drugs was a primary influence. With 2.3 million people behind bars, the United States leads the world in its incarceration rate, outpacing Russia and China.

Not only are more people arrested and incarcerated, the trend is that people are serving much more time behind bars once they are sentenced. In diverging from the usual indeterminate sentences which allowed for flexibility in the length of sentence pending an offender's correctional progress or growth, mandatory minimums and habitual offender laws focused instead on lengthy and severe punishment. Overall, the focus on correctional processing became less about rehabilitation and more about punishment, and the cost has been astronomical. Incarcerating Cutty, Avon, or anyone else, for one year costs between 25 and 50k (depending on the state and the level of risk, respectively).

But perhaps the more important issue here isn't how much was spent, but where that money comes from. Although the Homeboy Seminar alluded that the government had an infinite amount of money to spend, as it turns out, the money has to come from *somewhere*. To use a very basic metaphor, the finite number of tax dollars from Americans can be seen as a pie. When one group takes out a bigger slice of the pie, then there is less pie left for other people. Take, for example, California, which is currently in desperate financial straits. Former Governor Arnold Schwarzenegger had this to say:

> The priorities have become out of whack over the years ... I mean, think about it, 30 years ago, 10 percent of the general fund went to higher education, and 3 percent went to prisons. Today, almost 11 percent goes to prisons, and only 7.5 percent goes to higher education (Steinhauer, 2010: A12).

Sadly, California is not the exception, but the rule; similar patterns have occurred across the country with respect to shrinking education funds and swelling corrections budgets. *The Wire* explores this fiscal crisis best in Season 4, when the schools face incredible pressure from a multi-million dollar budget shortfall. During this storyline, the police are pitted against schools in a 'who's-going-to-get-a-better-piece-of-pie' standoff. What the show doesn't explore in any depth is the fact that corrections—prisons in particular—are eating larger slices out of that same fiscal pie with reckless abandon. State correctional spending has jumped more than 300% in a twenty year period. For example, the Pew Survey of the States (2009: 11) found that:

> [Corrections] growth rate outpaced budget increases for nearly all other essential government services tracked over the same period, from elementary and secondary education (205%) to transportation (82%), higher education (125%) and public assistance (9%). Only Medicaid spending grew faster than spending on corrections ...

In this case "Correctional" spending primarily refers to prisons, as it is estimated that states spend nearly 88% of the correctional budget on jails and prisons. Unfortunately, prisons and jails make up only a fraction of the total correctional population (there are roughly two and one half times the amount of folks under community supervision than in jail or prison). In the meantime, the community corrections population is left with the remaining 12% of the pie (Pew Center, 2008). As conservative policy analyst John Dilulio (1999) states, "Currently, we spend next to nothing on community-based corrections. We get what we pay for." Loosely translated, the few in prison eat up the budget, leaving scraps for the bulk of offenders who remain in the community on probation or parole. In the series, although many of the characters were under some loose form of "supervision" like probation or parole, this was portrayed as having a negligible influence in anyone's decision-making (with the exception of Cutty, who tries to go straight once released on parole, although there is still no real influence or support from the parole office).

With that said, the global recession and constricting budgets have brought some clarity to the fiscal spending spree related to the War on Drugs as of late (2007–2012), and legislatures around the country find themselves in a place where they are looking to cut back and re-organize priorities. Given the current economic straights we're in now, the punitive, lock-em-up solution is less and less tenable every day. The cost is forcing policy makers to reconsider whether these policies make us appreciably safer, and what the long lasting negative unintended consequences are.

Sustaining Cycles of Poverty and Crime

At some point in watching *The Wire*, viewers will invariably find themselves confronted with the depressing reality that things don't seem to change. Just as one drug kingpin is toppled (Avon or Stringer), another steps up (Marlo or

Prop Joe) to perpetuate the violence and illicit commerce. The reasons for this cycle are complex, but David Simon argues that the economic structure in these areas amount to "inverted capitalism." Specifically, with the exodus of American jobs to other parts of the globe, high rates of joblessness, and often blocked legitimate opportunities for inner city residents (due to sub-par education and poor health care, among other things), drug dealing fills a vacuum in these neighborhoods, offering employment—albeit illegal. In one stark discussion in Season 4, Episode 3, Bodie mocks Michael when he resists selling drugs, asking him: "What the fuck you want to go to school for? What you wanna be? An astronaut? A dentist? A pay lawyer, nigga?" His message is clear: his chances of success through mainstream, legitimate means are slim to none; his best opportunity for independence is likely going to be selling drugs.

High rates of incarceration compound this cycle. While in the previous section I outline the fiscal cost of mass incarceration, here I'd like to address perhaps what is the more important cost: lost lives and shrinking human capital. The unintended consequence of this is the "cradle to prison pipeline", and perhaps this has hit the African American community hardest. In their analysis, Petit and Western (2010: 10) note the impact on African Americans at the lower end of social wealth:

> Most of the growth in incarceration rates is concentrated at the very bottom, among young men with very low levels of education. In 1980, around 10% of young African American men who dropped out of high school were in prison or jail. By 2008, this incarceration rate had climbed to 37%, an astonishing level of institutionalization given that the average incarceration rate in the general population was 0.76 of 1 percent.

It is precisely this group on which *The Wire* focuses. The National Criminal Justice Commission stated that the number of African Americans behind bars in this country has reached the level of "social catastrophe" (Walker, 2011: 311). More African Americans in prison also means more black children with a parent away, unable to provide a stable home. As the data indicate, the percentage of African American children who have a parent behind bars increased dramatically between 1980 and 2008, significantly more than changes for white or Latino children (Western and Petit, 2010: 17).

Parental incarceration is related to a host of negative consequences for children, including a heightened risk to live in poverty and to become involved in the criminal justice system. Considering that incarceration severely limits employment opportunities for offenders and families, the cumulative effect of having so many people behind bars is enormous. Consider Cutty in Season

4—returning from prison, determined to go straight in a system where ex-felons are disenfranchised at many levels. The economic struggles of Namond and his mother in Season 4 also illustrate this well. His mother urges him to "step up" to provide for his family by selling drugs. The economic reality this storyline demonstrates is that when people go to prison, families are broken, and children grow up without mothers and fathers. This leaves those children increasingly vulnerable to the street, and the cycle implodes upon itself over and over. All the while, product continues to be sold, junkies continue to be made, and many neglected children turn into neglectful parents.[1]

Why Does *The Wire* Focus Mostly on Blacks? The Role of Race and the War on Drugs

One of the criticisms of using the *The Wire* as part of a college course text is that it uses stereotypes to depict African Americans as being either violent, drug addicted, or both. In an editorial in the *Boston Globe*, Ismael Reed (2010) points out that Blacks have no corner on the crime market, and that there are already many, many images of the black criminal. He states:

> The main reason that I oppose the teaching of "The Wire" is that it joins other shows such as "Training Day," "The Bad Lieutenant: Port of Call—New Orleans," and "Brooklyn's Finest" in locating drug use and distribution in the inner city, when most of it occurs elsewhere.

It is correct that the bulk of the five seasons of *The Wire* take place in the inner city, using primarily African American characters (although to be precise, Season 2 addresses the global drug and human trafficking piece using mainly white

---

1. It is for this reason that when I've taught courses using *The Wire* that I've assigned Season 4 as dramatic text. Because Season 4 dives right into lives of children in the inner city (notice I used the term "children" and not "super-predators," which is how these kids are often portrayed in the media), students become immersed in the characters and the impossible choices which they face daily: Michael needing to care for his younger brother, despite his mom's junkie penchant for spending the family's welfare money on drugs; Randy trying to outrun the perception in the neighborhood that he is a "rat"; or Dukie's daily struggle to have a home, a shower, or even clean clothes. *The Wire* painstakingly presents these characters, demonstrating how difficult it would be for any of these characters to break the cycle of desperation they were born into to have mainstream success. (Spoiler alert: if you haven't finished Season 4, stop reading now!) Indeed, the only one of the kids in Season 4 who seems to have a chance at legitimate success was Namond, and this is because Bunny Coleman adopted him to get him out off the corner.

characters). And to Reed's point, having worked in the inner city during the height of the drug war in the 1990s, I also am familiar with the steady stream of suburban white folks coming into the inner city, buying drugs off young minority kids. Still, his arguments don't capture the whole picture.

Reed misses the point that African Americans *are* a big piece of the urban inner city War on Drugs. But rather than try to sidestep the race issue, it's important here to tackle this head on: this is a product of some of the policies which I talked about earlier. More to the point, Robinson and Scherlen (2007) point out the War on Drugs has historically been less about drugs and more about *who was using them*. They carefully chronicle how both cocaine and opium were used in the U.S. without regulation or criminalization, and claim that trade and ethnocentrism played a major role in the criminalization of certain drugs. Further, Massey and Denton have done an exceptional job of historically accounting the formal and informal roads that made the contemporary urban ghetto disproportionately black. (See *American Apartheid*, 1997, for a discussion on red-lining neighborhoods, federal mortgage programs, and federal highway programs which separated blacks and whites, as well as real estate funneling to channel de facto segregation.) More recently, critics point out that drug usage was actually declining when the drug war was officially declared (Alexander, 2010), yet panic of minority "crack fiends" and urban violence fueled the implementation of harsh penalties for both high ranking drug traffickers and casual users alike. (By the way, if you're interested in a series that dramatizes drug abuse in the suburbs, *Breaking Bad* may be *The Wire's* white, suburban counterpart.)

Like Reed, however, I worry that the casual viewer of *The Wire* will miss some of the bigger pieces at play here, and that stereotypes may be perpetuated. To that point, numerous independent studies have pointed out that drug use is neither particularly black nor particularly urban and that black and white youth both use and sell drugs at remarkably similar rates (Alexander, 2010). It's not the usage that is different; it's the response. Indeed, there are a growing number of critics of the criminal justice system who question whether the mass incarceration of African Americans (fueled in great part by the War on Drugs) may be "the new Jim Crow" (Alexander, 2010). With the revelation that some inner city blocks were "million dollar blocks"—meaning that it cost the government upwards of a million dollars to incarcerate residents from this small area—many critics question whether incarceration, and not welfare or health care, has become the "principle instrument of our social policy" for many inner city residents (Loury, as quoted by Alexander, 2010). (Imagine if all that money were spent on evidence-based effective social services that help to lift people out of poverty in sustaining ways, rather than locking up whole swaths of the community.)

Nowhere is the disparity between black and white sentencing more evident than in the 100 to 1 crack/powder cocaine sentencing disparities which were law for more than two decades. Until its repeal in 2010, the federal penalties for possession of 5 grams of crack triggered the 5 year mandatory minimum prison sentence, while it took 100 times this amount of powder cocaine to trigger the same sentence. Given that crack and powder cocaine are virtually the same chemical substance, the 100 to 1 ratio seemed wildly disproportionate. While crack markets did bring significant violence to cities in the 1980s and 1990s, others point out that the major difference between the two substances largely centers around *who* was using them. Crack cocaine was predominantly consumed by poor urban African Americans, while powder cocaine by middle or upper class whites. Even with the new guidelines, the ratios still heavily punish crack over powder cocaine use and trafficking, at about the rate of 18 to 1.

Another point of racial disparity in the drug war involves the response to illegal use of prescription drugs. While the War on Drugs has largely been fought against communities of color, often in urban environments like those seen in *The Wire*, enforcement of laws against illegal prescription drug abuse has not been a focus for this war to date. This is particularly relevant because some estimates suggest prescription drug abuse is both more popular than cocaine, heroin and methamphetamines *combined*, and responsible for many more deaths (in Florida prescription drugs kill nearly five times as many people as other illegal drugs) (CNN, 2010). In fact, according to a federal study in 2006, opium analgesics have become more popular among teenagers than marijuana. Between 1999 and 2005, unintentional death from prescription drug overdoses skyrocketed, second only to automobile accidents (Davenport, 2011). Like the differences between crack and powder cocaine users, the rates of illegal prescription drug abuse also vary by race, ethnicity and social class. Consider this: How many doctor's offices have you heard about being raided, *Wire* style, to target pill mills?

In addition to these differences in enforcement, there is also concern that racial disparities may influence prosecution patterns of drug offenses as well. Although the mandatory minimum sentences enacted in the 1980s and 1990s were meant in part to reduce the discretion of justice officials, there is some evidence that discretion wasn't eliminated; it was simply moved from the judge to the prosecutor, and race may continue to influence decision-makers, perhaps in subtle, less obvious ways than in earlier generations. In particular, the federal government has used the "substantial assistance" (aka: snitching) safety valve more often for white, educated defendants than for uneducated minorities, even when controlling for case specifics and offender history (Spohn and Fornago, 2009).

Because of these disparities—the lack of zeal in going after prescription drug "pill mills", combined with drug law enforcement and prosecution that often targets urban, largely minority communities, many minorities have come to feel that the War on Drugs is, in effect, a war on them. This sentiment— the feeling that inner city residents are at war with the police and vice versa— resonates throughout all five seasons of *The Wire*.

Rather than deny the reality of the racial dimensions of the drug war, or claim the stereotype is overplayed (which it indeed may be in the mainstream media), *The Wire* at least presents it with humanity in a complex, sophisticated way. Race does matter here, and to move forward, we need to acknowledge it in ways that promote that same humanity.

What Else Is There? Hamsterdam and Other Alternatives

The Wire lays bare so many ineffective drug policies. 'Just say no' doesn't work. Police sweeping kids off corners doesn't work. "Dope on the table" never really chokes off supply long enough to make a difference on the street. So what else can be done? Unfortunately, toward this end, *The Wire* leaves us hanging. At the end of the series, the creators of *The Wire* published an opinion editorial in *Time Magazine* answering just this question. In it, they stated they would no longer "tinker with the machinery of the drug war," and as a result, if they were asked to serve on a jury where a person was accused of a non-violent drug offense, they would vote to acquit, regardless of the evidence brought against the defendant (*The Wire* Creators, 2008). Unfortunately, they didn't answer the bigger policy questions in the op-ed. Jury nullification isn't a serious policy response to the bigger issues at play here. The policies that drove us to our current crisis, particularly in the inner cities, need to be re-evaluated at a grander level.

Critics of the drug war (and there are many at this point) suggest that targeting *demand* (rather than supply) could have more significant impact in reducing drug problems in the U.S. Currently, the United Nations estimates that there are 250 million illicit drug users worldwide, and of those, only 10% are considered dependent. Rather than targeting supply, these researchers suggest that targeting these 10% for treatment could have the potential to reduce demand considerably and thereby cut into drug related crimes. There are several variations of demand-centered responses.

The closest *The Wire* gets to exploring any of these demand-side policy alternatives was Major Bunny Colvin's Hamsterdam experiment in Season 3. For those who haven't seen it (I'll try hard not to spoil this story line, because it's one of the most important in all five seasons), the Major essentially tried to cordon off a de-criminalized area for drugs. He presented low and mid-level drug dealers with a form of détente: sell in a circumscribed area and the police will leave you alone; sell anywhere else and face stiff penalties. Whether this fictional experiment was a success or failure is debatable, but it did present a decent picture of what a truly de-criminalized zone might look like. And perhaps this is what *The Wire* does best: it demonstrated the complexity of this issue; once Hamsterdam was fully operational it looked like something out of *Dawn of the Dead*.

Interestingly, sections of the Downtown Eastside of Vancouver (in real life) have created a quasi-Hamsterdam—only through legal methods, and with considerable thought toward public health concern. In this particular area of Vancouver, they practice "harm reduction" toward drug use and abuse, meaning that people can legally use, but not sell, drugs (the next chapter on harm reduction strategies by Hamilton and Block provides more details on these types of programs). Unlike Hamsterdam (which the "old head" Deacon criticized because it didn't provide for any health care for the addicts), in Vancouver people who are addicted can stand in line at Insite, a safe facility, that will provide them with a clean plastic crack pipe (because it's safer than glass, and less likely to spread HIV or Hep B), clean needles, and a hygienic place to shoot up. If they overdose, a clinician is on hand and prepared to bring them back to life. Essentially, they use their drugs in a safe environment, off the street, designed to contain the harmful effects of the drug to the user. After several years of this policy, HIV rates by IV drug users are at their lowest point in three decades in Vancouver. The result is that the spread of disease is down and treatment is up, and the stigma of being a drug user has been lifted slightly. As of 2010, not a single addict died while at facility (Power, 2010).

That said, critics have pointed out that this facility, like Hamsterdam, might be one of the most depressing places on earth. Even pregnant women, like everyone else, are welcome to shoot up at Insite, with the theory being that it's better the women shoot up in a safe environment where they get some health care than out on the street, where they get none (Power, 2010). The model, however, demonstrates that there are different alternatives to the War on Drugs, but by no means does it mean that there are easy or pretty solutions.

Still, despite the ugly visualization of what some may consider a facility that services the walking dead, harm reduction methods have produced similar results across the globe in a variety of studies. Generally, treatment tends to go up, drug related diseases and drug related crime trends down, and most importantly, it doesn't seem to have created a surge in new users—although this last piece is highly contested.

Portugal took a slightly different road and has de-criminalized all drug use throughout the country. Like Vancouver though, trafficking drugs remains a crime. The money that was previously spent on courts and enforcement is now channeled into treatment; and now when someone is caught with drugs, they go before a panel of social workers and are encouraged (but not coerced) to seek treatment. When the policy changes went into effect in 2001, critics charged that the decriminalization of drugs would lead to many new users. However, after several different independent studies (including one by the CATO Institute), there was no new major surge in drug users. There was also a slight decline in heroin usage, as well as an increase in people seeking treatment (Hatton and Medoza, 2010). Perhaps the key to both the Vancouver and Portugal alternatives is that these interventions look at drug abuse as primarily a public health—not criminal justice—issue.

Perhaps part of Portugal's success is that it eliminated some of the criminal justice response, thereby affecting the black market around drugs. It is well known that drug abuse feeds the machinery of organized crime. The theory behind decriminalization is that if drugs were to become decriminalized, or even legalized, the underground criminal enterprise may also shrink, as it did when the prohibition on alcohol was lifted. Still, critics point out that Portugal is a very different country from the U.S., and question whether this strategy could work here. Currently, although decriminalization of medical and small amounts of marijuana has gained some traction in many individual states over the last decade, it still remains illegal under federal statute, leaving many states, such as Washington and Colorado, in an awkward and contradictory position.

More mainstream alternative responses which have been tried in the United States include drug courts, which intensively track drug offenders through the court system and appropriate treatment programs. Drug courts involve judicially mandated treatment with expedited court processing, and the program approaches the offender as an agent that *can* and *should* change his/her behavior. The evidence continues to mount that drug users who go through drug court programs are both less likely to be re-arrested and more likely to stay sober than similarly situated drug offenders who go through traditional court processes (Rossman, Roman, Zweig, Rempel, and Lindquist, 2011). Other similar programs include HOPE in Hawaii as a model for probation, which also stresses drug treatment and frequent and random drug tests, with expedited court processes that respond to drug use quickly with shortened incarceration, rather than lengthy prison sentences. But both of these options are still largely criminal justice responses.

Although I've briefly detailed other alternatives, it should be clear that none of the above is anywhere close to a magic bullet, or precludes using incarceration as one response within the toolbox to decrease drug abuse. As the Global Commission on Drug Policy suggests, the criminal organizations which traffic these illicit drugs need to be dealt with effectively through the justice system. But there's a crucial difference between the Marlos and "the Greeks" in the upper echelon of the drug world, and the Bodies and Namonds at the bottom rungs. The Major Crimes Unit in *The Wire* understood just that distinction and strategized around it, but it did so with very fickle support from police brass. This type of smart police operation—as Lester Freamon suggested, "follow the money"—pursues the key stakeholders rather than the small fry, and in order for it to be done right it needs *solid institutional support* to make it viable. Units like these can help the justice system do a better job of distinguishing between the different types of players, from low level drug traffickers who've been coerced to move drugs by abject poverty or threats to higher level officials who control the market for profit.

Likewise, the violence that accompanies the drug war, like that perpetrated by Avon or Omar, requires a swift response from the justice system to ensure public safety. The bigger question is: Could alternative approaches (de-criminalization, harm reduction) used in the United States structurally impact the amount of violence by shrinking the underground, as it did when prohibition ended?

Conclusion

The political climate has changed since the end of the series. Presently, the Obama administration has taken a slightly different tact than earlier administrations, explicitly rejecting the "War on Drugs" terminology, and demoting the (previously dubbed) "drug czar" position out of the Presidential Cabinet. This strategic move, along with the Fair Sentencing Act of 2010, suggests that the administration does not believe the drug war is as important as has been considered by previous federal administrations. Further, with fiscal budget crunches in every state, legislatures currently are looking for ways to save money, and many recently have targeted mandatory sentences to be either modified or repealed. It remains to be seen whether these changes mark a new period—perhaps even the beginning of the end—in America's War on Drugs or whether these reforms will tinker at the margins of this massive governmental effort.

For now though, one of the main fronts in the War on Drugs continues to be fought by local police in communities like those in featured in *The Wire*.

As scholar Peter Moskos (2008: 159) notes, "Drugs became a police problem as many problems do: Nobody else wanted to deal with it. Society's buck stops with the police." In response, policing in inner city neighborhoods has fundamentally changed. Major Bunny Colvin explains:

> This drug thing, this ain't police work. Naw. It ain't. I mean I can send any fool with a badge and gun up on them corners and jack a crew and grab vials. But policing ... who you [gonna] call? Pretty soon everybody gonna be walking around like warriors. Like gonna be running around on a damn crusade ... slapping on cuffs and racking up body counts.... And when you at war, you need a fucking enemy. And pretty soon damn near *everybody* on *every corner* is your fuckin' enemy! And soon the neighborhood that you supposed to be policing, that's just occupied territory. You follow this? The point I'm making is this: soldiering and policing— they ain't the same thing. And before we went and took the wrong turn and start up with these war games, the cop walked a beat. And he *learned* that post. And if there were things that happening, whether it be a rape, a robbery or a shooting, he had people out there helping him, feeding him information.... The worst thing about this so-called drug war, in my mind, is that it just ruined this job (Season 3, Episode 10).

In particular, the racial disparities involved in enforcement of the drug war have had—and will continue to have—important and often negative implications for inner city communities, often undermining the community's connection to and belief in the legitimacy of the police.

The Wire shows the casualties of the War on Drugs in sobering detail, albeit fictional. It presents a world where the drug war is acute—a separate and disconnected third world within America's borders. Part of the significance of *The Wire* is that it paints a vivid picture of cities ripped with failure and hopelessness, of criminal markets that reach across the globe, and of well-intentioned law enforcement trying to do the right thing—whatever it might be.

References

Alexander, Michelle. 2010. *The New Jim Crow: Mass Incarceration in the Age of Color Blindness.* New York: The New Press.

Bikel, Ofra (producer). 1999. *Snitch.* WGBH Educational Foundation.

CNN. 2010. Prescription Drug Abuse. (Campbell Brown). http://www.gatehouseacademy.com/blog/2010/02/11/shocking-video-on-cnn-pain-clinics-in-florida/.

Davenport, Christian. 2011, January 1. Doctors who prescribe oft-abused drugs face scrutiny. *The Washington Post.*

Dilulio, J. J. 1999, March 12. Two million prisoners are enough. *The Wall Street Journal.*

Global Commission on Drug Policy. 2011, June. *Report of the Global Commission on Drug Policy.*

Greenwood, Peter. 2006. *Changing Lives: Delinquency Prevention as Crime-Control Policy.* Chicago: University of Chicago Press.

Hatton, Barry & Martha Mendoza. 2010, December 27. Portugal's drug policy pays off; US eyes lessons. *The Washington Post.*

Hornik, Robert, Jacobsohn, Lela, Orwin, Robert, Piesse, Andrea & Graham Kalton. (2008). Effects of national youth anti-drug media campaign on youth. *American Journal of Public Health* 98, no.12. p. 2229–2236.

In Living Color. Accessed through: http://www.youtube.com/watch?v=7juk QX2pl2Q.

Moskos, Peter. 2009. *Cop in the Hood.* New Jersey: Princeton University Press.

NewsOne. 2010, May 13. Despite spending 1 trillion dollars, the drug war has failed. Posted by Associated Press. Accessed on January 17, 2011 from: http://newsone.com/nation/associated-press/despite-spending-1-trillion-the-war-on-drugs-has-failed/.

Pew Center on the States. 2009 March. *One in 31: The Long Reach of American Corrections.* Page 11.

Power, Matthew. 2010, Feb 1. The Vancouver Experiment. *Slate.* http://www.slate.com/id/2242828/entry/2242868.

Reed, Ismael. 2010, September 10. "No, it relies on cliché's about Blacks and drugs." *The Boston Globe.* Opinion Editorial. http://www.boston.com/bostonglobe/editorial_opinion/oped/articles/2010/09/30/no_it_relies_on_clichs_about_blacks_and_drugs/.

Robinson, Matthew and Renee Scherlen. 2007. *Lies, Damned Lies and Drug War Statistics.* Albany, NY: State University of New York Press.

Rossman, Shelli, Roman, J, Zweig, Janine, Rempel, Michael and Christine Lindquist. 2011, June. The multi-site adult drug court evaluation: Executive Summary. The Urban Institute.

Simon, David. Interview with Bill Moyers. 2009, April. http://www.pbs.org/moyers/journal/04172009/watch.html.

Spohn, Cassia and Robert Fornago. 2009. U.S. Attorneys and substantial assistance departures: Testing for interprosecutor disparity. *Criminology* 47: 813–845.

Steinhauer, Jennifer. 2010, January 6. Schwarzenegger Seeks Shift From Prisons to Schools. *New York Times.* http://www.nytimes.com/2010/01/07/us/07calif.html.

United Nations Office on Drugs and Crime. 2010. *World Drug Report.* http://www.unodc.org/documents/wdr/WDR_2010/World_Drug_Report_2010_lo-res.pdf.

Walker, Sam. 2011. *Sense and Nonsense about Crime, Drugs and Communities.* Belmont, Ca: Wadsworth.

Wallace-Wells, Ben. 2007. How America lost the war on drugs. *Rolling Stone.*

Western, Bruce. 2007. *Punishment and Inequality in America.* New York: Russell Sage Foundation.

Western, Bruce & Becky Petit. 2010, Summer. Incarceration and Social Inequality. *Daedalus.* American Academy of Arts and Sciences.

White House Drug Policy. Accessed from: http://www.whitehousedrugpolicy.gov/publications/policy/ndcs10/ndcs10_data_supl/ds_list_of_tables.pdf.

The Wire Creators (Ed Burns, David Simon,& George Pelecanos). 2008, March. *The Wire's* War on the War on Drugs. *Time Magazine.*

Study Questions

1. According to Balboni, what are some of the challenges or obstacles in ending the War on Drugs, or to decriminalizing or legalizing drugs?

2. Was it appropriate for Nixon to shift drug use and addiction from a medical issue to a criminal justice issue? What are some of the repercussions, failures, and/or successes in doing so over the last 30 years?

3. Discuss how current criminal justice and law enforcement tactics have succeeded or failed in reducing production and importation of various illegal drugs.

4. The cost of the War on Drugs to individuals, the criminal justice system, and the government is almost immeasurable. What are the consequences of criminalization of drugs to individual citizens? Communities as a whole? How have incarceration rates been affected? Discuss the monetary costs to state and federal government.

5. How is the War on Drugs affecting African-American communities in America? How could the criminal justice system revise its practices to account for the monetary and social devastation of minorities?

6. What solutions have been suggested or implemented to address the effects criminalization of drugs and addiction? What other approaches might be visited? Are there any positive aspects about the War on Drugs?

Chapter 11

Harm Reduction Strategies: The Hamsterdam Perspective

Zachary Hamilton and Lauren Block

Introduction

In Episode 2 of *The Wire*'s third season Major Howard "Bunny" Colvin addresses the Baltimore Police Department's Western District patrol officers during their morning daily briefing. The previous night an officer was shot while working undercover. The undercover operation, which was conducted to address the department administration's demands that district commanders lower crime rates by any means possible, cemented in Colvin's mind that the crime problem would not be solved by traditional police work. His address in the morning's daily briefing is one of the series' most provocative monologues. In it he describes how, within an urban city environment, a moderate amount of public drinking is allowed. Although technically illegal, police are encouraged to "look the other way" as long as there is an (albeit blatant) attempt to conceal the act by placing the beverage in a paper bag. This long understood notion that victimless, or quality-of-life crimes, may be ignored in the interest of public harmony is a topic that is not often discussed in *The Wire*, which typically focuses on the competitive and violent game of heroin distribution. Colvin's monologue ends with the provision of a key analogy, "there is no paper bag for this stuff," suggesting that, even though it is also a victimless offense, there is no acceptable way to hide heroin use from the public view.

The context of this monologue and the experimental solution to follow are centered on an infrequently utilized strategy referred to as Harm Reduction. Most frequently associated with interventions that impact drug use, harm reduction is an umbrella term for any intervention that is intended to reduce the problematic effects of a behavior pattern (Logan and Marlatt, 2010). As demonstrated in Season 3, the harm reduction model is not the status quo for U.S. drug policy, which typically surrounds the use of law enforcement and treatment strategies to deter drug use through a zero-tolerance abstinence approach. This chapter aims to describe the harm reduction approach in connection to, and in contrast with, current U.S. drug policy. By injecting scenes from Season 3 and real world policy examples we intend to provide a relatable introduction to application of harm reduction strategies, demonstrating their impact within the intersections of criminal justice and public health.

U.S. Drug Policy

Drug policy in the United States has traditionally focused on two common approaches to control the distribution and use of illegal narcotics. The first approach, demand reduction, focuses on reducing and eliminating the use of drugs and associated harms by providing drug treatment services to those individuals already addicted, and using education and prevention efforts to discourage others from using illegal drugs in the future (Marlatt and Witkiewitz, 2010). The second approach, supply reduction, uses law enforcement to prevent the flow of illegal drugs into the U.S (Marlatt and Witkiewitz, 2010). This includes the focus of federal and state agency resources on controlling U.S. borders, airports, and highways, and working with other countries in the hopes of disrupting the flow or reducing the availability of drugs.

Local law enforcement agencies also use a variety of tactics to disrupt the distribution of drugs within their own cities, such as the targeted enforcement tactics (crackdowns) on drug markets, which, in essence, is the primary role of the Major Crimes detail portrayed in *The Wire*. These crackdowns often involve the seizure of drugs and arrest those individuals in possession, who are then processed through the criminal justice system. When these efforts are effective, their outcomes are striking and satisfying, often culminating in a press conference where drugs and weapons "taken off the streets" are displayed to assure the public that the system is working. Possibly due (in part) to the visual display of tangible effects, the U.S. provides disproportionately greater resources toward supply reduction tactics compared to those demand reduction interventions (Wodak, 2009). In 2008, the Office of National Drug Control Policy only spent 23% of its budget on treatment services, 12% on prevention efforts, and 64% on supply reduction tactics (Center for Substance Abuse Research, 2008).

While numerous studies have demonstrated successful drug treatment services (Gerstein and Harwood, 1990; Hubbard et al., 1989; McLellan, Luborsky, Woody, and O'Brien, 1982; Simpson and Savage, 1980), the traditional focus of many programs has been an abstinence-only philosophy, with an overall goal to immediately stop the use of drugs without the aid of opiate inhibitors (i.e. beuprenorphine and methadone). This all-or-nothing approach forces a drug user to choose: either you're a Junkie or not—you're either clean or you're an addict (Logan and Marlatt, 2010). Although having an ideological evil to fight (such as drug markets and dealing) goes a long way to soothe the general public's conscience regarding the nation's efforts to eliminate consequences of drug use, those who work with users or struggle with addiction know that this is a hard policy line to toe.

Harm Reduction

In *The Wire*, Major Colvin views the sale and use of heroin as the least of many concerns for his district. For those that have taken in the lessons from previous episodes, or have an understanding of the sheer volume and impact of the drug trade, it is well-known that police enforcement strategies will never eradicate the distribution and use of drugs in America. There will always be drugs and there will always be drug users. Finally, as with most illegal enterprises, there is always someone willing to risk arrest to make a profit (i.e. there will always be dealers).

Accepting these core illegalities to be true, it is important to understand how additional acts of illegality often surround the drug trade. Because the drug trade is illegal, police do not serve the interest of those involved. Dealers must establish and maintain their territory of distribution, often with violence (i.e. murder, assault, and intimidation). Users (more specifically termed "Junkies") typically obtain money to purchase goods through illegal means, often through additional victimless crimes (i.e. prostitution) or property crimes (i.e. burglary, theft, vandalism, etc.). These peripheral illegalities are presented in countless examples throughout *The Wire*.

Colvin begins to understand why neighborhoods have deteriorated as a result of the drug trade. Within the Western District, businesses are sparse and often shielded behind bulletproof glass; citizens are afraid to walk the streets and fear reprisal from those employed by the drug trade; truant children, termed "Hoppers," roam the streets working themselves through the ranks of the drug enterprise with daily commission of illegal behaviors both violent and drug related. To Colvin, the deterioration witnessed is not due to the inability to stop the use and distribution of drugs, but to the violence and omnipresence of the drug enterprise impeding the natural flow of citizen life.

The controversial idea that Major Colvin begins to put into action centers on the demarcation of acceptable and unacceptable illegality. If one can accept, or permit, the core behaviors of use and sale of drugs, one can then make a stronger attempt to prevent the violence that surrounds the creation and maintenance of the distribution territory. That is, in order to prevent the peripheral illegality that surrounds the drug trade, one must isolate the core behaviors to an acceptable area, or business district—giving the corners, parks, streets and open areas back to the residents. In Episode 3 Major Colvin attempts to create his "paper bag" neighborhood inside the Western District of Baltimore. His idea is to create a "free zone" where dealers and users can exist without the threat of arrest. He identifies a set of blocks that are virtually vacant, exist within a low trafficked neighborhood, contain no businesses and offer a substantial distance from the nearest school.

Once this heroin "business district" is established the officers then must convince dealers to sell in these outlined areas. Paddy wagons of junkies are then driven to the location and dropped off to purchase in the streets, and neighborhood vacant row houses then become shooting galleries for use of drugs recently acquired. While police patrol the border of the free zone and the remaining Western District, leaving a haven for the core activities of the drug trade, no arrests for drug law violations take place within the area. Prior to its creation, open-air drug markets existed on dozens of corners and within the grounds of housing projects. After its creation, the free zone becomes the only drug market (within the Western District).

A reference is offered to the dealers to consider the free zone their "Amsterdam," and after an enjoyable mispronunciation from an uninformed dealer, the area becomes lovingly referred to as Hamsterdam. Although seemingly a radical departure from any strategy to ever be utilized in Baltimore, the idea of the free zone is not new and has existed for decades in various forms. This strategy, known as "Harm Reduction," is not based within law enforcement literature but has been aptly described in the Public Health field.

Defining Harm Reduction

The harm reduction model suggests that addiction is a mix of biopsychosocial risk factors and treatment must be tailored to the individual. The goal of this model is to help cope with the addiction and its consequences in whatever method that works best, and where treatment may exist on a continuum from abstinence to moderation. This perspective recognizes that, within a society where drugs are present, the goal of eliminating all drugs to form a drug-free society is unlikely to occur and that abstinence is not a realistic goal for many drug users. Instead of marginalizing individuals by demonizing their behavior, the harm reduction perspective suggests that, despite our disappointment with their continued use, it is better to let individuals continue to use drugs safely than to banish them to back alleys and abandoned buildings where there is a greater potential to incur disease and become victims of predatory crimes (Marlatt and Witkiewitz, 2010).

It is important to note that harm reduction recognizes that abstinence is the ideal way to avoid the harms associated with drug use. However, abstinence-based treatment is not desired, nor successful, for every drug user (Reid, 2002). An old joke that states "how many social workers does it take to change a light bulb ... only one, but the light bulb really has to want to change" illustrates this dynamic. Stopping the use of drugs is a difficult life change and results in withdrawal, lifestyle changes, and removing a key source of pleasure often causes a great deal of anxiety. Furthermore, refusing to administer treatment until one becomes and stays abstinent only further isolates the individual and ignores the negative consequences of their continued drug use. The knowledge of these zero-tolerance policies often creates anxiety that prevents more users from seeking treatment. Harm reduction focuses on taking steps that will reduce the harms associated with addiction, hoping that the individual will eventually choose to abstain when they are capable of doing so (Reid, 2002).

Harms to Be Reduced

The U.S. reliance on supply and demand reduction drug policies has been heavily critiqued by an increasing population, including public health workers, agents within the criminal justice system, academics, legislators in the U.S., and worldwide, and a growing number of citizens. One of the main arguments against the current drug policies used in the U.S. is simply that they do not work (MacCoun, 1998). The violence and crime associated with drug markets plague U.S. cities and our courts, and prisons continue to be overcrowded with drug offenders despite the nation's more than 30-year War on Drugs (Tonry, 1995). The use of law enforcement and criminal sanctions will unlikely eliminate the presence of illegal drugs, as such policies only have a limited impact on crime rates. As long as the U.S. continues to fight an unwinnable war, the harms imposed by drug markets will also continue. Furthermore, studies have shown that the harsh tactics used by law enforcement in attempts to control and prevent the use of illegal drugs actually exacerbates some of the harmful consequences associated with drug use, such as increasing instances of unsafe injection practices and unprotected sexual practices which can lead to the spread of sexual and blood-borne illness as well as overdoses (Burris et al., 2004; Koester, 1994; Maher and Dixon, 2001; Nadelmann, 1989). Hamsterdam was initially conceived to reduce the harm created by the violence known to surround open air drug markets. What Colvin is forced to realize is that there are many more harms to be reduced and/or prevented. The current section describes the scope of the problem that surrounds injection drug use.

Heroin

As Hamsterdam exemplifies, heroin use, addiction, and the associated harms continue to plague communities across the United States. According to the 2008 National Survey on Drug Use and Health, approximately 213,000 people aged 12 and older reported using heroin in the month preceding, a significant increase from 2007 (estimated at 153,000) (Substance Abuse and Mental Health Services Administration, 2009). From 2002 to 2008, it was estimated that between 91,000 and 118,000 people tried heroin for the first time each year. That number significantly increased to 180,000 (among people aged 12 and older) in the 2009 National Survey on Drug Use and Health (SAMHSA, 2010). Furthermore, the 2009 survey reported that the number of people who had been categorized as abusing or being dependent on heroin was approximately 399,000, up from 213,000 in 2007 (SAMHSA, 2010).

Opiates such as heroin are known for their ability to relieve pain and to produce a sense of euphoria in their user. Unfortunately, such drugs are also known for their crippling effects associated with opiate addiction. Heroin is a short-acting opiate, meaning the user will experience the effects of the drug quickly, but they will also begin feeling the symptoms of withdrawal quickly, usually within a few hours of the drug being administered (Tapert et al., 1998), often sparking the user to inject another dose in order to avoid these symptoms. As the frequency of these injections increase, a tolerance begins to build, resulting in a need for larger and larger doses to still experience the feelings of euphoria, and the user starts to develop a dependence on heroin (National Institute on Drug Abuse, 2005).

Heroin use is associated with much harm. It takes a toll on an individual's health and social functioning. Chronic heroin use has been associated with a variety of health problems, including abscesses, collapsed veins, infection of the heart lining and valves, and liver or kidney disease (NIDA, 2005). These health problems are compounded by the fact that many injection drug users rely heavily on emergency room services because they often lack access to regular medical care (French et al., 2001). Furthermore, by obtaining heroin from street dealers the user will be unaware of harmful additives, which increases the risk of ingesting a dangerous substance, and the strength of the drug, which increases the chance of an overdose (Tapert et al., 1998). In addition, as an addict's life revolves around scoring the next hit, responsibilities such as a job or family fall by the wayside. It is not surprising that heroin use has also been associated with criminal activity, as one needs to find ways to support their habit that are not always legal.

Crime

The relationship between drug distribution and violence became common in headlines during the crack cocaine epidemic during the late 1980s and early 1990s, coinciding with large increases in drug-related violent crime in urban cities across the U.S. (Baumer et al., 1998; Blumstein and Rosenfeld, 1999). Then, as the crack cocaine markets began to fade in the 1990s, so did the violence (Ousey and Lee, 2002). However, there is still evidence that violent crime rates continue to be associated with fluctuations in drug markets. Homicide rates in large U.S. cities have been shown to be positively associated with arrest rates for distribution of heroin and cocaine (Ousey and Lee, 2004). A recent study of Miami neighborhoods found evidence that drug activity was associated with high rates of aggravated assault and robbery (Martinez, Rosenfeld, and Mares, 2008). Just as drug markets are bound to attract drug users, high crime rates are also bound to bring law enforcement, setting the stage for these two groups to ultimately interact with one another and, unfortunately, physical confrontations between law enforcement and injection drug users (IDUs) have been shown to be a source of many health-related harms to IDUs (Cooper et al., 2004).

Disease

Many injection drug users will resort to injecting in nearby areas that are hidden from view, such as abandoned buildings, alleys, or parked cars, in order to avoid having their drugs taken by police. Under these circumstances, the injection process is more likely to be rushed and unsafe (Aitken et al., 2002; Dixon and Maher, 2002). There are many harms that can occur when the injection process is rushed, including vascular damage when the syringe is injected quickly (Maher and Dixon, 2001), and the failure to clean hands and the injection site prior to injection (Broadhead et al., 2002), which can lead to abscesses and infection (Murphy et al., 2001). Furthermore, IDUs are more likely to share injection equipment, which increases the risk for spreading a blood-borne virus (Maher and Dixon, 2001), and they may fail to test the drugs for strength prior to injecting, which increases the risk of overdose (Broadhead et al., 2002).

Another popular location IDUs often retreat to is what is known as a "shooting gallery" (Des Jarlais and Friedman, 1990). Shooting galleries are typically indoor locations that are hidden from public view where IDUs can go to buy and use drugs (such as the row houses used in Hamsterdam). However, they are also places where injection-related risk behaviors run rampant. Within shooting galleries, IDUs will often share syringes and store used syringes to be used again in the future (Neaigus et al., 1994). Steps that help sterilize the injection equipment are unlikely to be taken, as shooting galleries lack alcohol pads or a source of clean water needed to keep injecting safely (Chitwood et al., 1995). Unsurprisingly, shooting gallery attendance is also associated with an increased risk of HIV infection (Zolopa et al., 1994).

There is a great deal of evidence that shows injection drug users are at a high risk of contracting blood-borne viruses such as HIV, hepatitis C (HCV), hepatitis B (HBV), and tuberculosis (TB), and that injection drug use contributes to the spread of these viruses (NIDA, 2005). The risk factors that make IDUs more vulnerable to such viruses include the sharing of injection equipment such as needles and syringes and injecting at "shooting galleries" and other public areas. Nearly 16% of HIV infections in the U.S. and another 10% globally are attributed to injection drug use (WHO, 2011). In Eastern Europe and Central Asia estimates for transmission through IDUs are as high as 80% (WHO, 2011). Furthermore, 20% of IDUs are HIV positive (Mathers et al., 2008), however, only 8% of IDUs worldwide receive HIV-related prevention/harm reduction services (UNICEF, WHO, and UNAIDS, 2007). These risk factors for IDUs become exacerbated by limited access to much needed resources— including sterile needles, safe injection sites, drug treatment, and other social services—marginalization by society, and the presence of laws that aim to punish drug users (Burris et al., 2004). In addition, both male and female users often turn to prostitution (also referred to as sex work) as a quick source of cash in order to fuel their addiction and stave off withdrawal. The internalized need for money/drugs in order to avoid the painful effects of withdrawal, poor judgments and lack of resources (i.e. condoms), and threats of violence lead to an inability for sex workers to negotiate safe sex practices, providing yet another potential method for the transmission of HIV and other sexually transmitted diseases. Furthermore, most IDUs who exchange sex for drugs do not consider themselves "sex workers" and are less likely to negotiate condom use or engage in health services (Rothenburg et al., 2000). Recent U.S. estimates indicated that the prevalence of HIV among sex workers is nearly 12% greater when compared to general population estimates (UNAIDS, 2006), and the odds of contracting HIV increase further when sex workers are using, under the influence, or practice injection drug use (Agarwal et al., 1999).

This discussion provides brief descriptions of the dangers that follow drug use. Although unintended, these dangers and their associated costs are caused by the illegal nature of the business. That is, because distribution, sale and use are prohibited the acts must take place in secrecy. This secrecy prevents the utility of police support forcing those involved to protect themselves and their drug businesses territory through their own illegal and violent means. The psychopharmacological properties of drugs lead to poor hygiene and unsafe sexual and injection practices, all of which incur greater health costs to the individual and society. These peripheral dangers are the crux of the harm reduction perspective and the creation of the strategies used to counteract them.

Creation and Utilization

Harm reduction is an umbrella term used to describe all strategies that do not punish or require abstinence from drug use, including: Needle/Syringe Exchange Programs (NEPs and SEPs), Methadone Maintenance Treatment (MMT), Safe Injection Facilities (SIF)/Drug Consumption Rooms (DCR) and sexual education and condom distribution. However, before discussing applications and types, one should first understand the history surrounding the existence of harm reduction.

Due to the marginalization of drug users and the contrasting ideology of the general public, harm reduction programs are often created by grass-roots advocacy groups who have an understanding of drug use, addiction and their associated harms. Amsterdam is home to perhaps some of the most infamous drug policies in the world. However, while parts of the world may view the city as a drug user's haven, many of the successful harm reduction programs used throughout the world have their roots in Amsterdam.

The basis for drug policy in the Netherlands is the Opium Act, first established in 1919 (Korf and Buning, 2000). While the Dutch themselves were not experiencing widespread opium use, they did control one of the world's largest providers of opium and coca, in what is now Indonesia. The pressure to develop an official drug policy came from the United States, who was experiencing a growing problem with opium use. As a result, the Netherlands Opium Act focused on controlling the trade of opium and cocaine, and was further amended to outlaw the sale and possession of cannabis (Korf and Buning, 2000).

These changes remained in effect for only a short period due to the growing belief that these drugs produced little harm. The decriminalization of "soft drugs" such as cannabis began in the Netherlands; in 1976 the Opium Act was amended to decriminalize the sale and possession of small amounts of cannabis (Korf, Riper, and Bullington, 1999). In Amsterdam, today, individuals can possess small amounts of cannabis (up to 5 grams) for personal use without being subject to arrest or prosecution. Small amounts of cannabis can also be purchased within coffee houses where sale has been permitted. However, the so-called "hard drugs" such as heroin and cocaine are not available for legal purchase, although there are many programs that aim to reduce the harms associated with their use (Korf and Buning, 2000).

As mentioned, IDUs expose themselves to a host of health and social problems, no matter which drug they choose to use. One of the most serious health concerns for IDUs is the possible exposure to a blood-borne virus, such as HIV or hepatitis, as a result of sharing and borrowing needles (NIDA, 2005). Due to their emphasis on harm reduction policies, however, the Netherlands has been proactive in providing needles and syringes to their IDUs (Korf and Buning, 2000). For example, in Amsterdam, there are no laws against purchasing or possessing needles, making sterile needles easily accessible from pharmacies, shops, and vending machines and able to be carried by IDUs without recourse. The first needle exchange program (NEP) in the world was also established in 1984 by the Amsterdam Junkie Union, an advocacy group comprised of IDUs concerned with the spread of HBV (Lane et al., 2000). There are now approximately 40 countries that have established NEPs, including the United States (Wodak and Cooney, 2006).

Beginning in the 1970s, the Netherlands also became one of the first countries to develop what are known as "drug consumption rooms," (Dolan et al., 2000) designed to provide a place for drug users to inject safely, receive medical care and counseling, and have showers, laundry facilities, and food. As of 2003, there were 21 DCRs located in cities throughout the Netherlands (Kimber et al., 2003).

Applications of Harm Reduction

In the current section we describe the primary applications of many of the programs that have been established under the umbrella of harm reduction. While each is discussed as an individual intervention, many are provided jointly as a "one-stop-shop" where referrals to treatment may also be obtained if so desired (Drucker et al., 1998; Kimber et al., 2003; Wood et al., 2004).

Needle Exchange Programs (NEP)/Syringe Exchange Programs (SEP)

While the NEP was opened in Amsterdam due to fears surrounding HBV, it was the ensuing AIDS epidemic that eventually caused the widespread development of NEPs across the world. For decades injection drug use has consistently been shown to play a major role in the spread of HIV and HCV in the U.S. The Centers for Disease Control and Prevention (CDC) estimates that since the beginning of the HIV epidemic, the behaviors associated with injection drug use have accounted for one-third of all HIV cases and continue to contribute to new HIV cases each year (CDC, 2004). As a result, exchange programs began to be recognized around the world as a way to reduce sharing and borrowing of needles among IDUs (Lane et al., 2000).

One of the most severe consequences of heroin use is related to the needles used by IDUs. The CDC recommends that when drugs such as heroin are injected, a completely safe injection occurs only when a sterile needle is used one time and by only one person (U.S. Public Health Service, 1997). However, clean needles are not always readily available and users may require multiple needles just to get through the day and avoid the onset of withdrawal. Furthermore, in the U.S. there are still many cities where purchasing sterile needles is often difficult and expensive, requires a prescription, or is still illegal, as is the possession of needles (Gostin et al., 1997; Koester, 1994).

NEPs and SEPs provide IDUs with new, sterile needles in exchange for their used, dirty needles (Drucker et al., 1998). The logic behind the NEP is that if IDUs are provided with clean needles and dispose of the used ones, it will reduce the amount of time that a needle spends in circulation, and therefore, the amount of times it is used or shared with others. By providing a location to dispose of dirty needles, it also reduces the risk of unsafe disposal in garbage bins or on the street where they could potentially stick another person (Peterson et al., 1998).

Since IDUs are often homeless and tend to avoid certain areas due to the presence of law enforcement, NEPs take many different forms in order to reach them. These may involve a clinic, a café, mobile vans, and even folding tables on the street to make them more accessible (Peterson et al., 1998). Some programs require patrons to register while others leave participation anonymous. Most NEPs will also provide bleach and alcohol prep pads to assist with disinfecting the needle and skin, in addition to providing free condoms and safe sex education, and referrals to drug treatment, medical care, and other social services.

The laws surrounding possession of needles and syringes, the stigma surrounding injection drug use and AIDS, and a federal ban on their funding have all contributed to a difficult road for the acceptance of NEPs in the United States. As of 2010 there are currently 211 SEPs operating in 32 states, the District of Columbia, Puerto Rico and the Indian Nations (UN AIDS, 2006). In order to impact current HIV transmission rates, the recommended distribution rate is 200 needles per IDU per year (WHO/UNODC/UNAIDS, 2008), whereas the U.S. distribution rate is only 22 needles per IDU per year, one of the lowest in the world (Mathers et al., 2010).

Despite this fact, many cities (particularly in the U.S.) still have laws against the over-the-counter sale and purchase of syringes without a prescription, which makes it difficult for IDUs to obtain sterile injection equipment. The justification for such laws is often that providing accessibility to syringes encourages continued drug use (Buchanan et al., 2003). However, this argument is not supported by empirical evidence; in actuality, prescription laws likely do more harm than good. A study comparing cities with laws forbidding non-prescription sales of syringes to those cities without such laws were found to have similar rates of injection drug use, while possessing higher rates of HIV (Friedman, Perlis, and Des Jarlais, 2001). Cities with laws limiting the availability of syringes have also been shown to have higher prices for those syringes purchased on the street, making it even more difficult to obtain safe injection works (e.g. needles, syringes, rubbing alcohol, sterile pads and clean water) (Rich et al., 2000). While NEPs and SEPs are one type of service that can be made available to IDUs to provide them with sterile needles and allow them to dispose of their used needles without the need for and cost of the prescription, in the United States there are still many barriers to their development, including the twenty-year ban on federal funding for NEPs (DHHS, 2010).

Safe Injection Facility (SIF)

While NEPs were developed to specifically address the spread of infectious diseases such as HIV and HCV, there are still other problems associated that current health initiatives for IDUs fail to address (Dovey, Fitzgerald, and Choi, 2001). More specifically, NEPs and other services for IDUs here in the U.S. are often limited in providing a safe location in which to inject due to the criminal sanctions attached to illicit drug use. Safe injection facilities (SIF) aim to reduce instances of public drug use and associated harms while also providing IDUs with access to much needed services such as medical care and referrals to drug treatment.

Similar to the DRCs in Amsterdam, Switzerland operates what they refer to as "supervised injecting centers" where IDUs are provided with a clean room and sterile works to use for their injection (Dolan et al., 2000). These centers also contain a café and provide medical care and counseling with healthcare professionals when needed. As of 2003, 33 supervised injecting centers were operating throughout Switzerland (Kimber et al., 2003). Similar SIFs are currently operating in Vancouver, British Columbia, Australia, Germany and Spain, and plans to implement SIFs in other European countries have begun. There has never been such a facility sanctioned in the U.S. (Wood et al., 2004).

Methadone Maintenance Treatment (MMT)

MMT can be considered both a treatment and a harm reduction strategy. The short-term effects reduce the harm associated with heroin use, while long-term goals seek to stop use all together. Methadone, and to a lesser extent be-uprenophine, are pharmacological agents that prevent the withdrawal effects associated with heroin desistence, but do not provide the euphoric effects produced by opiate narcotics. During the 1950s and 60s, methadone was originally prescribed to heroin users to help manage their symptoms during the withdrawal period, lasting only one to two weeks, at which time methadone administration is stopped. However, these studies also found that the vast majority of users would relapse back to heroin once the methadone was out of their system and their cravings began again (Duvall, Locke, and Brill, 1963; Hunt and Odoroff, 1962). In the mid-1960s, trials began at the Rockefeller University in New York under the direction of Dr. Vincent P. Dole and Dr. Marie E. Nyswander that experimented with methadone maintenance, where instead of stopping the use of methadone, it continued to be administered to heroin users over a period of weeks and months (Joseph, Stancliff, and Langrod, 2000). The trials chose participants who were severely addicted—many with at least 10 years of addiction—and had multiple failures at other drug treatments and long criminal histories related to their drug use. Results of the trials showed that while the methadone maintenance was successful in containing the participants' symptoms of withdrawal, it also eliminated their cravings for heroin and built a tolerance for the euphoria or sedation effects of methadone (Joseph et al., 2000).

A major benefit of methadone is that it drastically reduces the harms associated with heroin use. First, the effects of one dose of methadone lasts up to 36 hours, drastically reducing the frequency of administering the drug compared to heroin (Tapert et al., 1998). Second, methadone use does not lead to an escalating tolerance like heroin use, which allows for a stable dose to be administered each time. Third, with the methadone constantly in the system, it is soon discovered that heroin use no longer has the same effects, resulting in the reduction or complete stoppage of use. Last, addicts are no longer distracted by the constant need to buy heroin. Therefore, a single dose of methadone each day could allow for heroin addicts to avoid the symptoms of withdrawal, the cravings, and the criminal activities related to obtaining heroin (Drucker, 2000).

Once methadone maintenance had been established as a safe and effective treatment for heroin addicts, treatment programs quickly spread across the U.S. (Drucker, 2000). However, during the moral crusade surrounding the advent of abstinence-only programs and the war on drugs, MMT was often demonized as "replacing the use of one addictive drug with another," and thus, the once rapidly expanding program soon grew stagnant. It was not until the start of the AIDS epidemic in the U.S. that it became clear there were serious health concerns related to injection drug use in which MMT could play an important role. Since methadone is administered orally, MMTs not only reduces the use of heroin but also the potential spread of HIV and other injection related diseases (Drucker, 2000).

Safe Sex Provisions and Care

As mentioned sex workers who are also IDUs are at much greater risk for contracting negative health effects. Studies have indicated the sex workers who are also IDUs are more likely to inject daily, exchange sex for drugs and share injecting equipment (Benotsch et al., 2004; Platt et al., 2005), putting them at higher risk for contracting HIV and other sexual and blood-borne diseases, as well as overdose. When IDUs negotiate sex for money and/or drugs, there is often little leverage to negotiate condom use and sterile injection works. Given that most of the money that is earned by IDU sex workers goes towards the purchase of drugs for their addiction, one way to encourage safe sex practices is to distribute free condoms. As a general harm reduction practice major cities have been distributing free condoms for decades. In fact, New York City began combating STDs with free condom distribution in 1971 (DiBranco, 2010). As one form of harm reduction, clinics and outreach centers seek out this risky population providing not only condoms but typically offer literature on safe sex practices and health and wellness, as well as referrals to shelters and other harm reduction practices (e.g. NEPs/SEPs).

Although many harm reduction practices have been implemented and remain operational, many fail as often their sustainability is dependent on local and governmental support. Implementation requires a shift from the current status quo of drug preventions (typically the moral model) to the progressive tactics of harm reduction. The following section will describe why and how implementation is impeded.

Implementation and Barriers

By Episodes 6 and 7 of Season 3 of *The Wire*, Hamsterdam is fully operational. Dealers and Junkies are freely exchanging goods while police patrol from a distance. Those involved in the drug market are made aware that, while distribution and possession are acceptable acts, violence (or any form of aggression) is not. Unlike the successful grass-roots organizations that gain the support of the public, the secret and yet authoritarian implementation of Hamsterdam created barriers that impeded its chances of success. Although considered novel, finding support for the modification of the status quo to a harm reduction method is difficult. Particularly among line staff that is both unfamiliar and resistant to new occupational roles, it can be a difficult hurdle for the implementation of harm reduction strategies. In Episode 9 the pushback from frustrated officers is observed, particularly those once involved in narcotic enforcement and those who relish "busting heads the Western District way." This pushback is due to the changing of roles from enforcement to glorified security guard or babysitter. Eventually, Hamsterdam becomes a less exotic version of Lord of the Flies. Given the recent police acceptance of dealing, Hoppers, no longer employed by dealers as lookouts and runners, are simply truant children running and playing in the streets. With the threat of violence and the veil of judgment lifted, Junkies bring their children with them to score and the vacant row houses become havens for sex and drug use. This blatant hedonism no doubt creates some of the officers' frustration; where those once illegal acts that normally occurred out of sight are now in purview of the police. Officers trained under the status quo, zero-tolerance, moral model are forced to reconcile the compromise that is harm reduction. That is, while it is great to have a reduction in violence and the associated harms of drug use, one is forced to watch as individuals harm themselves through drug use, sex work and ambivalence. The internal moral conflict felt by officers, results in the pushback and the boiling point of that pushback (Herc calling the press) represents the beginning of the demise for Colvin's experimental neighborhood.

Disgust for the Marginalized

Although advocates of harm reduction strategies often lay blame on the conservative status quo of the moral model, it is important to recognize why such interventions have a difficult time being implemented and sustained. Drug users are marginalized in our society. The reason for this marginalization is multi-dimensional and, depending on the person, has a potential mixture of religious, health, political and ideological components involved. Particularly in the U.S., drug users are treated by non-drug users as though they possess a disease that we are frightened will infect us or someone we care about. However, because users choose to begin and continue their addiction, they can be blamed for hurting themselves and, in turn, our society. The blame associated with addiction provides the rationale needed to treat drug users and dealers as "less deserving," and in many instances within the U.S., as criminal.

Right or wrong, this marginalization process makes those involved in illegal drug use considered the "underclass," which is the status quo of all societies. Harm reduction strategies attempt to remove, or at least reduce, the marginalization of drug users, providing services and resources to those that were once considered "less deserving". This break with the status quo often causes the type of pushback witnessed in Season 3 and impedes real world implementation of interventions and programs.

National Pushback

There is no place that better exemplifies the marginalization of drug users than the U.S. While an increasing number of countries embrace harm reduction, the U.S. continues their zero-tolerance approach towards drug use, even with knowledge that such policies are having drastic consequences on the HIV/AIDS epidemic (Lurie and Drucker, 1997). The current ban on the federal funding for NEPs has existed in the United States since 1988 (Vlahov et al., 2001). While the ban was lifted by Congress in December of 2009, giving hope that funding could now be provided to states and localities to support NEPs, it would prove to only be a temporary victory (Lucas, 2009). Congress reinstated the ban on the federal funding for NEPs in December of 2011 (Barr, 2011). The ban continues to be justified by those who argue that NEPs/SEPs provide few benefits to IDUs, and actually produce further harm to communities, an argument that has never been supported by empirical evidence. As long as the ban is in place, it will continue to contribute to a serious lack of needle exchange programs in the U.S. and leave the burden of providing funding for NEPs/SEPs on state and local governments.

Unfortunately, the ban will also continue to create costly health consequences for the U.S. Lurie and Drucker (1997) estimated that between 4,000 to 10,000 new HIV infections could have been prevented between 1987 and 1995 if NEPs had been established, which represents only a portion of the ban period. The healthcare costs associated with treating just these HIV cases is estimated to be between a quarter and a half-billion dollars.

Localized Pushback

Unfortunately, it would also appear that even in those cities where legal NEPs have been established, barriers still exist. Similar to the Hamsterdam experiment, when pushback occurs it is often local police and officials who often ignore the sanctioned efforts of local harm reduction strategies and continue to operate under an abstinence-only model. Several findings have documented this enforcement pushback and intimidation phenomenon. One study found evidence that law enforcement presence in the area around a legal NEP subsequently decreased attendance levels, especially among African-Americans and males using the program (Davis et al., 2005). There is evidence that law enforcement officials have also been known to harass IDUs attempting to access legal NEPs and even arrested users possessing syringes they received from an NEP (Bluthenthal, 1997; Davis et al., 2005; Heimer et al., 1996). A nighttime NEP was set up in Vancouver, British Columbia to provide needles to IDUs after other similar facilities had closed for the day. In turn, the Vancouver police department set up officers on the corner where the NEP was located. Results showed a significant decline in the number of needles being exchanged compared to before the police intervention began (Wood et al., 2003). A study conducted in cities in Massachusetts found that law enforcement in Boston and Cambridge still continued to arrest IDUs who were attending legal NEPs and carrying their identification card (Case, Meehan, and Jones, 1998). Another study conducted in California found that IDUs attending legal NEPs were more likely to receive citations and be arrested by law enforcement than those IDUs attending an illegal NEP (Martinez et al., 2007).

Given these findings, it is not surprising that some studies also indicate IDUs report unwillingness to access NEPs or carry syringes on them for fear of being stopped or arrested by law enforcement (Bastos and Strathdee, 2000; Bluthenthal et al., 1999). Furthermore, those IDUs who report they are concerned with law enforcement stopping them while carrying such paraphernalia were also more than one and a half times more likely to report the sharing of syringes (Bluthenthal et al., 1999). These findings buttress the conception that U.S. drug policy, or the laws that are implemented to prevent and control IDUs, are also causing them considerable harm.

Other tactics used by law enforcement have also been found to have similar effects on IDU behavior (Kerr, Small, and Wood, 2005). While police crackdowns and raids are often aimed at displacing illegal open air drug markets and the public disorder associated with them, research has shown they also indirectly impact IDUs. With an increased police presence around a drug market, IDUs spend more time searching for drugs to buy and finding a location to use them where they will not be seen (Dovey et al., 2001). For example, a district of the New York City police department conducted crackdowns on drug-related activity, and interviews conducted with IDUs living in the area found that they were more likely to take their injecting to unsafe locations in order to avoid police presence (Cooper et al., 2005).

In addition to the increased health and safety risks IDUs are exposed to as an indirect result of police presence, research has also indicated users are less likely to attend the services available to them for fear of law enforcement contact (Kerr et al., 2005). Outreach programs already report having a difficult time locating and maintaining ties to IDUs, indicating police presence drives an already isolated population even further underground and impedes their access to the much-needed health and social services.

Given the strong link between sex workers and IDUs, some police tactics combat prostitution through targeted enforcement of those who utilize harm reduction practices. Washington, D.C., a city that possesses the highest HIV infection rate of HIV/AIDS in the U.S., enacted the Omnibus Public Safety Emergency Amendment Act in 2006, allowing law enforcement to enact new "Prostitution Free Zones." Unlike the free zone of Hamsterdam, in these areas of D.C., it is unlawful for two or more persons to congregate in a public space for the purposes of engaging in prostitution or related offenses. A violation is incurred if an officer is knowledgeable that a person is a participant of prostitution-related offenses (DC Act 16-445), and a person found to be in violation can be fined and jailed for up to 180 days. The evidence needed to convict a person of being in violation is simply the possession of an unspecified number of condoms. Similar instances of using condoms as evidence of prostitution have been reported in New York and San Francisco (DiBranco, 2010). Therefore, organizations that provide free condoms in promotion of safe sex practices have the ability to implicate their target population because of local law enforcement practices designed to utilize harm reduction practices as evidence of illegality, thus rendering sex workers fearful of protecting themselves. Until recently, U.S. policy requires that any organization that receives HIV/AIDS funding to demonstratively oppose prostitution by requiring funded agencies to sign an anti-prostitution pledge (CHANGE, 2008; CHANGE, 2010). In the field, these local and national policies have yet to identify documented positive results; however, there have been numerous findings of their harmful effects including endangerment of the lives of sex workers, their clients and their families (CHANGE, 2011).

The negative health and social consequences for IDUs as a result of typical law enforcement practices aimed at illegal drug markets has been well-documented (Burris et al., 2004; Kerr et al., 2005). And while there is some evidence that law enforcement has been successful in achieving goals of public order and the impression of public safety, strategies such as police crackdowns also come with many drawbacks (Caulkins, 1993). For example, crackdowns can lead to harsh tactics, civil rights violations, and the possibility of only displacing drug dealers and users to other surrounding neighborhoods or indoor locations.

Whatever model a person, society or nation views as the best, or believes should be prominent, what we have hopefully conveyed through this chapter is that a single, one-size fits all model (such as that operated by the U.S. for the past 30 years) is not likely to work as a default response to all drug policy. As nations and localities continue to experiment and apply harm reduction methods, it is crucial to gain the support of all organizations, especially law enforcement. Demonstrated here, invoking the change in status quo is hard and not always accepted by those with power and influence. To insure success of harm reduction strategies practitioners must gain the support of policy makers and law enforcement officials prior to and during implementation and operation.

Impact of Harm Reduction

Because Hamsterdam is kept secret, Colvin is aware that his experiment has an expiration date. By Episode 9 the officers assigned to patrol Hamsterdam are finally frustrated with their "babysitting" duties. The press is called and Colvin is allowed to have a week before the story is released to the public.

In Episode 10 he presents his results to the Commissioner and the other Senior Officers at the regular COMPSTAT meeting. His findings indicate a 14% decline in crime, a substantial decrease. He then comes clean and explains how he was able to achieve the large drop in such a short period of time. When pressed to reveal his strategy Colvin states, "I moved them [the dealers] off the corners ... to the areas in my district of the least harm." To which Deputy Commissioner Rawls, exclaims, "Don't you realize what he has done? He's legalized drugs!"

Effectiveness

Up to this point we have discussed what harm reduction is and how it works but have yet to discuss if it works. That is, is it effective? Since the goals of harm reduction differ, the outcomes to determine effectiveness also differ. Evaluations of harm reduction interventions focus on the harms they are designed to impact, such as: decreased use of dirty needles, reduction of risky sexual behaviors, improved overall health, decreases in fatalities caused by overdose and a reduction of drug use; with the ultimate goal of desistance from drug use. This section discusses the current state of findings that surround the various harm reduction strategies described previously.

Methadone Maintenance Treatment (MMT)

The success of MMT as a harm reduction program has been well documented. Studies conducted on the impact of MMT have found numerous benefits for those heroin users participating in treatment, including: a reduction in heroin injecting (Ball and Ross, 1991), a decreased likelihood of risky behaviors related to injection drug use (Gibson, Flynn, and McCarthy, 1999), a decreased mortality rate (Hall, 1997), a reduction in criminal activity and arrests (Marsch, 1998), and improved social productivity (Drucker et al., 1998). When comparing those heroin users in MMT to those users not in treatment, heroin users not receiving MMT were more likely to report visiting shooting galleries, sharing needles, a higher average number of sexual partners, and behaviors related to contracting HIV and other diseases (Metzger et al., 1993). While relapse has been found to occur at high rates for those who leave MMT (Ball and Ross, 1991), the benefits continue for those who remain in treatment.

Needle/Syringe Exchange Programs (NEPs/SEPs)

Effectiveness of NEPs/SEPs is usually measured by the ability to reduce needle sharing and borrowing, behaviors seen as increasing the risk of contracting HIV and other blood-borne viruses. Studies have consistently shown that IDUs reporting use of an NEP show a decrease in the sharing and borrowing of needles (Ksobiech, 2003) and decreases in HIV prevalence (DeJarlais et al., 2005; Hurley, Jolley, and Kaldor, 1997). In addition, studies have failed to find increases in drug use or in the number of IDUs, and some have actually reported a reduction in drug use (Drucker et al., 1998). Furthermore, research has shown no evidence of an increase in the number of discarded needles in the area surrounding a NEP (Fuller et al., 2002).

Supervised Injection Facilities (SIFs)

Evaluations conducted on the supervised injection facility (SIF) in Vancouver, B.C. have shown participants to be less likely to engage in high-risk behaviors associated with injection drug use, such as sharing and borrowing needles (Kerr et al., 2005). Evidence has also shown that IDUs defined as "high risk"[1] were more likely to use the SIF (Wood, et al., 2005). Furthermore, interviews with IDUs reveal safe injection education to be helpful, and they found the practitioners to be knowledgeable and trustworthy (Fast et al., 2008).

In addition evaluations have also shown that the fears associated with the opening of the supervised injection facility, such as an increase in public nuisance associated with drug use, influx of drug dealers into the neighborhood,

---

1. Defined in terms of their potential harm to the community and themselves, such as those IDUs at an elevated risk of contracting HIV, IDUs who were frequent cocaine injectors, those living in unstable housing conditions and IDUs reporting public drug use.

discarded needles and syringes in the streets, and more criminal activity never came to fruition (Wood et al., 2006). Furthermore, a study of the arrest rates for drug trafficking and other drug-related crimes in the neighborhood where the SIF is located showed that there were no significant changes from the year prior to the year after the opening of the SIF (Freeman et al., 2005; Wood et al., 2006).

Evaluations of auxiliary services and referrals provided by harm reduction interventions showed that referrals to drug treatment, addiction counseling, and medical and housing assistance were commonly made and the number of IDUs participating in addiction counseling within the facility increased over time (Tyndall et al., 2005).

Safe Sex Provisions and Care

Given federal policies and law enforcement tactics used to combat prostitution in the U.S., it is not surprising that the most effective programs of safe sex provision and care have been observed elsewhere. For instance, in the Dominican Republic, where there is no specific provision against sex work, there are estimated to be more than 100,000 female sex workers (Haddock, 2007). By promoting a peer education program in conjunction with policies requiring condom use in every sexual encounter between sex workers and their clients, the Dominican Republic has succeeded in promoting consistent condom use and other safe sexual behaviors and the prevalence of HIV had consistently declined since 1990 (Moreno and Kerrigan, 2000). Similar programs have been established in Cambodia and Taiwan.

Although not as prevalent as evaluations of drug treatment interventions, encouraging evidence has been identified regarding effective outcomes of harm reduction methods. As knowledge and advocacy for such interventions continue to progress, the importance of gaining support from the grass-roots level and above is critically important, the following section will demonstrate that even the smallest amount of negative public reaction can be the catalyst that shuts down a harm reduction intervention.

Legalization and Negative Connotations

In Episode 11, Mayor Royce is informed of Hamsterdam's existence. Because of its effectiveness he forms a committee to explore the possibility of keeping the experiment going. The belief among the committee is that "legalization" has too strong of a negative connotation and if the program can be renamed, it may have a chance of public acceptance. Unfortunately, after the press reveals video from inside the free zone, all of those involved realize the public and political backlash is too great to keep it alive. Episode 12 closes with a police crackdown of Hamsterdam and concludes with the vacant houses being bulldozed, as Bubbles states "like they took a big eraser and wiped it all clean".

Public Reaction

The U.S. law enforcement strategy known as the "War on Drugs" invokes a sense of mission. One in which, as a nation, will not stop until drug use is eradicated, and by winning the war will, in turn, protect the nation's citizens and vulnerable populations, namely impressionable children. What has been observed in three decades since the war's declaration is that, without a representative for the opposition to declare defeat, a sense that "winning" the war, or a banner of "mission accomplished" will never be waived.

As one digs deeper into the impact of drug use (such as: HIV transmission, overdose and incarceration) one sees that the war is declared against its own citizens. In order to fight a war against our own people, policy makers and drug enforcement agents must declare the cause a moralistic pursuit, in which an opposition exists (i.e. Junkies and Dealers), and those persons are downright "evil" and/or bad for society. This vilification allows members of society to create the "Us vs. Them" mentality needed to fight a domestic war. However, as demonstrated in numerous occasions in *The Wire* series, dealers and junkies who either die, become incarcerated, or get out of the game for any reason are quickly replaced by a new generation of players.

This is the traditional law enforcement strategy of drug prevention: continue to chase an ideal of a drug-abstinent society. For U.S. politicians and policy makers, the moral model possesses intergenerational acceptance and to pursue a new direction (e.g. harm reduction) will be met with harsh resistance. When the strategy is effective, a police drug bust allows for a news conference to display piles of drugs being taken off the street, invoking a temporary sense of mission accomplished for the good guys. At the other extreme, courts have interpreted illegal possession as used needles, where residue left in a syringe constitutes criminal possession (Burris et al., 2002)[2]. However, press conferences are never held when a person is convicted for possession of drug paraphernalia, and thus, the punishment and marginalization of low level of-

---

2. Typically the penalty for residue possession is a misdemeanor offense with persons convicted often sentenced to jail time and/or fines of $1,000–$5,000. However, some states view residue as a felony offense, punishable by 5–10 years in prison (Burris et al., 2002).

fenders (junkies/users) continues. Although the extent and visibility of this punishment often goes unnoticed.

Strategies that utilize harm reduction, in contrast, practice compromise to deal with society's ills, attempting to help not punish these low level offenders. There is no futile pursuit of evildoers or eradication of drugs; there is instead an acceptance that certain persons, for whatever reason, feel the need to abuse drugs. This perspective suggests that, while preventing drug use entirely is impossible, one can allow users to commit their bad acts in a way that is safe and reduces the harm on the players and the other citizens. Although viewed as a more humanitarian approach to the problem, in the U.S. these strategies are often painted as being "soft on crime", a label that policy makers and politicians hope to avoid.

An example of the backlash that can occur in reaction to harm reduction programs occurred during and after the documented closing of a NEP in Windham, Connecticut (Broadhead, Van Hulst, and Heckathorn, 1999a and 1999b). In 1992 Connecticut passed legislation allowing for state support of non-prescription sale of syringes and NEPs, making Windham one of six exchange programs in operation by 1994. Although numerous national organizations have praised needle exchanges as a preventive measure for the transmission of HIV and other IDU-related illnesses, and despite a demonstration of preliminary success within Windham, the program was nonetheless shut down in 1997.

The demise of the Windham program is a common story to many failed harm reduction interventions. A politically motivated public figure (in this case the State's Attorney) accused the program of "causing" the drug problem rather than solving it. This is a common attack of harm reduction strategies as, by their very nature, do not attempt to decrease drug use and thus, never demonstrate visible "effectiveness" (i.e. less drugs, dealers and users in the streets). Because of this premise, they become easy scapegoats for a city's problems, as one can claim that drug addicts and dealers are allowed to corrupt new users and that creating a safe haven for users encourages migration of such populations to the areas in which exchange programs operate.

Harm reduction programs are often further condemned by sensationalized news stories depicting the harmful effects of drug use. In Windham's case, the local paper reported a story of a two year-old girl accidently jabbing herself with a used needle found in her yard. Although likely an isolated incident, unrelated to the practices of the needle exchange, once blame was attached to the program's practices the ship began to sink. As witnessed by the Windham exchange project, once the public has a reason to fear a program's clients and cast judgment on competency, no amount of scientific evidence or citizen testimonials can save the program. Quickly the town reverted to the tried and true law enforcement strategy. In contrast to the public reaction, post-closure interviews revealed significant increases in self-reported needle sharing among Windham IDUs after the program halted operations. However, neighborhood surveys revealed the "closure of the needle-exchange appeared to have no significant impact on the larger drug scene" (Broadhead, Van Hulst, and Heckathorn, 1999a: 59).

Buchanan and colleagues (2003) described a similar cultural resistance to needle exchanges in Massachusetts, and imply that in the U.S., it is difficult to convince the public to switch from a law enforcement strategy to harm reduction tactics. They suggest that when scientific evidence butts heads with a moralistic crusade against a social problem, science tends to lose. In a discussion of harm reduction methods, Governor Christy Todd Whitman (an opponent of harm reduction strategies) surmised the moralistic backlash to harm reduction, stating that "It would tactically encourage illegal drug use. Government should not be in the business of facilitating illegal activity" (Buchanan et al., 2003: 431). Thus, when a social ill, like drug use, can be viewed in terms of possessing a moral right and wrong choice, a compromise of that moral authority is difficult to come by (despite overwhelming scientific evidence to the contrary). Furthermore, arguments against harm reduction tactics are often broken down into two sides, reducing the harm to current drug users/addicts, or sending a clear message to impressionable parts of society (typically children) that drug use is morally wrong. Unfortunately for the current users/addicts that might benefit from a harm reduction model, defining right and wrong to children in the U.S. is a more favored topic of public conversation and policy. Thus, creating policy that sides with the drug user and other "evil doers" can kill a political career.

In contrast, many developed countries (e.g. Western Europe, Canada, New Zealand and Australia) and even some low-and middle-income countries (e.g. Nepal and Brazil) do not view intravenous drug use as a moral crusade but as a national health epidemic. For these countries harm reduction methods such as needle exchange, prescription opium use or supervised injection facilities are a social service solution, similar to that of food stamps and Medicaid. However, instead of providing food and general medical coverage, one prevents the spread of blood-borne illnesses and overdoses. In fact, in many of these countries, syringes are universally sold over the counter (Tempalski, 2007).

It should be clear that, no matter what vague or mission-oriented name one attempts to rename it, harm reduction strategies often elicit a negative public reaction. Although some neighborhoods that have a history of drug sales and use might welcome harm reduction strategies, certainly most communities would not want needles sold at their local pharmacy (as that would indicate that heroin use is occurring near them). This is referred to as the Not In My Back

Yard mentality (NIMBY). Now, needle exchanges are a mild form of harm reduction, in which those with a liberal perception of drug use might be able to accept. That is, the greater intensity of the strategy, the greater the clash with cultural tradition. The notion that legalized heroin or safe injection sites could exist in the U.S. is a distant unforeseeable reality. This is why Colvin knew that, once the press arrived, the Hamsterdam experiment was over.

Conclusion

In the final scene of Episode 12, prior to the closing of Hamsterdam, Major Colvin drives Councilman (soon to be Mayor) Carcetti down for a one last look at the free zone. Before Carcetti steps out of the car Colvin states, "what you are going to see ain't pretty, but it's safe."

Convincing the general public to accept an alternative strategy is the most challenging part of implementation. As Tempalski (2007) describes, it is difficult to implement needle exchange and other harm reduction strategies even in neighborhoods hardest hit by drug use. The hardest part of implementing harm reduction is ignoring the "brown paper bag" that is suspending moral outrage for the sake of health and safety of the most marginalized of society. Successful harm reduction clinics and other facilities have been established. Unlike Colvin's experiment, the most successful programs have received support from government authorities and law enforcement officials prior to implementation. When the influential groups are on board early, the local resistance is greatly weakened (Tempalski, 2007). If the harm reduction movement is to move forward in the U.S., the most difficult part is removing the stigma from "Junkies and Dope Fiends" at the local level. This takes convincing the general public that abstinence for drug users is difficult to achieve and the policies that surround abstinence ultimately criminalize the drug users, escalating the medical and social consequences of drug use (Clear, 2003). It is also clear that harm reduction cannot simply rely on scientific evidence but must also do the grunt work of convincing others to retreat from, or at least compromise about, their ideological moral crusade and instead commit to improving the health and well-being of all people.

References

Agarwal, A.K., Singh, G.B., Khundom, K.C., Singh, N.D., Singh, T., & Jana, S. (1999). The prevalence of HIV in female sex workers in Manipur, India. *Journal of Communicable Diseases*, 31, 23–28.

Aitken, C., Moore, D., Higgs, P., Kelsall, J., & Kerger, M. (2002). The impact of a police crackdown on a street drug scene: Evidence from the street. *International Journal of Drug policy*, 13, 189–198.

Bastos, F.I., & Strathdee, S.A. (2000). Evaluating effectiveness of syringe exchange programmes: Current issues and future prospects. *Social Science and Medicine*, 51(12), 1771–1782.

Ball, J.C. & Ross, A. (1991). The effectiveness of methadone maintenance treatment: Patients, programs, services, and outcome. New York, NY: Springer-Verlag Publishing.

Barr, S. (21 December 2011). Needle-exchange programs face new federal funding ban. KHN News. Available at http://www.kaiserhealthnews.org/stories/2011/december/21/needle-exchange-federal-funding.aspx.

Baumer, E., Lauritsen, J.L., Rosenfeld, R., & Wright, R. (1998). The influence of crack cocaine on robbery, burglary, and homicide rates: A cross-city, longitudinal analysis. *Journal of Research in Crime and Delinquency*, 35(3), 316–340.

Benotsch, E., Somlai, A.M., Pinkerton, S.D., Kelly, J.A., Ostrovski, D., Gore-Felton, C. & Kozlov, A.P. (2004). Drug Use and sexual risk behaviors among female Russian IDUs who exchange sex for money or drugs. *International Journal of STD & AIDS*, 15: 343–347.

Blumstein, A. & Rosenfeld, R. (1999). Trends in rates of violence in the USA. *Studies on Crime and Crime Prevention*, 8, 139–167.

Bluthenthal, R.N. (1997). Impact of law enforcement on syringe exchange programs: A look at Oakland and San Francisco. *Medical Anthropology*, 18, 61–83.

Bluthenthal, R.N., Lorvick, J., Kral, A., Erringer, E.A., & Kahn, J.G. (1999). Collateral damage in the war on drugs: HIV risk behaviors among injection drug users. *International Journal of Drug Policy*, 10, 25–38.

Brickman, P., Rabinowitz, V.C., Coates, D. Cohen, E., & Kiddler, L. 1982. Models of helping and coping. *Am. Psychol.* 37: 364–384.

Broadhead, R.S., van Hulst, Y., & Heckathorn, D.D. (1999a). The impact of a needle exchange's closure. *Public Health Reports*, 114, 439–447.

Broadhead, R.S., van Hulst, Y., & Heckathorn, D.D. (1999b). Termination of an established needle-exchange: A study of claims and their impact. *Social Problems*, 46(1), 48–66.

Broadhead, R.S., Kerr, T.H., Grund, J.C., & Altice, F.L. (2002). Safer injection facilities in North America: Their place in public policy and health initiatives. *Journal of Drug Issues*, 32(1), 329–356.

Buchanan, D., Shaw, S., Ford, A., & Singer, M. (2003). Empirical science meets moral panic: An analysis of the politics of needle exchange. *Journal of Public Health Policy*, 24(3/4), 427–444.

Burris, S., Welsh, J., Ng, M., Li, M., & Ditzler, A. (2002). State syringe and drug possession laws potentially influencing safe syringe disposal by injecting drug users. *Journal of the American Pharmaceutical Association*, 42(Suppl. 2), S94–S98.

Burris, S., Blankenship, K.M., Donoghoe, M., Sherman, S., Vernick, J.S., Case, P., Lazzarini, Z., & Koester, S. (2004). Addressing the "risk environment" for injection drug users: The mysterious case of the missing cop. *The Milbank Quarterly*, 82(1), 125–156.

Case, P., Meehan, T., & Jones, T.S. (1998). Arrests and incarceration of injection drug users for syringe possession in Massachusetts: Implications for HIV prevention. *Journal of Acquired Immune Deficiency Syndrome and Human Retrovirology*, 18(Suppl 1), S71–S75.

Caulkins, J.P. (1993). Local drug markets' response to focused police enforcement. *Operations Research*, 41(5), 848–863.

Centers for Disease Control and Prevention. (2004). HIV prevention in the third decade: Specific populations. Atlanta, GA: Centers for Disease Control and Prevention.

Center for Substance Abuse Research. (2008, March 10). FY2009 Federal drug control budget released; Prevention continues to receive dwindling proportion of funding. Available at http://www.cesar.umd.edu/cesar/cesarfax/vol17/17-10.pdf.

CHANGE. (2011 July 6). Women's Health Rights Advocates Applaud Court Ruling Against Bush-era HIV/AIDS Policy Against Sex Workers. CHANGE's press release on the 2011 court ruling. Available at: http://www.pepfarwatch.org/the_issues/anti_prostitution_pledge/.

CHANGE. (2008 August). Implications of U.S. Policy Restrictions for HIV Programs Aimed at Commercial Sex Workers. CHANGE's Policy Brief. Available at: http://www.genderhealth.org/files/uploads/change/publications/aplobrief.pdf.

CHANGE. (2010 October). Human Trafficking, HIV/AIDS, and the Sex Sector: Human Rights for All. Report by CHANGE and American University Washington College of Law. Available at: http://www.genderhealth.org/files/uploads/change/publications/Human_Trafficking_HIVAIDS_and_the_Sex_Sector.pdf.

Chitwood, D.D., Griffin, D.K., Comerford, M., Page, J.B., Trapido, E.J., Lai, S. & McCoy, C.B. (1995). Risk factors for HIV-1 seroconversion among injection drug users: A case-control study. *American Journal of Public Health*, 85(11), 1538–1542.

Clear, T. (2003) Personal communication with Barbara Tempalski. Executive Director, Harm Reduction Coalition. New York City, New York.

Cooper, H., Moore, L., Gruskin, S., & Krieger, N. (2004). Characterizing perceived police violence: Implications for public health. *American Journal of Public Health*, 94(7), 1109–1118.

Cooper, H., Moore, L., Gruskin, S., & Krieger, N. (2005). The impact of a police drug crackdown on drug injectors' ability to practice harm reduction: A qualitative study. *Social Science and Medicine*, 61, 673–684.

Davis, C.S., Burris, S., Kraut-Becher, J., Lynch, K.G., & Metzger, D. (2005). Effects of an intensive street-level police intervention on syringe exchange program use in Philadelphia, PA. *American Journal of Public Health*, 95(2), 233–236.

DC Act 16-445. 2006. Prostitution Free Zone. District of Columbia, Metropolitan Police. Available at http://mpdc.dc.gov/mpdc/cwp/view,a,1238,q,560843.asp.

Department of Health and Human Services. Implementation Guidance for Syringe Services Programs. CDC. (2010, July). Available at http://www.cdc.gov/hiv/resources/guidelines/PDF/SSP-guidanceacc.pdf.

Des Jarlais, D.C. & Friedman, S.R. (1990). Shooting galleries and AIDS: Infection probabilities and 'tough' policies. *American Journal of Public Health*, 80(2), 142–144.

Des Jarlais, D.C., Perlis, T., Arasteh, K., Torian, L.V., Hagan, H., Beatrice, S., Smith, L., Wethers, J., Milliken, J., Mildvan, D., Yancovitz, S., & Friedman, S.R. (2005). Reductions in hepatitis C virus and HIV infections among injecting drug users in New York City, 1990–2001. *AIDS*, 19(Suppl 3), S20–S25.

DiBranco, A. (2010). New York and San Francisco use condoms as evidence of prostitution. Change.org. Available at http://news.change.org/stories/new-york-and-san-francisco-use-condoms-as-evidence-of-prostitution.

Dixon, D., & Maher, L. (2002). Anh Hai: Policing culture and social exclusion in a street heroin market. *Policing & Society*, 12(2), 93–110.

Dolan, K., Kimber, J., Fry, C., Fitzgerald, J., McDonald, D., & Trautmann, F. (2000). Drug consumption facilities in Europe and the establishment of supervised injecting centres in Australia. *Drug and Alcohol Review*, 19, 337–346.

Dovey, K., Fitzgerald, J., & Choi, Y. (2001). Safety becomes danger: Dilemmas of drug-use in public space. *Health and Place*, 7(4), 319–331.

Drucker, E. (2000). From morphine to methadone: Maintenance drugs in the treatment of opiate addiction. In J.A. Inciardi & L.D. Harrison (Eds.)

Harm reduction: National and international perspectives (1st ed., pp. 27–45). Thousand Oaks, CA: Sage Publications, Inc.

Drucker, E., Lurie, P., Wodak, A., & Alcabes, P. (1998). Measuring harm reduction: The effects of needle and syringe exchange programs and methadone maintenance on the ecology of HIV. *AIDS*, 12(Suppl A), S217–S230.

Duvall, H., Locke, B., & Brill, L. (1963). Follow-up study of narcotic drug addicts five years after hospitalization. *Public Health Reports*, 78(3), 185–193.

Fast, D., Small, W., Wood, E., & Kerr, T. (2008). The perspectives of injection drug users regarding safer injecting education delivered through a supervised injecting facility. *Harm Reduction Journal*, 5, 32.

Fischer, B., Oviedo-Joekes, E., Blanken, P., Haasen, C., Rehm, J., Schechter, M.T., Strang, J., & van den Brink, W. (2007). Heroin-assisted treatment (HAT) a decade later: A brief update on science and politics. *Journal of Urban Health*, 84(4), 552–562.

French, M.T., McGeary, K.A., Chitwood, D.D., & McCoy, C.B. (2000). Chronic illicit drug use, health services utilization and the cost of medical care. *Social Science & Medicine*, 50, 1703–1713.

Friedman, S.R., Perlis, T., & Des Jarlais, D.C. (2001). Laws prohibiting over-the-counter syringe sales to injection drug users: Relations to population density, HIV prevalence, and HIV incidence. *American Journal of Public Health*, 91, 791–793.

Fuller, C.M., Ahern, J., Vadnai, L., Coffin, P.O., Galea, S., Factor, S.H., & Vlahov, D. (2002). Impact of increased syringe access: Preliminary findings on injection drug user syringe source, disposal, and pharmacy sales in Harlem, New York. *Journal of the American Pharmaceutical Association*, 42(Suppl 2), S77–S82.

Gerstein, D., & Harwood, H. (Eds). (1990). Treating drug problems (Vol. 1). Washington DC: National Academy Press.

Gibson, D.R., Flynn, N.M. & McCarthy, J.J. (1999). Effectiveness of methadone treatment in reducing HIV risk behavior and HIV seroconversion among injecting drug users. *AIDS*, 13, 1807–1818.

Gostin, L.O., Lazzarini, Z., Jones, T.S. & Flaherty, K. (1997). Prevention of HIV/AIDS and other blood-borne diseases among injection drug users: A national survey on the regulation of syringes and needles. *Journal of the American Medical Association*, 277(1), 53–62.

Haddock, S. (2007). Policy empowers—Condom use among sex workers in the Dominican Republic. *Population Action International*, 2(1), 1–7.

Hall, W. (1997). Australia's Methadone Program. Randwick, Australia: National Drug and Alcohol Research Center.

Heimer, R., Bluthenthal, R.N., Singer, M., & Khoshnood, K. (1996). Structural impediments to operational syringe-exchange programs. *AIDS and Public Policy Journal*, 11, 169–184.

Hubbard, R.L., Marsden, M.E., Rachal, J.V., Harwood, H.J., Cavanaugh, E.R., & Ginzburg, H.M. (1989). Drug abuse treatment: A national study of effectiveness. Chapel Hill, NC: University of North Carolina Press.

Hunt, G.H. & Odoroff, M.E. (1962). Follow-up study of narcotic drug addicts after hospitalization. Public Health Reports, 77(1), 41–54.

Hurley, S.F., Jolley, D.J., & Kaldor, J.M. (1997). Effectiveness of needle-exchange programmes for prevention of HIV infection. *Lancet*, 349(9068), 1797–1800.

Joseph, H., Stancliff, S., & Langrod, J. (2000). Methadone maintenance treatment (MMT): A review of historical and clinical issues. *The Mount Sinai Journal of Medicine*, 67, 347–363.

Kerr, T., Small, W., & Wood, E. (2005). The public health and social impacts of drug market enforcement: A review of the evidence. *International Journal of Drug Policy*, 16, 210–220.

Kerr, T., Tyndall, M., Li, K., Montaner, J., & Wood, E. (2005). Safer injection facility use and syringe sharing in injection drug users. *Lancet*, 366, 316–318.

Kimber, J., Dolan, K., Van Beek, I., Hedrich, D., & Zurhold, H. (2003). Drug consumption facilities: An update since 2000. *Drug and Alcohol Review*, 22, 227–233.

Koester, S.K. (1994). Copping, running, and paraphernalia laws: Contextual variables and needle risk behavior among injection drug users in Denver. *Human Organization*, 53(3), 287–295.

Korf, D.J. & Buning, E.C. (2000). Coffee shops, low-threshold methadone, and needle exchange: Controlling illicit drug use in the Netherlands. In J.A. Inciardi & L.D. Harrison (Eds.) Harm reduction: National and international perspectives (1st ed., pp. 111–135). Thousand Oaks, CA: Sage Publications, Inc.

Korf, D.J., Riper, H., & Bullington, B. (1999). Windmills in their minds? Drug policy and drug research in the Netherlands. *Journal of Drug Issues*, 29(3), 451–472.

Ksobiech, K. (2003). A meta-analysis of needle sharing, lending, and borrowing behaviors of needle exchange program attenders. *AIDS Education and Prevention*, 15(3), 257–268.

Lane, S.D., Lurie, P., Bowser, B., Kahn, J., & Chen, D. (2000). The coming of age of needle exchange: A history through 1993. In J.A. Inciardi & L.D. Harrison (Eds.) Harm reduction: National and international perspectives (1st ed., pp. 47–68). Thousand Oaks, CA: Sage Publications, Inc.

Lintzeris, N., Strang, J., Metrebian, N., Byford, S., Hallam, C., Lee, S., Zador, D., & RIOTT Group. (2006). Methodology for the Randomized Injecting

Opioid Treatment Trial (RIOTT): Evaluating injectable methadone and injectable heroin treatment versus optimized oral methadone treatment in the UK. *Harm Reduction Journal*, 3, 28.

Logan, D.E. & Marlatt, G.A. (2010). Harm reduction therapy: A practice-friendly review of research. *Journal of Clinical Psychology*, 66(2), 201–214.

Lucas F. (2009 December15) Obama likely to sign $1.1 trillion omnibus with 5,224 earmarks, taxpayer-funded abortions, needle exchange, White House says. CSN News. Available at: http://cnsnews.com/news/article/58528.

Lurie, P. & Drucker, E. (1997). An opportunity lost: HIV infections associated with lack of a national needle-exchange programme in the USA. *Lancet*, 349, 604–608.

Maher, L. & Dixon, D. (2001). The cost of crackdowns: Policing Cabramatta's heroin market. Current Issues in Criminal Justice, 13(1), 5–22.

Marlatt, G.A. & Witkiewitz, K. (2010). Update on harm-reduction policy and intervention research. Annual Review of Clinical Psychology, 6, 591–606.

Marsch, L.A. (1998). The efficacy of methadone maintenance interventions in reducing illicit opiate use, HIV risk behavior, and criminality: A meta-analysis. *Addiction*, 93(4), 515–532.

Martinez, A.N., Bluthenthal, R.N., Lorvick, J., Anderson, R., Flynn, N., & Kral, A.H. (2007). The impact of legalizing syringe exchange programs on arrests among injection drug users in California. *Journal of Urban Health*, 84(3), 423–435.

Martinez, R., Rosenfeld, R., & Mares, D. (2008). Social disorganization, drug market activity, and neighborhood violent crime. *Urban Affairs Review*, 43(6), 846–874.

Mathers, B.M., Degenhardt, L., Phillips, B., Wiessing, L., Hickman, M., Strathdee, S.A., Wodak, A., Panda, S., Tyndall, M., Toufik, A., & Mattick, R.P. (2008). Global epidemiology of injecting drug use and HIV among people who inject drugs: A systematic review. *Lancet*, 372(9651), 1733–1745.

Mathers, B.M., Degenhardt, L., Ali, H., Wiessing, L., Hickman, M., Mattick, R.P., Myers, B., Ambekar, A., & Strathdee, S. (2010). HIV prevention, treatment, and care services for people who inject drugs: A systematic review of global, regional, and national coverage. *Lancet*, 375, 1–15. doi: 10.1016/S0140-6736(10)60232-2.

MacCoun, R.J. (1998). Toward a psychology of harm reduction. *American Psychologist*, 53(11), 1199–1208.

McLellan, A.T., Luborsky, L., Woody, G.E., & O'Brien, C.P. (1982). Is treatment for substance abuse effective? *Journal of the American Medical Association*, 247, 1423–1427.

Metzger, D.S., Woody, G.E., McLellan, A.T., O'Brien, C.P., Druley, P., Navaline, H., DePhilippis, D., Stolley, P., & Abrutyn, E. (1993). Human immunodeficiency virus seroconversion among intravenous drug users in- and out-of-treatment: An 18-month prospective follow-up. *Journal of Acquired Immune Deficiency Syndromes*, 6, 1049–1056.

Moreno, L. & Kerrigan, D. (2000). HIV prevention strategies among female sex workers in the Dominican Republic. *Research for Sex Work*, 3, 8–10.

Murphy, E.L., DeVita, D., Liu, H., Vittinghoff, E., Leung, P., Ciccarone, D.H. & Edlin, B.R. (2001). Risk factors for skin and soft-tissue abscesses among injection drug users: A case-control study. *Clinical Infectious Diseases*, 33(1), 35–40.

Nadelmann, E. (1989). Drug prohibition in the United States: Costs, consequences, and alternatives. *Science*, 245, 939–947.

National Institute on Drug Abuse. (2005, May). Heroin: Abuse and addiction. Available at: http://www.nida.nih.gov/PDF/RRHeroin.pdf.

National Institute on Drug Abuse. (2009). Principles of drug addiction treatment (2nd ed.). Available at: http://www.drugabuse.gov/PODAT/PODATIndex.html.

Neaigus A., Friedman, S.R., Curtis, R., Des Jarlais, D.C., Furst, R.T., Jose, B., Mota, P., Stepherson, B., Sufian, M., Ward, T., & Wright, J.W. (1994). The relevance of drug injectors' social and risk networks for understanding and preventing HIV infection. *Social Science and Medicine*, 38(1), 67–78.

Ousey, G.C. & Lee, M.R. (2002). Examining the conditional nature of the illicit drug market-homicide relationship: A partial test of the theory of contingent causation. *Criminology*, 40, 73–102.

Ousey, G.C. & Lee, M.R. (2004). Investigating the connections between race, illicit drug markets, and lethal violence, 1984–1997. *Journal of Research in Crime and Delinquency*, 41(4), 352–383.

Palepu, A., Tyndall, M.W., Leon, H., Muller, J., O'Shaughnessy, M.V., Schechter, M.T., & Anis, A.H. (2001). Hospital utilization and costs in a cohort of injection drug users. *Canadian Medical Association Journal*, 165(4), 415–420.

Perneger, T.V., Giner, F., del Rio, M., & Mino, A. (1998). Randomised trial of heroin maintenance programme for addicts who fail in conventional drug treatments. *British Medical Journal*, 317, 13–18.

Peterson, P.L., Dimeff, L.A., Tapert, S.F., Stern, M., & Gorman, M. (2000). Harm reduction and HIV/AIDS prevention. In G.A. Marlatt (Ed.), Harm reduction: Pragmatic strategies for managing high-risk behaviors (1st ed., pp. 218–297). New York, NY: Guilford Press.

Platt, L., Rhodes, T., Lowndes, C.M., Madden, P., Sarang, A., Mikhailova, L., Renton, A., Pevzner, Y., Sullivan, K. & Khutorskoy, M. (2005). The impact of gender and sex work on sexual and injecting risk behaviors and their association with HIV positivity amongst injecting drug users in an HIV epidemic in Togliatti City, Russian Federation. *Sexually Transmitted Diseases*, 32(10): 605–612.

Reid, R.J. (2002). Harm reduction and injection drug use: Pragmatic lessons from a public health model. *Health & Social Work*, 27(3), 223–226.

Rich, J.D., Foisie, C.K., Towe, C.W., McKenzie, M., & Salas, C.M. (2000). High street prices of syringes correlate with strict syringe possession laws. *American Journal of Drug and Alcohol Abuse*, 26, 481–487.

Rothenburg, R.B., Long, D.M., Sterk, C.E., Pach, A., Potterat, J.J., Muth, S., Baldwin, J.A., & Trotter, R.T. (2000). The Atlantic Urban Networks Study: A blueprint for endemic transmission. *AIDS*, 14(14), 2191–2200.

Simpson, D.D. & Savage, L.J. (1980). Drug abuse treatment readmissions and outcomes: Three-year follow-up of DARP patients. *Archives of General Psychiatry*, 37(8), 896–901.

Substance Abuse and Mental Health Services Administration. (2009). Results from the 2008 National Survey on Drug Use and Health: National Findings (Office of Applied Studies, NSDUH Series H-36, HHS Publication No. SMA 09-4434). Rockville, MD.

Substance Abuse and Mental Health Services Administration. (2010). Results from the 2009 National Survey on Drug Use and Health: Volume I. Summary of National Findings (Office of Applied Studies, NSDUH Series H-38A, HHS Publication No. SMA 10-4586Findings). Rockville, MD.

Tapert, S.F., Kilmer, J.R., Quigley, L.A., Larimer, M.E., Roberts, L.J., & Miller, E.T. (1998). Harm reduction strategies for illicit substance use and abuse. In G.A. Marlatt (Ed.), Harm reduction: Pragmatic strategies for managing high-risk behaviors (1st ed., pp. 145–217). New York, NY: Guilford Press.

Tempalski, B. (2007). Placing the dynamics of syringe exchange programs in the United States. *Health and Place*, 13, 417–431.

Tyndall, M.W., Kerr, T., Zhang, R., King, E., Montaner, J.G., & Wood, E. (2005). Attendance, drug use patterns, and referrals made from North America's first supervised injection facility. *Drug and Alcohol Dependence*, 83, 193–198.

UNAIDS. (2006). 2006 Report on the Global AIDS Epidemic. Geneva: UNAIDS.

UNICEF, WHO, UNAIDS. (2007). Towards universal access: Scaling up priority HIV/AIDS interventions in the health sector: Progress Report, April 2007. Available at: http://www.searo.who.int/linkFiles/News_and_Events_UA_Progress_Report.pdf.

U.S. Public Health Service. (1997, May 9). HIV prevention bulletin: Medical advice for persons who inject illicit drugs. Available at http://www.cdc.gov/idu/pubs/hiv_prev.htm.

Vlahov, D., Des Jarlais, D.C., Goosby, E., Hollinger, P.C., Lurie, P.G., Shriver, M.D., & Strathdee, S.A. (2001). Needle exchange programs for the prevention of human immunodeficiency virus infection: Epidemiology and policy. *American Journal of Epidemiology*, 154(Suppl 1), S70–S77.

Wodak, A. (2009). Harm reduction is now the mainstream global drug policy. *Addiction*, 104, 340–346.

Wodak, A. & Cooney, A. (2006). Do needle syringe programs reduce HIV infection among injecting drug users: A comprehensive review of the international evidence. *Substance Use & Misuse*, 41, 777–813.

Wood, E., Kerr, T., Small, W., Jones, J., Schechter, M.T., & Tyndall, M.W. (2003). The impact of a police presence on access to needle exchange programs. *Journal of Acquired Immune Deficiency Syndrome and Human Retrovirology*, 34(1), 116–118.

Wood, E., Kerr, T., Montaner, J.S., Strathdee, S.A., Wodak, A., Hankins, C.A., Schechter, M.T., & Tyndall, M.W. (2004). Rationale for evaluating North America's first medically supervised safer-injecting facility. *Lancet*, 4, 301–306.

Wood, E., Tyndall, M.W., Li, K., Lloyd-Smith, E., Small, W., Montaner, J.S.G., & Kerr, T. (2005). Do supervised injecting facilities attract higher-risk injection drug users? *American Journal of Preventative Medicine*, 29(2), 126–130.

Wood, E., Tyndall, M.W., Lai, C., Montaner, J.S.G., & Kerr, T. (2006). Impact of a medically supervised safer injecting facility on drug dealing and other drug-related crime. *Substance Abuse Treatment, Prevention, and Policy*, 1, 13.

Wood, E., Tyndall, M.W., Montaner, J.S., & Kerr, T. (2006). Summary of the findings from the evaluation of a pilot medically supervised safer injecting facility. *Canadian Medical Association Journal*, 175(11), 1399–1404.

World Health Organization. (2011). HIV/AIDS: Injecting drug use and prisons. Available at: http://www.who.int/hiv/topics/idu/en/index.html.

World Health Organization/United Nations Office on Drugs and Crime/Joint United Nations Programme on HIV/AIDS. (2008). Technical guide for countries to set targets for universal access to HIV prevention, treatment, and care for injecting drug users (IDUs). Available at: http://www.who.int/hiv/idu/target_setting/en/.

Zolopa, A.R., Hahn, J.A., Gorter, R., Miranda, J., Wlodarczyk, D., Peterson, J., et al. (1994). HIV and tuberculosis infection in San Francisco's homeless adults: Prevalence and risk factors in a representative sample. *Journal of the American Medical Association*, 272(6), 455–461.

Study Questions

1. How is "Hamsterdam" considered a "Harm Reduction" technique? According to the authors, what have other countries used as harm reductions techniques? Compare and contrast your examples.

2. What challenges does the Criminal Justice system face when it comes to abstinence-based treatment for offenders who abuse illegal substances? Do you view abstinence-based treatment as a legitimate or realistic solution?

3. What unforeseen support did Colvin receive following the establishment of "Hamsterdam?"

4. According to the authors, what are the pros and cons of harm reduction strategies? Do you think the U.S. will abandon the zero-tolerance laws concerning drugs in the near future?

5. What prevented Mayor Royce from continuing the "legalization" project?

6. What was the Windham exchange project? According to the authors, what prevented the Windham exchange project's success?

Section 4

Criminological Theory and *The Wire*

In the following and final section, the authors link key criminological theories, concepts, and practice to *The Wire*. Although readers will note that many, if not all, of the previous chapters touched on theoretical issues, the essays that make up this final section are unique in that each one tackles a set of theoretical concepts and readings ranging from those focused on the individual or interactional level, to those focused on the community level. For example, Stephen Rice leads off in Chapter 12 with a discussion focused on how well *The Wire* depicts interactions between citizens and police, as well as those between organizations. He goes on to give several examples of these interactions within the context of the show, which he links to criminological ideas such as procedural injustice and how individual-level processes are embedded within neighborhood dynamics. Readers who may be interested in furthering their knowledge in these areas should note the references given in this chapter (and others of course), as they represent some of the landmark studies in their respective disciplines.

In Chapter 13, Gabriel Cesar and Kevin Wright tackle one of the most significant and multifaceted issues to impact the criminal justice system in the later twentieth and entire twenty-first centuries: prisoner release, reentry, and reintegration back into the community. Due in a great part to massive increases in incarceration caused by what many thoughtful individuals argue are system-based changes in crime control strategies, sentencing, and discretion, during the last few decades, criminal justice and other scholars and practitioners have been dealing with an increase in the number of prisoners returning to their communities. As the authors note, this fact has not been overlooked by those working in the system, as well as those who oversee it. In fact, there has been a massive movement to identify those treatment programs, or program components, which are most effective at aiding personal change through addressing the criminogenic risks and needs of transitioning offenders.

The authors note, however, that recidivism-focused treatment and reentry programs are often devoid of context—they fail to incorporate a more comprehensive understanding of successful inmate reentry and reintegration. Noting the importance of individual-based treatment and support programs, the authors argue for a multilevel social support approach where not only are individual-level factors addressed, but also those issues that greatly influence success at the community and system levels. Using a case-study approach to highlight a multilevel social support strategy to inmate release and reintegration, Cesar and Wright outline the trials and travails of Dennis "Cutty" Wise, whose story in *The Wire* provides an interesting context in which we can begin to understand and dissect the core internal and external pressures at play at each level of analysis.

In Chapter 14, the focus turns to how certain aspects of a community may affect its crime rates and public safety. Such a community-level analysis typically involves considering why highly disorganized communities regularly have higher rates of crime and delinquency. In this chapter, Kyle Thomas and Matthew Nobles examine how this neighborhood ecological approach is prevalent throughout *The Wire*. The authors argue that Simon astutely identifies the root cause of crime as being structural, rather than individual-based. Inner-city Baltimore is segregated, there is a distinct lack of employment opportunities, the educational system is dysfunctional, and citizens live in abject poverty. Worst of all, its citizens are trapped and must learn to carry on in such an environment as best they can. Some choose crime as a means of survival. Thomas and Nobles note that addressing these structural shortcomings can have important real-world implications, and are the key to reducing urban crime.

In Chapter 15, Laurie Drapela notes that within the criminal justice system women have been continually overlooked and marginalized on both sides of the law. Laws that dictate how we punish were created and perpetuated from a time when it was thought that women certainly could not commit the same crimes as men. As a result, the laws, courts systems, and correctional facilities are designed for male offenders and merely adapted for female offenders.

Critics of *The Wire* address the perceived underrepresentation of women within the series as a reflection of their place within American culture as a whole. Women are often secondary, shallow characters to the strong and well-developed male characters. Within the series, as in the criminal justice system, women are only valued and discussed through attributing masculine traits to them. Not allowing them to be recognized for the same accomplishments while still exuding feminine qualities or approaching dilemmas with "female solutions," further perpetuates the inequality between the sexes. The author points out that there are strong female characters within the series; however, they are still representative of the familiar ways in which television portrays women. *The Wire* may have missed an opportunity to advance the development of female characters on the whole by failing to utilize empirical data that more accurately describes women's participation in society.

In the final chapter, Christopher Sullivan and James McCafferty address the unique way in which *The Wire* approaches and taps into the historical and contemporary theories and empirical research surrounding juvenile delinquency and adjudication. The chapter revolves around the interactions between the justice system, schools, and broader societal institutions and the four boys who are the show's main focus in Season 4. Throughout the chapter, there is consideration of how well the portrayal of the characters and their relationships fit with empirical data and what it means for a comprehensive understanding of how to best respond to youth delinquency in urban areas. The authors stress that although these are fictional characters, the issues faced and portrayed in *The Wire* are quite real and accurately represent those faced by the at-risk youth we see in urban schools and neighborhoods. Finally, the authors emphasize that there are moments in the program that reflect reality, in that the life-course of each at-risk youth is not set in stone. Choices and decisions made by the writers of *The Wire* can be used to better understand the causes of juvenile delinquency and the ways in which schools, the justice system, and other societal influences respond to it.

Chapter 12

Injustice, Emotions, and West Baltimore Collectives

Stephen K. Rice

Introduction

Just as House Speaker Thomas "Tip" O'Neill famously noted that all politics tends to be local, interactions between police and the individuals they serve tend to transcend the societal and find their basis in the visceral—in the "hot," "wet" interactions which condition whether community members choose to cooperate with or defy authority. Within the field of criminology, such processes receive illumination within the areas of procedural injustice (Tyler, 1990), determinants of defiance (Sherman, 1993), perceived violations of justice rules by police (Agnew, 2001), and also how individual-level processes (e.g., stressors, strains) are embedded within neighborhood dynamics (Agnew, 1999). In short, the interactional level of explanation will always hold a key role in the criminological imagination.

Media Exemplars and *The Wire*

Over the past decade, several television dramas illustrate the vivid interaction between formal and informal organizations, figures of authority, and the individuals they serve. These include Tom Fontana's (and Augustus Hill's) *Oz*, that of Em City's perspiration, musculature, and the fight for status and power by Aryans, Homeboys, Wiseguys, Irish, and other collectives; and David Simon's *Treme*, that of Indians, music, the NOPD, and deep water.

David Simon's *The Wire*'s dramaturgical accounting of school bureaucrats, dockworkers, the body politic and their representatives, jurisprudence, and narcotics dealers and enforcers sworn to uphold the law also connectively illustrate themes so central to criminological theory and scholarship. So by extension, *Crime and Justice in the City as Seen Through "The Wire"* provides an outstanding opportunity for students to "three-dimensionalize" key constructs from their academic studies within one of television's most successful dramatic series.

Students already have access to empirical research on topics such as fear of crime and expected safety in Baltimore (e.g., Robinson, Lawton, Taylor, and Perkins, 2003). Strong attention to the themes outlined in the essays presented in this text will allow students to "place" this type of empirical research and their classroom studies within Simon's stunning visuals and storylines and to also potentially serve as useful classroom debate topics/counterpoints to the professional dialogues and pedagogical initiatives that have been launched nationally on *The Wire*. Among these were a distinguished panel at the Law and Society Conference and special topics courses at schools such as Berkeley, Harvard and Washington State University, the latter of which is taught by volume Co-Editor David Brody with *The Wire* Seasons 3 and 4 utilized to study drug markets, Compstat, police behavior and attitudes, decriminalization, and gang life (Brody, 2008).

Many Ties to Criminological Constructs

The Wire's plot groupings relate to many areas of focus within criminology to include Payne (2009) on student and school characteristics and student deviance (see "Dukie" Weems and his cohort at Edward Tilghman Middle School in Season 4), Douglas (1992) on risk, blame and failed collectives (see the rise and fall of the Barksdale Organization over several seasons[1]), Hagan (2010) on the politics of crime policy (see both the corrupt and well-meaning Maryland State and Baltimore City politicians and administrators over several seasons), and a robust literature tapping Engel, Calnon and Bernard (2002), Markovsky (1995), Murphy and Tyler (2008), Agnew (1999), my work (Rice and White, 2010) and others attending to micro-level police-public contact in areas such as real or perceived racial profiling, citizen demeanor, compliance behaviors, community-level strain, and cognitive appraisals of police fairness and legitimacy/procedural justice.

---

1. Also see the interesting conversation at riskcontainment.com ("The Prospect of Hanging," 2011) on Avon Barksdale's capacity to limit his risk.

Where Short's (1998) address to the American Society of Criminology made the observation that scholarship focusing on "The City" as its laboratory declined in the years following the heyday of the Chicago School, it too is reasonable to cast David Simon and Ed Burns as latter day Parks and Burgesses, Shaws and McKays, Cavans, Wirths, and Whytes. Even the popular online video series TED.com identified vigorous reexaminations and reimaginations of The City as efforts that can inspire the world ("Announcing the 2012 TED Prize Winner," n.d.).

Within the tapestry of *The Wire*, one need not look further than Rafael Alvarez's *The Wire: Truth be Told* (2004: 4–5) to expand on this focus:

> *The Wire* is not about Jimmy McNulty. Or Avon Barksdale. Or crime. Or punishment. Or drugs. Or violence. Or even race.
>
> It is about The City. It is about how we live as Americans at the millennium ... sharing a common love, awe, and fear of what we have rendered in Baltimore, St. Louis, Chicago, New York, Los Angeles.
>
> At best, our metropolises are the ultimate aspiration for the American community, the repository for every myth from rugged individualism to the melting pot. At worst, our cities—or those places in our cities where most of us fear to tread—are vessels for the darkest contradictions and most competitions that underlie the way we actually live together.

To Alvarez, ecology holds great sway within *The Wire*, and most certainly relates to Sampson's (1993: 426) calls for dynamic contextualism in the manner in which time and place combine to explain the "unfolding" of human lives. And this unfolding not only pertains to obvious characters such as D'Angelo Barksdale or Stringer Bell. It too is represented in Officer Pryzbylewski ("Prez"), the officer who blinds a Franklin Terrace Towers juvenile wrongfully in Season 1, later cutting his teeth as a teacher at Edward Tilghman Middle by Season 4.

Within the context of Agnew's (1999) macro level strain, community characteristics such as economic deprivation, inequality, and population density are all too evident in the form of West Baltimore and the impact of spatial location, culture, ghetto schools, and concentrated disadvantage on incarceration and perpetuated imbalance across generations (see Chapter 3 by Chaddha and Wilson). Even "Hamsterdam," the imperfect enforcement-free zone from Season 3, pathologizes and evinces a process of "othering" (Young, 2007) related to social cleavage and alternative goals and identities. Relative to more common, across-neighborhood symbols of concentrated disadvantage, *The Wire* features comparatively few symbols of relative deprivation—or at least those that encapsulate perspectives from all social strata (politicians such as Davis, Carcetti and Royce notwithstanding). As one blogger notes:

> There is … a big portion of society—in fact, the portion that used to be called Society—that never really makes it into (David) Simon's view of the world. You have to wonder how that impairs his ability, and his projects' ability, to tackle the issues they claim to depict so accurately.
>
> It's a weird sense of reverse ghettoization: wealthy North Baltimoreans see the origins of social ills in the form of the occasional member of the underclass who comes into their neighborhoods to steal from them; advocates of the underclass see the origins of social ills in the form of the wealthy who come into their neighborhoods to steal from them.
>
> Simon is a master of the second version of the narrative, and he does it beautifully, powerfully, and unforgettably. But at some point it seems as if maybe, to effect [sic] any real kind of change, we need a new story ("The Wire and Treme").

The Wire also illustrates union labor history at play. For example, Dainville's (2004) discussion of space, place and globalization and the 1889 London dockworkers' strike tie nicely to the stevedores' and The Greek's activities during Season 2—that of a loosely coupled system of illegal human (e.g., thirteen dead women from Budapest) and non-human product exchange unencumbered by traditional boundaries of social interaction and the nation-state. Whether it be lobbying Senator Mikulski to help push through dredging with not-so-subtle tithes at St. Casimir's, or patterns of exchange of "hot boxes," through their rise and fall Frank, Nick, and Ziggy evoke the type of "unitary ambiance" (Dainville, 2004) seen in the London dockworkers' strike—that of traversing functionally separate ecological zones (e.g., the checkers local, the East Baltimore dealers) to create vibrant political economies.

Police Legitimacy, Emotions, and the Collective

Consistent with recent scholarship (e.g., Capers, 2011) on perceptual legitimacy, rules of evidence, and police brutality in *The Wire* and principally Seasons 1, 2, and 3, a focus on police ↔ citizen/community interaction provides an excellent opportunity for the scholar or student intent on exploring the intersections of *The Wire*, media studies, policing, and criminological constructs. As such, *The Wire* is an excellent medium for exploring subtopic areas such as procedural justice, distributive justice, group processes, emotions and injustice, motive-based trust and perceptions of racial profiling.[2]

In particular, the tension between procedural and distributive justice is studied by most students of policing. Procedural justice refers to the fairness of the means by which distributions are made, fairness which takes shape through standards of consistency, suppression of bias, accuracy of information, mechanisms of rectification, and ethicality of standards (Leventhal, Karuza, and Fry, 1980; Lind and Tyler, 1988). Distributive justice refers to the distribution of resources within a group that corresponds to that which is expected on the basis of a normative principle; criteria for a "just" distribution may be based on principles of cooperation related to equity, equality, and need (Deutsch, 1975).

Police scholars hypothesize that in the era of community policing, police are more reliant on citizens' exercise of voluntary compliance and self-control than punitive arrest in face-to-face encounters. Perceived unfairness or disrespect on the part of sanctioning agents—and their resultant illegitimacy—has been linked to increased crime (Tyler, 2000), particularly when the behavioral reaction to perceived injustice is coupled with unacknowledged shame and defiant pride by those who are poorly bonded to the sanctioning agent or the community the agent represents (Sherman, 1993).

While the areas of procedural/distributive injustice (not to mention emotions and injustice and inter-group processes) are too rich to explore here comprehensively, it may be helpful to situate some of *The Wire's* additional major themes within them for the purpose of future scholarship and pedagogy. In doing so, it is key to remember that despite the longstanding model of self-interest rooted in Hobbes (1651) and reinforced in theories of human behavior within social, behavioral and psychoanalytic traditions (Miller, 1999; Sears and Funk, 1991), more nuanced conceptions of human motives have been advanced relating to public life and social justice (Mansbridge, 1994). Further, the inter-agent model of social justice focuses on the mechanisms at work in interactions between a citizenry and agents of social control and whether reactions to personal experience with legal authorities are affected by group processes and emotional reactions to perceived injustice. Group process theory asks whether legitimacy—an inherently collective process—can influence justice evaluations and reactions that have been examined primarily at the individual level.

Within the context of *The Wire,* the potential tie-ins are vast. Leveraging research such as Tyler and Fagan (2008) on legitimacy and cooperation, or

---

2. For example, in Season 4 officer "Herc" Hauk is accused of racial profiling an African American minister, an incident which ends dramatically with the leafing of a bible amid questions about the legality of the stop and search. Hauk is later cleared.

why people choose to help police fight crime in their neighborhoods, one need not look further than the previously mentioned episode in Season 1 with Prez, Carver and Herc at the Towers. Expressed succinctly, Tyler and Fagan (2008) argue that perceived police legitimacy conditions community cooperation, and legitimacy finds its basis in the perceived justice of the authority exercised by police. At the Towers that night, Carver and Herc begin stop, question and frisk activities in a manner far short of reasonable suspicion standards, through that process emasculate one male and verbally defy all Tower residents within earshot, after which point Prez inflicts serious harm on a non-threatening juvenile with the butt of his firearm. "Cooperation" from Tower residents comes swiftly in the form of thrown bottles and televisions.[3]

Tyler and Fagan (2008) point out that a key antecedent to legitimacy is procedural justice—the "hot," "wet" interactions I referenced earlier. As they explain, "A performance model of policing ... link(s) public views about cooperation to their judgments of the effectiveness of police performance in fighting crime and urban disorder. It ... suggest(s) that to be viewed as legitimate the police need to communicate to those in the community that they can credibly punish wrongdoers, as well as that they are effectively fighting crime" (Tyler and Fagan, 2008: 252). In this scene, Prez, Carver and Herc demand an odd amalgam of both compliance and cooperation and, of course, receive neither.

Perceptions of the fairness of treatment are also strongly linked to the public's willingness to comply with the law. Although citizens may have access to strict, objective measures related to crime control (e.g., community crime rate), community disorder (e.g., prostitution, drug use) and police adherence to norms of conduct (e.g., shootings) at their disposal, more generalized, subjective indicators of police performance have been found to be extremely important predictors of public compliance and cooperation.[4] One need only look at the

---

3. I have not yet come across a *The Wire* discussion focusing on the tossing of televisions. At least two appeared to be thrown, without an indication of other household items that can cause injury (e.g., microwaves, furniture). Given that this scene takes place in season 1, one wonders whether Simon and Burns meant the televisions to be *reflexive* devices—as means toward incorporating the viewer into to the scene (and essentially, the series) by subtly reinforcing that this is not television. It's West Baltimore.

4. In an influential study, Sunshine and Tyler (2003) compared the influence of subjective legitimacy to that of five aspects of police performance in shaping public cooperation with the NYPD. They found that the subjective judgment of legitimacy had a significant influence on whether the public supported increases in the size and budget of the police, on whether people supported giving the police broader discretionary authority, and on the degree to which the public cooperated with the police in fighting crime. More importantly, their legitimacy measures outperformed nearly all "objective" aspects of police perform-

interactions between Bubbles and Kima to witness a relationship that's not only informed by self-interest but also some level of humanity borne from fair treatment.

Group Processes and Perceptions of Injustice

As touched on earlier, *The Wire* also illustrates group processes. According to the group-value model of procedural justice (Lind and Tyler, 1988) and the related relational model of authority (Tyler and Lind, 1992), members of groups desire to seek self-relevant information through evaluations of the quality of interactions with group representatives, and that interactions with authorities who represent such groups (typically in hierarchical social relationships) are used as sources of information about individual self-worth (Tyler, Degoey, and Smith, 1996). The relationship between treatment quality and acceptance of authorities and their decisions is thought to be stronger when the authority and group member share the same cultural background (i.e., the authority is ingroup) than when the authority and group member are from different cultural backgrounds. Ingroup relations provide relational information about the group member's position within the valued ingroup, which in turn shapes self-concept. In short, individuals are not only concerned with a dispute itself, but with their relationships with authorities and institutions (Lind and Tyler, 1988).

Whereby the "meaning" of criminal justice can be both symbolic and variable (Hagan and Albonetti, 1982), there too is evidence that motive-based trust can be distributed differentially across a population and that perceptions of the underlying fairness of police/public contacts are impacted by a constellation of variables governed by street-level, ad hoc, emotional reactions to perceived injustice and profiling (Rice and Piquero, 2005). The theoretical premise that police will find it easier to gain deference when the authority and the person with whom he or she is dealing share group membership may not be easily sustainable in police-citizen-community contacts, however, because it is noted that police officers are often viewed by the public as members of a single group, not as White or Black but as "blue" (Tyler and Huo, 2002).

---

ance in predicting cooperation with the police. On balance, high quality police performance does not necessarily equate to high quality community support when a department lacks the counterbalance of perceived procedural fairness.

The Wire provides several opportunities for group process framings. Even more so, its entire structure seems to call for it. As Chaddha, Wilson and Venkatesh (2008:84–85) recognize:

> *The Wire* develops morally complex characters on each side of the law, and with its scrupulous exploration of the inner workings of various institutions, including drug-dealing gangs, the police, politicians, unions, public schools, and the print media, viewers become aware that individuals' decisions and behavior are often shaped by—and indeed limited by—social, political, and economic forces beyond their control.
>
> Anyone who watches Season 4 will come away with a clear understanding of how the public school system has failed these students and why the atmosphere in these schools is so devastating. Over the course of that season, *The Wire* combats the misguided belief that inner-city students themselves are largely responsible for their lack of education achievement.

As such, *The Wire* trumpets collectives (here, Chaddha et al., 2008 don't even include stevedores), and when one adds in the finer details of the Barksdale operation and BPD, relational models of authority (Tyler and Lind, 1992) are brought to bear.

Bandes (Chapter 2, this volume) illustrates this in her chapter by focusing on "Bodie" Broadus from Season 1, a street level dealer who experiences hierarchical angst (as "pawn") after playing chess with D'Angelo. As Bandes outlines:

> Several years later, Bodie finally understands D'Angelo's chess lesson. Bodie's realization and rejection of his status as one of the 'baldheaded bitches' leads to his murder:
>
> Preston 'Bodie' Broadus: "I feel old. I been out there since I was 13. I ain't never fucked up a count, never stole off a package, never did some shit that I wasn't told to do. I been straight up. But what come back? ... They want me to stand with them, right? But where the fuck they at when they supposed to be standing by us? I mean, when shit goes bad and there's hell to pay, where they at? This game is rigged, man. We like the little bitches (pawns) on a chessboard" (p. 18).[5]

---

5. Homan's (1974) argument about emotional responses to injustice is straightforward: those treated fairly will experience positive emotions and those treated poorly are likely to feel anger. According to Homan's work and to the exchange approach to justice, the severity of a perceived injustice is likely to affect individuals' emotional, psychological, and behavioral reactions (Hegtvedt and Johnson, 2000). Hegtvedt and Markovsky (1995) found that individuals who receive awards that are lower than expected are likely to experience

Here, Bodie not only speaks to group processes but also perceived injustice and emotions and that of a City yearning to break free from Jane Jacobs' forewarning in The Death and Life of Great American Cities (1992: 5): of a City where Job would have been thinking of Chicago (or Baltimore) when he wrote:

> Here are men that alter their neighbor's landmark ... shoulder the poor aside, conspire to oppress the friendless.

> Reap they the field that is none of theirs, strip they the vineyard wrongfully seized from its owner ...

> A cry goes up from the city streets, where wounded men lie groaning ...

References

Agnew, R. (1999). A general strain theory of community differences in crime rates. *Journal of Research in Crime and Delinquency, 36,* 123–155.

Agnew, R. (2001). Building on the foundation of general strain theory: Specifying the types of strain most likely to lead to crime and delinquency. *Journal of Research in Crime and Delinquency 38,* 319–361.

Alvarez, R. (2004). *The Wire: Truth be told.* New York: Pocket Books.

Announcing the 2012 TED Prize Winner—The City 2.0 (n.d.). Retrieved from http://www.tedprize.org/announcing-the-2012-ted-prize-winner/.

Bandes, S.A. (2011). And all the pieces matter: Thoughts on *The Wire* and the criminal justice system. *Ohio State Journal of Criminal Law 8,* 435–445.

Brody, D. (2008, Fall). Examining urban crime, policing, politics, and delinquency through *The Wire.* Retrieved from http://img.slate.com/media/42/wire%20syllabus%202008.pdf.

Capers, I.B. (2011). Crime, legitimacy, our criminal network, and *The Wire. Ohio State Journal of Criminal Law 8,* 459.

Chaddha, A., Wilson, W.J., & Venkatesh S.A. (2008). In Defense of *The Wire. Dissent,* 55 (Summer):83–86.

Chaddha, A., & Wilson, W.J. (2011). "Way down in the hole": Systemic urban inequality and The Wire. *Critical Inquiry 38,* 164–188.

Dainville, A.C. (2004). *Contesting globalization: Space and place in the world economy.* London: Routledge.

negative emotions, especially when coupled with a perception that he or she was not responsible for the injustice.

Deutsch, M. (1975). Equity, equality, and need: What determines which values will be used as the basis of distributive justice? *Journal of Social Issues, 31*, 137–148.

Douglas, M. (1992). *Risk and blame: Essays in cultural theory.* New York: Routledge.

Engel, R.S., Calnon, J.M., & Bernard, T.J. (2002). Theory and racial profiling: Shortcomings and future directions in research. *Justice Quarterly, 19*, 249–273.

Hagan, J. (2010). *Who are the criminals? The politics of crime policy from the age of Roosevelt to the age of Reagan.* Princeton, NJ: Princeton University Press.

Hagan, J., and Albonetti, C. (1982). Race, class, and the perception of criminal injustice in America. *The American Journal of Sociology 88*, 329–355.

Hegtvedt, K.A., & Johnson, C. (2000). Justice beyond the individual: A future with legitimation. *Social Psychology Quarterly 63*, 298–311.

Hobbes, T. (1651). *Leviathan.* London: Andrew Crooke.

Homans, G. (1974). *Social behavior: Its elementary forms.* New York: Harcourt Brace Jovanovich.

Jacobs, J. (1992). *The death and life of great American cities.* Vintage.

Leventhal, F.S., Karuza, J. Jr., & Fry, W.R. (1980). Beyond fairness: A theory of allocation preferences. In G. Mikula (Ed.), *Justice and social interaction* (pp. 167–218). New York: Springer-Verlag.

Lind, E.A., & Tyler, T.R. (1988). *The social psychology of procedural justice.* New York: Harcourt Brace Jovanovich.

Mansbridge, J.J. (1994). Public spirit in political systems. In H.J. Aron, T.E. Mann, & T. Taylor (Eds.), *Values and public policy* (pp. 146–172). Washington: Brookings.

Markovsky, B. (1995). Toward a multilevel distributive justice theory. *American Sociological Review, 50*, 822–839.

Miller, D. T. (1999). The norm of self-interest. *American Psychologist 54*, 1053–1060.

Murphy, K., & Tyler, T. (2008). Procedural justice and compliance behavior: The mediating role of emotions. *European Journal of Social Psychology 38*, 652–668.

Payne, A.A. (2009). Girls, boys, and schools: Gender differences in the relationship between school-related factors and student deviance. *Criminology 47*, 1167–1200.

Rice, S.K., & Piquero, A.R. (2005). Perceptions of discrimination and justice in New York City. *Policing: An International Journal of Police Strategies and Management 28*, 98–117.

Rice, S.K., & White, M.D. (Eds.). (2010). *Race, ethnicity, and policing: New and essential readings.* New York University Press.

Robinson, J.B., Lawton, B.A., Taylor, R.B., & Perkins, D.D. (2003). *Journal of Quantitative Criminology 19*, 237–274.

Sampson, R.J. (1993). Linking time and place: Dynamic contextualism and the future of criminological inquiry. *Journal of Research in Crime and Delinquency 30*, 426–444.

Sears, D. O., & Funk, C.L. (1991). The role of self-interest in social and political attitudes. In J. Mansbridge (Ed.), *Advances in experimental social psychology 24*, 2–91. New York: Academic Press.

Sherman, L. W. (1993). Defiance, deterrence, and irrelevance: A theory of the criminal sanction. *Journal of Research in Crime and Delinquency 30*, 445–473.

Short, Jr. J. F. (1998). The level of explanation problem revisited: The American Society of Criminology 1997 Presidential Address. *Criminology 36*, 3–36.

Sunshine, J., & Tyler, T.R. (2003). The role of procedural justice and legitimacy in shaping public support for policing. *Law & Society Review 37*, 513–547.

The prospect of hanging concentrates the mind: Avon Barksdale on managing risk, part two (2011). Retrieved December 31, 2011, from http://risk containment.com/?p=850.

The *Wire* and *Treme:* David Simon keeps it "real" (2010, Sept 29). Retrieved January 3, 2012, from http://niftyrictus.blogspot.com/2010/09/wire-and-treme-david-simon-keeps-it.html.

Tyler, T.R. (1990). *Why people obey the* law. New Haven, CT: Yale University Press.

Tyler, T.R. (2000). Social justice: Outcome and procedure. *International Journal of Psychology, 35*, 117–125.

Tyler, T.R. (2002). A national survey for monitoring police legitimacy. *Justice Research and Policy 4*, 71–86.

Tyler, T.R., Degoey, P., & Smith, H.L. (1996). Understanding why the justice of group procedures matters: A test of the psychological dynamics of the group-value model. *Journal of Personality and Social Psychology, 70*, 913–930.

Tyler, T.R., & Fagan, J. (2008). Legitimacy and cooperation: Why do people help the police fight crime in their communities? *Ohio State Journal of Criminal Law 6*, 231–275.

Tyler, T.R. & Huo, Y.J. (2002). *Trust in the law: Encouraging public cooperation with the police and courts*. New York: Russell Sage Foundation.

Tyler, T.R. & Lind, E.A. (1992). A relational model of authority in groups. In M. Zanna (Ed.), *Advances in experimental social psychology* (Vol. 25, pp. 115–191). New York: Academic Press.

Young, J. (2007). *The vertigo of late modernity.* Sage Publications.

Study Questions

1. The author notes a focus on "the city" in drawing a comparison between Ed Burns and David Simon (the show's creators) and Chicago School scholars. In expanding upon this idea, describe some possible linkages that come to mind.

2. What factors or community characteristics depicted within the show does the author identify in relation to macro level strain?

3. At one point, the author notes that there is a lack of additional perspectives from all social strata—what impact do you think this has on the overall story of *The Wire*? Why?

4. In this chapter, the author notes the numerous subtopic areas depicted within *The Wire*. Which of these topics or subtopics is of the most interest to you? Why?

5. Explain the main differences between procedural and distributive justice. Provide some possible examples from the show.

6. Provide some examples of how *The Wire* is illustrative of group processes. In your example, how does the relationship(s) between individuals (citizens) and the authorities (police) or institutions further shape the perceptions of fairness held by the citizenry?

Chapter 13

That Ain't the Only Way to Be: The Reintegration of Dennis "Cutty" Wise From an Individual-, Community-, and System-Level Perspective

Gabriel T Cesar and Kevin A. Wright

Introduction

Oriole Park at Camden Yards is widely regarded as one of the most well-designed and beautiful ballparks in all of Major League Baseball. Modeled after the classic ballparks built in the early 1900s, the stadium unites brick with steel and features an imposing warehouse just beyond right field that has stood for over a century. Southeast of Camden Yards is Federal Hill, a historic neighborhood that now features high-priced townhomes and fancy restaurants and taverns owing to the process of gentrification. North of Federal Hill, east of Camden Yards, is the well-known Inner Harbor area where tourists can catch a dolphin show at the aquarium, peruse the books of a mammoth bookstore situated in a converted power plant, or watch with wonder as fudge is made—the creators flinging the gooey chocolate in the air while singing gleeful songs. College students and young professionals in search of a vibrant night life will find it here at Power Plant Live and further east in nearby Fells Point. In short, Baltimore, Maryland has much to offer in the way of entertainment opportunities for tourists and a fulfilling lifestyle for its permanent residents.

Much less known, however, are the streets of Baltimore portrayed in *The Wire*. These areas—the bulk of which lie west of Camden Yards—are characterized by dilapidated housing and few opportunities for mainstream entertainment or gainful employment. Here, residents do not crack and eat crabs at a restaurant while overlooking the gentle waters of the harbor, but instead look at the rundown streets through the neon signs in the windows of New York Fried Chicken. There are no trolley tour stops and no professional sports teams. A fulfilling lifestyle is replaced with a lifestyle marked by crime and victimization, where "the game" structures life for both its participants and its onlookers. It is into this world that Dennis "Cutty" Wise returns after a spending 14 years in prison.

Offender reentry is one of the most pressing issues in criminal justice and criminology today. With mass incarceration eventually comes mass decarceration, and over 700,000 offenders are returning from state and federal prisons to U.S. streets each year (West, Sabol, and Greenman, 2010). Over the last several decades significant advancements have been made in documenting the evidence-based components of successful offender rehabilitation and reentry. Despite these improvements, recidivism rates remain high, with nearly half of offenders released in 2004 having been returned to prison within a three year period (Pew Center on the States, 2011). In this chapter we focus on Cutty's story to document the myriad obstacles to successful reintegration faced by ex-offenders. In particular, we advance the idea that reentry policies and programs must attend to the individual-, community-, and system-level components of recidivism in order to ensure the successful reentry of individuals like Cutty.

Criminology and Corrections

The need for effective reentry programs to ease the transition process of ex-offenders back into society has not gone unnoticed among criminal justice scholars and practitioners. Indeed, over the last decade the "evidence-based movement" has taken hold in corrections in general (e.g., Mackenzie, 2000) and offender reentry in particular (e.g., Listwan, Cullen, and Latessa, 2006). The result has been a significant roster of best practices and program characteristics designed to encourage successful reintegration on the part of ex-offenders. Yet even the most well-designed reentry programs have produced disappointing outcomes in terms of reduced recidivism (Wilson and Davis, 2006). Usually, these discouraging results are explained away by invoking a disconnect between theory and practice, whereby proper implementation of program blueprints would have led to the expected reductions in recidivism.

A more critical explanation for the lack of program success is that we simply fail to appreciate the full range of factors that influence reoffending. Offenders being released today are qualitatively different than those released in the past, and a crucial reason for this is that offenders are serving longer sentences as a result of America's imprisonment binge in the 80s and 90s (Irwin and Austin, 2001; Pratt, 2009). This translates into two inconvenient truths regarding the reintegration prospects of ex-offenders. First, offenders themselves have significant risks, needs, and life-deficiencies that make a law-abiding lifestyle difficult. Imagine an offender who was locked up in 1990: the president was George Bush (the first one), 9/11 had not yet occurred, the crack epidemic (and corresponding market) was just entering a decline, and the Internet was just beginning. Consequently, upon release in the 2000s, the world has changed and the offender has not. Second, any social supports or networks the offender may have had prior to incarceration are likely to have disappeared. Family and friends move or pass away, the fire of old relationships are extinguished, and employment connections and prospects dry up. Thus, the passage of time while institutionalized puts offenders at an additional disadvantage, compounding an already bleak outlook for remaining crime-free.

A more holistic understanding of reoffending thus acknowledges the many obstacles to reintegration that are in place at various levels of analysis. Viewed differently, we have many impressive criminological theories that seek to explain why individuals engage in criminal behavior. Yet these theories are often discarded when we attempt to reason why ex-offenders engage in *repeat* criminal behavior. Cutty's story provides a snapshot of various criminological theories—he lives in a community marked by concentrated disadvantage and limited resources, he displays antisocial attitudes and his closest peers exhibit the same thoughts and behaviors, and the stigma of incarceration is but one stressor in a life characterized by strain and frustration. Why is it, then, that our lasting image of Cutty in Season 5 is one of a free man, while most of his oldest confidants and youngest protégés are either locked up or deceased?

We believe that the concept of social support (Lin, 1986) is central to explaining why Cutty has yet to return to prison. Social support has been defined as "the perceived or actual instrumental and/or expressive provisions supplied by the community, social networks, and confiding partners" (Lin, 1986: 18). In particular, Cullen (1994) argues that social support serves as an organizing theme for the many seemingly disparate theories of criminal behavior that exist at various levels of explanation. We extend this idea to argue that it may also function as an organizing concept for understanding successful offender reintegration across the individual-, community-, and system-levels of offender reentry. This application comes as part of a renewed interest in the links between criminological theory and corrections (see, for example, Cullen and Jonson, 2011)—a necessary step in solving the correctional quagmires associated with budget deficits, prison crowding, and less-than-acceptable recidivism rates (Wright and Rosky, 2011). Thus, while Dennis "Cutty" Wise is merely a fictional character in a television series, his narrative offers a glimpse into some of the answers to the offender reentry problem.

The Individual Level

Offender reentry has traditionally been about the individual, with individual risks to reoffending guiding the decision to release offenders as well as determining how to best supervise them within the community. Offender rehabilitation in particular has also focused almost entirely on changing the offender; for example, the use of cognitive behavioral techniques to modify antisocial attitudes and behaviors has emerged as an empirically-validated method of reducing recidivism (Lipsey, Chapman, and Landenberger, 2001). Ideas about reoffending at the individual level are thus appropriately situated in psychology. In their theory of the psychology of criminal conduct, Andrews and Bonta (2003) identify what they call the "Big Four" risk factors toward criminal behavior: antisocial attitudes, antisocial associates, antisocial personality, and a history of antisocial behavior. In addition, they recognize problems with family, problems with work or school, problems in adequately using leisure time, and substance abuse as all contributing to an increased likelihood of criminal behavior. In other words, Andrews and Bonta have essentially described the typical ex-offender in identifying those individuals most likely to engage in criminal behavior (and perhaps repeat criminal behavior). Cutty Wise represents this typical ex-offender.

Released from prison, Cutty comes home to Baltimore, but quickly finds it has little to offer. He receives a "coming home" gift from his criminal associates, but the G-Pack (slang for a thousand-dollar package of drugs such as heroin or cocaine) only brings more trouble. He has a place in the home of his grandmother, Mee-maw, who is happy to see him after 14 years. But his Mee-maw is poor and aging, and the home is in a largely abandoned block of forgotten track housing. He meets with his old girlfriend, who has moved on to a conventional life and is uninterested in revisiting the past. In short, Dennis Wise has served his time for murder, but is left to fend for himself in a resource deprived, crime-ridden environment where his options appear, at least initially, to be limited to abject poverty and menial labor or a return to crime, violence, and potentially, prison and death.

Conceptually, Cutty is forced to choose between a conventional, albeit disadvantaged life or the lifestyle he was raised into as defined by the "code of the street" (Anderson, 1999). This code is characterized by antisocial attitudes, aggressive behaviors, and often times criminality, and any perceived deviation from this script is viewed by adherents as a personal challenge and a threat to their way of life. Put simply, the code of the street dictates that affronts to one's reputation are tantamount to violent victimization, that violence is to be answered in kind, and that reliance on formal authority is a clear sign of weakness. Against this cultural backdrop, Cutty is required to meet the sometimes-lofty goals of community corrections. He is expected to transition from the structured life of a prisoner to one where he must independently secure housing and employment, report to a dispassionate parole officer, and resist the temptation to hang around the people and places that are most comfortable to him.

Although Cutty does not immediately desist from crime, pro-social changes are seen in him as he secures and maintains landscaping work, slowly comes to the realization that "the game ain't in me no more…," and starts pursuing the goal of a youth boxing gym. His eventual realization that he has outgrown criminality is powerful in the context of the code of the street. In that aggressive, retributive honor society, to renounce one's participation in "the game" can be viewed as an admission of weakness and fear. For a "heavy" like Cutty, such an admission carries particular danger. Ultimately, then, this realization denotes the internal changes in self-perception that are at work in Cutty as he re-acclimates to life on the outside (to be returned to below). The admission also demonstrates his willingness to move away from his old, violent identity as a street criminal, but toward what new identity? How is it that Cutty might once again become Dennis Wise? More generally, how might an ex-offender, willing to relinquish his antisocial attitudes and behaviors, be helped along the path to pro-social behaviors?

Across the lifecycle, social support increases the likelihood that offenders will turn away from a criminal pathway.

Offender rehabilitation has been defined as "the centrality of interactions with the offenders aimed at motivating, guiding, and *supporting* constructive change in whatever characteristics or circumstances engender their criminal behavior or subvert their pro-social behavior" (Lipsey and Cullen, 2007: 302, emphasis added). In essence, then, arguments and empirical evidence in favor of rehabilitation and offender treatment are arguments in favor of the provision of social support to ex-offenders. A significant body of work has indeed established that rehabilitation can be effective in reducing recidivism (for a review, see Lipsey and Cullen, 2007). In particular, the "principles of effective intervention" (Gendreau, 1996) detail the components of successful treatment programs aimed at attending to the individual risks to reoffending identified above. Programs that adhere to these principles have been found to produce sizeable reductions in recidivism (Smith, Gendreau, and Swartz, 2009; Lowenkamp, Latessa, and Smith, 2006). Thus, social support (both instrumental and expressive) to individual offenders in the form of offender rehabilitation remains a key component to a comprehensive understanding of successful reintegration.

Unfortunately, we know very little about the types of programming Cutty may have received both within prison and after his release. It is unlikely, however, that he received anything extensive, as high quality treatment programs tend to be an anomaly (Lowenkamp et al., 2006; but see Listwan, Jonson, Cullen, and Latessa, 2008). It cannot be ignored, however, that Cutty's antisocial attitudes and behaviors were, in fact, ultimately modified in a manner that discouraged continued criminal involvement. We therefore argue that individual offender rehabilitation is but one piece of the reentry puzzle (albeit an important one), and Cutty's narrative tells us that social support from other sources is an essential ingredient in encouraging successful reintegration. Again, part of the promise of social support is that it is an organizing concept that bridges multiple dimensions. Stated differently, social support on the part of family members or a community may function the same way as formal offender treatment when it comes to the individual risks to reoffending.

The Community Level

Changing the attitudes and behaviors of offenders provides a necessary yet insufficient step toward ensuring successful offender reentry. As Currie (1998: 171) notes, "[e]ven the best efforts at rehabilitation of offenders will be undermined unless they are linked to a broader strategy to improve conditions in the communities to which offenders return." Indeed, researchers are beginning to uncover community-level effects on recidivism that function independently of individual risks. For example, returning to a neighborhood that is characterized by poverty is likely to increase the chances of an offender recidivating (Kubrin and Stewart, 2006), and these effects have been found to be more pronounced for minority ex-offenders in particular (Reisig, Bales, Hay, and Wang, 2007). These ideas about reoffending at the community-level are situated primarily in the sociology and urban studies literature. Although scholars of these traditions do not necessarily ignore the psychology of criminal behavior, the emphasis is instead placed on how community characteristics can limit ex-offenders to a lifestyle of anything but crime. It is not hard to envision—would a completely reformed and rehabilitated Cutty be able to leave prison and immediately abandon his old ways in search of a successful, conventional lifestyle on the rugged streets of West Baltimore?

As noted in the introduction to this chapter, the community to which Cutty returns is certainly in need of improvement. Fatherless homes, poverty and crime-stricken neighborhoods, dilapidated schools, and hopeless or corrupt officials characterize the Baltimore depicted in *The Wire*. Ultimately the neighborhoods are defined by social disorganization (Shaw and McKay, 1942), and informal social control among community members is limited while criminal subcultures flourish. Few opportunities for gainful employment exist, and it is difficult to envision a successful lifestyle for any member of the community, much less one that is now marked by the stain of a criminal record (Pager, 2007). It is again through the receipt of social support that Cutty is able to navigate the seemingly impossible path to successful reentry.

The more social support in a person's social network, the less reoffending will occur.

"Private social support" refers to the residential community to which an offender returns, which includes the familial and social networks available to assist in the reintegration process (Bazemore and Erbe, 2004). For Cutty, private social support is limited to his impoverished grandmother and his criminal associates. While the role of his grandmother is not featured heavily in the storyline, her contribution to supporting Cutty upon release cannot be overstated. By providing him a home, both physically and emotionally, she offers him more than many ex-offenders can hope for upon their return. To be sure, securing adequate housing is often among the first and most formidable hurdles for ex-offenders to overcome (see Richards, Austin, and Jones, 2004 for a discussion of material challenges facing returning ex-offenders). Mee-maw poignantly tells Cutty, as she slips him some pocket cash, "times like these you have to shine; in your face, in your clothes, and in your *pocket*."

As for Cutty's sources of private social support through social networks, his friends—after 14 years in prison—are effectively reduced to Avon Barksdale and his associates. And while they intend to support him socially, that support is implicitly to come at the price of continued criminality. As Colvin and colleagues (2002) have pointed out, "social support (whether from a legitimate or illegitimate source) assists individuals in controlling their social environments, which gives them some degree of control balance or even control surplus." This illustrates Cutty's dilemma: at the risk of parole violation, he could accept the support offered by his associates, and his continued allegiance to them will allow him to supercede the myriad tribulations associated with conventional life in his impoverished community. The "control surplus" that would result would allow Cutty to make ample money, as well as maintain a social status above his struggling neighbors. Cutty's menial labor job, his acerbic parole agent, and the general plight of his situation upon release from prison exacerbate this predicament.

Seemingly undeterred, Cutty seeks out an old girlfriend, Grace. She is reluctant to even talk to the ex-convict, and is disinterested in a walk down memory lane. A schoolteacher at Ida B. Wells Elementary, she has clearly developed a level of social capital that she is unwilling to compromise by associating with Cutty, and intimates that she was disappointed by his incarceration years before. Nevertheless, after Cutty admits he has forsaken the game, and the attendant luxury cars for a "bus pass", she ultimately offers him a modicum of help. She takes his number, and notes she will pass it along to the Deacon of her church, who is trying to fill custodial positions at her school.

The desistance process, even when bolstered by supportive employment networking connections, is not always an instant phenomenon (Sampson and Laub, 1993). Often, the process is marked by fluctuations in criminality and integration before complete desistance and formation of new roles are realized. Such is the case with Cutty. He meets with the Deacon, but the Deacon offers only a G.E.D., which does not interest Cutty. He is likewise nonplussed at the prospect of religion. Finally, dismayed as well that Grace did not attend the meeting, Cutty leaves.

After being romantically rebuffed by Grace, and finding no resolution with the Deacon, Cutty has a disheartening conversation with his landscaping boss. The owner of the small company tells Cutty the truth: life as an unskilled ex-convict on the straight and narrow is hard, defined every day by sore backs, low wages, and generally dismal prospects. As the ex-offender and day-laborer hops out of the bed of the pickup truck after the day's work, the owner reminds him: "every day". The next time we see Cutty, he is returning to work as an enforcer for his drug-dealing associates. Instantly, he is rewarded with a weapon, clean clothes, and a party. More importantly, he regains his former and more comfortable identity as a soldier, and a seasoned, effective participant in the honor culture of the street. This move by Cutty to embrace a more comfortable role obviously imperils his successful and pro-social reentry.

However, he does not completely relinquish the burgeoning social ties that start to form as a result of Grace's assistance. And after a stint working as muscle for Avon Barksdale's drug crew, Cutty returns to work at the landscaping company, where he has another compelling conversation with his boss. Tellingly for the present chapter, the boss asks if Cutty might seek help from family members (private social support), to which Cutty replies he has only his grandmother, who has given what she can. The boss then wonders aloud if a social worker of some kind (parochial social support) might prove helpful. Cutty responds that he had met with Grace's friend from church, but that he was "not ready" at the time.

When he quit the Barksdale gang, Avon poignantly decreed that he was free to move on, but noted that Cutty knew no other way of life. This becomes evident once Cutty has come to the realization that the game is not for him any longer, but that a life of menial labor does not suit him either. Still searching for his rightful path, Cutty finds himself back in the Deacon's office. Unsure of what he is asking for Cutty stumbles through his thoughts until he utters that maybe what he needs is not help for himself, but to help others. And although the Deacon again suggests religion, and Cutty again adamantly declines, a baptism of sorts takes place nevertheless. "Cutty, is it?" asks the Deacon. "No. Dennis Wise ..." is the reply. With that, the stage is set for Cutty's transition into a law abiding life, in which he uses his wisdom, experience, and toughness to help others instead of hurt them. This transition is ultimately facilitated by the assistance of community-level parochial social support.

The less social support there is in a community, the higher the recidivism rate will be.

"Parochial social support" refers to support provided by the health and social service network of a community (Bazemore and Erbe, 2004). Season 3's "Hamsterdam" is a perfect allegory for the plight of over-burdened social service agencies. When the Deacon brings Cutty to the edge of the "Free Zone" to introduce him to some representatives of service agencies, all are busy distributing condoms, meals, clean needles, and other interventions to drug users, prostitutes, homeless and others in the street. It is clear that they are far too busy to stop for long and discuss the future of the newly christened Dennis Wise. Undeterred by the havoc of Hamsterdam, the Deacon shows Cutty the work being done, and in so doing, shows him how much work remains. When it comes out in conversations with other social workers that his main interest and expertise is in boxing, another corner is turned in the path to successful reintegration for Dennis "Cutty" Wise.

It is important to point out for the present chapter that the Deacon, for all his stern fortitude, never judges Cutty harshly, and does not condemn him for disagreeing. His place on the front lines of social service has made him wise, but not cynical. He knows the risks involved for an ex-offender returning to impoverished inner city streets with no education, no work experience, and a criminal record. Nevertheless, when the ex-offender is ready, the Deacon is there to facilitate Cutty's involvement in his own reintegrative process. After a trip to an existing boxing gym where some of the neighborhood boys work out, a social worker, introduced by the Deacon, takes Cutty to an old, cluttered warehouse. Undaunted by the need for excessive refurbishing before he can start his own boxing gym, Cutty says: "this is my trip, man; I need to go from A to B all by myself." Bravado aside, it is clear from the story of Cutty Wise up until this point that left to his own devices, it would have been all but impossible for the returned ex-offender to reemerge from his life of disadvantage and crime. But with some well-placed assistance from his community, the thug, inmate and ex-con formerly known as Cutty finds himself positioned to become a much-needed asset to the community he once victimized.

Like the Deacon and his boss, Cutty is from a background similar to the youth he attempts to reach and coach. He is able to relate to them in a way that more traditional, "academic" interventionists might not be able to achieve. This offers Cutty an identity in which he can once again utilize his wisdom, toughness, and street experience, but now in a constructive way. In fact, faced with daunting budget deficits and aging, dilapidated equipment, Cutty appeals to his old drug boss, Avon Barksdale, for financial sponsorship. Visibly nervous and wagering his old-school street credibility, Cutty goes over the needs for the gym, describing how it would help the kids. After a tense moment, Avon agrees to Cutty's request for what is to Avon a nominal sum. In response to his request for ten thousand, Cutty receives fifteen. In his benevolence, Avon Barksdale becomes an unlikely source of parochial social support.

On the opposite end of the community support spectrum, as the gym nears completion, the Deacon lets Cutty know that permits will need to be obtained; licenses, authorizations, and inspections will need to be put in place. All of this is news to Cutty, who returns from a hopeless whirlwind tour of various city offices feeling "like a balloon, with the air shooting out my ass". Here we see parochial social support at its highest form. The Deacon invokes assistance from a prominent Minister, who, in turn, calls on State Delegate Watkins to intercede. This assistance facilitates the process in a way that Cutty Wise would never have been able to achieve on his own. As such, it demonstrates the reintegrative power of parochial social support. Admittedly, the serious criminologist is forced to allow for a good deal of artistic license regarding all of this assistance. Clearly, the vast majority of released offenders will lack access to top-tier drug lords, and many fewer still will have the relationships necessary to cultivate multi-thousand dollar investments for philanthropic social service endeavors. Similarly unlikely is the thought of State Delegate intervention on behalf of paroled murderers. Nevertheless, these storylines underscore the lack of resources and professional aptitude suffered by most released ex-offenders. It also illustrates dramatically how social support like investment of resources, attention, and assistance from institutions, both formal and informal, can positively impact the reintegration process.

The System-Level

A return to prison is usually the result of one of two events: a new arrest or a parole violation (though they are not mutually exclusive). Thus, recidivism can represent system behavior (i.e., the decision of whether to revoke parole upon a violation) in addition to the actual behavior of offenders (i.e., the offender breaking the law). In other words, variations in reaction to deviance by the system and its agents can affect reoffending outcomes independent of the offender's personal attributes or community characteristics. Research has shown that the characteristics of a community supervision system can indeed impact recidivism. For example, an increased intensity of supervision (i.e., more drug tests, more face-to-face meetings) has been found to increase the likelihood of a parole violation net of individual risks (e.g., prior criminal history) (Grattet, Lin, and Petersilia, 2011). Both the individual attributes of Cutty and the collective attributes of Baltimore could describe why Cutty might continue to engage in criminal behavior. A full understanding of offender reintegration, however, must consider the influence of system-level practices on reoffending.

We know very little regarding the relationship between Cutty and his parole officer, but from what we can see, the relationship is not a positive one. When Cutty asks about the existence of a possible employment opportunity, his parole officer replies, "I don't know and I don't care. Just get a job." There seems to be little effort on the part of the parole officer to ensure that Cutty is linked up with the social services and employment opportunities that he requires. Instead a laundry list of parole requirements are rattled off: obtain gainful employment, refrain from associating with known criminals (a difficult task when the community of return is composed of current and former criminals), and keep the office informed of any changes in residence. A significant portion of ex-offenders—even those that succeed—break some form of supervision requirement (Visher and Courtney, 2006) and Cutty is no different. In the end, it is possible for an offender like Cutty to be revoked for violating a condition (e.g., failure to report) of parole while otherwise remaining crime-free (see Richards et al., 2004).

A supportive correctional system reduces recidivism.

A supervision system that is rich in resources and low on constraints (in contrast to the parole system depicted in *The Wire*) might allow for a more socially supportive parole officer. Farrall (2002; 2004) has argued that community corrections officers are in the unique position to aid in the development of the social capital (i.e., provide social support) of ex-offenders. This can be accomplished by working to strengthen family ties or by assisting in employment searches. Such an approach would be a return to the classical reintegration approach taken by parole officers. Unfortunately, attempts at a transition back to this orientation have often amounted to increased supervision only (Austin, 2001). Nevertheless, Visher and Courtney (2006: 8) found that within one month of release 71% of parolees in their sample described their parole officer as "helpful with their transition home, especially by understanding their situation and providing encouragement."

For Cutty, social support necessarily came from outside his parole agency. Additionally, intensified scrutiny could easily have resulted in a technical violation, and a return to prison, which would have prohibited his eventual reintegration. Along those lines, Travis and Petersilia (2001) proposed a managed reentry period with a system of graduated sanctions in place to respond to transgressions. This approach would reduce discretion on the part of parole officers while still providing them with the tools to encourage successful reintegration. Thus, a socially supportive parole officer, armed with a bevy of increasingly punitive responses to violations, may serve to increase the likelihood of successful reintegration by ex-offenders who may experience a few minor setbacks. And Cutty certainly qualifies as an offender who suffers a few setbacks on his long path to desistance.

Cutty in the Community

As Season 3 draws to a close, Cutty Wise has exited prison with little more than Mee-maw and a G-pack. He has fluctuated for a time between legitimate employment and criminal activity. Through Cutty's eyes during his initial release, we see the harsh truth of a life lived by the code of the streets, where robbing, stealing, beatings and murders occur with apparent impunity. As Cutty regains his identity as Dennis Wise, we are witness to the perils of life as a laborer and social worker: Cutty works long days, struggles with his would-be boxing students, and is initially lost in a cyclone of red tape. Although it is clear that much of his behavioral improvement, pro-social advances, and employment prospects would have been far less likely without the assistance of social support from key players, there is something about Cutty himself that contributes to his unlikely "success."

The crime for which Cutty has been incarcerated is telling. As relayed by Wee-Bey Brice in the prison yard, Cutty shot his victim, Elijah Davis, in broad daylight, and then called police himself to report it. This cold-blooded killing is revered by fellow street criminals as showing intentional viciousness and singular clarity. In the context of his eventual desistance, this same sense of focus and drive is likely at work. Certainly, we see Cutty vigorously performing tasks at his landscaping job; later we watch as Cutty takes the helm of the boxing gym project, impressing the Deacon. And when his earliest recruits rebel and leave, he doggedly retrieves them from their loitering posts in Hamsterdam and re-initiates their training.

This transformation of negative skills into positive forces is part of what Maruna (2001) has referred to as "redemption scripts." In his qualitative study of both offenders who desisted, and those who persisted in offending, he found several recurring themes, whereby offenders attempted to make sense of their past and predictions about their futures. One key finding for Maruna (2001: 99) was that "regardless of the specific framework, ex-offenders who desist seem to find some larger cause that brings them a sense of purpose." This seems to be precisely what Cutty is working through cognitively during his initial meetings with the Deacon. In the past Cutty has been a strong, independent actor on the street. Released from prison, struggling toward a new identity, Cutty seems reluctant to resign himself to a life of day-labor and mundanity. Maruna (2001: 105) explains it eloquently: "[f]or all its problems, being a criminal provides individuals with at least momentary escapes into excitement, power, and notoriety. If going straight means accepting docility, self-hatred, and stigma, there is little reason to desist from such escapes."

For Cutty, the boxing gym offers an opportunity to achieve both of the goals described above from Maruna's discussion of internal redemption. First, by helping the kids in the neighborhood where he grew up, Cutty is able to improve, at whatever level, the quality of life in Baltimore. This allows him to imbue meaning on his life as a criminal and time "wasted" in prison, as cautionary lessons which he can share with young men headed down similar paths. Maruna points out that not all or even most ex-convicts are likely to become social workers or volunteers, but notes that it is a prominent theme in the self-styled narratives in his sample. Given Cutty's particular focus, and the remarkable level of social support he receives along the way, it is not surprising that he is able to achieve what many ex-offenders only dream of.

Second, founding the gym allows Cutty to establish a new, prominent, and pro-social identity within the conventional world. The "docility" of day-labor is replaced with teaching of the "sweet science" to a growing, changing group of youngsters. The "self-hatred" of a man who has killed, beaten, and disappointed is replaced by the self-respect of someone who has overcome adversity, and now helps others do the same. Finally, the "stigma" of a convicted felon is replaced with the positive reputation as a community leader, a coach, and a social worker. In short, despite the prominence of social support for Cutty at multiple levels, a sense of human agency and a want to change plays a significant role in his successful offender reintegration (Laub and Sampson, 2003).

Conclusion

Cutty's story tells us a significant amount of information regarding the challenges of offender reentry. It also paints a daunting picture of what must be done in order to ensure ex-offenders remain crime-free. We must find ways to attend to individual offenders and their communities that does not place additional system-imposed pressure on staying out. One key consideration in implementing future correctional policies is the question of who bears the responsibility of caring for offenders. Currently, ex-offenders like Cutty are largely left to their own devices and are expected to bear the responsibility of reintegration themselves. According to this line of thought, offenders chose to offend, and for that, they are expected to figure out themselves how to stop offending.

The problem with this, again, as we see in Cutty, is that the ecological background of many offenders leaves them without education, work experience, or even hope in the form of pro-social attitudes. Born into resource-deprived neighborhoods, characterized by social distance from mainstream society, poverty, and violence, many released offenders are paroled into the same conditions that set the stage for their criminality in the first place. Without support from family and pro-social friends in the form of housing, employment and financial assistance, it is hard to imagine any drastic improvements in individual behavior or circumstances of released ex-offenders. Similarly, without strong parochial institutions like churches, social service agencies, and educational organizations to assist in the reintegration process, meaningfully pro-social reentry will likely continue to elude us on a broader scale. Finally, as long as supervision systems focus on increased scrutiny, general deterrence, and incapacitation, the current vicious, wasteful cycle of mass incarceration, decarceration, and reincarceration is likely to continue. The answer, then, is that the responsibilities of the framework of reoffending set forth here do not fall squarely on any one entity, and the challenge instead is organizing the necessary components and communicating the importance of shared responsibility.

We have suggested here a focus on social support at every level of the reentry process as a way of fostering the successful reintegration of released ex-offenders. This means doing something "for" offenders instead of doing something "to" them (Cullen, Chamlin, and Wright, 1999). But lending assistance to former criminals is not just feel-good policy; it is fiscally responsible and promotes public safety. In today's restricted economy, state and federal resources are increasingly spread thinner and thinner. While in the past there has been a "get tough" push to increase incarceration rolls, build new prisons, and hire more guards, it has become clear that indefinite mass incarceration is a strain on individuals, communities, and correctional systems. Increasing the number of ex-offenders who are viable, reintegrated citizens frees up governmental resources, improves and returns individuals like Cutty to their neighborhoods as an asset and promotes independence and prosperity in releasees.

For his part, Cutty is a man of principle. Even as a murderer he is a "stand-up" guy. When he committed the crime for which he was incarcerated, he accepted the punishment openly, by calling the police on himself. After his release, when he decides he can no longer participate in the violent street life he grew up in, he tells the crime boss to his face that he is done. When he lets his anger come between him and his young students, he seeks them out, apologizes, and takes responsibility. But all along the way, Cutty has social support. He has a grandmother who loves him, friends who, in their own ways, look up to him and institutions who back up his dream of helping kids through boxing. For the ex-offender whose life is not born on the pages of a Hollywood screenplay, social support is all the more important to successful reintegration.

As viewers of *The Wire*, we are provided a unique window into Cutty's life. As such, it becomes easy to sympathize with him and the direness of his situation. In reality, we typically do not have that opportunity. A final implication of this chapter is to advocate for a return to the first person interviewing that defined some of the classics in early criminology (e.g., Shaw, 1930). Doing so will allow for a more comprehensive understanding of the components of successful reintegration from the view of ex-offenders, criminal justice agents, and social service providers. By developing a broader understanding, which considers individual-, community- and system-level characteristics, scholars and practitioners will be able to make better decisions, develop more effective strategies, and most importantly help to improve the future for people and communities suffering from crime, poverty and disadvantage.

Much of *The Wire* depicts an understanding of initial and continued forays into criminal behavior due to the limited opportunities available to residents for conventional lifestyles. What is often forgotten is that these contexts (both structural and cultural) remain when ex-offenders return from a period of incarceration. Existing theoretical frameworks, and the evidence-based programs based on these foundations, often focus on changing the offender without changing the environment to which he or she returns. In short, "the game" was waiting for Cutty upon his return, and his chances of leaving the game were diminished further due to the presence of a criminal record and the added expectations associated with his supervision conditions. An exchange that Cutty has with one of the troubled youth of *The Wire* is particularly telling:

> **Cutty:** I guess what I'm tryin' to say is ... not everything comes down to how you carry it in the street. I mean, it do come down to that if you gonna be in the street. But that ain't the only way to be.
> **Dukie:** Round here it is.
> **Cutty:** Yeah. Round here it is. World is bigger than that, at least, that's what they tell me.
> **Dukie:** Like ... how do you get from here to the rest of the world?
> **Cutty:** I wish I knew.

Until we begin to consider the multiple dimensions involved in offender reentry, Cutty's success story will likely be an anomaly.

References

Anderson, E. (1999) *Code of the street: Decency, violence and the moral life of the inner city.* New York: Norton.

Andrews, D. A., and James Bonta (2003) *The Psychology of Criminal Conduct.* Cincinnati, OH: Anderson.

Austin, James (2001) 'Prisoner Reentry: Current Trends, Practices, and Issues', *Crime & Delinquency* 47(3): 314–334.

Austin, James, and John Irwin (2001) *It's About Time: America's Imprisonment Binge.* Belmont, CA: Wadsworth.

Bazemore, Gordon, and Carsten Erbe (2004) 'Reintegration and Restorative Justice: Towards a Theory and Practice of Informal Social Control and Support', in Shadd Maruna and Russ Immarigeon (eds.) *After Crime and Punishment: Pathways to Offender Reintegration*, pp. 27–56. Cullompton, Devon: Willan.

Colvin, Mark, Francis T. Cullen, and Thomas Vander Ven (2002) 'Coercion, Social Support, and Crime: An Emerging Theoretical Consensus', *Criminology* 40(1): 19–42.

Cullen, Francis T. (1994) 'Social Support as an Organizing Concept for Criminology: Presidential Address to the Academy of Criminal Justice Sciences', *Justice Quarterly* 11(4): 527–560.

Cullen, Francis T., John P. Wright, and Mitchell B. Chamlin (1999) 'Social Support and Social Reform: A Progressive Crime Control Agenda', *Crime & Delinquency* 45(2): 188–207.

Cullen, Francis T., and Cheryl L. Jonson (2011) *Correctional Theory: Context and Consequences*. Thousand Oaks, CA: Sage.

Currie, Elliott (1998) *Crime and Punishment in America*. New York: Henry Holt and Company.

Farrall, Stephen (2002) *Rethinking What Works with Offenders*. Cullompton, Devon: Willan.

Farrall, Stephen (2004) 'Social Capital and Offender Reintegration: Making Probation Desistance Focused', in Shadd Maruna and Russ Immarigeon (eds) *After Crime and Punishment: Pathways to Offender Reintegration*, pp. 57–84. Cullompton, Devon: Willan.

Gendreau, Paul (1996) 'The Principles of Effective Intervention with Offenders', in Alan T. Harland (ed.) *Choosing Correctional Options that Work: Defining the Demand and Evaluating the Supply*, pp. 117–130. Thousand Oaks, CA: Sage Publications.

Grattet, Ryken, Jeffrey Lin, and Joan Petersilia (2011) 'Supervision Regimes, Risk, and Official Reactions to Parolee Deviance', *Criminology* 49(2): 371–399.

Kubrin, Charis E., and Eric A. Stewart (2006) 'Predicting who Reoffends: The Neglected Role of Neighborhood Context in Recidivism Studies', *Criminology* 44(1): 165–197.

Laub, J.H., and Sampson, R.J. 2003. Shared beginnings, divergent lives: Delinquent boys to age 70. Cambridge, MA: Harvard University Press.

Lin, Nan (1986) 'Conceptualizing Social Support', in Nan Lin, Alfred Dean, and Walter Ensel (eds) *Social Support, Life Events, and Depression*, p. 17–30. Orlando, FL: Academic Press, Inc.

Lipsey, Mark W., and Francis T. Cullen (2007) 'The Effectiveness of Correctional Rehabilitation: A Review of Systematic Reviews', *Annual Review of Law and Social Science* 3: 297–320.

Lipsey, Mark W., Gabrielle L. Chapman, and Nana A. Landenberger (2001) 'Cognitive-Behavioral Programs for Offenders', *Annals of the American Academy of Political and Social Science* 578: 144–157.

Listwan, Shelley J., Cheryl L. Jonson, Francis T. Cullen, and Edward J. Latessa (2008) 'Cracks in the Penal Harm Movement: Evidence from the Field', *Criminology and Public Policy* 7(3): 423–465.

Lowenkamp, Christopher T., Edward J. Latessa, and Paula Smith (2006) 'Does Correctional Program Quality Really Matter? The Impact of Adhering to the Principles of Effective Intervention 2006', *Criminology and Public Policy* 5(1): 201–220.

MacKenzie, Doris L. (2000) 'Evidence-Based Corrections: Identifying What Works', *Crime & Delinquency* 46(4): 457–471.

Maruna, Shadd (2001) *Making Good: How Ex-Convicts Reform and Rebuild their Lives*. Washington, DC: American Psychological Association.

Pager, Devah (2007) *Marked: Race, Crime, and Finding Work in an Era of Mass Incarceration*. Chicago: University of Chicago Press.

Pew Center on the States (2011). *State of recidivism: The revolving door of America's prisons*. Washington, DC: The Pew Charitable Trusts.

Pratt, Travis C. (2009) *Addicted to Incarceration: Corrections Policy and the Politics of Misinformation in the United States*. Thousand Oaks, CA: Sage.

Reisig, Michael D., William D. Bales, Carter Hay, and Xia Wang (2007) 'The Effect of Racial Inequality on Black Male Recidivism', *Justice Quarterly* 24(3): 408–434.

Richards, Stephen C., James Austin, and Richard S. Jones. (2004) 'Thinking About Prison Release and Budget Crisis in the Blue Grass State', *Critical Criminology* 12(3): 243–263.

Sampson, Robert J., and John H. Laub (1993) *Crime in the Making: Pathways and Turning Points through Life*. Cambridge, MA: Harvard University Press.

Shaw, Clifford R. (1930) *The Jack-Roller: A Delinquent Boy's Own Story*. Chicago: University of Chicago Press.

Shaw, Clifford R., and Henry D. McKay (1942) *Juvenile Delinquency and Urban Areas*. Chicago: University of Chicago Press.

Smith, Paula, Paul Gendreau, and Kristin Swartz (2009) 'Validating the Principles of Effective Intervention: A Systematic Review of the Contributions of Meta-Analysis in the Field of Corrections', *Victims and Offenders* 4: 148–169.

Travis, Jeremy, and Joan Petersilia (2001) 'Reentry Reconsidered: A New Look at an Old Question', *Crime & Delinquency* 47(3): 291–313.

Visher, Christy A., and Shannon M.E. Courtney (2006) *Cleveland Prisoners' Experiences Returning Home*. Washington, DC: The Urban Institute.

West, H.C., Sabol, W.J., & Greenman S.J. (2010). *Prisoners in 2009*. Washington, D.C.: U.S. Department of Justice.

Wilson, James A., and Robert C. Davis. (2006) 'Good Intentions Meet Hard Realities: An Evaluation of the Project Greenlight Reentry Program', *Criminology and Public Policy* 5(2): 303–338.

Wright, Kevin A., and Jeffrey W. Rosky. (2011) 'Too Early is Too Soon: Lessons from the Montana Department of Corrections Early Release Program', *Criminology and Public Policy* 10(4): 881–908.

Study Questions

1. What is the importance of social support to successful offender reentry?

2. How is the typical offender described by Andrews and Bonta? What are the individual-level obstacles faced by ex-offenders when reentering society? How is this portrayed in the character Dennis "Cutty" Wise?

3. As discussed by Shaw and McKay, how does social disorganization influence offender reentry? What are the potential effects of both legitimate and illegitimate sources of private social support? How are these illustrated by the social challenges faced by Cutty?

4. It is said that the behavior of the system component of recidivism is also important; what do the authors mean by stating this? What part can a parole officer play in recidivism?

5. What policy implications can be gleaned from what we have read about individual-, community-, and system-level support? Given these implications and the information provided in this chapter, what recommendations would you make in order to improve on the existing policy?

6. We have a decent picture of prisoner reentry and support structures (or lack thereof) as presented in the show. In order to gain a deeper understanding of programs that currently exist, go online and conduct a search to find information pertaining to post-release offender support services in your immediate community (or in the closest viable system) and describe them. Are there any improvements to be made? Why or why not?

Chapter 14

Perspectives on Structure, Normative Conflict, and Social Disorganization in *The Wire*

Kyle J. Thomas and Matthew R. Nobles

Introduction

Indicative of the field's roots in sociology, many early criminological theories developed in the "golden era" of the Chicago School in the 1920s and 1930s sought to explain how macro-organizational factors contributed to differences in crime rates across space and social classes. In contrast to classical theories that are oriented to the individual offender, these macro theories emphasize social structure, subcultures, and the transmission of deviant or delinquent values in the aggregate. A larger theme from this theoretical perspective is that the nature of *place* can be itself inherently criminogenic, and that the people living in criminogenic places are disadvantaged both by lacking legitimate opportunities and by overexposure to illegitimate opportunities. Similar prominent criminological theories have since been developed that share many of these qualities (Anderson, 1999; Cloward and Ohlin, 1960; Sampson and Wilson, 1987; Wolfgang et al., 1967)—most importantly, that the ecological concentration and social isolation of individuals in disadvantaged communities leads to structural barriers and cultural adaptations conducive to delinquency.

The criminogenic effects of social isolation, structural barriers and culture are pervasive throughout *The Wire*. The young African Americans residing in the "High Rises" of inner-city Baltimore routinely discuss the futility of educational attainment, rejecting it merely as an institution of white America.

279

Cutty, Poot, and other inner-city Baltimore residents experience significant hardships when trying to find and adjust to legitimate employment—stemming from their lack of education and their inability to utilize social capital to achieve lawful ends. Moreover, Stringer Bell's attempts to transform Avon Barskdale into a respectable business entrepreneur also fails after Avon admits that he is "just a gangster" (Season 3, Episode 11) and cannot put the game behind him. Many of these young males instead turn to the streets and criminal organization for status, causing them to see crime as a part of everyday life, to value the respect they receive for violently defending or taking corners and to use violence to regulate individuals who violate the code of the game. The deleterious effects of this culture become exacerbated by the relatively poor socializing job done by the schools, churches, and families of the Baltimore residents, as is evident in the developmental experiences of Michael, Namond, and Randy. Indeed, the structural barriers and competing oppositional culture removes much of the conventionality and innocence in the children and adolescents who are forced to grow up on the corners of inner-city Baltimore.

This chapter examines the role of structural disadvantage and normative conflict in crime, and more specifically identifies their important role as catalysts of criminal behavior throughout *The Wire*. First, we provide a brief description of the core tenets and evolution of prominent structural-cultural theories of crime, discussing their relevance in explaining how community factors can impact the socialization, development, and ultimately the offending of inner-city residents. Second, we discuss how these structural barriers and cultural adaptations affect inner-city Baltimore and shape the lives of many of the characters of *The Wire*, also discussing how the breakdown of conventional institutions and the prominence of criminal organizations influence the development of some of the younger residents who are forced to grow up in these adverse conditions. Finally, we conclude by discussing the policy implications of these theoretical perspectives and the need for policymakers and criminologists to recognize the importance of structure and normative conflict when searching for the causes and solutions of crime.

Theoretical Origins: Chicago School

At its core, the Chicago School of criminology emphasizes the value of context. The social and cultural context in the city of Chicago was characterized by unique upheaval and transition during the early 20th century. Industry and construction, fueled by railroad expansion and Chicago's role as a key port city, resulted in a profound shift in the economic environment. In addition to a sustained influx of immigrants from Ireland, Germany, and various Eastern European nations, the Great Migration (1910–1930) brought African Americans from the South in pursuit of industrial jobs and the promise of a better future. The interactive population explosion and ethnic diversification contributed to various social problems, including overcrowding in the urban core of the city and, eventually, the prominence of both organized and street crime. Meanwhile, these trends were observed and modeled by University of Chicago sociologists, who attempted to correlate macro-level social structural transitions with crime and delinquency. Sociologists Park and Burgess (1925) interpreted Chicago's growth and development, with all of its concomitant social problems, as a fundamental process of urban ecology. Their theory proposed a series of concentric zones extending from Chicago's downtown outward to the suburbs. Each zone, according to the authors, was characterized by similar ecological behaviors, the most critical of which involved competition for scarce resources such as housing and employment. Moreover, Park and Burgess (1925) postulated that competition between social zones resulted in spatial differentiation and similarly characterized social properties within each zone. Although this theoretical framework was written fundamentally about population and applied demography, it does have utility for understanding crime as a manifestation of ecological competition. Crime could be alternatively interpreted within zones as carrying an intrinsic "property" motive tied to scarce resources, or between zones as a critical process that involves gaining a strategic, competitive advantage over a favored class. The primary contribution the social ecological perspective offers, however, is to provide a bridge to context-specific subcultural theories that emerged in the later Chicago School.

Social Structure and Crime

Subsequent Chicago School theories integrated themes of social and spatial differentiation while expanding the scope to include greater emphasis on cultures. In a seminal work, Shaw and McKay (1942) argued that structural factors—specifically poverty, residential mobility, and racial/ethnic heterogeneity—contribute to *social disorganization*, defined as "the inability of local communities to realize the common values of their residents or solve commonly experienced problems" (Bursik, 1988: 521). The phenomenon of social disorganization differentially affects communities or neighborhoods characterized by concentrated disadvantage by definition, and thus the theory is often considered to be primarily concerned with geography or spatial proximity. Community social disorganization, however, is particularly conducive to high rates of delinquent behavior through a process of cultural transmission, in which "traditions of delinquency are transmitted through successive generations of the same zone in the same way language, roles, and attitudes are transmitted" (Shaw and McKay, 1942: 28). Social disorganization, therefore, is a theory that incorporates both tangible properties of spatial differentiation throughout the city, as well as intangible properties that describe the evolution of subcultures and informal social control.

Although social disorganization theory is commonly associated with symptoms of physical incivilities and urban blight, the theory offers considerably more nuance in explaining the articulation between structural context and crime. Rather than adopt a reductionist approach that argues for simple compositional effects (e.g., "bad people live in bad neighborhoods"), Shaw and McKay (1942) suggested that communities become disorganized through a multi-stage process, which begins with structural deficiencies like poverty, ethnic/racial discrimination, and a dearth of legitimate opportunities. These factors are associated with social consequences involving the erosion and deprioritization of traditional values, resulting in the community's isolation from larger society, and the breakdown in institutions that are most effective in socializing conformity (i.e., family, church, schools). This breakdown, in turn, leads individuals to hold relatively weak moral beliefs that can regulate behavior. Weak ties held among community members, particularly juveniles, allows gangs and other pro-criminal groups to socialize people in community settings, and thus, powerful deviant norms are developed and transmitted in these areas that compete with the conventional institutions promoting conformity. Finally, individuals residing in these communities are at a profound structural disadvantage when it comes to achieving legitimate success, and in turn, seek status from illegitimate means.

From Social Structure to Subcultures

The Chicago School's emphasis on social and structural context was also influential to subsequent generations of theorists, who were similarly focused on the problems of violence and life in the inner city. Shaw and McKay's (1942) conceptualization of social disorganization as a theory about cultural transmission of pro-crime values, particularly in neighborhoods marked by poverty and racial/ethnic heterogeneity, figured prominently in redefining crime as a *subcultural* phenomenon. Wolfgang and Ferracuti (1967: 103) defined subculture as "a normative system of some group or groups smaller than the whole society," implying that subcultures contrast with the parent culture but do not exist independently of it. The norms, values, and beliefs that are embraced by a subculture, therefore, may overlap in part with the dominant culture, but also gain identity from differentiation. One such example involves a normative system in which "a whole [sub]culture may accept a value set dependent upon violence, demand or encourage adherence to violence, and penalize deviation" (Wolfgang and Ferracuti, 1967: 155)—a system that the authors termed the *subculture of violence*.

The subculture of violence model represents an extension of earlier Chicago School theories in the sense that socially disorganized communities, previously defined as *lacking* features necessary for adaptation (e.g., cohesiveness), may be more formally viewed as *actively* embracing pro-violence conduct norms as a coping strategy. The conceptual similarity also extends to measurement, since Wolfgang and Ferracuti state that aggregate rates of deviant behavior could be effectively predicted using structural correlates of subculture, including "class position, ethnicity, occupational status, and other social variables" (Wolfgang and Ferracuti, 1967: 151), which are commonly identified covariates of crime rates in disorganized communities. Finally, according to Wolfgang and Ferracuti (1967), immersion in the subculture of violence results in greater acceptance of deviant and pro-crime norms and subsequent personality integration for some individuals through a process of differential learning. This process is conceptually similar to Shaw and McKay's (1942) exposition of the social disorganization causal process, in which pro-crime values are transmitted throughout successive generations when traditional values and institutions break down. Like Shaw and McKay (1942), Wolfgang and Ferracuti (1967) inherently promoted a framework for understanding crime as a function of social structure, normative conduct, and class conflict.

These broad Chicago School themes have been further extended in recent years, updating perspectives on social structure, norms, and crime for contemporary society. Anderson (1999), emphasizing contrasts in normative conduct, provided a striking case study throughout his examination of neighborhoods located along Germantown Avenue in North Philadelphia. Philadelphia offers interesting parallels to classical examples in the Chicago School tradition, in that present-day Philadelphia is a major city for industry and immigration, it is characterized by large and diverse racial and ethnic populations, and it has consistently high rates of violent crime. Thus, many of the social structural dynamics of 1920s Chicago are reflected in present-day Philadelphia, a remarkable commentary on the universal nature of these themes despite decades of ostensible progress.

Chicago School themes have persisted in other ways as well. Through a series of qualitative interviews, Anderson (1999) described the diversity of backgrounds sampled in Philadelphia's neighborhoods, noting that access to legitimate opportunities for advancement—generally, those involving "traditional" institutions like education and employment—are either blocked to most disadvantaged individuals or are actively disdained. Instead, the social norms, values, and behaviors of the inner city, which stress masculinity, "success" in terms of physical intimidation and sexual conquests, and ultimately, forcing respect from others through violence where necessary, are collectively referred to as the *code of the street*. Anderson (1999) also notes that details of the codes vary according to context, and that privately held values may give way to "street" code depending on the situation. For example, some types of disrespect are expected to be confronted by physical violence as a means to protect one's respectability and street credibility. In this way, Anderson identifies overlapping subcultural relationships in which some inner city residents are cognizant of their role in street subculture and are frequently regarded as active participants, despite general unwillingness.

Structural Disadvantage and Crime in *The Wire*

The theoretical and literary contributions of the Chicago School have highlighted the importance of context in understanding the criminal behavior of disadvantaged youth in inner-city American cities. For early Chicago School theorists and later scholars who were influenced by their work, communities are not just a setting and backdrop in which human behavior takes place, but rather are a foundation and an element deeply integrated into those who reside in the areas. Community, then, involves reciprocal influences. This is similarly true in *The Wire*, where David Simon has uniquely captured the interdependence of the structural community and the residents of those communities—the characters of *The Wire* are embedded in their community context just as much as the community is embedded in the characters. Interestingly, there are many other parallels between the social structural characteristics discussed by Shaw and McKay (1942) and Anderson (1999) and those portrayed in inner-city Baltimore throughout the series; and it is evident that the social disorganization and cultural transmission of delinquent values are the central contributors to the prevalence of drug markets and high levels of violence.

Economic stratification and marginalization are constant themes throughout *The Wire*. Many of the recurring characters transitively discuss how the high rises and Franklin Terrace differ from the other, more wealthy parts of the city. The discrete nature of such stratification is poignantly pointed out by

Stringer Bell and Avon Barksdale, two of Baltimore's more prolific gangsters (Season 3, Episode 11). They reminisce about being young soldiers who would sit across the river and admire the wealthy, and predominately white, inner-harbor area of Baltimore.

> **Avon:** Look at this shit! Can you fucking believe this? I mean, I got a crib that's overlooking the harbor. This is the same place ... we used to run through this mother fucker ... we had every security guard in there following us.
> **Stringer:** They should have.
> **Avon:** True. True. And then there was that one time....
> **Stringer:** At the toy store....
> **Avon:** Hell yeah! I told you not to steal the badminton set. What are you going to do with a fucking net and a racquet? We ain't got no yard!

After Stringer begins to discuss his current wealth, Avon tells him to "forget about that for a while. Just dream with me." "We ain't got to dream no more", Stringer then replies, highlighting that their success in "the game" has put them in a level of economic and social status that they did not think they would ever attain. The landscape of stratification is brought up again in the fourth season, this time through the eyes of Carcetti and his wife. As they stand on the inner-harbor and look across the river at the rundown ghetto of Baltimore, Carcetti claims that it "can be a great city again" (Season 4, Episode 6). These moments illustrate themes that were discussed by Park and Burgess in their description of social ecological zones in 1920s Chicago: every zone had a motif and a unique set of normative and behavioral expectations that reinforced differences in social class, race, or ethnicity.

The process of competition, politics, gain and loss illustrated throughout *The Wire* is fundamentally similar to the social Darwinism and the human ecology outlined by Park and Burgess and other Chicago School theorists. Society is structured by geographic area, and there is an intense competition for resources that ultimately leads to fundamental dichotomies of winners and losers. As one area improves in its quality, resources, and infrastructure, other areas of the city can be infiltrated and the process of disorganization and disorder can spread. This process is symbolized through Bunny Colvin's attempt to isolate the drug game in the Season 3 episode "Hamsterdam." Colvin, recognizing that the violence deriving from turf wars is rising, develops a policy to isolate all drug deals to a single part of the city, and to act as the arbiter on boundary lines within the area (see Hamilton and Block, Chapter 11 in this volume). Colvin begins to see the positive results of the program, as formerly dangerous parts of the city begin to improve, and children are seen happily playing outside with little fear of violence. Hamsterdam, however, was still the home of several law abiding citizens and the area quickly becomes disorganized and run down. The law abiding citizens are subsequently forced to move to other locations in the city. When questioned about the ethicality of the program, Colvin claims that the decay in one area is ultimately necessary for improving the other (Season 3, Episode 11). Indeed, the "losers" in the ecological struggle between classes and geographic areas eventually reside in an urban setting characterized by decay and disorganization, which ultimately results in high levels of violence that would be intolerable, perhaps even unimaginable, in other parts of Baltimore. This sentiment is echoed by McNulty, Freamon and Bunk in Season 5 as they question the inequality, decay and violence they encounter every day as police officers in inner-city Baltimore. Freamon asks contemptuously, "Do you think that if 300 white people were killed in this city every year, they wouldn't send the 82nd Airborne?" (Season 5, Episode 2).

Indirect Controls

The structural differences between the inner-city and suburban parts of Baltimore are also highlighted when contrasting the recreational and leisure activities of the corner boys and those of the children of the other prominent characters within the series. In a subtle but telling bit of contrasted imagery, McNulty tries desperately to attend his sons' club soccer games where the middle-class boys are seen wearing matching uniforms on a seemingly well-kept field in suburban Baltimore (Season 3, Episode 4), reinforcing the social stratification that is surely a constant reminder to the disadvantaged living in the inner city: not even recreation is equal-access. Other, more complex *Wire* narrative threads also touch on this theme. In Season 4, we are first introduced to Michael Lee, Namond, and Randy in a back alley as they attempt to catch birds in a makeshift bird trap using a milk crate and string. Cutty, in an attempt to get boys off the streets, develops the only organized recreational activity we see in the inner-city throughout *The Wire*: a boxing gym. After several attempts, Cutty has difficulty finding any legitimate investors who are willing to support the development of the gym. Ironically, Cutty turns to his old drug-boss Avon Barksdale who funds the boxing gym using money he has obtained through the drug trade. The analogy offered through Cutty's difficulty obtaining support, and ultimately securing it through illegitimate means, is that lack of official support for pro-social recreational activities directly weakens an institution that might have otherwise been effective in socializing youth towards conformity. These institutions, when healthy and functional, can effectively supervise the youth and keep them off the streets, where they can potentially be influenced by others already enmeshed in "the game."

The structural disadvantage within inner-city Baltimore is even more evident throughout Season 4 of *The Wire*, which emphasizes the inadequacy of the educational system in inner-city Baltimore. It is apparent in the opening scenes within the confines of the Edward J. Tilghman Middle School, for example, that it is woefully underfunded to the extent that the administration is more concerned with maintaining resources than they are with providing an education. In a Season 4 episode titled "Refugees," Assistant Principal Donnelly hires Cutty to be the school's truant officer, not to ensure that the children are in school for the sake of education, but because ensuring that the students are in school for "one day in September and one day in October" secures the school more funding. Moreover, it is evident that the school is largely occupied with maintaining safety rather than providing education. There are frequent sweeps at the middle-school in search of weapons that could be used to assault other students. Mr. Pryzbylewski initially encounters much difficulty in educating his students, as much of the time in his class is spent preventing fist fights and other assaults. In one instance, however, a female student is "cut" by another student using a razor blade. While Mr. Pryzbylewski is shocked that such an event occurred within the walls of the middle-school, Ms. Donnelly is able to find some light in the situation, as the girl who was stabbed was not HIV-positive.

Institutions and Opportunity

Similar to the Chicago School theorists, the creators of *The Wire* go to great lengths to identify obstacles to legitimate means of advancement. For instance, the poor educational system in inner-city Baltimore ultimately diminishes the opportunities for residents to gain and maintain lawful employment. Even children who are eager to attend school are reminded of the futility of educational attainment. In Season 4, Michael is originally portrayed as an average corner boy from inner-city Baltimore. However, he begins to show an interest in school and aptitude for learning. Bodie attempts to convince Michael to work the corner during the school week. Michael refuses citing his desire to be at school. In response, Bodie mockingly asks "Yo, what the fuck want to go to school for? What you want to be? An astronaut? A dentist? A pay-lawyer nigga?", ultimately reminding Michael of the neighborhood from which he comes. This sends a clear message: when you grow up on the streets, opportunities to legitimate employment are few and far between, and working the corners is what you do. It is more than an enterprise; it is an identity, and a way of life.

Series creator David Simon has stated that Season 2 of *The Wire* is a meditation on the death of work and the betrayal of the American working class. This is evidenced by an extended metaphor on the plight of the working-class in Baltimore, represented by the stevedores working the ports. Work is scarce for the stevedores, as the poor infrastructure has reduced the opportunities for them to support their businesses legitimately. Ironically, the lack of business has hampered any opportunities to pay for facility improvements and Sobotka, the head of the stevedores union, attempts to lobby politicians for financial support. Still, Sobotka and his organization lack the funds to gain this necessary support, and the organization turns to drug smuggling to meet their financial needs. Sobotka's son and his nephew similarly see few legitimate prospects for financial gain and turn to crime as well. In the end, Sobotka's nephew is convicted of murder, his son is forced into the witness protection program and Sobotka himself is murdered at the hands of the criminal organization for which he worked (Season 2, Episode 11). Sobotka's demise is a metaphor for the death of work in inner-city Baltimore and the subsequent consequences that arise from those structural changes. The inner-city is no longer a viable ecology for legitimate opportunities for advancement, as those jobs have gone elsewhere, particularly to the suburbs. Park and Burgess (1925) likely would have anticipated this eventuality in their discussion of social ecologies; the workers with the greatest opportunities for legitimate advancement will naturally come from the most advantaged areas of the urban environment. Simultaneously, as work leaves, working-class individuals are faced with the conundrum of conceding defeat or searching for alternative, often illegitimate, ways to survive.

Shaw and McKay (1942) discuss social disorganization as a theory as much about the community as about the subcultures that spawn delinquency and crime. A key component of this interplay is the inability of communities to marshal resources and create stability over time. In *The Wire*, even among the developers who are willing to invest in the inner-city, considerable barriers exist. Stringer Bell was one of the most popular inner city residents in early seasons. Although he made his fortune as Avon Barksdale's right hand man in the drug game, his primary goal was to use the money he earned and invest it back in the lower income areas of Baltimore through legitimate business means. Stringer Bell's real estate development plan encountered many problems, as construction was halted several times because he was unable to attain contracts through the city government to begin his development. Indeed, many of the problems he encountered were initiated by corrupt politicians who were seeking bribes and other political gains from Stringer. Unfortunately, and ironically, Stringer's aspirations to reinvest and develop the disadvantaged areas of

Baltimore were thwarted when he was executed by Omar Little and Brother Mulzahn (Season 3, Episode 11). Despite the fact that Stringer, a former gangster, was involved in legitimate business practices, his attempts at positive development were ultimately halted by the workings of corrupt real estate developers and politicians who control power and communicate with violence in the inner-city.

Social Disorganization, Normative Conflict and Crime in *The Wire*

Many structural impediments face the residents of inner-city Baltimore in *The Wire*. Institutions intended to provide access to legitimate opportunities and to adequately socialize residents to conformity are weak. However, for cultural theorists, such structural disadvantage is only part of the equation, because a competition between institutions develops: one set of institutions promote conformity and achieving success through legitimate means, while other institutions (e.g., "the street") encourage residents to internalize antisocial values. Anderson (1999), for instance, has argued that the alienation that develops from the structural disadvantage and lack of legitimate opportunities can lead to the development of a culture that opposes dominant society and its agents, that begins to permeate schools and other institutions.

The permeation of this insurgent subculture only increases violence in the inner-cities, and it further alienates inner-city residents from mainstream society. Young males and females in the inner-city are socialized to believe that employment opportunities are limited, and that the institution of education is merely an agent of white America that serves little purpose for their future success. Instead, an alternative subculture develops whereby a desperate search for respect leads individuals to believe that honor is earned through one's ability to defend oneself, particularly by using violence. In this subculture, individuals who embrace middle-class values such as education are labeled as "soft" and mere agents of white America. These individuals are then vulnerable to ridicule and assault. By contrast, those who attain money through illegitimate means (drug sales), defend themselves when challenged, and use violence ruthlessly are respected by the players in "the game." Thus, in these alienated and disorganized communities, young males and females are socialized to believe that violence, and crime in general, is encouraged and rewarded as a mainstream normative perspective.

Oppositional Culture Case Studies: Michael and Namond

The most telling appearance of an oppositional culture is found in the character development of Michael Lee. We are first introduced to Michael and his friends in Season 4 of *The Wire*. They initially appear to be like many juvenile boys their age—discussing the attractiveness of female schoolmates, and engaging in relatively minor acts of delinquency like throwing urine-filled water balloons at another group of boys. Moreover, in the early parts of Season 4 it was apparent that they were relatively naïve about the activities of the corner boys. While many of their early behaviors are reflective of an average boy's delinquent conduct, we also see that their experiences at home, at school, and in the community differ greatly from those located in middle-class communities, which plays an influential role in these boys' maturation. Michael, Dukie, and Randy all grow up in households where their guardians invest little into their development in terms of providing a moral compass or supervising their activities. In these ways, Michael and his friends seem typical of juvenile delinquents described by many Chicago School theorists.

Throughout the series, these characters also experience adversity in different ways. Michael seems to be the most responsible figure in his household and acts as the father figure to his younger brother. Dukie's guardians are more concerned about achieving their next high than assuring his needs are met, which prompts Mr. Pryzbylewski to bring him lunch and buy him school clothes. Interestingly, Namond's parents display the most concern over their child but they actively encourage Namond to become more involved in street life and the drug trade. Indeed, at the beginning of Season 4 we see that, while these boys often appear to be relatively innocent in their behavior, their family offers little in terms of structure and adequate socialization, with some parents even encouraging the boys to be criminal. This inclusion of young inner city males, before their submersion into a street lifestyle, humanizes the other characters of *The Wire*. These individuals are not immoral black men who have actively chosen a life of drugs and crime; they themselves are victims of circumstance.

As *The Wire* progresses, Michael starts to harden. Michael initially begins to excel in Mr. Pryzbylewski's class. Given his mother's consuming addiction, his primary concern is the safety of his little brother. Although Michael reluctantly accepts a position as a drug runner to buy school supplies for his brother, he initially refuses several offers of permanent employment in the drug game. Michael is also relatively shy and introverted in the early parts of the season, and never initiates violent confrontations. In fact, the only time Michael is seen using violence is when he is protecting weaker members of his group such as his brother and Dukie. As the show continues on, however, the culture of the street begins to turn Michael into a cold-blooded killer. Marlo's men, particularly Chris Partlow, persistently attempt to recruit Michael into "the game," noting that the Stanfield organization is "always in the market for a good soldier." Chris makes Michael promises, offering to "take care of Michael" and "make him part of the family," pledging to be around if Michael ever needs anything. This all occurs in the absence of a real family life for Michael. He had always been on his own and was forced to raise and take care of himself. But now there is a group of individuals willing to be there for Michael, to offer resources and a sense of identity, to fill in the void that his mother had not filled, and even promising to protect him from any problems.

Eventually Michael turns to Marlo and his men for help. After Michael's stepfather, who had sexually assaulted Michael in the past, returns from prison, Michael fears for his brother's safety. He explains to his mother that he does not want him in the house, but his mother refuses to listen to his concerns. Michael then turns to Marlo Stanfield, telling Marlo that he has a "problem that he can't bring to no one else." Marlo then orders Chris and Snoop to kill Michael's stepfather, and they brutally beat him to death in the back of an alley (Season 4, Episode 9). With this decision, Michael formed an alliance with Marlo and Chris. Now that they were there for him when he needed, Michael would need to be there for them. He had pushed "all in" to the game.

This sequence of events set in motion the deviant socialization process that would turn Michael into the hardened killer that he eventually became. He is initially given lessons on how to deal drugs, how to run a corner, and how to manage younger dealers, all of which Michael picks up quickly and prove to be tasks at which he excelled. This leads Michael to rise quickly through the ranks of the Stanfield organization and eventually become the protégé of Chris and Snoop. In a scene that is reminiscent of a military training exercise, Chris and Snoop teach Michael how to kill in the abandon buildings in Baltimore using a paintball gun (Season 4, Episode 12). After shooting Chris and Snoop with the paintball gun, Michael notes that next he will give "one to the head" to finish off a rival soldier quickly. Eventually, the extensive training that Michael receives from Chris and Snoop is utilized, and Michael's death toll begins to accumulate.

Michael's socialization towards a "street code" occurs during the season in *The Wire* that is primarily concerned about schooling in inner-city Baltimore. It is interesting, then, to compare the learning process that Michael goes through to that of the learning process that occurs in the confines of high schools, as well as other occupational trainings. Michael is curious, and eager to ask questions to improve his understanding of "the game." He consistently asks Chris questions about his specific method of killing when going to a job (such as showing up an hour early to make sure the targets are not setting him up), but Michael also asks Chris about the rationale behind many of the murders (i.e., why violence is being used on a specific individual). This directly speaks to a "code of the street" that is similarly discussed by Anderson (1999), where violence is seen as acceptable or necessary in certain situations. Most telling is the rationalization given to Michael before Chris and Snoop attempt to murder June Bug. When asked by Michael why the boy deserved to die, Chris and Snoop respond that the guy had disrespected Marlo by calling him a "dick sucker." They admitted that this may not have been true, but it was the word on the street and such *disrespect could not go unpunished*. Michael was beginning to learn when violence on the street was normative, and when it was not.

We could see that this socialization process fundamentally changed Michael as a person. The quiet and strong teenager had been turned into a seasoned criminal. Even Namond, one of his best friends, noted that "Mike ain't Mike no more" (Season 4, Episode 12). Michael's socialization and tutelage had been so effective by the end of the series that he was beginning to socialize others into the "code of the street." After Dukie began carrying a gun for protection, Michael lectured him on the implications (Season 4, Episode 5). He told Dukie that carrying a gun would not stop people from harassing him, and in fact, all it meant was that people on the street would challenge whether Dukie was actually ready to use it. Indeed, his socialization had become so effective that Michael was able to get the drop on Chris and Snoop when they tried to set him up to be executed. The final dialogue between Michael and Snoop was indicative of the socialization process that Michael experienced throughout the series, as well as the culture of the street that punishes violations of the code with violence (Season 5, Episode 9). This exchange occurs right before Michael executes Snoop.

> Snoop: Smart nigga, how'd you know?
> Michael: Ya'll taught me. Get there early. Why? What did I do wrong?
> Snoop: Chris locked up behind bars for something he done for you. You downtown with the police.
> Michael: I ain't say a word.
> Snoop: You say that. But it is how you carry yourself. Always asking why? When you should be doing what you are told.

Michael's transition from a shy teenager to a ruthless killer is perhaps an extreme example of the normative values and socialization that can occur in socially disorganized communities. Still, we see that the code of the street and the normative socialization influences the other boys on the streets of Baltimore. Randy, for instance, becomes noticeably harder throughout the series. In the beginning of the series he naively becomes involved in the murder of Lex after giving Lex a message that ultimately led him into a trap (Season 4, Episode 1). This involvement troubled Randy deeply, and he later provides some information regarding the murder to the police. This results Randy being labeled as a "snitch" and he is subsequently ostracized and beaten by other community members. The strength of the street code is especially highlighted when Mr. Pryzbylewski, a former police officer, instructs Randy to no longer talk to the police. Randy violated the code of the street, and he paid for it with violence. When we see Randy again at the end of the series, it is evident that he had learned from his mistake: he is noticeably bigger, stronger and harder; refusing to talk to the police and assaulting fellow boys in his home.

This emphasis on socialization and normative conflict is more interesting when contrasting the development of Michael and Randy to that of Namond Brice. Namond begins the series invested in the drug game. His father, Wee-Bey, was one of Avon Barksdale's most loyal and ruthless soldiers. He often gives Namond advice on how to be a successful dealer. Wee-Bey even forces Bodie to take on Namond as a drug runner, and when Namond begins to show disinterest in the profession of dealing, his mother refuses to buy him new clothes for school. Namond, however, begins to take an interest in school, and this interest is quickly discouraged by his parents. Wee-Bey consistently changes conversations about Namond's schooling to Namond's drug dealing. Moreover, his mother even begins to refuse to drop him off at school, dropping him off on the corner to deal drugs instead. Both Namond's mother and father consistently encourage him to be actively involved in the drug game in order to gain respect, and in doing so, repeatedly try to convince him of the futility of education.

It becomes apparent, however, that Namond is not cut out for the street. To be sure, he repeatedly discusses his intentions to be a prominent soldier and dealer, but does little to back up this talk. His inadequacy as a gangster comes to a head when Namond is robbed of a drug supply by Kenard (Season 4, Episode 12). Rather than defending his honor and exerting punishment on Kenard, Namond refuses to use violence against Kenard and watches as Kenard is beaten by Michael. When talking to detective Carver, Namond accepts his shortcomings as a soldier, noting that his lack of violence will disappoint his mother and others. "I can't go home," he says. "She expects me to be like my father, but I ain't him" (Season 4, Episode 12). Indeed, the permeation of the street code extends into the family, as Namond fears the punishment that he will receive for violating the code and not standing up for his honor. As the series progresses, Namond becomes an example of how positive and conventional institutions can be a catalyst for change, even in socially disorganized communities. After beginning to excel in a special class ran by former Baltimore police commander Bunny Colvin and being disowned by his mother, Colvin adopts Namond and brings him into a stable family environment that promotes conformity to conventional rules. Colvin, his wife, and the greater educational structure that Namond experiences ultimately leads him to get out of the dangers of inner-city Baltimore, and to leave behind a life on the streets as a soldier.

The experiences and character development of Michael, Randy, and Namond highlight the influential role that deviant and oppositional cultures play in the lives of inner-city African Americans. In a season devoted to the inadequacy of schools and formal education in inner-city Baltimore, *The Wire* shows us that there is a competing street institution that is socializing residents to reject education and legitimate employment, and to value things like honor and violence. Ultimately, then, it is not just that important institutions of control are weak and there are few opportunities to attain success legitimately. Many of the inner-city males are taught to get ahead using any means necessary — including violence and drug dealing. As Namond Brice points out, this "any means necessary" attitude is also present in other classes: baseball players use steroids, corporations are guilty of insider trade, cigarette companies advertise to children. On the streets there are just different rules and ways to get ahead — violence and dealing.

Transitions and Stability

A major contribution of the Chicago School theorists and those who have been influenced by their work is their emphasis on context over individuals. One of the most intriguing findings of Shaw and McKay's (1942) seminal work is that areas characterized by social disorganization consistently had the highest rates of crime, even though the individuals who resided in these communities (in their case ethnic groups) changed. The implications of such findings are obvious: in a field that has traditionally been dominated by individual-level explanations of offending, and in turn individual solutions to crime, the focus on context has been woefully neglected. When addressing the crime problem we cannot simply focus on the individuals who we see as "bad apples," because the context plays an important role in the developing the individuals who engage in criminal behavior and without targeting many of these root causes, the crime problem will surely perpetuate. This is precisely the point of Shaw and McKay's study — even after the individuals who were driving the crime problem in one period left, others who were similarly influenced by the context that developed their criminality were there to fill the vacated roles.

Interestingly, David Simon provided a similarly bleak outlook on the future of inner-city Baltimore as *The Wire* concluded. It was evident that the structural characteristics that Simon had emphasized as crucial to the disorder and decay of Baltimore had gone largely unaddressed. Accordingly, the fifth season saw a changing of the guard as the original gangsters' shoes were filled by the young, and initially innocent, boys to which the audience was introduced in Season 4. Some of the most important and ruthless participants in the series were dead, in prison, or out of "the game" by the series end. Bodie, one of Barksdale's most important soldiers, was shot and killed in the Season 4 finale "Final Grades," but we saw almost immediately that his role had been filled by another eager young soldier. Stringer Bell was similarly shot and killed in Season 3. Despite most of the central members of the Barksdale organization having been killed or incarcerated throughout the series, "the game" was still omnipresent, with successive generations playing identical roles. Marlo took over Barksdale's territory. Chris became his muscle and number two, and the same organizational structure that terrorized inner-city Baltimore persisted with new faces.

The consequences of the normative conflict evidenced in *The Wire* extended beyond the organized criminal element. Even some of the more "isolated" characters were replaced by younger boys. Omar was known widely for his ruthlessness, his adherence to "the game" and his dislike of the drug organizations who dealt on the inner-city streets. It was clear that he had previously been wronged by authority figures, and his distrust for the pitiless drug market that wrongs even the innocent played an influential role in his character development. Throughout Season 4, we begin to see Michael Lee's life unfold in a similar fashion. Michael Lee's distrust of authority figures stems from the abuse he received at the hands of his father. Although he joins the drug game as muscle in Marlo's crew, it is also evident that he despises the "no rules" behavior that it embraces after he is betrayed by Marlo. Michael leaves the drug game and skips town to hide from Marlo's crew. However, mimicking Omar's moves, Michael returns as a stick-up artist and shoots a player in "the game" in the knee. The process of intergenerational transmission is thusly illustrated on the individual level: Michael has become Omar.

"Bubbles," a relatively compassionate and vulnerable drug addict, is portrayed as a sympathetic figure throughout *The Wire*. He spends much of the five seasons struggling with addiction and attempting to make a better life for himself as he seeks reconciliation with his family. Interestingly, Bubbles' story is one of the positive endings at the conclusion of the series, as he is able to get clean and is last seen at his sister's house for dinner. Around the same time, however, we see Duquan begin to follow the path of Bubbles into drug addiction, an allusion to the cyclical nature of intergenerational transmission of pro-crime subcultural values. Like Bubbles, Duquan is also a relatively vulnerable and compassionate character. He is invested in school and avoids all violent confrontations, while his friend and protector Michael gets heavily involved in "the game." Further, he is regularly bullied by the tougher kids on the block, positioning him explicitly in the role of a victim. As his chances for legitimate employment fall short, Dukie's story concludes with a scene of him injecting heroin with another junkie. Thus, Dukie has become Bubbles.

Conclusion

The endings of the characters in *The Wire* speak to the paradox of crime prevention strategies within the United States. The immediate and politically appealing strategies are to target the individuals and groups who are involved in the drug trade and committing crimes. However such a strategy realizes, at best, only short-term effects. A policy that features incarceration as its central tenet does not speak to the relative health and functionality of pro-social institutions, such as schools and families. Thus, the structural barriers that lie at the center of crime causation are left unaltered, and the same processes graduate young adults into identical criminal roles that those policies sought to eliminate. Families are still broken. Schools are still inadequate. Employment opportunities are still limited. And so the cycle of disorganization and crime continues. The depth of *The Wire* humanizes this process in a way that many other fictional portrayals do not, and therein rests perhaps its greatest singular message. In creating a metaphor that communicates the parallel moralities and normative conflict inherent in urban subcultures, *The Wire* shows us, brilliantly and often uncomfortably, that crime does not originate primarily from "bad people," but from bad situations. Simon's point is that if we as a society are to seriously address the crime problem and urban inequality in the United States, we need to address the structural disadvantage that is its primary cause.

We conclude this chapter by relaying a fitting excerpt from Anderson's (1999) seminal ethnography, *Code of the Street*:

> A vicious cycle has been formed. The hopelessness many young inner-city black men and women feel, largely as a result of endemic joblessness and alienation, fuels the violence they engage in. The violence then serves to confirm the negative feelings many whites and some

middle-class blacks harbor toward the ghetto poor, further legitimizing the oppositional culture and the code of the street for many alienated young blacks. But when jobs disappear and people are left poor, highly concentrated, and hopeless, the way is paved for the underground economy to become a way of life.... Only by reestablishing a viable mainstream economy in the inner-city, particularly one that provides access to jobs for young inner-city men and women, can we encourage a positive sense of the future. Unless serious efforts are made to address this problem, and the cycle is broken ... alienation and violence ... will likely worsen (Anderson, 1999: 325).

References

Anderson, Elijah. 1999. *Code of the Street: Decency, Violence and the Moral Life of the Inner City.* New York: W. W. Norton & Company, Inc.

Bursik, Robert J. 1988. Social disorganization and theories of crime and delinquency. *Criminology* 26: 519–552.

Park, Robert E. and Ernest W. Burgess. 1925. *The City.* Chicago: University of Chicago Press.

Shaw, Clifford R. and Henry D. McKay. 1942. *Juvenile Delinquency and Urban Areas.* Chicago: University of Chicago Press.

Wolfgang, Marvin E. and Franco Ferracuti. 1967. *The Subculture of Violence: Toward an Integrated Theory in Criminology.* London: Tavistock Publications.

Study Questions

1. Discuss how the characters of *The Wire* that are involved in "the game" reflect the criminological theories stemming from the Chicago School. How do the informal controls and institutions of the neighborhood contribute to their overall experiences?

2. How does Shaw and McKay's social disorganization theory expand upon Park and Burgess's concentric zone theory? How does this, and other criminological theories discussing other social ecology, influence participation in crime?

3. Discuss the similarities between Anderson's "code of the street" and Wolfgang and Ferracuti's "subculture of violence". How do these concepts further expand the earlier theories of the Chicago School when dealing with crime?

4. How does *The Wire* perpetuate the theoretical perspective that the nature of "place" can be inherently criminogenic? Discuss the economic stratification and structural differences within neighborhoods featured in *The Wire* as the issues pertain to Chicago School theories.

5. How do the limited access to legitimate opportunities, subculture of violence, and the code of the street contribute to normative perspective within urban subcultures? Describe how this is illustrated through the characters in *The Wire*. Does this follow the theories of the Chicago School? Why or why not?

6. What are the advantages of focusing on the context of a community, rather than or in addition to the individuals within a community, when discussing options for dealing with crime in a specific location?

Chapter 15

Women of *The Wire* and The Sociological Imagination

Laurie A. Drapela

Introduction

The Wire is regarded as one of the "best shows on television" (Heffernan, 2006; Simon, 2008); some critics even say it is the best show in television history (Goodman, 2006). Television critics and scholars alike have lauded its ability to engage the television viewing audience with storylines and characters that unflinchingly portray the intersections of race and social class in the modern American ghetto. Such praise is usually reserved for musings about the show at a global level, however a careful analysis of how the female characters are portrayed in the series yields a much more nuanced and critical evaluation of its impact on the television genre. The following essay summarizes these critiques, advances a conceptual framework with which to view *The Wire's* female characters, and articulates how research from sociology and criminal justice could be incorporated to further enhance the television viewing audience's "sociological imagination" about female characters in crime dramas. I have two principal objectives in doing so: 1) to underscore to the reader the fundamental problems with the portrayal of female characters in *The Wire*; and, 2) to inspire a dialogue among scholars, writers, actors, and producers about creating female characters in future series who embody the engrossing race/class intersections so prevalent among the male characters in the series.

Critique Summary:
The Role of Women in *The Wire*

Critics writing about the female characters in the series tend to reach consensus on one single point: Fundamentally, *The Wire* is about men. Female characters do not "drive the action," so to speak; they serve as foils to a male narrative about crime, justice, and inequality (Khan, 2007; Lippman, 2009; Marshall, 2009; Jones, 2008; Timm, 2008). Where these critics depart from one another concerns their perceptions of the quality of these characters and whether such representations are acceptable to them as writers, scholars, and television consumers. Laura Lippman's (2009) essay on *The Wire's* female characters acknowledges that the limited number of women in the series are there to serve male storylines, but she also notes that they are written and portrayed in a way that allows them to be flawed human beings, just like the men, rather than the typical "plucky heroine" chestnuts so common among television crime dramas. Despite this compliment to the writers and actors who construct these women, she concedes that "… like it or not, we must credit men with these human scale portraits. Yes, many of the women in *The Wire* appear in secondary roles, but that is a simple truth about the world it portrays—and the point of view through which it is filtered" (Lippman, 2009: 60).

Contrast such a pragmatic viewpoint with other critics who contend that the series utterly failed women with both its limited roles as well as the stereotypical shallowness with which those roles were constructed. Most articulate among them is Sophie Jones (2008), who contends that *The Wire's* creators deftly construct male characters who survive in West Baltimore's illicit economy in a way that allows a mostly white middle class viewing audience to form attachments to them; as well as prompt these viewers to reflect on how their own lives' chances are affected (or enhanced) by their place in the race and social class hierarchy. The female characters do not get such opportunities to stretch the viewers' 'sociological imaginations,' however. There are many of the usual crime drama "stock female stereotypes" here; and gender is absent from the "sophisticated, expansive worldview" which prompts the viewer to consider that "it is misleading to think about race without considering the economy without taking into account education, and so on" (Jones, 2008: np). She concludes that it is a shame "[t]hat one of the most progressive TV shows in the medium's history consistently demonstrates its ignorance of and disinterest in gender politics …" (Jones, 2008: np). A similar viewpoint is echoed by a member of the illicit economy who, when asked by a noted sociologist how *The Wire* could be improved, opined the following:

"Women," Tony T said. "Where I come from, women run most of the things [that the show] talks about. It's the women that have the power in the ghetto. This show totally got it wrong when they made it all about men. Women are the politicians, they can get you a gun, they got the cash, they can get you land to build something on" (Venkatesh, 2008a).

Courtney Marshall (2009: 151) takes more of a middle-ground approach. In her analysis of the series' portrayals of three black mothers—Donnette, Brianna Barksdale, and De'Londa Brice—Marshall argues that the creators "walk a fine line between making them stereotypical and making them victims." As is the case with Lippman, both critics note that these flawed female characters are the work of male writers, but Marshall asserts that there is functionality to these women's flaws that make their choices believable, given the circumstances under which they must survive. All three women are socializing their young in an area of extreme poverty; participation in the illicit economy is the way to financially provide for their families. In doing so, they also teach their children "civic values, even if those values are criminalized" (Marshall, 2009: 150).

Brianna Barksdale is the most involved of the three in the illicit economy, being the sister of Avon Barksdale, who controls the West Baltimore drug market. She operates a funeral home as a clean front for the drug operation and enjoys the trappings of an upper middle class lifestyle as a result. When her son D'Angelo is arrested while transporting a shipment of drugs into Baltimore, Marshall (2009: 155) describes how Brianna uses her "maternal instincts ... to challenge her brother ... call[ing] him on his lax supervision and is very angry that he would jeopardize her son's freedom so carelessly." Marshall argues that Brianna's dual role as mother to Avon's nephew and "manager" in one of his businesses places her in a vaulted position for a female criminal, an unusual occurrence in television crime dramas. That the character of Brianna is able to use her emotional leverage with D'Angelo to the benefit of the Barksdale family, dissuading him from turning state's witness against the drug trafficking operation, is further testament to her efficacy as both a mother and a manager (although this maneuver gets D'Angelo killed later on in the series, a point I will revisit).

The other two characters are given similar treatment by Ms. Marshall, who goes on to explore how their choices as women and mothers are affected by their place in West Baltimore's illicit economy. Her analyses are an important middle ground in critics' writings about *The Wire's* women, for they advance the idea that there is some depth to the relatively few female characters highlighted in the series. Rather than deride the creators of the series for the typical representations of black women ('the fallen woman,' the Machiavellian mother who prioritizes material comfort and social standing above the welfare of her child, the drug addict, the whore), Marshall asserts that these three women's dual roles as caregivers and criminals gives them dimensions not heretofore seen among black females in television crime dramas. That these women participate in the illicit economy while socializing their young and performing the role of breadwinner forces the viewer to consider how poverty constrains the choices of women who are raising families in the American ghetto. Such a notion is consistent with one poverty scholar's observation that, "One must ... take into consideration that there is a material foundation to the development of a moral framework" (Venkatesh, 2006: 61).

This chapter will continue such a nuanced approach in its analyses of how the women in the series are portrayed. I will explore two dimensions related to Ms. Marshall's critiques: 1) an assessment of the relationship between a female character's masculinity and the level of efficaciousness in her professional life; and, 2) how research from sociology and criminal justice are necessary elements in stimulating viewers' 'sociological imaginations' of the female characters in crime dramas, using two characters from *The Wire* as case studies.

Advancing a Conceptual Framework for Viewing Women in *The Wire*: The Masculinity-Competence Continuum

The Wire is indeed a police drama, which means there will inevitably be some diversions from 'true' police procedure or 'actual' cases, for the purposes of plot/character development that can build an audience. As Lippman (2009) notes, some creative license is expected, for entertainment should not function as documentary filmmaking. Even so, there are some predictable character development devices here, the most prominent of which I refer to as the "Masculinity-Competence Continuum." Put simply, the more masculinized a female character in a crime drama is written/portrayed, the more efficacious she is portrayed in her professional life. Such a continuum is not unknown in crime television dramas; consider Detective Claudette Wyms and Captain Monica Rawling from FX's *The Shield*. Both women are highly masculinized in their affect and are some of the most powerful female police officers in the history of the genre (contrast their career success with the series' more feminized Danielle "Danni" Sofer). *The Wire* reproduces this spectrum with its portrayal of women.

The first season introduces two of the women who will be most prominently featured during the rest of the series: Detective Shakima Greggs (Narcotics

Unit, Baltimore Police Department) and Deputy District Attorney Rhonda Pearlman (Maryland State's Attorney's Office). Season 3 marks the arrival of 'Snoop,' an assassin working for Marlo Stanfield's drug operation. This character presents herself in such a highly masculinized fashion that she is easily mistaken for a man. She is also one of the most efficient killers in the West Baltimore setting, no insignificant designation given the violent nature of the world she inhabits. Seasons 2, 4, and 5 include Beatrice 'Beadie' Russell, a Port of Baltimore Police Officer who is a neophyte to complex criminal investigations. Each of these women occupy a place on this continuum; with Snoop and Greggs competing for the most masculine/competent end of the spectrum and forming Russell forming the "most feminized, least competent" end. Rhonda Pearlman marks the middle of the continuum.

Shakima Greggs (hereafter referred to as "Kima") is developed as a cop who earns her bona fides with the male detectives on a new Criminal Investigation Division (CID) detail (hereafter known as the "Barksdale Detail"). She establishes her competence with the male investigators in this unit by demonstrating her investigative skills, as well as her skill in working with her confidential informant, "Bubs," a Westside addict who knows the housing projects very well. She gathers intelligence about the syndicate while talking like one of the boys, presenting a masculine affect (jeans, ball cap, etc.), and exerting her authority over her underlings (Detectives Herc and Carver) as a male detective would. During one scene in the first season, Kima and Detective Jimmy McNulty are discussing what they love most about "the job" and how it affects their personal lives. This is a very critical element to the 'masculinity-competence continuum'—the more devoted to the job the female cop is, the more dysfunctional her personal life becomes (if she has one at all). McNulty and Greggs bond over their shared frustrations about romantic partners who do not understand the professional world they are so much a part of. Kima's love and talent for the job masculinizes her in the eyes of her male counterpart, who himself is described by the other detectives as being "good po-lice" (among many other things).

As Kima's professional bonds strengthen with the male detectives on the detail (McNulty in particular), series creator David Simon employs a traditional device in cop shows—that of the "officer down" plot twist—to allow his male detective characters further opportunity to explore the issues of Kima, her identity as a cop, her gender, and her sexuality. Kima is shot as part of an undercover buy that goes bad. She is posing as a player's "girl" when both are shot by criminal elements hired to eliminate the player. She is dressed in highly feminine, form-fitting attire, and looks "hot" in the way of a traditional street female. (At one point, Detective Ellis Carver praises her for "looking the part," to which she shoots him the finger while giving him a wry look, emulating masculine behavior.) In the aftermath of Kima's shooting the male detectives react with rage toward the shooting of one of their own (as they would with a male detective) but the intensity of the rage is laced with frustration about their inability to protect Kima from getting shot. Though not overplayed by any of the actors, viewers can feel from their rage that the failure of men to protect "one of their own" who is a woman is emasculating to them.

Once Kima is transported to the hospital, the series creators interplay race, gender, and sexuality in the following scenes with a finesse rarely achieved in American television. As the police brass congregate at the hospital for news of Kima's condition, the top cop in the jurisdiction, the Police Commissioner, mistakes a white detective for the senior officer on the Barksdale detail, who is in fact an African-American lieutenant named Cedric Daniels. When the white detective directs the commissioner to Lt. Daniels; the Commissioner smiles and covers the breach with, "Oh ... of course."

The Police Commissioner has no such desire to cover himself when he refuses to offer any words of comfort to Kima's lesbian partner, however. His refusal to acknowledge Kima's wife as family that could use a kind or comforting word from the department demonstrates how invisible both women are to a traditional, white, masculine power. It also diminishes Kima's sacrifice in the line of duty by bringing her sexuality to the forefront. Eventually, the Deputy of Operations, who is an African-American man, says out loud, "I guess I'll do it myself." He goes over to say a kind word to Kima's wife (also African-American); making it clear that the slight on Kima was both a racial issue as well as one where her homosexuality was at play.

Kima proves herself the ultimate, masculine "tough cop" when she refuses to respond to Bunk Moreland's prompting that she identify one of her suspected attackers at a photo lineup taking place from her beside. At this point, Kima is conscious, relatively responsive, but very weak and her health is still in grave danger. She identifies "Little Man" with relative ease, but cannot positively identify "WeeBey" Brice as the other shooter in the attack. Despite Bunks' gentle but persistent prodding to identify the second suspect, she looks at him deep in his eyes and says, "Yeah. Sometimes things just gotta play hard." So not only does Kima show herself to be a physically resilient and courageous police officer, she also shows herself to have a strong sense of moral courage as well. A cop's cop; "real po-lice" according to Bunk and McNulty. Kima secures her position on the "high masculinity, high professional competence" portion of the continuum when her personal life with partner Cheryl unravels and they separate later on in the series. The driving forces behind the separation are Kima's return to street-level policing and the infidelity she engages in once Cheryl is consumed with mothering their new infant.

Contrast Kima with her polar opposite at the end of the continuum, Beatrice 'Beadie' Russell. During Season 2, Russell is working as a port patrol officer who discovers a freight canister holding thirteen dead women who ostensibly were being trafficked to the U.S. to work as prostitutes. She is a novice/neophyte to serious criminal investigations, but—to her credit—takes the opportunity to learn more about CID practice when she is transferred to the BPD detail investigating the deaths. She is brought along to observe and occasionally contributes to the investigation (e.g., gathering intel from an old boyfriend on how the port computer system tracks shipping containers). Never at any time does she drive the investigation; this is left to the male detectives—Lester Freamon, Roland Pryzbylewski, Cedric Daniels, and Jimmy McNulty. She is also one of the more traditionally feminized women in the series, in terms of her presentation of self, as well as her work/family balance. She is a divorcee with two children who only took the port patrol job because of its salary and benefits. There are no discussions with her and the male characters about loving the job, the calling of the job, the price of the job on a personal life, and so on. She develops a romantic relationship with McNulty that coincides with his stint "on the wagon" in Season 3 and is not infrequently described by critics as a "Madonna/savior" type of female character (Lippman, 2009; Jones, 2008). Though we see Beadie later in the series, it is only as a romantic foil to McNulty's cycle of sobriety and all-to-anticipated departure from the wagon. As far as the masculinity-competence continuum goes, she is the most feminized and the least competent in her professional duties as a "po-lice."

Assistant State's Attorney Rhonda Pearlman falls in the middle of this continuum. She is an officer of the court who presents herself in a traditionally feminine way; and she is a reasonably competent officer of the court. Her professional competence is on occasion undercut by her muted reactions to male detectives' paternalistic and condescending behaviors. For example, in the first season of the series, Detectives Freamon and Pryzbylewski begin following the cash being laundered by members of the Barksdale drug operation. They find that some of the cash is being laundered as campaign contributions to local politicians. As elected officials learn that the police are investigating the source of their campaign contributions, Ms. Pearlman's supervisor, the State's Attorney for the City of Baltimore, voluntary shares with her the source of his campaign contributions, as well as the knowledge that all of the contributions with questionable pedigrees have been returned to their respective contributors. Ms. Pearlman is professional, but direct with her boss about being unsure why she is the recipient of this information. It is then and only then that she learns about the direction the CID detectives are taking their investigation.

While she is able to credibly deny that she has any knowledge of this aspect of the case, she is also shown up before her superior to be on the outside edges of the detail—pulled in only when an electronic surveillance warrant is needed, and kept out of everything else. When she inquires of Freamon and Pryzbylewski about the substance of the activity, Freamon condescends to her by asking "Aren't you glad you didn't know?" She expresses concern at being left out of the loop, but ultimately agrees that it was advantageous to her in this particular instance and moves on. This reaction is curious for a DA whose ignorance of the investigation's progress has been laid bare in front of her boss. Moreover, this would have been an opportune moment for her character to exert some leverage over the detectives by reminding them of her ability to get them access to their wiretaps and other surveillance activities. Prosecutors are some of the most powerful actors in the criminal justice system because they possess the "power of the charge" and ultimately decide which illegal activities will receive the State's attention and which ones will not (Lippman, 2011). Very little of that power is evident here. In short, Ms. Pearlman is neither a driver of the action, nor is she incompetent in her work. She is a little more of a player in the narrative than a foil, but not by much.

The classification scheme I have advanced contributes to the normative consensus that *The Wire* is essentially a male narrative with female foils. It also shows that while there are some interesting variations on the typical female characters found in crime dramas, there are some all-too-familiar representations of women in television found as well.

Extending Viewers' 'Sociological Imaginations' of Female Characters in Crime Dramas: *The Wire*'s Brianna Barksdale and Rhonda Pearlman as Case Studies

In the third portion of this analysis, I argue that the integration of knowledge from sociological/ethnographic research could have dimensionalized the female characters in *The Wire*, entreating the viewers to engage their 'sociological imaginations' by considering: 1) how participation in either the illicit or legitimate economies constrains life choices for women in a way that is distinct from men; and, 2) integrating themes from this research to flesh out female characters to minimize some illogical behaviors exhibited by them during the course of the series. I focus on examples of two women in particular here: Brianna Barksdale and Rhonda Pearlman.

Brianna Barksdale

As previously noted, one of *The Wire's* greatest achievements is stimulating the television viewing audience by bringing an urban authenticity to the storylines and characters of the series. Such authenticity is achieved by filming on location in West Baltimore, often times using persons who have extensive histories in either the local illicit economy, the community, or policing (Penfold-Mounce, Beer, and Burrows, 2011). That the insights about race and poverty for which *The Wire* is so well known are produced by non-sociologists further enhances its "bona fides" as the kind of work that C. Wright Mills would have credited as possessing a 'sociological imagination' (1959). Its realism enables the viewer to attach to the characters in the series, internalize their dilemmas, and imagine how the institutions the viewers function in every day constrain—or enhance—their own life's chances.

With such an emphasis on authenticity in *The Wire,* the portrayal of Brianna Barksdale's understandings of her son's arrest and death seems quite out of place. During Season 2, D'Angelo Barksdale, Brianna's son and Avon Barksdale's nephew, is found hanged in a storeroom of the prison library where he worked. D'Angelo was serving a 20-year sentence for drug trafficking; and his arrest and imprisonment is an ongoing source of tension between Brianna and her brother. During a heated discussion on the incident, Brianna blames Avon for putting her son's freedom at risk. Avon reminds her of the risks he has undertaken over the years to financially support her and D'Angelo. Bowing to his financial authority, she does not push him further about his lapse of responsibility for D'Angelo's arrest. Marshall (2009) notes that in this scene Brianna uses her position as Avon's sister—as well as her extensive knowledge of the ways the illicit economy is supposed to work—to assert her power within the family and the organization by demanding an explanation for Avon's poor judgment, as well as assuring him that D'Angelo will not share any information about the family's business with police.

I assert that this scene is one where *The Wire* could have used the character of Brianna Barksdale to push back against the notion that women in the illicit economy are simply the beneficiaries of men's labors (Marshall, 2009: 155). Brianna could have brought it to Avon's attention that she maintains a clean front for the organization, allowing him a place to launder money and other support functions for the drug operation. She could have detailed how many other female family relations do so for him; that the operation starts at cash and corners but must have more to it than that if it is to sustain and build growth. Such a scene would have shown how the illicit economy in the ghetto has ties to legitimate businesses (they actually conduct funerals at the funeral home) and how women are a critical power in that nexus between the ghetto's illicit and licit economies.

A careful read of recent sociological studies on black urban poverty provides some authentic material on the economic leverage women possess in the modern ghetto. In his ground-breaking work on the ways that poverty shapes micro-level economic decisions and partnerships, Sudhir Venkatesh's (2006) study of a poor Chicago neighborhood underscores two fundamental points about life in the American underclass: 1) women have the economic and social power in the household, determining the residency as well as the labor demands extracted of those residents; and, 2) to maintain the economic and social functioning of these households, they often blend work and income from the licit and illicit economies. Though many of the women in his research are not managers in the "shady" economy like Brianna Barksdale, they are stakeholders in it because they either participate in it directly, or extract money, goods, or services from household members who are. Some women in his study sublet their apartments to gang members so they could process cocaine and heroin, or served gangs in other capacities (e.g., lookouts). Others worked as prostitutes. Despite these activities, these women are not portrayed as desperate, nor are they destitute. They hold dreams of what their lives will be like when things turn around for them economically. In the meantime, however, they flex between the legitimate and illicit economies to provide for their families and keep a safe environment for their children—even if it means going "toe to toe" with the local gangs (Venkatesh, 2006).

Another portrait of the gravitas black women possess in the modern ghetto can be found in Venkatesh's *Gang Leader for a Day* (2008b). "Ms. Bailey," a long-term resident of Chicago's Robert Taylor Homes, is one of the most powerful forces shaping the quality of life in for "Homes B" residents (2008: 145–183). Her power derives from her deep inter-connectedness—sociologists call it social capital (Coleman, 1988)—between members in the licit and the illicit economies. Because of her length of residence in the ghetto, she is able to track which families have "made it out" of the Homes and regularly solicits them for donations of food, clothing, appliances, liquor, and other items. She redistributes these items to families inside the Homes who are in need and are in her favor, giving her a measure of power over such families.

Managers of the illicit drug trade that flourishes in "The Homes" also defer to Ms. Bailey's authority. 'J.T.,' one of the upper-echelon managers in the illicit economy sells drugs in the lobby of her building only during the evening hours, per her demand. When a gang shooting takes place between JT's gang and a rival syndicate, Ms. Bailey is instrumental in brokering a truce between them by getting a coalition of community members together to manage the 'sit down.'

At the end of the meeting, it is Ms. Bailey who sets the terms of the compensation JT's gang is to receive (his gang member was killed during the incident); both leaders agree the settlement is something they can live with.

One consequence of *The Wire's* failure to portray women as a critical part of the illicit economy is that consumers and critics alike will accept Brianna's utility to the Barksdale organization as one primarily borne of maternal influence: "Brianna can articulate motherhood and deploy it to sanction her own participation in the business. She successfully mobilizes the construction of motherhood to stake her claim in Barksdale politics" (Marshall, 2009: 155). Were the "real life; authentic" research efforts of Venkatesh and others incorporated into the development of her character, viewers would understand her presence as one of mutual need and economic necessity with Avon (e.g., drug lords need to launder cash; trustworthy family members need work and are knowledgeable about the business); not simply favors bestowed on a sister by a kind-hearted brother.

Once D'Angelo is apprehended, the tension between Brianna and Avon is further escalated when he decides to share information about Barksdale operations and homicides with the police in return for reduced criminal charges. About the time that D'Angelo learns that the State cannot provide him witness protection, Brianna locates him in custody and persuades him to re-hire the Barksdale's attorney and take the years, "for the family." Once in prison, D'Angelo distances himself from Avon and is found dead shortly thereafter, an apparent suicide. Detective Jimmy McNulty begins investigating D'Angelo's death as a homicide, interviewing his paramour Donette, who in turn shares McNulty's suspicions with Brianna. It is not until *then* that Brianna begins asking very direct and very uncomfortable questions about D'Angelo's death of Avon and his drug operations partner, Stringer Bell. (Stringer later admits to Avon that D'Angelo was killed on a contract put out by Bell; but Avon never shares this information with his sister.)

That a street-wise black female who grew up in "the life" does not become suspicious (or even give voice to her own suspicions) about the mysterious circumstances of her son's death until awakened by a white cop is highly illogical. Aside from such a gaffe, the problem with this portrayal of a major female African American character in a crime drama is that it reproduces negative stereotypes about black women by relying on a familiar television crime drama device: it's the white cop that has to clue in the black lady from the neighborhood about what's really going on in her immediate environment. While such a slight to African American women was not the intention of *The Wire's* writers, producers, and actors, the fact that such a well-crafted series could leave such an impression means that there is a lot of good, constructive work yet to be done inside television crime to nurture the audience's 'sociological imagination' about the gravitas of black women.

Rhonda Pearlman

Another example of how social science research could be incorporated into a female character to expand the audiences 'sociological imagination' concerns Rhonda Pearlman and her romantic misadventures. In the beginning of the series, she is Detective McNulty's paramour; and the viewing audience learns that the affair between herself and Jimmy was a catalyst in his divorce from wife Elena. Later in the series, Ms. Pearlman enters a romantic relationship with Cedric Daniels, the estranged husband of Marla Daniels, a newly-elected member of the city council. Both men are married when Pearlman becomes romantically involved with them and critics have noted that this female character is "utterly convincing as a driven prosecutor, ... [but] an enigma when it comes to her love life—or, more correctly, her lust life" (Lippman, 2009: 58). Others have included Pearlman's character in a general indictment of female characters who use their sexuality to advance in a male-dominated world (Timm, 2008).

Such musings on Pearlman's poor judgment in her personal life fail to consider how her age and her place in the career later constrain her mate selection opportunities. Although it is never discussed in the series, she is likely in her middle thirties, having completed college, then law school, then several years as a prosecutor trying to advance up the career ladder (Carson, 2002). By the time she is established enough as an attorney, there are likely to be very few single men left that are her age and are professionals looking to marry. The men in her profession? If demographic statistics are any indication, most of them married in their late twenties (Cohn, 2009), possibly to women whom they met in law school and their wives either delayed their careers or abandoned them entirely to raise children.

While Ms. Perlman works just as hard as her male counterparts to establish a respectable professional reputation, the men get to go home to wives and children at the end of the long workday. Perlman goes home to a quaint but empty cottage with stacks of work on the kitchen table and a bottle of wine (and an occasional visit from a drunk McNulty) for companionship. Research on female attorneys' perceptions of the costs of having successful law practices underscore the difficult choices women feel they must make between having a career and having a family (Slotkin, 2008). The percentage of women who feel they can "have it all" in terms of marriage, career, and family has actually *decreased* since 1983 (Samborn, 2000; Slotkin, 2002).

This research could have been personified in the series by including a male peer character in the DA's office for comparison about the work/family balance between career men and women. *The Wire* could have shown that the social cost of lengthy educations and long working hours have different consequences for women pursuing careers than men. Perlman's romantic choices in light of such comparisons (either be alone or be the third party in a marriage) would have humanized her dilemma and made the audience understand her choices, even if they didn't agree with them. At the very least, it would have made the audience entertain the notion that social advancement has social costs for women that can have unintended consequences for both the individual and the society at large. In the absence of such a character or plot device, the audience is left wondering why a woman who is so smart at work is so dumb at love.

Final Considerations: *The Wire's* Achievements and Future Directions for the Development of Female Characters in Crime Dramas

Despite the critiques of *The Wire's* women offered here, I also agree with L.S. Kim's assessment of why it is still possible for me to consider it one of the most innovative shows in television: "I think that the force of the program's innovation is so impressive that we kind of forgive or forget some of the questions and doubts about the representation of women" (Timm, 2008: np). In addition to this forgiveness, there is real measure of inspiration among the viewers about what is now possible in American television. The creators of this series do a *brilliant* job developing male characters whose lives personify the intersections of race and class in a modern American city. That David Simon and Ed Burns were able to create male characters that either participate in the illicit economy or make varying attempts to fight the drug war, and make us care about their fates, is a testament to their screen writing as well as the skills and life experiences they brought to the medium from their former day jobs. In a previous life, Simon was a journalist and Burns was a cop and then a teacher. They wrote what they knew from those days at those jobs.

In an interview with *Mystery One*, Mr. Simon described how disillusioned he became with the *Baltimore Sun's* management after a particularly difficult series of contract negotiations with the writers back in 1987. He was able to receive a leave-of-absence opportunity and write *Homicide: A Year on the Killing Streets* (1991). This type of job benefit allowed him to transition his writing from short features to a book length manuscript, and eventually, he was able to support himself and transition his craft into screen writing. Critics and scholars who are dissatisfied with the portrayal of women in *The Wire* would do well to take notes and strategize how they would seize career opportunities for developing female television characters that would build on the techniques Simon and Burns so skillfully deployed for male characters. "The most innovative series in television" is the beginning of writers developing "social science fiction" as crime dramas—not the end.

References

Carson, C.N. (2002). The lawyer statistical report: The US legal profession in 2000. Chicago, IL: American Bar Foundation. Retrieved from http://www.americanbar.org/content/dam/aba/migrated/marketresearch/PublicDocuments/lawyer_statistical_report_2000.authcheckdam.pdf.

Cohn, D. (2009, October 15). The states of marriage and divorce: Lots of exes live in Texas. Pew Research Center. Retrieved from http://pewresearch.org/pubs/1380/marriage-and-divorce-by-state.

Coleman, J. (1988). Social capital in the creation of human capital. *American Journal of Sociology*, 94, S95–S120.

Goodman, T. (2006). Yes, HBO's 'Wire' is challenging. It's also a masterpiece. *The Hollywood Reporter*. Retrieved http://www.sfgate.com/cgi-bin/article.cgi?file=/c/a/2006/09/06/DDG7BKV7HK26.DTL.

Heffernan, V. (2006). Higher learning in the drug trade for four Baltimore students. The New York Times. Retrieved http://tv.nytimes.com/2006/09/09/arts/television/09wire.html?scp=1&sq=%22The%20Wire%22%20HBO&st=cse.

Jones, S. (2008, August 25). Women and 'The Wire.' PopMatters. Retrieved from http://www.popmatters.com/pm/feature/women-and-the-wire.

Khan, U. (2007, July 24). Why, oh Wire? The Guardian. Retrieved from http://www.guardian.co.uk/commentisfree/2007/jul/24/whyohwire.

Lippman, L. (2009). The women of *The Wire* (No, Seriously). In R. Alvarez (Ed.), *The Wire: Truth be told* (2nd ed., pp. 54–60). New York: Grove Press.

Lippman, M. (2011). *Criminal procedure*. Thousand Oaks, CA: Sage Publications.

Marshall, C. (2009). Barksdale women: Crime, empire and the production of gender. In T. Potter & C.W. Marshall (Eds.), *The Wire: Urban decay and American television*. New York: Continuum International Publishing Group Inc.

Mills, C.W. (1959). *The sociological imagination*. Oxford: Oxford University Press.

Penfold-Mounce, R., Beer, D., & Burrows, R. (2011). *The Wire* as social science fiction? *Sociology,* 45, 152–167.

Samborn, H.V. (2000). Higher hurdles for women. ABA Journal, 30, September. Retrieved from http://heinonline.org/HOL/LandingPage?collection=journals&handle=hein.journals/abaj86&div=174&id=&page=.

Simon, D. (Executive Producer & Director). (2008). *The Wire.* [DVD.] Available from http://www.hbo.com/the-wire/index.html.

Simon, D. (1991). *Homicide: A year on the killing streets.* New York: Owl Books.

Slotkin, J.H. (2008). Rabenmutter and the glass ceiling: An analysis of role conflict experienced by women lawyers in Germany compared with women lawyers in the United States. *California Western International Law Journal,* 38, Spring. Retrieved from http://www.lexisnexis.com/hottopics/lnacademic/?

Slotkin, J.H. (2002). Should I have learned to cook? Interviews with women lawyers juggling multiple roles. *Hastings Women's Law Journal,* 13, Summer. Retrieved from http://www.lexisnexis.com/hottopics/lnacademic/?

Timm, J. (2008, February 27). Could 'The Wire' be misogynistic? Some fans of the crime drama are troubled by how women are portrayed on the show. Macleans, CA. Retrieved from http://www.macleans.ca/culture/entertainment/article.jsp?content=20080227_73638_73638.

Venkatesh, S.A. (2006). *Off the books: The underground economy of the urban poor.* Cambridge, MA: Harvard University Press.

Venkatesh, S. (2008a). What do real thugs think of *The Wire*? Part nine. *The New York Times.* Retrieved from http://www.freakonomics.com/2008/03/10/what-do-real-thugs-think-of-the-wire-part-nine/?scp=2&sq=real%2520thugs%2520wire&st=cse.

Venkatesh, S. (2008b). *Gang leader for a day: A rogue sociologist takes to the streets.* New York: Penguin Books.

Study Questions

1. In this chapter, Drapela discusses critiques of the ways in which *The Wire* has portrayed female characters. Describe the main points of concern from critics such as Lippman, about the ways in which women in *The Wire* are represented. Do the creators of *The Wire* have a responsibility to better represent the female segment of society?

2. Do women need to be characterized by masculine qualities in order to be better understood and received by the general public? Can a woman be strong and self-sufficient while still retaining typically female qualities?

3. According to Drapela's review of critics, what sociological challenges do black females encounter while trying to live, raise a family, and provide financially on both sides of the law? Is this accurately portrayed in *The Wire*?

4. Compare and contrast the three female characters highlighted in this chapter. Do these characters contribute to furthering the discussion surrounding the many unique issues women face in the criminal justice system? Or do they follow the same familiar formula used historically in American television and popular fiction?

5. In what ways could the writers of *The Wire* have better addressed the true sociological involvement of black urban women in legitimate and illegitimate activities? Discuss the research findings surrounding the legitimate and illegitimate ways in which women contribute.

6. Does *The Wire's* portrayal of female characters engage viewers "sociological imagination"? Why or why not?

Chapter 16

"… One of Those At-Risk Children": Adolescent Development, Juvenile Delinquency, and System Response in *The Wire*

Christopher J. Sullivan and James T. McCafferty

Introduction

During the first several scenes of Episode 1 of *The Wire,* the viewer is introduced to a setting that endures throughout the show's five seasons: D'Angelo Barksdale, who has just left court after being found not guilty of homicide, is relegated by his uncle to work with a crew of youth who distribute drugs in one of many housing projects in West Baltimore. This group, which is part of a larger network of African-American adolescent and adult males, eventually engages in violence with rival crews and within itself to maintain its position in the city's drug trade. The interactions between this group and other street youth, as well as broader social systems related to education and criminal justice, for example, relate well to historical and contemporary theory and empirical research on juvenile delinquency. The fictitious portrayal of the development and daily interactions of these youth with others in their communities serves as an excellent context within which to discuss and understand contemporary juvenile justice policy and theory.

Although the core Barksdale group's development is considered at various points in the series, the "origin story" underlying this initial vision of how the show and juvenile justice relate to each other receives concerted attention in Season 4. Here the show's creators and writers initiate a school and juvenile crime plotline that coalesces with a number of key issues in the contemporary study of delinquency and societal response. The focus turns to the development of four youngsters who are born into this setting and with that, focuses the viewer's attention on the many issues important to understanding how one might transition from being an innocent kid to a hardened criminal offender, along with how the justice system might respond during this time. It also offers an occasional portrayal of malleability and hope for the future that colors discussions of youth development and juvenile justice generally. Namond Brice's escape from the life of a "corner boy" suggests that, whatever the other aspects of the narrative, youth from these communities can indeed do well under the right circumstances and given a proper amount of support (Furstenberg et al., 1999).

Broadly speaking, much of *The Wire* focuses on delinquency in the urban environment, which is a theme of interest to criminologists that dates back to the work of Shaw and McKay (1942). Although there are a number of threads of the show that may be relevant to understanding juveniles, crime, and criminal justice, this chapter explores a few key points in depth. First, we consider the neighborhood culture in terms of how it might affect adolescent development, driving them towards lifestyles and activity patterns that have long term negative repercussions. Some of this will be accomplished through a juxtaposition of Elijah Anderson's (1999) work on the "Code of the Street" with the key themes and narrative of the show. Second, the discussion turns to the related issue of legal cynicism and youths' interactions with the justice system as demonstrated in the show. This allows for some assessment of the relevance of these portrayals in thinking about how to deal with serious delinquency. Third, we consider notions of risk/protection for antisocial behavior as they are discussed in the show and evidenced by developmental considerations in the narratives of some of Season 4's main characters. Finally, we review the show's implicit statements about what can be done with youth who are at high risk of serious delinquency and how this fits with some of the evidence base regarding effective programming. Emphasis on factors that put a youth at risk for juvenile delinquency harkens back to the work of William Healy, continuing with the research of Sheldon and Eleanor Glueck, followed by more recent work focused on identifying risk and protection and the interventions that might offer some remedy (Loeber and Farrington, 1998). In the end, this chapter provides a sense of how the content of the show might affect the way students, scholars, urban leaders, and policymakers think about adolescent development and serious juvenile delinquency and society's response to it.

Street Culture and Adolescence

Anderson's (1999) "Code of the Street" was published shortly before *The Wire* first aired in 2002. There are some key parallels in terms of how the two works frame urban culture—particularly when one considers its role in the socialization and development of kids who grow up in these areas. The Season 4 story arc concerning the four main teenage characters, Michael, Randy, Namond, and Duquan, and the manner in which they interact among themselves and with others is heavily guided by the codes identified by Anderson. In most respects, what *The Wire* offers the viewer in most "street" scenes is an artistic interpretation of the code described by Anderson.

The geographic focus of Anderson's work is primarily Germantown Avenue—a major thoroughfare in Philadelphia. The setting of *The Wire* in West Baltimore is shown much like the "ghetto" parts of Germantown Avenue described in Anderson's ethnography. In this portrayal of Baltimore ghettos, like the ones in Philadelphia, many residents live by an unwritten code guiding their adopted street morals. The code of the street is responsible for creating a hierarchy of values among the street-life participants that is defined through machismo, violence and a constant need for respect. The characters in *The Wire* that tend to get the most screen time are those who come from "street" families. That is, these characters have adopted (or are in the process of adopting) the code and are actively engaged in crime and violence in the neighborhood.

At the time of their introduction, the four key characters are in the 8th grade and seem to be well aware of the code and the need for credibility in the streets. More importantly, the characters understand that if an individual does not find themselves towards the upper part of this social structure, it could leave him open to being preyed upon (e.g., Bubbles's experiences with the street bully throughout Season 4 are instructive in that sense). Namond, for one, is keenly aware of the issue of credibility in his early scenes, including when he is being provoked and insulted by other boys in front of a group of people. After being insulted, Namond reacts immediately to sustain his reputation and, perhaps, advance his street-credibility if he can dominate the other boy in a battle of insults. He repeatedly challenges and belittles Duquan, especially after he is slighted by others, in a seeming attempt to preserve his own standing.

The children in these neighborhoods trade insults when one feels that he has not been shown the respect he deserves. Respect, according to Anderson, is loosely defined as being treated "right" by other people. That is, an individual expects to be treated in a particular way and, in some cases, expects to be given "props" for having negotiated more street credibility and being higher on the social ladder of the neighborhood environment. The early scenes of the boys are filled with youthfulness and 'boys-will-be-boys' scenarios in which they carry out milder versions of the code more reminiscent of the minor delinquency of Bart Simpson or Dennis the Menace. An early scene provides a lighter moment of youthful transgressions when the group of boys flings urine-filled balloons at another group that did not show them the respect that they thought they deserved. As the season progresses, however, some of these characters begin to adopt the violent tendencies strongly valued by the code. This aggressive part of the code defines one's reaction to provocation by another: it is no longer acceptable for these young men to trade simple retaliatory "your-momma" jokes, but in order to gain street credit they are expected to react with physical violence to prove their domination over another. Significantly, these teens are often expected to do so by older community members (e.g., Chris Partlow's "mentoring" of Michael) and even their parents (e.g., Namond's mother pressing him to engage those who slight him on the street with violence). Their development, or going from boy to man, is primarily benchmarked against the degree to which they ascribe to the code in their attitudes and actions.

At the time of their introduction, these four boys are just beginning their socialization towards the drug trade, but not all four make for good players in that game. As the narrative unfolds, the boys will have very different levels and types of involvement that will change over time (e.g., initially Namond is active in the trade but by the end of the show he is completely removed from such activities). Across the final two seasons of the show, the boys witness, are privy to knowledge of, or, in some cases, participate in violence associated with the drug trade. Their value to the Stanfield organization is largely defined by their adoption of and ability to perform the behaviors dictated by the code of the street. More specifically, Marlo, Chris and Snoop must assess who is willing to participate in the drug trade, commit violent acts if necessary, and, above all, keep their mouth shut in front of the police.

In Season 4, Episode 8, Bunny Colvin summarizes the seemingly simple job requirement to become a good corner boy as, essentially, living by the code. The code on *The Wire* frequently requires these young boys and men to participate in acts of violence and to adhere to a strict code of silence. Similarly, at the heart of Anderson's code is an explanation of these high rates of violence among young African-American males in disadvantaged neighborhoods. Anderson notes that those who follow and adhere to these rules can protect themselves from risk of victimization. In fact, Anderson's work states that even families that do not value the violence inherent in the code teach these rules to their children so that, although they are "decent," they will know how to protect themselves from potential predators. Each of the boys is aware of the code, especially Namond who makes a concerted effort to follow the rules and to negotiate street credit through aggression—he just is not very good at it (e.g., he can verbally insult others, but cannot win a street fight). In the end, Michael is the only one among the four main characters who possesses enough of the qualities of the code to enter an important role in the Stanfield organization.

The code of the street also defines much of the language and euphemisms used by these boys. The use of certain terms like "the game" when referring to the drug trade is perfectly acceptable on the street and the meaning of the term is known there; however, Dennis "Cutty" Wise advises the kids in his gym that there is not to be any "street talk" while in the gym. Cutty is making an attempt to break these kids of their street language in an effort to make their lives, behaviors and speech mirror more mainstream culture. Later, Cutty sees that his efforts are failing outside of his gym. At one point he attempts to engage Michael and another boy at a professional boxing match—generally about life and specifically about preparation and training in terms of boxing. Cutty's conversation is short—he cannot overcome the boys' tendencies toward the street code.

The Wire offers some scenes from the better, more suburban areas of Baltimore (i.e., Carcetti's home, Bunny's home). The code serves little purpose in these parts of town because, seemingly, respect is assessed in terms of pro-social attitudes and behavior. Many of the characters from these neighborhoods are interested in changing the ghetto and are frequently seen going in to those neighborhoods as part of their professional roles. However, rarely are characters from the ghetto shown outside their part of town. Anderson suggests that these characters are cut-off from mainstream society and may have no means of escape from their underclass neighborhoods, especially after internalizing the code. For example, when dining in a steakhouse in Baltimore's Inner Harbor, Namond and his classmates quickly become aware of their fish-out-of-water status and are embarrassed and ashamed. Later, in Season 5, the viewer sees Cutty and Duquan discussing the possibility of leaving the neighborhood. After watching his poor self-defense skills and seeing that he could be something other than another corner boy, Cutty advises Duquan to leave Baltimore, but neither can come up with any concrete plan for such a move. Essentially, Duquan and his peers are stuck in their world which routes their development heavily towards the options that they see in their neighborhood (drug dealer, soldier, or junkie).

Interestingly, Anderson questions the depiction of the ghetto residents in *The Wire*: "What [the writers] have left out are the decent people" (Bowden, 2008). In his book, Anderson suggests that most families in the ghetto are aware of the code and understand the consequences should the code be broken; however, in opposition to the prevalence of violence in the show, he notes that most families do not value violence as a way of life. *The Wire* does not offer the viewer storylines from "decent families" in Baltimore. Instead, *The Wire* provides glimpses of decent folk, such as Randy's foster mother who is strongly authoritative and seemingly persistent with her parenting style. Additionally, *The Wire* provides multiple examples of street people, behaving at times like they had been raised in a decent-family home with pro-social beliefs and behaviors. Some of the more interestingly nuanced scenes involving Michael surround his parenting of his younger half-brother Bug (e.g., picking him up after school, feeding him at meal time) and sheltering of Duquan in an apartment provided by Marlo in exchange for Michael's work as an enforcer and crew leader in the Stanfield organization. Anderson's critique is valid in that decent-families are largely absent across the run of the show. At the same time, there are glimmers that positive development is possible in spite of the hold that the neighborhood and its code have over the families and kids living there. For example, the acknowledgment of this code on the part of Cutty and Bunny and their willingness to help the kids move toward a positive developmental trajectory is essential in offering the possibility of positive outcomes.

"Legal Cynicism" in Corner (and Stoop) Kids

The issue of legal cynicism and the interaction between communities and the agencies that serve them has received increasing attention on the part of urban leaders and scholars in recent years. At the center of this broad issue is a question of citizen-viewed legitimacy in the law. Criminologists have theorized that the perception of legitimacy can explain who will and will not follow the law (Tyler, 1990). Compliance with the law, according to Tyler, is dependent upon a range of views, including the consideration of procedural justice (fairness in an outcome) and distributive justice (the favorableness of an outcome). In other words, if citizens have beliefs that justice actions are fair and there is equity in behavior by system actors, citizens will tend to look at the law as serving a legitimate function and will therefore be more likely to obey the law. Typically, criminal justice system legitimacy in urban areas is low, especially among those who actively engage in high-risk activities. The police and other legal agencies in *The Wire*, suffer from the same lack of legitimacy and this trickles down to the youth who live in the neighborhoods portrayed in the show.

Perceptions of fairness can be formed on several grounds. For example, the news media often covers issues of disproportionate minority contact with the police, including the question of racial profiling by officers during traffic stops (i.e., DWB—"Driving While Black"). Often, the narratives of those who are mistreated by the police, such as Rodney King, or whose victimization is perceived to be mishandled by the system, such as Trayvon Martin, have been catalysts for community leaders and other concerned residents to raise questions about the legitimacy of law and the actions of justice practitioners. In the world of *The Wire*, it is clear that Herc upsets police-community relationships when he pulls over a local African-American minister on false information that he is a drug dealer. While the media portrayal of criminal justice behaviors and questions of legitimacy brought forth by social leaders is important—the youths in *The Wire* are socialized to legal cynicism through interactions with family members and their peers. This socialization process is apparent throughout the series and informs these kids that the police are not to be trusted under any circumstances. At certain points in Season 4, the youths have experiences that they perceive as validation for these views. For example, Officer Walker's actions, even when the boys know they have done something wrong, appear to them to be arbitrary, brutal, and hypocritical, further reinforcing their notions that the system is out to get them (Fagan and Tyler, 2005). This point is really driven home when he is shown breaking the fingers of the juvenile auto thief "Donut" after being led on a destructive car chase through the neighborhood.

The question of how kids interact with the police has been one of interest to social scientists for some time. Perhaps the earliest study of the effect of demeanor on arrests focused specifically on police-juvenile interactions (Piliavin and Briar, 1964). *The Wire* offers a variety of juvenile views on the police and experiences of corner kids. One theme is consistent across juveniles, drug dealers, and adults: don't trust the police. The writers have shown this especially well in Bunk's interactions with Lex's mother—she knows from word on the street that her son has likely been murdered on Marlo's order, but she will not admit that to a police officer. Lex's mother is forced to decide between cooperation with the police whom she does not trust and abiding by the street code that ultimately was used as the justification for her son's death.

What police interactions with citizens "look like" is important to justice research; however, for the purposes of these adolescents, the more salient effect may come from how they have been socialized towards the law and how their life experiences with the police perpetuates or refutes these beliefs. It also appears that these suspicions are carried over to other government institutions. Namond's classroom monologue regarding the parallels between school and prison drive home a generalized anger and mistrust towards society. Among the key obstacles that must be overcome in attempting to address the problems experienced in urban areas like those portrayed in the show is the need to develop a mutual interest around the task of dealing with shared difficulties, crime and delinquency among them.

As mentioned in the previous section, the code of the street may inhibit efforts to foster a relationship between the community and the police. There are several aspects of the show that fit in with this narrative of legal cynicism. In particular, Randy's interactions with local agencies and the street community exemplify the difficulties associated with cooperation with the system. His story line draws heavily on the notion that those who reside in these communities are intent on dealing with their own problems without the help of the authorities. Consequently, those who do cooperate (i.e., "snitch") face serious repercussions. Randy's experience began with bullying at school, but quickly escalated to his foster mother's house being set on fire. Bodie, a disgruntled but otherwise loyal soldier in the drug trade who was an important character throughout the show's first four seasons, ultimately falls victim to this code as well. When Bodie is spotted sitting on a park bench with Officer McNulty, an indicator of the rejection of legal cynicism and a willingness to snitch, his credibility is lost and this leads to his abrupt murder.

The criminal justice system has attempted to address issues surrounding witness intimidation, but it is improbable that the alternatives would be fully accepted. In some circumstances, people may be offered short-term police protection before being sent back to their neighborhoods. Even Randy's foster mother—a moral, trustworthy character—is worried about overt police protection in her neighborhood so the officers are placed in unmarked cars. These efforts fail of course, leading to her demise. In other cases, criminals that cooperate with the system can be offered a downward departure at sentencing. This option may sound enticing, but the characters in the show do not appear to mind getting arrested (e.g. kids allowing themselves to be arrested for Little Kevin when he is standing right next to them) or going to jail (e.g., Bodie's comments on the failure of the criminal justice system after Poot's early release from a prison sentence). Additionally, the tag of "snitch" may inexplicably follow an individual, regardless of where they wind up. In Randy's final scene in Season 4, he returns to the bedroom in his group home to find "Snitch Bitch" scrawled on his bunk. He attempts to defend himself, but is last seen getting viciously attacked by a large group of boys. This scene offered an epilogue for the lessons the boys learned as they developed throughout Season 4.

The At-Risk Youth in *The Wire*

Understanding the development and continuance of careers in criminal behavior is a topic of considerable interest in the contemporary study of crime.

Identifying qualities like age at onset, length of career, type of offending and patterns, frequency of offending, and desistance from crime are now important objectives in understanding crime and criminality. Inevitably, this interest has led to a desire to identify those factors that might be seen as predictors of involvement in delinquency and crime. The idea of the at-risk youth is a continual undercurrent of Season 4 of *The Wire*. At one point in the discussion regarding the social skills intervention program being implemented at Edward Tilghman Middle School, an aide to the project conveys her skepticism to school administrators by indicating that the involved youth were "profoundly damaged" and change was unlikely. In essence she was expressing a view about the depth of risk faced by these youth and also raising some questions about the relative tractability of their problems. This resonates with developmental research on enduring individual differences versus state dependent change in criminal and other antisocial behaviors (Sampson and Laub, 1993; Wright, Tibbetts, and Daigle, 2008).

In unraveling the story of the boys' pathways toward delinquency and/or addiction, *The Wire* ties in closely to the understanding of risk factors that likely portend bad outcomes for those characters. For example, in synthesizing the material from Season 4 of the show, one can see considerable overlap between the things happening in the lives of these youths and the common lists of risk and protective factors for poor developmental outcomes that are often put together by researchers and organizations interested in juvenile justice and child welfare. A risk factor is an assessable personal attribute or circumstance that is highly predictive of future criminal behavior while a protective factor predicts an individual's likelihood of adopting long-term pro-social behaviors and attitudes. Table 1, listed in the Appendix below, provides an extensive (though not exhaustive) list of risk factors by domain cross-referenced with themes and specific scenes from the show (adapted from Hawkins et al., 1998).

The domains represent general areas of the juvenile's life and each contains specific elements that cover some aspect of a juvenile's life or disposition. For example, family life, and parenting in particular, is seen as an important marker for pro-social or antisocial behavior in adolescence (Simons, Simons, and Wallace, 2004). The story arc surrounding Namond perfectly illustrates some of the factors in this domain that might serve to put a youth at risk. Due to his father's serving time in prison, Namond resides in a single-parent household led by his mother. While this parental criminality and family structure provide risk, more immediate and persistent difficulty likely comes from his mother's brand of antisocial/authoritarian parenting style. When she appears in Season 4, De'Londa Brice is frequently seen deriding her son about his inability to be a "man" like his father and his failure to make much progress as a drug dealer. In particular, she scoffs at the idea that he called Bunny to bail him out because he did not want to go to the Baltimore's juvenile holding facility ("Baby Booking"). Thus, the only parental modeling and reward structure that Namond receives at that point trends strongly towards antisocial behavior. Later on, the creators of the show drive home the results of prosocial guidance and mentoring where, in Season 5, the viewer sees Namond succeeding in a city debate competition while his adopted father Bunny and his wife look on approvingly (Episode 9).

While the risk in the family domain is quite prominent in the show, individual, peer, school, and community risk factors are covered extensively as well. The individual risks are evident in a number of ways, but come to the forefront when the Tilghman social skills program staff discusses the litany of clinical diagnoses that they have presumably observed in the youth with whom they are working. These individual problems are evident in the behavior displayed by these youth as well. Bouts of hyperactivity and impulsive behavior frequently interrupt class lessons and the responses given to questions posed by teachers often elicit responses that suggest favorable attitudes towards antisocial behavior (e.g., the reaction of Prez's class as they learn that he is a former police officer). In terms of peer risk, it is clear that the youth featured in Season 4 have ample opportunity and reinforcement for getting involved with peers who show attitudes and behaviors that accommodate delinquency. At the school and the community level, *The Wire's* main focus is on neighborhoods and institutions that can put youth at risk and/or exacerbate problems in other areas of their lives. The frequent references to the low level of achievement on statewide testing, for example, indicates that these are schools that fall into the lowest percentiles of student academic achievement.

Unfortunately, a list of frequently observed "protective factors" cross-referenced to the show would likely be much shorter in length. These are factors that researchers have identified as predictors of a greater likelihood of pro-social behavior, but few ultimately seem to result in positive outcomes on the show. Only Namond's adoption keeps any of these boys from a life of crime or addiction. Still, if there is a potential source of protection it comes from the pro-social models that emerge from the school and/or community. Each of the four main characters seems to have some level of support from positive models/mentors. Duquan, for example, has support from many adults in the school and, in fact, the loss of these bonds may be seen as a factor in his later trajectory towards drug addiction in Season 5 of the show. Assistant Principal Donnelly sends home clean clothes for him before the start of the school year.

Duquan's relationship with Mr. Pryzbylewski is even stronger as Prez gives him food, lets him in school early to shower, brings home his clothes to be laundered and allows him to set up and work closely with the classroom computer. Duquan is grateful for this support and seeks it out again after he is promoted to the high school (of course, it is later taken advantage of when he hustles Prez for drug money). Additionally, when seeking refuge from the streets, the boys are frequently seen in Cutty's gym. As an informal mentor, Cutty both tries to prevent Michael from heading down the wrong path and also expends his limited social capital when asked by Sergeant Carver and Colvin to help with Namond's situation.

Intervention, Prevention, and *The Wire*

While much of the story surrounding these youth illustrates the risk markers that affect them on a number of fronts, there is an undercurrent that makes clear that these are, by and large, still youths. This runs parallel to recent discussions of how the justice system might consider the role of youthfulness in delinquent behavior and account for it in policy and practice (Scott and Steinberg, 2008). There are several instances in Seasons 4 and 5 of *The Wire* where the imagery of youth involved in serious criminal activity is juxtaposed with their engaging in behaviors that are more clearly linked to (a) typical pro-social activities or (b) more normative deviant behavior that often characterizes adolescence. For example, in Season 4, Randy is involved in the sale of candy to his schoolmates while some of his peers are beginning to be involved in drug sales. At one point, he tells Mr. Pryzbylewski that he would like to open his own business someday. Additionally, late in that season, when he has lost his foster mother to a fire that stemmed in part from his cooperation with the police and is in the station awaiting a social service placement, he reads a comic book. One of the more insightful scenes of *The Wire's* Season 5 (Episode 3) occurs when Michael and Duquan engage in an enduring rite of passage for male adolescents on television—meeting their dates at an amusement park and winning them stuffed animals. Michael is then faced with a somewhat different reality as he returns to the drug corner that he runs at the end of the day. This sequence nicely illustrates the paradoxical images that are typically held with respect to juvenile offenders which can alternately see them as either serious offenders or redeemable kids who have simply gone off course (Bernard and Kurlychek, 2010). The difficult resolution of this problem is at the heart of many discussions about how youth should be handled in the juvenile (or adult) justice system and/or how delinquency may be prevented in the first place.

Since the advent of the juvenile court, prevention and treatment have been seen as primary objectives in dealing with delinquency (Fox, 1996). *The Wire* offers insight into how this might be undertaken in a couple of important ways. First is the importance of early intervention for at-risk youth appears to be essential (Farrington and Welsh, 2007). In "Home Rooms," Bunny easily convinces a researcher named Dr. David Parenti that early intervention is important for creating long-term pro-social behavior. Originally, the researcher, who is made to seem clownishly ignorant about serious offenders and violent crime, wants to foster change in those who have already reached their late teens and early twenties, but when he meets a hardened criminal for the first time, he is startled to learn that maybe 18 years old is too late for the type of intervention he is planning. Bunny's response to the arrestee in restraints is simple: "thanks for being you" and it serves as a winking recognition that the young adult before him is set in his criminal ways (Season 4, Episode 3).

The interventions shown on *The Wire* are often shown to do more harm than good for these children. One unfortunate theme in the show is that policies and rules made by politicians and bureaucrats designed to help address problems faced by youths, regularly make matters worse for those children directly impacted. While this is not necessarily the most likely outcome, it is a possibility (e.g., Dishion, McCord, and Poulin, 1999), particularly when there is a conflict between seeking justice and protecting the welfare of youth, and a program has not been carefully planned, implemented, and assessed. In fact, the interventions seem to fall short in part because of a general lack of trust in the motives of the individuals and agencies involved.

In no storyline is this issue more important than in Randy's interaction with the system. Before Assistant Principal Donnelly contacts the police concerning Randy's knowledge of Lex's murder, she seeks out Prez's expertise about the criminal justice system. Prez is rightfully worried about Randy getting "eaten up by the system" especially since he is already in foster care and the loss of his current placement would put him at even greater disadvantage. His fears are eventually realized when the police do not act in Randy's best interests. Randy's storyline in the show essentially ends when he enters a group home at the end of Season 4; signifying that he has been eaten-up and forgotten by the system. Randy's lone Season 5 appearance is when Bunk tries to use him to get information about Lex's murder.

Currently, there is some recognition that this may be a problem that affects the ability of urban police departments to serve the types of neighborhoods and kids portrayed in *The Wire*. Policy makers and program officials now attempt to formally improve legal socialization through, among other things, school-based programming. For two decades, school-based prevention and education programs such as Drug Awareness and Resistance Education (DARE) or Gang Resistance Education and Training (GREAT) or the presence of school-based resource officers have been touted as important for building strong relationships to the community. While the primary purposes of these programs may not necessarily be succeeding (e.g., curbing gang membership, drug use), there is some evidence that their latent goals of increased police legitimacy is being achieved through growth in favorable views of law enforcement among involved youth (e.g., Esbensen and Osgood, 1999).

Although these types of initiatives are not really covered in *The Wire*, there are some nods toward effective prevention programs, even if the show does not really portray them as such. Although each had a different role prior to Season 4, Bunny, Prez, and Cutty take on different positions when played against the at-risk youth in that set of episodes. In addition to their formal occupations as teachers or trainers, they also are frequently seen to serve a mentorship role. Recent comprehensive reviews of the evidence on mentoring programs suggests that they can help in achieving small but significant reductions in delinquency and other problem behaviors if implemented correctly (Jolliffe and Farrington, 2008; Tolan et al., 2008). So, although mentorship in *The Wire* is met with limited success, with only Colvin seeming to have achieved the desired outcome, there is some evidence to suggest that this strategy deserves further consideration with the types of kids portrayed in Season 4 of the show.

Although somewhat amorphous in terms of its modality, the program implemented at Tilghman Middle School contained variants of social skills training and cognitive-behavioral restructuring. Although such programs are often utilized differently and probably would not be advocated in lieu of youth engagement in academic activities, there is some evidence for the potential benefits of social skills development, particularly when delivered early in the course of development. Lipsey, Wilson, and Cothern (2000) reviewed 117 studies of non-institutionalized, delinquent youth and reported consistent, positive effects for interpersonal skills training. Cognitive behavioral approaches were also found to be effective in their review. Similarly, Greenwood (2006) finds that several of these types of programs, when implemented with quality control, achieve "proven" or "promising" ratings by organizations that look closely at "what works" for delinquent preventions (e.g., Surgeon General, University of Colorado's Violence Prevention Blueprint program). So, although the Tilghman program continually comes under question by administrators and local officials in the show, there do appear to be some elements that are supported by research on delinquency prevention. Again, while the outcome of these efforts in terms of their observed effects on the show's characters was not good, *The Wire* does offer some insightful information regarding what might be done to achieve better outcomes for the types of kids that are the focus of Season 4.

Conclusion

The Wire's creators have publicly asked the viewer to understand that while the characters of *The Wire* are fictional, these characters represent real people on the wrong end of the War on Drugs (Burns et al., 2008). Each of these four main characters had some type of contact with the criminal justice system and intervention in their lives with varying degrees of success (or failure). The concerned viewer who might mistake these characters as a true representation of reality should recognize Assistant Principal Donnelly's statement to Bunny that most of the children in the middle school would be considered stoop kids—not corner kids—and therefore not at high risk for serious delinquency. These characters represent a small, yet significant, proportion of at-risk and delinquent youth in their age group. Still, each of the elements analyzed here, and portrayed in the show, are important because they shape the type of youth who will be seen in urban schools and, unfortunately, in many cases, the juvenile justice system. This in turn affects the options that might be available to attain success for youth, families, and communities that face the types of difficulties that provide the basis for *The Wire*'s storylines.

In its final frames, *The Wire*'s writers leave viewers with the image that two of the characters that emerged in Season 4, Michael and Duquan, have assumed the places of two of the show's most enduring characters, Omar and Bubbles, in the bleak world they erected over the course of five seasons. At the same time, the show does offer a sense that change is possible. Namond's reappearance at the city debate championship illustrates that there is certainly a possibility of positive outcomes with concerted prevention efforts directed at individuals and more organic development of positive attachments to prosocial others. Similarly, Carver's discussion with Herc regarding their handling of Randy as a source of information where he mentioned that what they did in that case mattered (i.e. "it all matters"), was meaningful from the perspective of the social institutions that must work with kids, families, and communities to create an infrastructure that facilitates success. Together, these brief moments in the show offer a sense that the circumstances faced by youth in *The Wire* and the decisions made in light of them are not inevitable and can be learned from in order to reach a better understanding of the etiology of serious delinquency in urban areas and develop better responses.

Appendix

Table 1 Key Risk Factors for Serious Delinquency in *The Wire**		
Domain	Risk Factor	Select Example(s)
Individual	Hyperactivity/ Impulsivity	• Namond continually acts out during Mr. Pryzbylewski's math class. He often shouts out during class and is a constant interruption. He continues this behavior early in the special social skills training program.
	Antisocial Attitudes/ Beliefs	• Michael explains his antisocial beliefs towards teachers when he equates them to police officers. Michael believes that the purpose of both groups of people is to get kids in trouble with the law and to get them to snitch.
	Aggressiveness	• Michael defends Duquan when he is being picked on by Namond at the gym. Michael aggressively assaults Namond before fleeing the gym for good.
Family	Poor Parent-Child Relationships	• Namond and Michael's relationships with their mothers are especially poor. Namond's mother, De'Londa Brice, reinforces that school isn't important and that he should focus on establishing himself in the local drug selling organization. Michael's mother, Raylene, sells groceries (bought with food stamps) to support her drug habit. She spends most of her time in front of the television and does not actively engage with her children.
	Stressful Family Events	• Michael provides many examples of pro-social behavior throughout the early parts of Season 4. He also buffered himself from Marlo, Chris and Snoop's initial attempts to get closer to him. However, the introduction of Bug's father into his home is strong evidence of strain (Agnew, 1992) in Michael's life. Michael makes it known to his mother and this man that he does not want him there. When his efforts to convince the adults that this man should leave, Michael feels that he has no other choice but to seek Marlo's help to get rid of Bug's father.

		Table 1 continued
Family	Poor Family Management	• De'Londa's discipline appears harsh through her tone, but the discipline is nonexistent. She intentionally buys Namond clothes that do not meet the school's dress code and then tells him to wear them. The only real (yet highly misguided) discipline she shows is to scold Namond for bringing drugs home from work.
	Lack of Supervision	• Michael's mother is often seen on the couch, high, watching TV. Michael and Bug are not provided with any parental supervision. Michael has no other choice but to parent Bug and he is often seen feeding and taking care of him.
	Low Parental Involvement	• Duquan's family has little parental involvement. His family members are also known for selling his clean clothes for drug money. He comes home from school in one scene and learns that his family has been evicted from their home and they are not seen again. A young teenager, he moves in with Michael in an apartment funded by Marlo.
	Parental Criminality	• Namond's father, Ronald "Wee-Bey" Brice, was a lieutenant in Avon Barksdale's organization before its collapse. Namond is expected to carry on the family tradition and is placed—by his mother—on the street corner to sell drugs. • Bunny makes reference to the fact that the at-risk youths' parents and siblings were involved in the types of activities they are hoping to prevent for those in their program.
School	Poor Academic Performance	• The school is under-performing on Maryland State standardized tests. In anticipation of an upcoming achievement test, the school administration takes time away from every subject to teach language arts.
	Low Bonding to School	• The students have a poor attitude in Prez's class towards both him and math. Prez can only overcome these attitudes by explaining the advantages of knowing probability while gambling—a skill these kids use in street dice games.

Peer Group	Delinquent Peers	• When the boys seek revenge on Officer Walker or engage in fights with other groups of kids, there are different degrees of willingness to participate but all generally end up involved to some extent.
Community	Neighborhood Disorganization	• The streets of West Baltimore consistently display visual evidence of concentrated disadvantage in terms of the interiors and exteriors of buildings portrayed in the show.

Table 1 continued

* Common list of risk factors adapted from Hawkins et al. (1998).

References

Agnew, R. (1992). Foundation for a general strain theory of crime and delinquency. *Criminology, 30*, 47–87.

Anderson, E. (1999). *Code of the street: decency, violence, and the moral life of the inner city.* New York: W.W. Norton.

Bernard, T., & Kurlychek, M. (2010). *The cycle of juvenile justice.* New York: Oxford University Press.

Bowden, M. (2008). The angriest man in television. *The Atlantic*(Jan./Feb). Retrieved from http://www.theatlantic.com.

Burns, E., Lehane, D., Pelecanos, G., Price, R., & Simon, D. (2008). *The Wire's* war on the drug war. *Time* (Mar). Retrieved from http://www.time.com.

Dishion, T.J., McCord, J., & Poulin, F. (1999). When interventions harm: Peer groups and problem behavior. *American Psychologist, 54*, 755–764.

Esbensen, F.A. & Osgood, D.W. (1999). Gang Resistance Education and Training (Great): Results from the national evaluation. *Journal of Research in Crime and Delinquency, 36*, 194–225.

Fagan, J. & Tyler, T. R. (2005). Legal socialization of children and adolescents. *Social Justice Research, 18*, 217–242.

Farrington, D.P., & Welsh, B.C. (2007). *Saving children from a life of crime.* New York: Oxford University Press.

Fox, S. (1996). The early history of the court. *The Future of Children, 6*, 29–39.

Furstenberg, F.F., Cook, T.D., Eccles, J., Elder, G.H., & Sameroff, A. (1999). *Managing to make it: urban families and adolescent success.* Chicago: University of Chicago Press.

Glueck, S., & Glueck, E. (1950). *Unraveling juvenile delinquency.* New York: Commonwealth Fund.

Greenwood, P. (2006). *Changing lives: delinquency prevention as crime-control policy.* Chicago: University of Chicago Press.

Hawkins, J.D., Herrenkohl, T., Farrington, D.P., Brewer, D., Catalano, R.F., & Harachi, T.W. (1998). A review of predictors of youth violence. In Loeber, R., & Farrington, D. (Eds), *Serious & violent juvenile offenders: risk factors and successful interventions.* Thousand Oaks, CA: Sage.

Healy, W. (1915). *The individual delinquent: a text-book of diagnosis and prognosis for all concerned in understanding offenders.* Boston: Little, Brown.

Jolliffe, D., & Farrington, D.P. (2008). *The influence of mentoring on reoffending.* Stockholm, Sweden: Swedish National Council on Crime Prevention. Available at www.bra.se.

Lipsey, M., Wilson, D., & Cothern, L. (2000). *Effective intervention for serious juvenile offenders.* Washington, D.C.: Office of Juvenile Justice and Delinquency Prevention. Available at www.ojjdp.gov.

Loeber, R., & Farrington, D. (Eds) (1998). *Serious & violent juvenile offenders: risk factors and successful interventions.* Thousand Oaks, CA: Sage.

Piliavin, I., & Briar, S. (1964). Police encounters with juveniles. *American Journal of Sociology, 70,* 206–214.

Sampson, R., & Laub, J.H. (1993). *Crime in the making: pathways and turning points through life.* Cambridge, MA: Harvard University Press.

Scott, E., & Steinberg, L. (2008). *Rethinking juvenile justice.* Cambridge, MA: Harvard University Press.

Shaw, C.R., & McKay, H.D. (1942) *Juvenile delinquency in urban areas.* Chicago: University of Chicago Press.

Simons, R.L., Simons, L.G., & Wallace, L.E. (2004). *Families, delinquency, and crime.* New York: Oxford University Press.

Tolan, P., Henry, D., Schoeny, M., & Bass, A. (2008). *Mentoring interventions to affect juvenile delinquency and associated problems.* Available at www.campbellcollaboration.org.

Tyler, T. (1990). *Why people obey the law.* New Haven: Yale University Press.

Wright, J.P., Tibbetts, S.G., & Daigle, L. (2008). *Criminals in the making: criminality across the life course.* Thousand Oaks, CA: Sage.

Study Questions

1. How is criminological theory reflected in Sullivan and McCafferty's discussion of Michael, Randy, Namond, and Duquan from Season 4? How do the processes of urban socialization fit into the overall theoretical discussion?

2. Compare and contrast "the code" as it is discussed in reference to the urban areas of Baltimore and the more suburban neighborhoods of Baltimore.

3. What are the roles of both formal and informal institutions in guiding the socialization of urban and suburban youth? What about anti-social and pro-social behaviors?

4. What role do the media play in the concept of "legitimacy" within the CJ system? How is this similar or dissimilar to the "word on the street"? How are these explained by justice research?

5. Link a few of the risk factors and examples listed in Table 1 to possible intervention and prevention programs in the show. Describe some real-world intervention and/or prevention programs that would likely be used today. Do the real-world and show-based examples differ significantly? Why?

6. Do you think that the problems faced by urban youth are realistically addressed by the politicians and bureaucrats depicted in the show? In reality, do you think socio-legal policies make it more or less difficult for police departments to deal with urban neighborhood issues?

About the Authors

Jennifer Balboni is an Assistant Professor in the Department of Sociology and Criminal Justice and Co-Director of the Master of Arts in Criminal Justice program at Curry College. Prior to her graduate work in the late 90s, she worked with youth in inner city programs contracted through the juvenile court and social services.

Susan A. Bandes is the Centennial Professor of Law at DePaul University College of Law. She has published widely in the areas of criminal law and procedure, federal jurisdiction, law and literature, and law and emotion. Her book *The Passions of Law* was published by NYU Press in 2000. Prior to joining academia, she worked as a civil rights lawyer and a public defender.

Lauren M. Block is a PhD candidate in the Department of Criminal Justice and Criminology at Washington State University. Her research interests include the administration of criminal justice, race, ethnicity and inequality, law enforcement practices and policies, and social research methods.

Jonathan Bolen is a PhD student of criminology at the University of Nebraska at Omaha. He recently coauthored a book on the neurobiological underpinnings of criminal behavior. His research interests include law, policing, issues of social justice, and criminological theory, especially the integration and examination of biological variables.

David C. Brody is an Associate Professor and Chair of the Department of Criminal Justice and Criminology at Washington State University. He is the author of casebooks on criminal law and criminal procedure, and several dozen other scholarly articles and books. His research areas include judicial selection and evaluation, prosecutorial discretion, and indigent defense systems.

Alafair Burke is a Professor of Law at the Maurice A. Deane School of Law at Hofstra University, where she teaches criminal law and procedure subjects. She has written extensively about prosecutorial discretion and is also the author of eight best-selling crime novels.

Gabriel T Cesar is a Graduate Research Assistant and PhD candidate in the School of Criminology and Criminal Justice at Arizona State University. His research interests include criminological theory and the transmission of values within at-risk populations such as troubled youth, immigrant groups, and criminal offenders.

Anmol Chaddha is a doctoral student of sociology and social policy at Harvard University. His research interests include urban political economy and racial inequality.

Peter A. Collins is an Assistant Professor in the Department of Criminal Justice at Seattle University. His research interests include criminal justice organizations and management, public administration, offender reentry, rehabilitation, substance abuse treatment, cost-benefit research, and evaluation research.

Jonathon A. Cooper is an Assistant Professor in the Department of Criminology at Indiana University of Pennsylvania, where he teaches courses on policing and on race, ethnicity, social structure and justice. His scholarly interests include understanding the behavior of the police within an organizational framework.

Laurie A. Drapela is an Associate Professor of Criminal Justice at Washington State University Vancouver. Her research interests include probation officer discretion, the institutional impacts of prison siting, the implementation and operation of therapeutic courts, and offending desistance trajectories among youth. Her manuscripts have appeared in *Crime & Delinquency, The Journal of Youth and Adolescence, Deviant Behavior, Youth & Society,* and *The Social Science Journal.*

Zachary K. Hamilton is an Assistant Professor in Criminal Justice and Criminology at Washington State University. His primary area of expertise is offender reentry with a focus on returning inmates. He has authored numerous articles describing the issues relevant to this population and the integration public health options utilized to ameliorate the overuse of the criminal justice system with regard to substance abusers.

James McCafferty is a PhD Candidate in the School of Criminal Justice at the University of Cincinnati. He is currently working on research related to the predictive validity of juvenile risk assessments. His research interests include decision-making in the juvenile justice system and community-based corrections.

Peter Moskos is an associate professor in the Department of Law and Police Science at CUNY's John Jay College of Criminal Justice, a former Baltimore City

Police Officer, and the author of *Cop in the Hood* and *In Defense of Flogging*. A sociologist by training, Moskos focuses on police culture, crime prevention, qualitative methods, and ending the war on drugs.

Matthew R. Nobles is an Assistant Professor in the College of Criminal Justice at Sam Houston State University. His research interests include violent and interpersonal crimes, GIS and spatial econometrics, and quantitative methods. His recent work has appeared in *Justice Quarterly, Crime & Delinquency, Journal of Quantitative Criminology, Journal of Criminal Justice, Criminal Justice and Behavior*, and the *American Journal of Public Health*.

Peter F. Parilla is a Professor in the Department of Sociology and Criminal Justice at the University of St. Thomas in St. Paul, MN. He has taught criminology, criminal justice and urban sociology courses there since 1982. His research interests are in the areas of crime and delinquency and experiential education in criminal justice.

Sarah Reckhow is an Assistant Professor of Political Science at Michigan State University and a former Baltimore City Public Schools teacher. Her interests include urban politics, education policy, and racial and ethnic politics. She is the author of *Follow the Money: How Foundation Dollars Change Public School Politics*, a forthcoming book with Oxford University Press.

Stephen K. Rice is an Assistant Professor in the Department of Criminal Justice at Seattle University. His research interests include criminological theory, procedural and restorative justice, racial/ethnic profiling, emotions and crime, and regulation, compliance, and defiance in policing, courts, and corrections. He has published in journals to include *Criminology, Justice Quarterly, Journal of Quantitative Criminology*, and *Deviant Behavior*. He is lead editor of *Race, Ethnicity and Policing: New and Essential Readings* published by New York University Press in 2010.

Dawinder S. Sidhu is Assistant Professor of Law at the University of New Mexico School of Law, where he teaches constitutional law, national security, and employment discrimination. His research focuses on marginalized communities, such as the urban poor, post-9/11 detainees, and Muslim-Americans and Americans perceived to be Muslim.

Christopher J. Sullivan is an Associate Professor in the School of Criminal Justice at the University of Cincinnati. He received his doctorate from Rutgers University in 2005. His research interests include developmental, life-course criminology and juvenile delinquency and prevention policy.

Kyle J. Thomas is a graduate student in the Department of Criminology and Criminal Justice at the University of Maryland. His research interests are peer influence, decision-making, and theory testing. His work has appeared in *Law and Human Behavior, Journal of Research in Crime and Delinquency, Police Quarterly,* and *Criminal Justice Policy Review.*

Gennaro F. Vito is a Distinguished University Scholar and Professor in the Department of Justice Administration at the University of Louisville. He also serves as a faculty member in the Administrative Officer's Course at the Southern Police Institute and Vice Chair. Active in professional organizations, he is a past President, Fellow and recipient of the Bruce Smith Award for research and contributions to criminal justice from the Academy of Criminal Justice Sciences. He has published over 90 articles in refereed academic journals and is the co-author of nine textbooks in criminal justice. His research interests include capital sentencing, program and policy evaluation in corrections and policing, leadership and management.

William Julius Wilson is the Geyser University Professor at Harvard. He is a recipient of the 1998 National Medal of Science, and the American Academy of Arts and Sciences' Talcott Parsons Prize (2003). He has been elected to the National Academy of Sciences, the American Academy of Arts and Sciences, and the American Philosophical Society.

Kevin A. Wright is an Assistant Professor in the School of Criminology and Criminal Justice at Arizona State University. His research interests include criminological theory and correctional policy, with particular emphasis placed on how they intersect.

Wendy N. Wyatt is an associate professor of communication ethics in the Department of Communication and Journalism at The University of St. Thomas, Minnesota. Her research interests include issues of media and democracy, media literacy, and citizen responsibilities to the media.

Index

Note: *f* denotes figure; *n*, note; and *t*, table.

Nutter, Michael, 173
NYPD Blue, 15
Nyswander, Marie E., 219

O

Obama, Barack
    drug policies of, 203
    on "Omar Little," 58–59*n*
    on torture, 69–70*n*, 104
O'Connor, Sandra Day, 90
offender reentry, 260–74. *See also* Recidivism
    barriers to successful, 272
    community conditions and, 264–69
    "Cutty's" redemption and, 270–72
    environment for, 273–74
    programs for, 260
    psychology of the individual and, 262–64
    social support and, 261, 263–69, 272–73
    system-level support and, 269–70
offender rehabilitation, 263. *See also* Offender reentry
Office of National Drug Control Policy (ONDCP), 190, 208
Okri, Ben, 31
Olsen, Matthew G., 70*n*
O'Malley, Martin, 153*n*, 179, 181, 182, 183, 185
O'Neill, Thomas "Tip," 247
Opium Act (Netherlands), 215
oppositional culture, 289, 294
    "Michael Lee" and, 290–92
    "Namond" and, 293–94
    "Randy" and, 293
Osborne, David, 183
overcharging, 65
Oz, 247

P

Padilla, Jose, 75*n*
Padilla, Rumsfeld v., 75*n*
Park, Robert, 31. *See also* Chicago School
parole. *See* Offender reentry
Pendleton Act, 145–46
perceptual legitimacy. *See* Police legitimacy
places, criminogenic, 279–80
Plan Columbia, 192
police
    aggression of, 123
    crime-fighting view of, 119–21
    as moral defenders of good *vs.* evil, 126–27
    parallels between "Omar Little" and, 60–62
    social isolation of, 129
    suspicious and skeptical nature of, 124–25
police culture, 115–34. *See also* Noble cause corruption
    "bending the rules" in, 121–24
    code of silence in, 148
    elements of police work and, 117–18
    enforcement of police norms through, 23
    human agency within, 133
    loyalty and solidarity in, 127–30
    maintaining authority and, 124–27
    police crime-fighting role in, 119–21
    social science perspective of, 116
    street-cop *vs.* management-cop, 130–32
    subcultures within, 115–16
    zero tolerance policy and, 113–14